Picturing Culture

Picturing

Explorations of Film & Anthropology

CULTURE

JAY RUBY

THE UNIVERSITY *of* CHICAGO PRESS   CHICAGO *&* LONDON

JAY RUBY is professor of anthropology at Temple University in Philadelphia and has been exploring the relationship between cultures and pictures for more than thirty years. His most recent publications include *Secure the Shadow: Death and Photography in America* and *The World of Francis Cooper: Nineteenth-Century Pennsylvania Photographer.*

The University of Chicago Press, Chicago 60637
The University of Chicago Press, Ltd., London
© 2000 by The University of Chicago
All rights reserved. Published 2000
Printed in the United States of America

09 08 07 06 05 04 03 02 01 00   1 2 3 4 5

ISBN: 0-226-73098-0 (cloth)
ISBN: 0-226-73099-9 (paper)

Library of Congress Cataloging-in-Publication Data

Ruby, Jay.
   Picturing culture : explorations of film and anthropology / Jay Ruby.
       p. cm.
   Includes bibliographical references and index.
   ISBN 0-226-73098-0 (cloth : alk. paper) — ISBN 0-226-73099-9 (paper : alk. paper)
       1. Motion pictures in ethnology.   2. Visual anthropology.   I. Title.

GN347.R83   2000
306ʹ.02ʹ08 — dc21   99-089536

Condemned though he was for his historical genre painting, Jean-Léon Gérôme's "ethnographic" painting was highly praised. . . . Even conservative Charles Blanc could write: "Ethnography, there he excels." La peinture ethnographique was, of course, just a new name for L'orientalisme, the genre painting of North African and Near Eastern subjects that was the by-product of French colonialism, and had been popular in France since Marilhat, Decamps and Delacroix. Romanticism gave way to Positivism, the romance and exoticism of far-off places was (supposedly) replaced by scientific observation of the customs of the natives. But this was a matter of semantics; the motifs had hardly changed at all. PATRICIA MAINARDI, ART AND POLITICS OF THE SECOND EMPIRE: THE UNIVERSAL EXPOSITIONS

[T]he function of the kinetograph is to set down and permanently record exact images of men walking, trees waving in the wind, birds flying, machinery in active operation—in fine, to secure pictures of any or everything that is going (i.e., in motion), and then to show us a complete representation of these objects with their movement, just as though we were looking at the reality.

. . . [B]y preserving for future ages vitalized pictures of each passing generation or of historic events, the kinetograph may yet play a part of incalculable importance in human life.

GEORGE PARSONS LATHROP, "EDISON'S KINETOGRAPH"

Sol Worth told a story about first approaching Sam Yazzie, the spiritual leader of the Navajo community in which he wished to teach Navajos to make films so that he could study how they would structure these pictorial utterances:

Although Sam was old, tired, and still coughing a great deal, there was no mistaking the authority in his manner. Finally [John] Adair [Worth's coresearcher] felt that it was time to bring up the subject of our visit. Adair explained that we wanted to teach some Navajo to make movies and mentioned Worth's part in the process several times. By the time Adair had finished, Yazzie was looking at Worth frequently, seeming for the first time to acknowledge his presence as legitimate. When Adair finished, Sam thought for a while, and then turned to Worth and asked a lengthy questions which was interpreted as, "Will making movies do the sheep any harm?"

Worth was happy to explain that as far as he knew, there was no chance that making movies would harm the sheep.

Sam thought this over and then asked, "Will making movies do the sheep good?" Worth was forced to reply that as far as he knew making movies wouldn't do the sheep any good.

Sam thought this over, then, looking around at us he said, "Then why make movies?"

Sam Yazzie's question keeps haunting us.

SOL WORTH AND JOHN ADAIR, THROUGH NAVAJO EYES

Contents

Preface

I have been exploring the possibility of an anthropology of the visible for over thirty years. It is an inquiry into all that humans make for others to see—their facial expressions, costumes, symbolic uses of space, their abodes and the design of their living spaces, as well as the full range of the pictorial artifacts they produce, from rock engravings to holographs. A visual anthropology logically proceeds from the belief that culture is manifested through visible symbols embedded in gestures, ceremonies, rituals, and artifacts situated in constructed and natural environments. Culture is conceived of as manifesting itself in scripts with plots involving actors and actresses with lines, costumes, props, and settings. The cultural self is the sum of the scenarios in which one participates. If one can see culture, then researchers should be able to employ audiovisual technologies to record it as data amenable to analysis and presentation. Although the origins of visual anthropology are to be found historically in positivist assumptions that an objective reality is observable, most contemporary culture theorists emphasize the socially constructed nature of cultural reality and the tentative nature of our understanding of any culture.

I am not alone in this search, as witness the recent book of essays edited by Marcus Banks and Howard Morphy entitled

Rethinking Visual Anthropology (1997). In their introduction, Banks and Morphy outline in some detail—more, in fact, than readers will find here—what an anthropology of the visible might entail. The book's final essay—"The Visual in Anthropology," by David MacDougall—acts as a kind of bookend recap of the idea with an emphasis on the potential of pictorial media to radically alter the shape of anthropological knowledge. The existence of such confirming work gives me hope that in the near future, most cultural anthropologists will realize that visual anthropology is more than simply making audiovisual aids for teaching.

My research has concentrated in two arenas—the potential of film as a vehicle for transmitting anthropological knowledge and the development of a sociocultural approach to the history of photography. This book explores my thoughts about the former and ignores the latter. I have tried with limited success to assist in the creation of a field that most people call visual anthropology but that I prefer to characterize as the anthropology of visual communication, based on Sol Worth's conceptualization (1981). My fantasy is to make the study of visual/pictorial phenomena and the production and use of pictorial statements a part of the mainstream of cultural anthropology and in the process cause cultural anthropology to rethink itself.

This book explores two questions posed when the motion picture was first invented: can anthropologists use the technology of film to research the human condition, and can they produce films that in some way convey the knowledge they have gained from their fieldwork and subsequent analysis? (The term *film* is used throughout this book to stand for both motion pictures and videotapes.) The questions may appear esoteric—of interest to only a handful of scholars—and yet if it were possible to come to some resolution about these rather narrow queries, an enormous amount of knowledge about the nature of film and the medium's ability to convey intellectual concepts would be gained. In addition, some insight into questions about the logocentric limitations of theorizing in anthropology would also be acquired. Can pictures convey abstract thoughts, or are they confined to illustrating these thoughts? I confess at the beginning of this venture that a solution to these questions eludes me. Yet I continue to be interested in the apparent conundrum that film and anthropology represent; hence, this book. This is a progress report of sorts that attempts to pull together and critique my work over the past thirty years. As I tend to be hypercritical, some of the book discusses what doesn't work and why. If I am successful, readers will come away with a strong sense of roads no longer worth traveling and perhaps a hint of where we might go next. We must learn from the past even if we are very critical of its failures and mistakes. It is my hope that others will find the results sufficiently provocative to continue to search.

There are two basic paths one could take to explore film and anthropology—either making films or theorizing about them. Although I have made a few films and intend to make others in the future and have been a consultant for dozens more, I choose to critique the efforts of others and to theorize based on a critical examination of past efforts. Few filmmakers have been able to generate theories of filmmaking. In general, Western creative and intellectual life has not produced many people who are both makers and thinkers, Umberto Eco aside. Alan Sekula (1985) and Martha Rosler (1981) are among the very few photographers who have an active life as photographic theorists. In film, Sergei Eisenstein and Dziga Vertov started a trend that never caught on. *Man with a Movie Camera* is the only documentary film I know that is an explication of a theory. I was told by Jay Leyda (personal communication, 1979) that Vertov and his fellow filmmakers, called Kinoks, produced *In Spring* immediately after *Man with a Movie Camera* as a demonstration that their theories could form a basis of action. A number of avant-garde/experimental filmmakers also articulate theories about their own work. David MacDougall is one of the few ethnographic filmmakers who writes thoughtfully about his own work and these issues (1998).

In order to write this book, I had to look at thousands of films, talk to as many filmmakers as possible, and participate in debates and discussions at film conferences, seminars, festivals, and private screenings all over the world. I learned to think about film by attending the Robert Flaherty Film Seminars, first in 1968 and then more or less continuously until 1980 (see Barnouw and Zimmerman, eds., 1995 for a discussion of the Flaherty seminars). The seminar no longer exists in a form that I can recognize, mainly because the world of liberal/leftist white privilege that made it possible is gone. I miss both. Listening to Sol Worth, Willard Van Dyke, Erik Barnouw, and many others taught me to have a healthy distrust of the surface of everything I saw.

I was also able to organize my own film events. The Conferences on Visual Anthropology at Temple University during this period (1968–80) gave me access to many, many films and pioneering ethnographic/documentary filmmakers. There was a time when I viewed between five hundred and a thousand films annually. Most were utterly forgettable, but as I had a great tolerance then for watching, I was able to think about what succeeded and what did not and why. Either the films have gotten much worse or my capacity has diminished, but I cannot stand watching most documentary/ethnographic films today.

Before I knew enough to have much to say, I started teaching courses on visual anthropology at Temple University in Philadelphia. Today I am director of the world's most extensive graduate program in the anthropology of visual communication. To my great fortune, Eric Michaels was one of my earliest students. Sol Worth had just completed his fieldwork with John Adair for the Navajo Film Project when I arrived at Temple. As we both lived in Philadelphia and shared a common interest in the anthropology of the visible, we became colleagues, friends, and collaborators. With Karl Heider, Carroll Williams, and Worth, I secured a National Science Foundation grant for a Summer Institute in Visual Anthropology in 1972, at which the first professional organization and journal in this field were created. In 1977, just before he died, Worth and I were about to embark on a long-term ethnographic study of visible culture—what today would be called a reception study (Worth and Ruby 1981). With the addition of people like John Szwed, Dell Hymes, Erving Goffman, Ray Birdwhistell, Larry Gross, and George Gebner, Philadelphia was a wonderful place to consider questions of visible/pictorial communication. More recently, I have had the privilege of being a friend and colleague of Faye Ginsburg, director of New York University's Program in Media and Culture. We have read and critiqued drafts of each other's papers for the past decade. Her reading of the manuscript of this book was invaluable, and I am in her debt. Her critique was just the jolt I needed to realize what I had to do to complete the book. My quest benefited from all of these friends and colleagues. Although any errors contained here are mine, they all have greatly contributed to my thinking.

Some of my colleagues and friends have told me that this book is long overdue. Perhaps it is, but the realization that I should do it only came to me a few years ago when I co-organized a seminar on visual anthropology for a research center in the Southwest. I envisioned the event as something like the one that produced *Writing Culture* (1986, edited by James Clifford and George Marcus) and pretentiously thought of the seminar as being "Seeing Culture"—a summit of sorts that would pull together the disparate streams of thought involved in visualizing cultures and making pictures about that knowledge. The seminar was a failure, except that I realized that what I took for granted and therefore conveyed in a relatively concise manner in the seminar paper was not as common knowledge as I had assumed. I then decided to write this book and to massively rewrite that paper as its introduction.

During the spring of 1998, when I wrote the body of the book, I was involved in the making of my own videotape biography with my colleague Bapa Jhala. Through a series of videotaped encounters with Bapa, Niyi Akinasso (another Temple colleague), and some of our graduate students—Sam Pack, Susanne Kempf, Bruce Broce, and Nora Jones—I came to realize that it was time to "put my money where my mouth is," and so I prepared this book. Now that it is completed, I plan to embark upon a long-term ethnographic project in which I will produce video and photographic ethnographies as a further exploration of these ideas.

In addition, I had the good fortune during the spring of 1998 to teach a seminar on film and anthropology, something I have been doing for thirty years. This time, the combination of my writing, the taping, and the high quality of the students made it one of the finest seminars I have had the pleasure of teaching. I wish to thank Rob Lazarski, Bruce Broce, Joseph Gonzales, Sasha Waters, Kathryn Ramey, Ryan Sander, and Shanti Thakur for all their productive provocations. Richard Schechner, Dwight Conquergood, Jeff Ruoff, and Sigjuron "Ziggy" Hafsteinsson were kind enough to read portions of the manuscript and make useful criticisms. My wife, Janis Essner Ruby, was her usual exacting self as an essential copyeditor and indexer. David Brent, my editor, was supportive in just the right ways.

The plan of this book is to articulate some of the issues involved in the creation of an anthropological cinema and place them in a historical and theoretical context. The first part of the book is structured around an analysis of key North American image makers. Then the nature of anthropological knowledge and ethnography and film is discussed. There has to be a way of looking at culture, communication, and pictures that leads us to the place where aspects of culture are visible and the medium of film can convey those elements in a distinctly anthropological manner. I conclude with some propositions about possible futures for an anthropological cinema.

Preface

Introduction

The idea of my film is to transform anthropology, the elder daughter of colonialism, a discipline reserved to those with power interrogating people without it. I want to replace it with a shared anthropology. That is to say, an anthropological dialogue between people belonging to different cultures, which to me is the discipline of human sciences for the future. JEAN ROUCH IN *LE MONDE*

To begin . . . a moral tale for anthropologists, a fantasy in which an anthropological cinema exists—not documentaries about "anthropological" subjects but films designed by anthropologists to communicate anthropological insights.[1] It is a well-articulated genre distinct from the conceptual limitations of realist documentary and broadcast journalism. It borrows conventions and techniques from the whole of cinema—fiction, documentary, animation, and experimental. A multitude of film styles vies for prominence—equal to the number of theoretical positions found in the field. There are general-audience films produced for television as well as highly sophisticated works designed for professionals. While some films intended for a general audience are collaboratively made with professional filmmakers, most are produced solely by professional anthropologists, who use the medium to convey the results of their ethnographic studies and ethnological knowledge. University departments regularly teach the theory, history, practice, and criticism of anthropological communications—verbal, written, and pictorial—enabling scholars from senior professors to graduate students to select the most appropriate mode in which to publish their work. There are a variety of venues where these works are displayed regularly and serve as the basis for scholarly discussion. Canons of criticism exist that allow for a critical discourse about the ways in which anthropology is realized pictorially. A low-cost distribution system for all these anthropological products is firmly established. Videotapes/CD-ROMs/DVDs are as common as books in the libraries of anthropologists, and the Internet and World Wide Web occupy a place of some prominence as anthropological resources.

This fantasy is more like science fiction than anything else. It is not remotely close to being realized. But it is an ideal worth pursuing. The purpose of this book is to lay some groundwork to achieve this goal by critically exploring the historical relationship between film and anthropology in the United States. Based on this analysis, I suggest ways in which some form of the fantasy might become a reality.

When the phrase *anthropology and film* is heard, many people think of the so-called ethnographic films about exotic peoples. They are the films seen in classrooms and on U.S. public television and the Discovery channel. *Nanook of the North, The Hunters, Dead Birds, The Ax Fight,* and *The Feast* come to mind. These foundational works have represented the essence of the genre for several generations. This book deals with them and their makers. It does so in a way that is appreciative of their place in the historical development of films about culture and, at the same time, is critical of them as a model for how anthropologists should make films. I argue that ethnographic and documentary film, as commonly practiced, is only marginally related to anthropology and that these film forms are actually an impediment to the development of an anthropological cinema.

Ethnographic film is a most perplexing form of cinema, occupying a position equally marginal to documentary film and cultural anthropology. It seems to defy easy categorization, causing interminable debates about its parameters. Anthropologists started making motion pictures as soon as the technology existed. And yet ethnographic film remains a minor pursuit of the few and a pedagogical device used in a relatively uncritical manner by most teachers of culture. It is a genre in the United States dominated by filmmakers with no training or apparent interest in ethnography or, for that matter, anthropology.

An examination of the credits for the films screened at the Margaret Mead Film and Video Festival, Royal Anthropological Institute Ethnographic Film Festival, Cinéma du Réel, or the Festival dei Popoli indicates that few were produced in association with anthropologists and those that did involve an anthropologist followed the conventions of documentary realism with no apparent consideration of the propriety of these conventions. The popular assumption held by layperson and professional alike is that an ethnographic film is a documentary about exotic people. This inclusive view seems to underlie the selection of films shown at the American Anthropological Association meetings as well as the choice of which films are to be reviewed in *American Anthropologist*. In *Anthropological Excellence in Film*, a 1995 review of films selected by the Society for Visual Anthropology for screening at the American Anthropological Association meetings, over half of the films have no anthropologist listed as being involved in the production (Blakely and Williams 1995). This point of view is also manifested in Karl Heider's *Films for Anthropological Teaching* (Heider and Hermer 1995). Begun in the 1960s and currently in its eighth edition, the book comes as close as anything to representing an ethnographic film canon for U.S. anthropologists. In the introduction, Heider and Hermer restate Heider's 1976 belief that since they are the products of human endeavor, all films are ethnographic (Heider and Hermer 1995:1). In addition, they assert that "no film can stand by itself as a teaching instrument" (Heider and Hermer 1995:1). The implicit assumption represented by these anthropologists (that is, those in charge of selecting films for screenings, reviewing, and inclusion in the filmography) is that the primary function of ethnographic film is as an audiovisual teaching aid that serves as a supplement for written materials. It is a point of view guaranteed to relegate film to a minor form of anthropological expression.

The result of an inclusive view of ethnographic film is the development of a body of work better described as being documentary films about the cultures of exotic people rather than a pictorial expression of anthropologically constructed knowledge. Although potentially useful for teaching, these films remain outside any critical discourse about anthropological theory. Ethnographic film is as dissociated from anthropology as psychological film is from psychology or historical film is from history. It can therefore be concluded that anthropologists interested in utilizing the medium of film to communicate the results of their field research and analytic insights must look outside the conventions of ethnographic and documentary film for models to convey anthropology pictorially and to discover a film form appropriate for their purposes. I intend to offer some suggestions as to how that might be accomplished.

Until the 1970s, ethnographic film, like the documentary, was undertheorized and underanalyzed. Film studies simply ignored it, along with all nonfiction. Because it was assumed that documentarians should strive for objectivity, there was no need for any other theoretical embellishment. The goal of the filmmaker was to objectively record the reality in front of the camera. Debate has been hampered further by a number of factors. Anthropologists tend not to be very knowledgeable about film, semiotic, or communication theory, as can be seen in the writings of Karl Heider (1976) and Peter Loizos (1993). These scholars are prone to naive assumptions about the nature and limits of film and uncritically accept the received wisdom of professional filmmakers. Film critics' and theorists' understanding of anthropology is equally limited, as can be seen in the writings of Bill Nichols (1994), Fatimah Rony (1996), and Trinh T. Minh-ha (1989). Later in this introduction, I critique the inadequacies of Nichols's thinking about ethnographic film as an exemplar of cultural and film studies' analyses of the genre. Their criticisms of anthropology apply more to the profession several decades ago than to contemporary practice. Those who produce these films are constrained by marketplace considerations and their knowledge of ethnography and therefore tend to be timid about exploring the parameters of the genre.

As a result of these conditions, ethnographic film has been hindered by a lack of a conceptual structure sufficient to the task of theorizing about and producing films that communicate ethnographic knowledge. For a time, the literature was dominated by proscriptive and programmatic admonitions and "war stories" about how a film was made (Rollwagon 1988). In the 1970s, the beginning of a critical discussion emerged (Hockings 1975; Heider 1976; Ruby 1975). Whereas a few argued for standards and critical expectations more complex than earlier assumptions about the need to be objective and to concentrate on the "ethnographic" content while avoiding what some called "the cinema aesthetic," the majority were still trapped in the false dichotomy of "the science of anthropology" versus "the art of cinema." Other topics of discussion at this time were questions of accuracy, fairness, and objectivity; the appropriateness of the conventions of documentary realism; the value of film in the teaching of anthropology; and the relationship between a written and a visual anthropology. Theoretical explorations were often limited to arguing about whether or not a particular film was objective, accurate, complete, or even ethnographic.

When the crack in the wall of positivism became increasingly apparent, more scholars articulated the need to see documentary realism and social-science knowledge as the products of discernible epistemologies (Nichols 1981; Ruby 1980a). These debates continued within a number of overlapping intellectual and political circles. The end of colonialism and the Vietnam War and other global and domestic upheavals caused many academics to critically examine the assumptions of their profession and distance themselves from what was perceived to be a less than noble history of involvement with the "exotic Other." Some dissension was the result of a "New Left" political awakening, the emergence of an academic Marxism in the United States, feminism, and other oppositional forces. It resulted in the assumption that paradigmatic shifts in anthropology were essential (Hymes, ed., 1972; Ruby, ed., 1982).

By the mid-1980s, written anthropology's version of "the crisis of representation" was articulated (Marcus and Fischer 1986; Clifford and Marcus 1986). Critics intensified their call for an anthropology that openly admitted to its "dishonorable" past and positivist sins by becoming less authoritarian, more collaborative, and reflexive about its methods, content, and forms of presentation. Some anthropologists interested in the production of pictorial materials and the analysis of pictorial and visual manifestations of culture joined together under the rubric of the anthropology of visual communication (Worth 1976) in hopes of creating an intellectual and academic framework for the exploration of visual and pictorial culture and the pictorial transmission of anthropological knowledge.

The 1980s and 1990s saw the emergence of two major periodicals—*Visual Anthropology* and *Visual Anthropology Review*—as well as a number of books that set about to redefine the field. Some attempted to elevate the discussion of ethnographic film (Crawford and Simonsen 1991; Crawford and Turton 1992), while others sought to frame questions of film and anthropology within a larger conceptual whole (for example, Taylor 1994; MacDougall 1998; Devereaux and Hillman 1995). The encouragement of indigenous media makers and the accommodation of natively produced work into visual anthropology also became a major concern of visual anthropologists, as witness the work of Eric Michaels (see chapter 9), Terence Turner (1990, 1991, 1992), Vincente Carelli (Aufderheide 1995), and particularly Faye Ginsburg (1989, 1991, 1993, 1994, 1995, 1998). This work is discussed in chapter 8. There was also an increase in interest in integrating visual anthropology into the mainstream of cultural anthropology, as evidenced by books like Marcus Banks and Howard Morphy's 1997 *Rethinking Visual Anthropology* (Wright 1998; Taylor 1998). I find myself allied with Banks and Morphy's inclusive definition of the field of visual anthropology, with Faye Ginsburg's recent assessment of the field (1998), and the position David MacDougall assumes in his essay "The Visual in Anthropology Cinema" (in Banks and Morphy 1997). We all seem to be saying, in slightly different ways, that at the end of the twentieth century, ethnographic film finally seems on the verge of some serious theoretical debates and a critical reexamination of film as a way of communicating anthropological knowledge.

Among academics, critics, and practitioners interested in pictorial representation, there is widespread concern with finding solutions to the so-called crisis of representation. Since pictorial media are logically at the center of any debate about representation, it may be possible, for the first time, to bring ethnographic film into the midst of anthropological concerns. To do so means creating a critical approach that borrows selectively from film, communication, media, and cultural studies. The promise is the construction of a theory and practice of ethnographic film that challenge the logocentric basis of anthropological theorizing—that is, in the profound sense of the term, constructing a visual anthropology while at the same time making a clear demarcation between ethnographic film and other pictorial attempts to represent culture.

As a step in that direction, this book presents an argument for a narrowly conceived and restrictive conceptualization of ethnographic film and a radical departure from current production practices. Failing to rehabilitate ethnographic film as an anthropological activity, an additional option would be for anthropologists interested in filmmaking to divorce themselves conceptually from ethnographic film altogether. It may be that because the term has found a particular niche in popular parlance for such a long time, it is simply easier to abandon it altogether and to describe these filmic works with a more accurate phrase—anthropologically intended films.

The argument presented here is an expansion of a position I first articulated in 1974 and have continued to expand and revise since (Ruby 1982, 1986, 1991). I propose that the term *ethnographic* be confined to those works in which the maker had formal training in ethnography, intended to produce an ethnography, employed ethnographic field practices, and sought validation among those competent to judge the work as an ethnography. I believe this conception transcends the medium of presentation—that is, it can be applied to both written and pictorial ethnographies. As such, it can serve as the basis for theorizing about what makes a film ethnographic. I also realize that such a conceptualization excludes the majority of films now called ethnographic.

As interested as I am in a transdisciplinary exploration of these questions, I have no desire to escape the limits of my own professional identity and therefore must admit to an avowedly parochial purpose. Although I would like to see the emergence of a theory and practice of image production that bridge the gap between anthropology, film, and communication studies, the bottom line for me is the further development of a dialogue among anthropologists interested in things pictorial and the hope of bringing issues of an anthropology of pictorial and visual communication into the anthropological mainstream. Like Sam Yazzie (the Navajo medicine man who responded to Sol Worth's request to teach some Navajos to make films that he, Yazzie, was only interested if the filmmaking would help the sheep), my only real interest in things pictorial is if they will transform anthropology.

A History of Ethnographic Film as Constituted in Social Practice

To be certain my readers understand the parameters of this exploration, an abbreviated history of what is generally considered ethnographic film is offered along with an exploration of some of the infrastructure that supports it—a skeleton on which to hang the flesh of the next several chapters and something to use as a basis for my critique. A discussion of the problematics of commonly held assumptions about what constitutes ethnographic film also follows. In writing about films, there is always the problem that some readers will not have seen the films under discussion, while others will be all too familiar with them. I have striven for a middle road and hope I neither confuse those with little knowledge nor bore sophisticated readers.

In order to begin the discussion, I will adhere to a broadly conceived view of ethnographic film as being any documentary film about non-Western culture in order to give an overview of the field, even though it is a view to which I do not subscribe. To be accurate, I suppose I should place quotation marks around "ethnographic" here so as to distance myself from this inclusive definition. The purpose of this section is not to describe a critical canon I would support but rather one as popularly conceived and in common use.

The following thumbnail history of ethnographic film is from a U.S. vantage point and emphasizes the development of the field from naive attempts to generate researchable footage for feature-length works produced by amateur anthropologists to audiovisual aids for the teaching of cultural anthropology and, finally, public television programs. Those works that attempt to free themselves from these relatively narrow confines are also considered.

The earliest ethnographic films—one-reel, single-take episodes of non-Western human behavior—are indistinguishable from theatrical "actualities" popular at the beginning of the twentieth century, even though only a few were actually shown in theaters (Musser 1990). Anthropologists, like everyone else, were fascinated with the technology and its promise to provide an unimpeachable witness. Audiences were and still are fascinated with images of the exotic Other. These early films fixed the colonial gaze in a way that provides contemporary scholars such as Alison Griffiths (1998) and Fatimah Rony (1996) with a virtually limitless archive for displaying, describing, and critiquing the colonial view of the world.

Félix-Louis Regnault, perhaps the first anthropologist to produce researchable footage, proposed in 1900 that all museums collect "moving artifacts" of human behavior for study and exhibit (Rony 1996; chapter 1). Scholars, explorers, missionaries, professional travelers, entrepreneurs, and colonial administrators made footage for research and public display. Some was used along with lantern slides on the illustrated-lecture circuit, which eventually evolved into the travelogue industry. This was the profession Robert Flaherty explored prior to making *Nanook of the North* (see chapter 2, on Flaherty). The crude technology, the complexity of the logistics, the lack of familiarity with the equipment, and the vagueness of the makers' intentions greatly limited the camera's scholarly usefulness. However, the notion of generating reliable and researchable data with a movie camera has been an important motivation for many anthropologists' movie-making ambitions since the inception of the technology. In addition, the conflict between the commercial and anthropological uses of the cinema appears at the very beginning of the medium. The Bureau of American Ethnology commissioned filmmaker P. O. Phillips in 1901 to make "absolutely trustworthy records of aboriginal activities for use of future students, as well as for the verification of current notes of native dances and other ceremonies. . . . The BAE Annual Report reassured its members that despite the fact that the Armat Moving Picture Company [it supplied Phillips with a camera] was a commercial enterprise, it could be entrusted with the task of producing ethnographically accurate records" (*Bureau of American Ethnology Annual Report*, no. 23 [1901–2], p. xvi, cited in Griffiths 1998:263–64).

In the 1930s, Franz Boas, a founder of U.S. anthropology, and his student Margaret Mead, together with Gregory Bateson, extended Regnault's ideas about producing research footage and films (Jacknis 1984, 1987, 1988). The results of Mead and Bateson's fieldwork were several "published" films, such as *Bathing Babies in Three Cultures* (1941), designed to make their data available for other scholars (Jacknis 1988; Chiozzi 1993). The tradition of group research of filmed behavior they championed continued with Alan Lomax's choreometrics study of dance as cultural behavior (1968). Ray Birdwhistell (1980) and Edward Hall (1969, 1974) also proposed the cinematic study of body movement and the uses of space as culturally conditioned communications. The most ambitious attempts to create archives of researchable footage about culture are to be found in the *Encyclopedia Cinematographica* project at the *Institut für den Wissenschaftlichen Film* in Göttingen, Germany, and at the Human Studies Film Archives at the Smithsonian Institution in Washington, D.C. Similar archives and depositories exist throughout the world (chapter 1).

Film footage as researchable data never dominated ethnographic film. It is the medium's potential for teaching anthropology in the classroom and via television that remains the dominant motivation among producers in the United States. The creation of films about culture for public edification and amusement began as part of a general educational film movement in the 1920s and continues today on television with the U.S. Public Broadcasting Service and cable channels such as Discovery and the Learning Channel. Prior to that, films of "exotic" peoples were produced commercially, sometimes with the cooperation of anthropologists, and screened in theaters as "selected short subjects." For example, in 1928, the Pathé brothers obtained the assistance of the Department of Anthropology at Harvard when making *People and Customs of the World*. The work of Timothy Asch, as discussed in chapter 4, best exemplifies the production of films as a tool for teaching anthropology.

There were a number of early attempts to represent native life in feature-length theatrical films shot on location. Photographer Edward Curtis's *In the Land of the War Canoes*, originally titled *In the Land of the Head Hunters* (1914), a romantic epic of the Kwakwaka'wakw (formerly known as the Kwakiutl) of British Columbia (Holm and Quimby 1980), was a box-office failure, but it established a precedent for Robert Flaherty's *Nanook of the North* (1922), a portrait of the struggles of an Inuit (Eskimo) family of the Hudson Bay region of Canada against a harsh environment. The international success of *Nanook* prompted Paramount Pictures to finance Flaherty's second film, *Moana* (1926), and to distribute Merian Cooper and Ernest Scheodsack's *Grass* (1925), a study of the annual migration of the Bakhtari of Iran. In writing about the film, Cooper notes that films like *Grass* could be used in classrooms to teach cultural geography—a suggestion almost a half century ahead of its time. "In the study of Human Geography the motion picture can and will play an increasingly important part" (Cooper 1925:ix–x). While Flaherty went on to make several more films, it is *Nanook of the North* and *Moana* that are most often associated with ethnographic film. Flaherty's place in this history is discussed in chapter 2.

Although the academic world, by and large, ignored film until after World War II, Hollywood saw the box-office potential for productions that featured exotic locations and starred native people. The procedures that were instituted at the major studios were essentially incompatible with ethnography. These filmmakers wished to tell relatively simple stories that had a protagonist, conflict, a love interest, and a resolution that was always a happy ending. When Cooper and Schoedsack traveled to Siam (Thailand) to shoot *Chang* (1927), they carried a fully approved script, ensuring fidelity to executive preconceptions and to popular folk models of the lives of people exotic to the West. Hollywood developed its own traditions of Asian, African, and South Sea Island adventure drama that were increasingly at odds with anthropological concerns and accurate portrayals. Unfortunately, the film industry's interest in accurately portraying any culture has never been high, nor has its ability to do so. In a very real sense, Hollywood misrepresents everyone's culture—minority and mainstream alike.

In *The Silent Enemy: An Epic of the American Indian* (1930), director H. P. Carver employed an all-native cast to tell the tale of an Ojibwa warrior. The film begins with Chief Yellow Robe, the lead actor in Sioux regalia, confronting the camera directly to inform audiences, "This is the story of my people. . . . Everything that you will see here is real. . . . When you look at the picture, therefore, look not upon us as actors. We are Indians living once more our old life." Never has a film before or after *The Silent Enemy* been so authenticated. The film is a good example of an interesting irony caused by cinema's assumed mimetic nature. *The Silent Enemy* is a "realistic" portrayal of Ojibwa life only if you are ignorant of Ojibwa life—that is, the illusion of film realism works best if the audience knows little about the subject.

The advent of sound caused the film industry to move onto the studio stage and abandon the location adventure film about exotic cultures until the 1970s.

For forty years, movie audiences learned about the exotic Other through back-lot Tarzan films employing African Americans as natives and cowboy and Indian movies using Mexican Americans as Native Americans. Colin Young cites a quote from movie pioneer King Vidor that in making Westerns, directors should always seek out Native Americans as the Indian half of the cowboy and Indian drama. If none are available, use "Bulgarians" (1986). I assume Vidor is making an assumption that was common in Hollywood: audiences will accept anyone with slightly dark skin as the "universal" ethnic—Native American, Mexican, and so on. Because of the popularity of Hollywood's perverted vision of the exotic Other, anthropological filmmakers have been forced to disabuse some audiences of their expectations of seeing cannibals, headhunters, and other savage clichés when viewing films about cultures foreign to their experience. Unfortunately, the tradition continues with the tendency for television programs, even those whose intent purports to be educational, to pander to these folk models.

Only a few ethnographic films were produced by or with U.S. anthropologists in the 1920s and 1930s. The false assumption that native peoples and their cultures were disappearing—that they represented "a vanishing race" and that folk and peasant customs of some Western cultures were equally in peril—caused some "salvage" ethnographic film projects to be undertaken. For example, the Heye Foundation supported a series of films on Native Americans from 1912 to 1927 that were produced by Owen Cattell with the assistance of anthropologist Frederick Hodge. Similar projects were designed to recover "lost" European folk traditions and were motivated by a sense of nationalistic pride rather than a need for anthropological study. Prior to World War II, most eastern and central European countries had an official governmental department of folklore that produced hundreds of short films, most often about peasants dancing in colorful costumes and making preindustrial artifacts. In colonial countries such as India, agencies like the Anthropological Survey, Films Division, continued this tradition. Until recently, state television systems in many countries maintained a continuous, if weak, tradition of recording native societies for research, publicity, developmental advocacy, and nation-building activities. These films were shown in movie houses, often mandated by law; at some of the larger museums; and on a regular basis on television. As television is becoming more and more privatized in these countries and the "folk" are becoming industrialized, programs about folk and local culture are also disappearing.

Until the 1950s, films of any sort were seldom shown in university classrooms in the United States. As an undergraduate at the University of California at Los Angeles in the late 1950s, I remember seeing *The Hunters*, not as part of a particular course but as a departmental special event. By the time I started teaching in the mid-1960s, I used films in the classroom on a regular basis and was not thought odd. By the late 1960s, Temple University owned its own collection of films and used them in all its introductory cultural anthropology courses. Teaching anthropology with videotapes is commonplace today.

A number of impressive ethnographic films emerged in the 1950s and 1960s from diverse institutions in the United States that were directed toward university audiences as well as the larger world of documentary-film viewers. *The Hunters* (1958) was the first North American ethnographic film to gain worldwide attention in prestigious film festivals. The story of some hunters and gatherers living in the Kalahari desert, it continued the *Nanook* theme of humans struggling with a hostile environment in order to eke out a living. It is part of John Marshall's forty-year-long film study of the San (Bushmen) of southern Africa. He produced dozens of African and North American films, including *N!ai* (1980), a life history of a San woman, broadcast on U.S. public television, as well as the less well known Pittsburgh Police Film Series (Ruby 1992). Since the late 1980s, Marshall has combined his role as a filmmaker with that of an activist by assisting the San in their efforts to create a new cultural and economic identity for themselves in Namibia while he films the process. His latest effort—and by his own account, his last San film—is a multipart work tentatively entitled *A Kalahari Family.*

Robert Gardner became a part of the Film Study Center at Harvard University to assist Marshall in completing *The Hunters.* In 1964, he released his own film, *Dead Birds*, a study of ritualized warfare among the Dani of Irian Jaya (New Guinea) (Heider 1972). The film grew out of a project in which ethnographers, a novelist, and a filmmaker all described the same culture, permitting audiences to compare the presentations. Gardner, one of the founders of the first U.S. ethnographic film organization, Program in Ethnographic Film, has continued to produce films that often generate heated debate among some anthropologists as to whether or not they are validly regarded as ethnographic. Gardner's contributions are evaluated in chapter 3.

Timothy Asch, another Boston-area filmmaker who also started his professional life with John Marshall, worked collaboratively with anthropologist Napoleon Chagnon to create a series of popular films on the Yanomamo of Venezuela, including *The Feast* (1968), *The Ax Fight* (1971), and *A Man Called Bee* (1972). (See chapter 4 for details about Asch.) The films, along with written ethnographies and study guides, were a pioneering effort to develop a curriculum designed to teach cultural anthropology to college undergraduates. Asch, working with his wife, Patsy, pursued his interests in collaborative filming in Indonesia with James Fox, creating *The Water of Words* (1983), and in Bali with Linda Conner, making *Releasing the Spirits* (1990).

Although this book concentrates on work within the United States, it is impossible to explore the relationship between film and anthropology without at

Introduction

least mentioning the foundational work of French anthropologist-filmmaker Jean Rouch, founding director of the Comité du Film Ethnographique and former head of Cinématèque Française, who brought new impetus to the field in Europe, gaining the attention of both academics and cineasts. Although Rouch has written about his ideas for a filmic anthropology (1971, 1974, 1975, 1988), his writing does not match the sophistication of his film work. Perhaps the best source to learn about his ideas from him directly is an interview conducted by his long-term colleague and friend Enrico Fulchignoni (1990). So far, no scholar, including myself, has had the background necessary to critically evaluate Rouch's contributions. One would have to be a scholar of film, African cultures, and French anthropology. Unfortunately, many of his seminal films cannot be seen unless you go to Paris. Steve Feld has produced an excellent overview of Rouch (1990). Paul Stoller's book (1992) is the most extensive source in English, but his lack of knowledge of film severely hampers his understanding of Rouch as anthropological filmmaker. As Rouch is now in his eighties, the urgency of conserving his films and conducting a comprehensive study of his contributions increases daily.

In the early 1960s, technical advances made it possible for small crews to produce synchronous-sound location films. The equipment encouraged some filmmakers to record actions and events as detached observers, naively assuming that they were not significantly influencing the actions being followed. The so-called American direct cinema of Richard Leacock, Robert Drew, Donn Pennebaker, the Maysles brothers (Albert and David), and others helped to define this kind of documentary. Eventually, it led to what is known today as observational-style film, which became so attractive for some ethnographic filmmakers (MacDougall 1975; 1992a).[2]

Rouch adopted an opposite approach. He felt that the presence of the camera could provoke a ciné trance in which subjects revealed their culture. *Chronicle of a Summer* (*Chronique d'un été*) (1961) was produced with sociologist Edgar Morin and was the first *cinéma vérité* film (Dornfeld 1989). An entire issue of *Studies in Visual Communication* (volume 11, number 1, winter 1985) is devoted to an exploration of this film. In *Chronicle*, Rouch combined the ideas he borrowed from Flaherty with those of Soviet film theorist and practitioner Dziga Vertov. He took cameras into Paris streets for impromptu encounters in which the filmmaking process was often a part of the film, with filmmakers and equipment in the frame. Those filmed became collaborators, even to the extent of participating in discussions of the footage, which were, in turn, incorporated into the final version of the film. The consequences of Rouch's work were immediately evident in the films of French New Wave directors such as Jean-Luc Godard and Chris Marker, whose film *Le Joli Mai* is a direct response to *Chronicle*. Rouch's impact in the United States was delayed because so few of his films were accessible. I screened *Chronicle of a Summer* for the first time for anthropologists at the American Anthropological Association meetings seven years after its release.

Rouch has continued to develop his collaborative approach over a forty-year period in a number of films made with West Africans. Some criticized certain early efforts, such as *Les Maîtres Fous* (1955), as ethnocentric because of an assumed overemphasis on the bizarre, but others celebrated it as a definitive surrealist film (De Bouzek 1989; Roberts 1995).

Rouch's intention was to produce a "shared anthropology" in which those in front of the camera shared the power with the director. This idea reached an apex with his so-called ethnographic science fiction films, such as *Jaguar* (1965), *Petit á Petit* (1968), *Cocorico, Monsieur Poulet* (1983), and *Madame l'Eau* (1992). Rouch is not alone in France in his adventurous experiments in collaboration. In 1946, George Rouquier produced a film about a year in life on a farm as lived by his relatives. *Farrébique ou les Quatre Saisons*, in which the subjects were asked to enact their lives, is a kind of ethnodocudrama. Although it was screened at the 1947 Venice Film Festival as a French form of neorealism, it has been virtually ignored by U.S. anthropologists (Aibel 1987). Rouch is not alone in his interest in pushing the limits of documentary realism. For example, U.S. anthropologist Robert Ascher experimented with drawing directly on film to produce a "cameraless" interpretation of a myth—a technique found in experimental art films (Ascher 1990). As with Rouch, his efforts have been ignored.

Rouch may be a premature postmodernist, as Stoller contends (1992). However, his work in multivocality and reflexivity has been ignored by the so-called crisis of representation and writing culture folks. Their lack of understanding of Rouch's many contributions to the postmodern debates that have obsessed anthropology in recent years is perhaps the best example of how marginalized ethnographic film is to the mainstream of cultural anthropology. George Marcus, James Clifford, and others simply do not see his work as contributing to their interests.

Rouch's attempts at collaborative filmmaking are mirrored in a number of other collaborative projects. Most noteworthy is the Native Alaskan Heritage Film Project of Sarah Elder and Leonard Kamerling. Since the early 1970s, this team has produced more than twenty community films, such as *Drums of Winter* (1988), in which the people filmed played an active role in the film from conception to realization (Elder 1995).

Rouch's desire to allow us to see the world through the eyes of the natives was also shared by Sol Worth and John Adair in the Navajo Film Project (1970), in which Native Americans were taught the technology of filmmaking without the usual Western ideology (Worth and Adair 1972). The Worth and Adair project was part of a more general movement in the 1960s and 1970s toward the expansion of production to people who were traditionally the subject of films. This interest has blossomed into a worldwide increase in indigenously produced media. (See chapters 8 and 9 for additional discussion of collaborative and subject-generated work.)

The idea of a reflexive ethnography that actively seeks the participation of those who are studied and that openly acknowledges the role of the ethnographer in the construction of the culture's image reflects a growing concern voiced by both anthropologists and documentary filmmakers about the ethics and politics of actuality filmmaking—topics explored in subsequent chapters (5, 6, 8, and 9). Through the efforts of such people as Vincente Carelli in Brazil (Aufderheide 1995), Eric Michaels in Australia (1987a), and Terence Turner in Brazil (1992), indigenous people have produced their own videotapes, thus raising anew the possibility of making available new visions of the world. Given the shift in power and awareness in a postcolonial and postmodern world, some argue that the only ethnographic films that should be produced in the twenty-first century are those that result from an active collaboration and sharing of power between ethnofilmmakers and the subjects of their films. Faye Ginsburg's publications (1989, 1991, 1993, 1994, and 1995) are the best place to get an overview of this area. These ideas are explored in two chapters: chapter 8 looks historically and theoretically at the rise of "new" filmmakers, while in chapter 9, Eric Michaels's work is examined as an exemplar of the involvement of an ethnographer in indigenous media.

The varied educational values of ethnographic film are demonstrated in two large-scale projects. "Man: A Course of Study" (MACOS) was a 1960s mixed-media curriculum developed by the Educational Development Corporation of Newton, Massachusetts, under the guidance of Canadian anthropologist Asen Balikci and others (1966, 1989). It was part of the U.S. government funding of the improvement of science education through the National Science Foundation (NSF). Films on Netsilik Eskimo life, originally designed for use in a grammar school course, were repackaged for college-level courses, a commercial television special (*The Eskimo Fight for Life*, 1968), and a Canadian preschool children's series. Although "Man" is undoubtedly the most ambitious ethnographic educational project, it was not greeted with enthusiasm by conservative journalists and politicians in the United States, who saw the course as being subversive to the U.S. way of life because it taught students to be less ethnocentric and to be culturally relative about other people. Gilbertson claimed that the course "explicitly sets out to develop the notion that man is no more than a sophisticated animal" (1980:54). Peter Dow (1991) has written about MACOS's effectiveness among the children who took the course. Although the Netsilik films and Balikci's accompanying monograph (1970) were also popular in university teaching, a comparable study was not undertaken of college-age students.

A second project, "The Faces of Culture," was designed by a team of filmmakers, anthropologists, and television producers at Orange Coast College in Southern California as an introductory cultural anthropology course to be broadcast on local public television stations and offered for credit through local community colleges. Ira Abrams, filmmaker-anthropologist, was the original series producer. John Bishop, ethnographic filmmaker, assumed that role in the second edition of the series. Most of the shows were derived from already existing footage on the Yanomamo, San, Aymara, and others. The programs were designed to complement the readings from a required textbook. The course continues to be a venue in which many thousands of students regularly see ethnographic films. The impact of The Faces of Culture films on students is not known. Indeed, the reception of most nonfiction films is a subject that has only recently caught the attention of scholars. As strange as it may seem, we literally do not know what, if any, impact these films have on their audiences. The implication of reception studies for ethnographic film is discussed in chapter 7.

Whereas most European and U.S. ethnographic filmmakers travel to distant places to film exotic peoples, white Australians have been filming the Aboriginal people of their country since about 1900 (Dunlop 1983). The British-organized Torres Straits Expedition of 1898 was reputedly the first such expedition in which an ethnographer took a motion-picture camera into the field (Griffiths 1998). The Australian Commonwealth Film Unit, and later Film Australia, made it possible for Ian Dunlop to undertake long-term filming projects, such as his Peoples of the Western Australian Desert series. The Australian Institute of Aboriginal Studies for several decades employed a staff ethnographic filmmaker. In that capacity, Roger Sandall produced films on the ceremonial life of various Aboriginal peoples, including *The Mulga Seed Ceremony* (1969). Since the late 1980s, public showing of these films has been restricted, owing to the secret nature of some of the portrayed ceremonial acts.

Australia has a number of documentary filmmakers interested in native Pacific cultures, particularly Papua New Guinea. Gary Kildea and Dennis O'Rourke worked collaboratively with anthropologist Jerry Leach to make *Trobriand Cricket* (1976), a film requested by a native cricket team to explain their version of the game to outsiders (Leach 1988). O'Rourke went on to make a number of films, including *Cannibal Tours* (1978), a critique of tourism in Papua New Guinea. Utilizing found amateur footage from the 1930s, Bob Connolly and Robin Anderson produced an extraordinary film, *First Contact* (1983), which explores some Papuans' first experience with people outside of their world—gold prospectors, the Leahy brothers (Connelly and Anderson 1988). They went on to make two more films—*Joe Leahy's Neighbors* (1988) and *Black Harvest* (1991), about the fate of one of the Papuan Leahy children and his attempt to straddle the native and Australian worlds. A recent film,

Taking Pictures, retrospectively explores the work of these Australians about Papua New Guinea. Although none of these filmmakers is trained in or particularly interested in anthropology, they have involved themselves in events such as ethnographic film festivals and thus have had an influence on the development of the field.

U.S. filmmakers David and Judith MacDougall, graduates of the University of California at Los Angeles's ethnographic film training program, served as the Australian institute's resident filmmakers during the 1980s (Myers 1988) but are best noted for an African film trilogy, Turkana Conversations, including *Lorang's Way* (1979) and *The Wedding Camels* (1981), shot in a distinctive observational style that has caught the attention of cinéasts as well as anthropologists. The MacDougalls have also produced films in India and Sardinia. David MacDougall is unique in that he regularly writes about as well as makes films and conducts production workshops in a number of countries (1998). Next to Rouch, the MacDougalls are the most influential ethnographic filmmakers in the United States and Europe.

During the last quarter of the twentieth century, television became the most significant source of support for ethnographic film activity (see Ginsburg 1988 for an overview). In Great Britain, Granada's long-running television series *Disappearing World* established a fruitful tradition of collaboration between field ethnographers and filmmakers (Curling 1978; Singer and Woodhead 1988), resulting in such films as Brian Moser's *Last of the Cuiva* (1971), shot in eastern Colombia, and a series of programs on the Mursi of Africa by anthropologist David Turton and filmmaker Leslie Woodhead (Woodhead 1987). Granada's interest in ethnographic film caused it to be a major benefactor for the University of Manchester's program in ethnographic film and a supporter of the Royal Anthropological Institute's ethnographic film festivals. BBC-TV anthropological projects have included the series *Face Values,* produced in cooperation with the Royal Anthropological Institute, and *Worlds Apart,* in which series producers Chris Curling and Melissa Llewlyn-Davies explored the impact of former Nazi Leni Riefenstahl's photography in *The Southeast Nuba* (1983).

In the United States, *Odyssey* was a short-lived series in the late 1970s that covered all aspects of anthropology for public television. The series producer, Michael Ambrosino, was the first person to make science interesting to U.S. television audiences with the long-running series *Nova.* With Ambrosino's track record, the possibility of anthropology's becoming a regular feature of public television as it is in other countries caused much excitement among anthropologists interested in maintaining a strong public image of the discipline. It did not happen. As a member of the advisory board for the series, I can personally attest to the difficulties television producers and cultural anthropologists have in working together. The producers were primarily concerned with making good television and the anthropologists with creating a useful public image of the discipline. At times, the two purposes were incompatible. The production staff regarded the cultural anthropologists as fact checkers and facilitators, nothing more.

Ambrosino acquired the rights to several of Granada's *Disappearing World* programs. Because the "television hour" is shorter in the United Kingdom, the programs had to be lengthened and in the long run ended up being extensively revised. Because television producers do not generally own the rights to their work, filmmakers like anthropologist Melissa Llewlyn-Davies saw her work on the Masai appear on U.S. television in a version over which she had no control. Although this may be common television practice to use other people's work in that fashion, it is unheard of in the academic world. I can think of no better example of the fundamental differences between how the world of television and the academic world of anthropology operate. The conflicts with *Odyssey* reached such an impasse that all of the cultural anthropologists resigned from the board. The series was canceled after two seasons because of poor ratings and a lack of funding. No one has tried since to make anthropology a regular part of public television fare. Barry Dornfeld's recent ethnographic production study of the PBS series *Childhood* (1998) and Roger Silverstone's *Framing Science: The Making of a BBC Documentary* (1985) provide additional insight into the complexities of collaboration between scholars and television producers. For me, U.S. television, whether public or commercial, holds little promise for anthropology.

The problems experienced with the *Odyssey* series may be cultural, in that Nippon TV's *Man*, produced by the recently deceased father of the Japanese documentary, Junichi Ushiyama, successfully employed filmmakers and anthropologists for many years. It was among the most popular programs in Japan until Ushiyama's death caused the series to be canceled. Television systems in many parts of the world have scheduled series about non-Western cultures and acquired ethnographic films not originally made for television.

Timothy Asch, in addition to being a pioneering ethnographic filmmaker, was also responsible for the development of a graduate training program in ethnographic film at the University of Southern California, where Lucien Taylor and Ilisa Barbash's filmic study of Chris Steiner's transnational, multisited ethnographic research on the art world of African sculpture in the United States, *In and Out of Africa*, was made. Temple University's J. Jhala and Lindsey Powell's risk-taking and controversial video *Whose Paintings?* is an example of a film made collaboratively by a faculty member and a graduate student. Given the popularity of the graduate programs at the University of Southern California, Temple University, and New York University, a history of ethnographic film in the United States written a decade from now will undoubtedly contain many more examples of works done by anthropologists trained in these programs. I hope that students' vitality and predisposition to contest received wisdom will produce a great many challenging works.

The acquisition of necessary technical skills and the financing, production, and circulation of the films discussed above do not happen in some sort of socioeconomic vacuum. The required infrastructure both inhibits and promotes the development of these films and therefore needs to be discussed.

Ethnographic Film Infrastructure—Technology, Financing, Distribution, Training, Exhibition, and Professional Organizations

The production and reception of ethnographic film operate within a series of academic and commercial structures. As these socioeconomic entities encourage certain developments and discourage others, it is essential that these structures be explored. It is my contention that the commercial-film paradigm ethnographic filmmakers borrowed from the documentary-film world inhibits the development of an anthropological cinema. It is therefore necessary to examine these structures historically and critically. The argument I make in this book is that anthropologists interested in ethnographic film need to create an infrastructure more suited to their scholarly purposes. Lest anyone think that I am making the pretentious assumption that the commercial-film world sullies the ivory tower, I am not. I am suggesting that an anthropological cinema designed primarily to further the purposes of anthropology is probably not an economically viable undertaking and therefore has to conflict with the reasonable expectations of professional filmmakers, who must maintain their professional reputations and realize revenue from their activities. Academics do not need to make money from their publishing activities, whether written or pictorial. They should therefore approach the making of films as a scholarly activity and nothing else.

MACHINES, MONEY, AND ACCESS. While the initial interest in motion-picture machines was primarily a scholarly fascination with the study of movement (Braun 1992), the industry of making movies that merely amused people who would pay for the experience quickly became dominant. Filmmaking is an industry designed for profit. Any other uses of the technology have always been secondary. The educational, documentary, and ethnographic film worlds mirror the expectations of the industry. Some filmmakers have regarded the making of a documentary as a career stepping-stone. There is a cruel if inaccurate assumption that anyone over the age of forty who is still making documentaries must be a hack because "real" filmmakers with talent use the making of a documentary as a training ground until they are able to make "real" movies—feature-length fiction films.

Early 35mm cameras were bulky and extremely difficult to use in remote locations. They produced short clips of silent footage and then only when there was sufficient outdoor lighting. The advent of 16mm cameras meant that the size and weight and cost were lessened, but nothing else. In the 1930s, Margaret Mead and Gregory Bateson had to ask the Balinese to move their ceremony outside of the locale where it was normally held and to perform it during the day rather than at night in order to make *Trance and Dance in Bali*.

Although there were some marvelous experiments with location-sound documentaries like Edgar Anstey and Harry Watts's 1935 exploration of urban poverty in *Housing Problems*, in which audiences heard and saw interviews with slum dwellers in their own homes, it has only been a little over thirty years since two-person crews could operate with relatively lightweight synchronous-sound cameras and use film that was sufficiently light-sensitive to allow interior shooting with little or no lighting. Jean Rouch's 1962 film *Chronicle of a Summer* and Drew Associates' 1960 film *Primary* were experiments using prototypes of this equipment.

These innovations in 16mm production did offer a new potential, but sync-sound camera equipment cost at least $25,000, with another $25,000-plus for an editing workstation—figured in terms of 1960s dollars. The costs and technical skills required to film and edit discouraged most anthropologists from even thinking about becoming filmmakers. At best, they could try to find a professional filmmaker with whom to collaborate, and in doing so, they became obligated to accept the expectations of a professional filmmaker. Although professional-level video technology costs slightly less, the estimate for an ethnographic film produced with professional filmmakers still runs into the thousands of dollars per finished minute. Budgets of $250,000 and up for a one-hour film are not unusual.

Funding for all filmmaking outside the commercial industry has always been haphazard. Robert Flaherty obtained funds from a Hollywood studio, the U.S. government, a furrier business, and an oil company. Only a few granting agencies have the ability or interest to provide the huge sums that professionally made ethnographic films cost. The amount of money necessary for one film could support a score of field-workers who only write. Although a quarter of a million dollars is a pittance in terms of the film business, it seems excessive if the result is only a one-hour teaching aid.

There have been some exceptions in the funding world. Under the guidance of Paul Fejos (Dodds 1973), a filmmaker himself, and his successor, Lita Osmundsen, the Wenner-Gren Foundation was generous in its support of ethnographic film production and assisted in creating the first professional organization devoted to the field, Program in Ethnographic Film. Other private agencies, like the Rock Foundation, have at times supported the ethnographic film work of Tim Asch, Robert Gardner, and Asen Balikci. No private foundation actively solicits proposals for ethnographic film, and only a few will even consider them. I have been told by a successful independent documentary filmmaker that he spends four years fund-raising for every one year of production.

When the U.S. government became panicked over the possibility that the Soviets might be producing more and better scientists, the National Science Foundation was given funds to "improve science education." The funds supported the film work of Asen Balikci, Tim Asch, Robert Gardner, and other ethnographic filmmakers during the 1960s because it was assumed that they were making films for classroom use. For the Netsilik Eskimo project, Balikci was employed by Educational Development Corporation, the Boston-area organization mentioned earlier that used mainly NSF funds to package multimedia curricula for schools. More recently, the National Endowment for the Humanities (NEH) provided some financing for a few ethnographic films that it believed would enhance the image of the humanities on public television. I received one such grant in 1982 to produce an ethnographic account of an estate sale in rural Pennsylvania, *A Country Auction*. NSF no longer supports this activity. NEH has become increasingly less interested in funding anything except Ken Burns–type documentaries. Other governmental agencies, like the National Institutes of Health (NIH) or the National Endowment for the Arts (NEA), rarely support ethnographic film work.

Given the film-world model that has dominated this activity—that of using expensive and technically complicated equipment that requires highly skilled operators to make costly products for which only limited funds are available—it is no wonder that few anthropologists seriously considered making films. The time consumed in funding-raising and the cumbersomeness of bringing into the field a crew of filmmakers who seldom have the time to learn much about the culture to be filmed are daunting prospects when the reward is the production of an audiovisual teaching aid—a product at best marginal to the goals of an active researcher. There has to be a more intellectually challenging reason to make an ethnographic film.

The new video technology has the potential to change this economic and logistical situation. But before it can, there needs to be an intellectual framework that will justify a move away from the documentary-film world. Low-end hi-8mm video cameras and editing equipment cost a fraction of what 16mm or professional-grade video does, and the technology is relatively easy to master. Some credible ethnographic films have already been made in this fashion: Jeffrey Himpele and Quetzil Castaneda's *Incidents of Travel in Chichen Itza* (1997), J. Jhala and L. Powell's *Whose Paintings?* (1995) and K. Braun's *passing girl: riverside* (1998) are three examples. However, the assumptions about what constitutes a "good" film that are the result of decades of professionally made 16mm films requiring professional crews and hundreds of thousands of dollars have inhibited the development of this potential. I have been told informally that NEH will not even consider proposals for such modest productions. The grant officers in NEH invariably suggest that anthropologists applying to it should find a professional filmmaker with a proven track record to assume the role of director for their project. Dwight Hoover (1992) has explored the consequences of NEH's policy of requiring professional filmmakers in his ethnography of the making of the PBS series *Middletown*. Ethnographic film production has been dominated by the professional expectations of the film world regarding equipment, production values, and consequently, costs, not by the interests and needs of anthropology. It is time to change that.

Another consequence of this commercial-documentary model has been the development of a particular type of distribution. Ethnographic films produced by professional filmmakers with large budgets logically must have the "look" of a "good" film and realize the greatest possible profit. These are the reasonable expectations of a professional filmmaker. Unlike anthropologists, most filmmakers attracted to ethnographic work have no institutional support. They derive their income from their film work, not from an academic institution. Consequently, a nontheatrical educational film distribution system emerged, with companies seeking primarily to sell and secondarily to rent these films to a school market. Because the per-unit cost of a 16mm film greatly exceeds the per-unit cost of a book, and one could reasonably expect to sell significantly fewer film units than books, film-distribution companies and academic-book publishers developed in very different directions. Film distributors had to deal with rentals. A few textbook companies, like McGraw-Hill, did for a time distribute and rent educational films. What is important to realize is that whether we are talking about nonprofit educational companies like Julian Bryan's pioneering International Film Foundation or Paramount Pictures, the industrial model prevailed. Film distributors are in business, and the goal is to maximize revenue. Even university-run distribution systems must cover their considerable overhead and pay filmmakers royalties.

For a time in the 1950s and 1960s, public libraries and schools had acquisition budgets of some consequence. Some universities, such as the University of California at Berkeley and Pennsylvania State University, developed large audiovisual centers that produced, sold, and rented films. At the height of this system, the Film Librarians' Association sponsored an annual American Film Festival, at which competition winners could realize sales numbering in the hundreds of units. Although the entire world of 16mm film—theatrical and nontheatrical, features, documentary—has been replaced by video, the same distribution model prevails. Most ethnographic videotapes sell for hundreds of dollars. Few reach the level of consumer-video prices—that is, twenty-five dollars or less. As university acquisition budgets vanish, the marketplace needs of distribution companies greatly limit the circulation of ethnographic film. To be candid about this field, most academics end up having to make illegal copies of videos if they are serious about teaching with film. An alternative to the system of high-cost production and distribution is an essential element in the move to make film a serious anthropological activity. Jean Cocteau is reported to have said that until cameras and film are as cheap as pencils and paper, the cinema will never become a viable art form. I would extend that notion and say that until videos are as cheap as books, filmic explorations of culture can never compete with written versions.

TRAINING. The professional documentary-film paradigm of production and distribution described in the preceding subsection has a number of logical consequences for how filmmakers should be trained and venues in which films should be displayed. Although many ethnographic filmmakers are self-taught, formal training has been available since the 1960s at a number of places in the United States and abroad. These programs often depend on film schools for technical and production training—that is, when anthropology students are trained to make films, they are trained by professional filmmakers, not by anthropologists. I contend that anthropology students need to be trained by anthropologists as analysts of pictorial media and culturally structured communications before they can become image makers. It is one way to incorporate the production of film into the intellectual mainstream of anthropology and by so doing confront the logocentric biases of the mainstream.

Most film schools assume that film is a visual art rather than a medium of communication capable of producing a variety of messages—among them, those that are intended and profitably understood as art. I assert an alternative point of view, one offered with limited success over the past three decades in my writings (Ruby 1976a) and, more important, in the writings of Sol Worth, especially his now classic essay "Film as Non-Art" (1966), and in Sol Worth and Larry Gross's model of social communication (1981). I concur with John Grierson that "[c]inema is neither an art nor an entertainment, it is a form of publication, and may publish in a hundred different ways for a hundred different audiences" (Grierson in Hardy 1979:185).

If film is conceptualized as a medium of communication, then it is potentially capable of having many voices and intentions—scholarly, artistic, and so on. Each style or genre maintains different codes, which, when employed in an expected context, cause people to understand the meaning of the film in a culturally predictable manner. This point of view offers the possibility of conceptualizing film as a means of scholarly communication. Although some films are intended as art, it is illogical to assume that all can be profitably understood that way. For my purposes, film must be regarded as a medium of communication with the potential for transmitting anthropological understanding in a manner parallel to, but not necessarily less significant than, the printed word. To assume otherwise is to commit a form of conceptual suicide.

An examination of some of the earliest attempts to train ethnographic film-makers at the University of California at Los Angeles, the University of Southern California, the Anthropology Film Center in Santa Fe in association with Temple University, and the University of Manchester reveals that the emphasis was not on developing a firm theoretical basis for production from within anthropology but on teaching students how to make something professional filmmakers called a "good" documentary film. Consequently, the majority of the graduates from these programs became professional filmmakers, not professional anthropologists. Faye Ginsburg has written a thoughtful overview of the professionalization of the field of visual anthropology in which she discusses this and other related issues (1998). New York University's program in media and culture, founded by Ginsburg, and the recently revised program in the anthropology of visual communication at Temple University, which I direct, both attempt to integrate the analysis of media and the production of ethnographic film. At Temple, the emphasis is on producing cultural anthropologists whose major research interests revolve around visible and pictorial aspects of culture and the problematic of communicating anthropology through pictorial means. At the writing of this book, the first graduates are emerging from these programs. As they are designed to counter the prevailing tendencies, it will be interesting to see what becomes of their graduates.

EXHIBITION. Ethnographic film, like all film, needs venues in which films are screened and discussed. These venues are a setting in which critical standards are debated and canons develop. It is an essential element in any film paradigm. For over thirty years, I have attended film festivals, seminars, conferences, and so forth all over the world at which ethnographic film is the center of attention. The Festival dei Popoli in Florence and the Robert Flaherty Film Seminar were among the first, followed by the Conferences in Visual Anthropology that I organized at Temple University. The Margaret Mead Film and Video Festival is now the most important venue in North America, but ethnographic film events are found throughout the world in ever-increasing numbers.

I have become more and more frustrated with these events and find myself feeling that most of what occurs has little to do with anthropology and a lot more to do with the interests of professional filmmaking. Those of us concerned with the scholarly exploration of film as a vehicle for the transmission of anthropological knowledge have not located the physical space or social conventions in which to talk about these works productively. I submit that the "film festival" format (the most popular nomenclature and the format I used for events I organized at Temple University at the beginning of my career) is fundamentally at odds with the purposes of a visual anthropology. A different venue and new canons of public debate must be constructed if film is to become more central to the concerns of anthropology.

The overwhelming majority of film festivals are marketplace events designed to enhance the commercial value of the works shown. Distributors lend films because doing so will enhance their market value, even when the festivals are sponsored by academic institutions or organizations. The prestige of being in these events and the possibility of winning a prize—honorific or monetary—is commercially motivated. It has little to do with the normal activities of a scholar. Book prizes are far more limited and focused.

The works selected for these events are shown, when possible, in the best theatrical fashion. Whether a film or a video, the work is often projected as large as possible in an auditorium that will accommodate as many people as possible, thus maximizing the quality of the image if it is film and minimizing the possibility of discussion (theatrical seating inhibits active discussion by the audience). The Robert Flaherty Film Seminar is unusual in having screenings in a theater and discussions in another room designed for that purpose. The more common system favors the larger-budgeted 16mm and high-end video productions while stigmatizing the modestly produced hi-8mm video works designed to be viewed on a television monitor by a limited number of people.

The makers of these works are often invited to appear at film festivals. Because the interests, expectations, and knowledge of most filmmakers differ from those of most anthropologists, discussions lack a common set of assumptions. A filmmaking sensibility dominates. Rather than encouraging a serious discussion, the makers' presence often invokes two polar and virtually useless responses—adoration or character assassination. Discussion topics seem to fall into two basic tropes: (1) aesthetic judgments about the work, as in "I really liked your film . . . " or "I was bothered in your film by . . . ," and (2) questions about particular details of the life portrayed—what I call the "Do the Eskimos really do that?" variety. The personal assessment questions often involve technical issues of how the maker accomplished some effect or the maker is asked to justify a decision he or she made, as in "Why did you decide to dub and not subtitle?" This line of questioning often prompts the filmmaker to tell "war stories" about the making of the film. What is seldom discussed is the contribution the film makes to anthropology. It seems to me that visual anthropologists have passively accepted the needs and expectations of the film world rather than developing places and approaches to discussion more appropriate to their own needs.

One concrete example is necessary. At the annual American Anthropological Association meetings, films are shown in their entirety in a kind of visual ghetto separate from the "scientific" papers. Honorific prizes are awarded. The screenings are further separated from the scholarly papers by calling the combined screenings a "festival." They are sometimes grouped by locale and sometimes the maker is present, but there is little discussion. When it does happen, the talk is strictly among visual anthropologists and filmmakers. The films therefore never enter the mainstream of the meetings. I submit that if the makers of these films were interested in behaving like anthropologists and wished their work to enter the scholarly arena of debate, they could excerpt a fifteen-minute portion of their film (the time allotted for a paper) and submit it to a panel concerned with the anthropological issues the film addresses. While excerpting fifteen minutes from a larger work is difficult, it is no more difficult than excerpting a fifteen-minute talk from a twenty-page paper or even a book-length study, which is what anthropologists who write do all the time. This approach would ensure that their films would be considered within the scholarly debates generated by these meetings.

PROFESSIONAL ORGANIZATIONS. The first organization devoted to ethnographic film—Comité du Film Ethnographique—was created in the 1950s under the bureaucracy of UNESCO in Paris by Jean Rouch. The committee was involved in the development of the Festival dei Popoli—also the first film event devoted to the genre. In the United States, after the successes of *The Hunters* and *Dead Birds*, Robert Gardner, along with Asen Balikci and Karl Heider, obtained funds in 1966 from the Wenner-Gren Foundation to establish a committee of the American Anthropological Association, Program in Ethnographic Film (PIEF), at Harvard's Film Study Center (Gardner 1970). Irven Devore, Margaret Mead, Walter Goldschmidt, Colin Young, and Sol Tax served as advisers. All were anthropologists except Young, who was the director of UCLA's film school and was at the time in the process of establishing an ethnographic film-training program. PIEF's stated purpose was to facilitate training, production, and teaching. Heider produced the first of several editions of *Films for Anthropological Teaching* for PIEF.

In 1969, I assumed the leadership of PIEF and moved it to Temple. We established a newsletter, continued publishing Heider's filmography, organized annual film events that eventually became known as the Conference on Visual Anthropology, and convinced the American Anthropological Association that film screenings should be organized at the annual meetings in a manner parallel to the presentation of the scientific papers. In 1972, PIEF obtained funds from NSF to sponsor a Summer Institute in Visual Anthropology (SIVA) with Sol Worth, Karl Heider, Carroll Williams (director of the Anthropology Film Center), and myself as organizers. With visits from Ray Birdwhistell, Edward Hall, Alan Lomax, and twenty young faculty members and graduate students, among them Larry Gross and Steve Feld, SIVA was a place where PIEF was transformed from an organization devoted exclusively to ethnographic film to an organization designed to explore the whole of an anthropology of visual communication.

As the result of SIVA, the Society for the Anthropology of Visual Communication (SAVICOM) was created, and a journal, *Studies in the Anthropology of*

Visual Communication, under the editorship of Sol Worth, was begun. In the late 1970s, SAVICOM was dissolved, and in its place, the Society for Visual Anthropology (SVA) was created. The journal was acquired by the Annenberg School of Communication at the University of Pennsylvania. Larry Gross and I edited *Studies* until 1985, when it ceased publication. Today SVA produces its own journal, *Visual Anthropology Review,* while the International Commission on Visual Anthropology publishes *Visual Anthropology,* in conjunction with Gordon and Breach. Although the scholarly outlets for writing about ethnographic film are now firmly established, venues for the screening of these films and scholarly discussion of them remain problematic.

In short, without an infrastructure designed to enhance the anthropological consequences of ethnographic film, it will remain a minor subset of a commercial documentary-film world.

On the Necessity of Being Painfully Obvious;
or, the (Mis)Appropriation of the Ethnographic

As should be clear by now, no one has articulated a theory or practice of ethnographic film adequate to the task. More than twenty years ago, MacDougall pointed out that ethnographic film needs "a new paradigm, another way of seeing, not necessarily incompatible with written anthropology but at least governed by a distinct set of criteria" (1978:405). It has not been an easy task. In fact, the search continues. One reason for the apparent lack of progress is that those most interested in the creation of a new paradigm are not sufficiently knowledgeable about ethnography or anthropology to understand its potential. As I suggested earlier, some film theorists and cultural studies scholars (Nichols 1981, 1994; Minh-Ha 1989) tend to caricature and dismiss anthropology as stuck in a nineteenth-century positivist and colonialist mode in which ethnographic representations were presented as the objective truth about the Other. These critics fail to understand that an anthropology of visual communication (Worth 1981) as well as several-decades-old dissonant traditions within anthropology contain within them the essential conceptual elements for a new paradigm.

In addition, the dominant point of view is that the term *ethnographic* can be applied to a large variety of things—an inclusive definition so general as to render the concept meaningless. "It is probably best not to try to define ethnographic films. In the broadest sense, most films are ethnographic—that is, if we take 'ethnographic' to mean 'about people.' And even those that are about, say, clouds or lizards or gravity are made by people and therefore say something about the culture of the individuals who made them (and use them)" (Heider 1974:1). Although this overly inclusive definition was written more

Introduction

than twenty-five years ago, Heider's book remains in print and is undoubtedly the most widely read book in the field; therefore, a critique of its inadequacies is still necessary.

This broad conception of ethnographic creates a canonical dilemma. If ethnographic film is supposed to have something to do with ethnography, then where do films produced by nonethnographers fit? From the beginning of the genre, the majority of the films labeled ethnographic were made by people with little or no anthropological training and no apparent interest in anthropological theory building. Excluding Robert Flaherty, John Marshall, and Robert Gardner from a discussion of ethnographic film seems altogether absurd, but then so does calling all films that deal with culture ethnographic. If nonanthropologists can produce credible ethnographic films, why should anyone interested in making ethnographic films bother being trained as an ethnographer? If the genre is confined to films made only by trained ethnographers, an insignificantly tiny field results. If it is opened up to any film that makes a sophisticated statement about culture, the definition implies that one need not know anything about ethnography or anthropology to produce an acceptable ethnographic film. Either way seems inadequate and frustrating. I do not have the solution to the apparent conundrum of where is the ethnography in an ethnographic film. Nonetheless, I feel compelled to explore the problem.

There is a general tendency to be overly generous in the use of the term *ethnographic*—an error common to anthropologists, film scholars, and indeed, many people in a host of situations. Some characterizations are merely faddish and can be dismissed out of hand. When it is applied to anything related to the exotic Other—as in "ethnographic" art, "ethnographic" ceremonies, or an "ethnographic" subject—it is merely another manifestation of orientalism commonly found in popular parlance. Readers can see from the frontispiece quotation about Gérôme's paintings that this tendency is quite old.

In keeping with a general tendency to misappropriate, the term *ethnographic* is often used to describe any "serious" film about an exotic Other—by that, I mean John Boorman's *The Emerald Forest* or Nicholas Ray's *The Savage Innocents* is labeled ethnographic, whereas *Abbott and Costello Go to Africa* is not. This is a reasonable, if unsophisticated, error. Historically, anthropological ethnographies were concerned exclusively with non-Western people. Ethnographies that dealt with people in the United States tended to be called "community studies." "They" are ethnographic subjects, whereas "we" are sociological. Curiously enough, few mainstream fiction films are labeled sociological.

A similar logic causes people to characterize any film that deals with unconscious motivation as psychological and any film concerned with the past as historical. The makers of these films do not employ the methods, practices, or theories of these disciplines, nor are they interested in having their audiences understand the subject from that point of view. Even a production based on the scholarly work of a historian, such as Warren Beatty's *Reds*—a film created out of Robert Rosenstone's *Romantic Revolutionary: Biography of John Reed* (1975)—is so altered as to destroy the integrity of the source. Apparently, Hollywood does not believe that "good" history (that is, credible scholarship) can be made into "good" movies (that is, turn a profit).

Critics who attempt to evaluate these films in terms of how well they reflect current thinking within anthropology, psychology, or history quickly discover that the films thoughtlessly replicate popular folk models. For example, Boorman's depiction of a Yanomamo-like tribe in *The Emerald Forest* is nothing more than a cinematic articulation of the "noble savage being destroyed by the degenerate West" trope. He used elements from the cultures of several rainforest peoples as an authenticating background for his morality tale (see chapter 4 on Tim Asch for an amusing story about Boorman and Asch). If one is interested in exploring the ways in which the commercial-fiction-film world replicates the popular imagination, then these films are worth studying in terms of commonsense notions of the ethnographic. Although scholars may rant and rave about this misappropriation of the ethnographic, the psychological, and the historical, it will continue as long as it is assumed to sell a picture and as a way for popular writers to maintain an easily understood nomenclature. Perhaps it is time for anthropologists to stop labeling their films as ethnographic and instead call these works something like anthropologically intended films. Although undoubtedly clunky, the term is more precise.

If the term *ethnographic* is to retain any of its original meaning, it is most profitably applied only to those films produced by competent ethnographers and explicitly designed to be ethnographies. Standards of evaluation derived from anthropology should be applied. As ethnography stands for both a process of investigation and a product, determining whether a film is ethnographic should not be difficult. The approach seems almost commonsensical, and yet it is at variance with most people's views. The dominant assumption appears to be that one need not be an ethnographer to make ethnographic films, as this quote makes evident:

Tidikawa and Friends is the exposition of filmmakers who are attuned to what may be revealed of a way of life through the subtleties of movement and sound, rather than through a knowledge of cultural symbolism or social organization. As the film stands we think the presence of an anthropologist could have added very little. Indeed, it is possible that an anthropologist's presence would have detracted from the film's success. . . . *Tidikawa and Friends* demonstrates that sensitive and perceptive filmmakers can say a great deal about a culture with which they are not familiar if their explication remains on the level of their own medium of sight and sound. When properly edited by someone who understands them, there is consid-

Ethnographic practices are rather unique and distinguishable from other forms of cultural investigation, thereby separating the ethnographer from other cultural analysts. Long-term intense involvement with the people being studied is the norm. Ethnographers live in the field for as long as they can. Participant observation is the taken-for-granted field method, usually requiring a competence in the local language or the employment of a full-time translator. Filmmakers "more trained in filmmaking than in anthropology" who are "extra institutional" (Nichols 1994:66) face the economic reality that people who are not academically affiliated lack the economic support to be able to devote the time necessary to do ethnography. Few films termed ethnographic are the result of a study in any academic sense of the term or derived from extensive fieldwork. In addition, the assumption that films must maintain certain industry standards requires a several-person crew and expensive, often cumbersome, equipment, resulting in an average cost of several thousand dollars per finished minute, even when the crew spends limited time in the field. The professional expectations and economic realities of independent filmmaking seem to be a fundamental impediment for anyone who wants to do ethnographic fieldwork.

As a way of further articulating my approach to ethnographic film, I will contrast it with that expressed by film theorist Bill Nichols in "The Ethnographer's Tale" (1994). We are both concerned with the creation of a new paradigm. We differ as to where we look for the resources for its construction. Nichols is among the best-known cultural/film studies scholars who has critiqued what he regards as the inadequacies of anthropology. Dubious of what he considers the inherent limits of anthropology as a word-dominated positivist social science and the perceived naïveté of visual anthropologists, Nichols argues for an ethnographic film produced outside academia by people trained primarily as filmmakers, not ethnographers, and for theory to be derived from culture studies and literary models of textual analysis.

Nichols's challenge to ethnographic film is part of a general attack on traditional anthropological paradigms that he thinks was initiated by cultural studies and literary criticism. As a consequence of forces from outside the field, Nichols believes a shift has occurred "from a social science model to a cultural studies and textual analysis paradigm" (1994:78). Certainly he is correct that anthropology has been severely criticized for its colonialist, racist, positivist history, but he gives too much credit for these critiques and for the creation of alternative paradigms to the relatively recent "ethnography as text" movement articulated by George Marcus and Michael Fischer (1986) and James Clifford and Marcus (1986). These internal criticisms are part of a

Introduction

long history of oppositional traditions at odds with the colonialist, positivist, scientizing forces that once dominated anthropology. Long before cultural studies were even known in the United States, Stanley Diamond was editing a journal, *Dialectical Anthropology*, filled with articles denouncing the ethics, politics, and intellectual assumptions of mainstream anthropology. In 1972, Dell Hymes edited *Reinventing Anthropology*, in which these matters were discussed, and in 1982, I edited *A Crack in the Mirror: Reflexive Perspectives in Anthropology*, which also explored many of these issues. All of this work and much more predates the "crisis of representation" literature.

It is the intellectual ferment of academic Marxism, feminism, humanism, and calls for a reflexive and openly interpretative anthropology that provided the underpinning for the creation of a multiplicity of paradigms in anthropology, not simply cultural studies or literary criticism. If one is looking for models to radically alter ethnographic film, they have been available for some time within anthropology. Nichols is correct that many anthropologists involved with ethnographic film (Paul Hockings, Karl Heider, and Peter Loizos, to name the most prominent) seem oblivious to these ideas and continue to espouse discredited and outmoded notions of objectivity and reality and blindly believe in the scientific merit of realist-documentary conventions like observational cinema and false dichotomies between art and science. But theirs is not the only point of view being expressed from within ethnographic film. What is perplexing is that Nichols admits that a tradition exists "already represented, though often neglected, within sociology and anthropology that offers something of a bridge from paradigms lost to paradigms regained" (1994:78–79), but he cites no one, nor does he use this tradition to shore up his arguments. For example, why Nichols does not explore the films of Jean Rouch is curious. Rouch has been a pioneer in reflexive cinema and in the move toward "shared" anthropology and indigenous media (Stoller 1992). These are ideas central to Nichols's argument. The absence of these resources could cause a reader to think that Nichols lacks a familiarity with the relevant literature or perhaps that he wishes readers to think his point of view is more unique and original than it is.

Nichols advocates making films that are openly interpretative, highly reflexive, and able to be rationalized as being useful. For him, this is a cinema located in the worlds of woman/native/Other—a term borrowed from Trinh T. Minh-ha (1989). In short, Nichols sees the future in works made by the traditional subjects of ethnographic film. Nichols is not making the essentialist error of assuming that the natives know the truth about themselves. He is suggesting that academic anthropology is simply too limited to offer much assistance. Although I concur with the rejection of a positivist social-science paradigm and have argued elsewhere for an openly interpretative and reflexive anthropology (Ruby 1980a; Ruby, ed., 1982; chapter 6), I believe the future of ethnographic film is located in anthropologically grounded theories and anthropologically trained ethnographic filmmakers' taking control of the genre.

Nichols is convinced the hope for the future lies with "individuals more trained in filmmaking than in anthropology" (1994:66)—specifically with films made by woman/native/Other. The emergence of the "subject" as author is one of the more exciting developments of this era. It represents a significant shift in power toward people who were traditionally the subject of ethnography. Native representations dispute the false claims of positivist anthropology and open up the possibility of *Rashomon*-like versions of actuality (Ruby 1991). Documents about a culture by members of that culture offer a unique and valuable perspective. But I fail to understand why that qualifies them as ethnography. The logic of that argument would cause all realist novels to be regarded as equally "ethnographic"—as they are documents of a culture by a member of that culture.

Films by woman/native/Other and ethnographic films are distinct in two significant ways—the relationship of the producer to the community and the purpose of the production. A fundamental, if not defining and historical, characteristic of ethnography has been that it expresses the view of an outsider. More recently, scholars marginalized to the culture under study and, in a few cases, such as Alfonso Ortiz (1969) or Francis Deng (1984), sufficiently bicultural as to be simultaneously native and ethnographer, have broadened the notion of who can produce an ethnography. The chief value and inherent limitation of all ethnography still remains that it is the product of professional outsiders—people whose lifelong loyalties, commitments, obligations, and so forth do not lie exclusively with the community represented. The agendas of people representing a culture in which they are native have to be different from those who are not. Once it is acknowledged that no one can speak for or represent a culture but only his or her relationship to it, then a multiplicity of viewpoints is possible and welcome—some from within and others from without and all the marvelously gray areas in between.

The motivation of woman/native/Other to acquire the technology of image production is often to correct what is regarded as "misrepresentation" by the dominant culture, class, and gender. Whether these "new" producers are mainly concerned with the preservation of aspects of their traditional culture or with the politics of their public image, they are constrained by forces different from those of an ethnographer who has professional loyalties and obligations that lie outside the community. Although some ethnographers have or develop a lifelong commitment to the people they study, their stake in the community's image will never be the same as that of those native to it. The intention of an ethnography is to contribute to an anthropological discourse about human behavior. Native producers seldom have either the interest or the competence to make such a contribution—at least, not in any direct fashion.

Native productions are more usefully understood as pictorial documents that usually require some contextualizing, translating, and explaining in order to be comprehensible to nonnative audiences. I have argued elsewhere (1995a; chapter 8) that the role of the visual anthropologist as facilitator of indigenous production should increase, resulting in ethnographies of native production and reception (Michaels 1987a; Turner 1992). The flowering of pictorial representation among people who have traditionally been the subject of the camera's gaze is exciting. It should be encouraged and assisted. Labeling it as an ethnography will not aid; it will only confuse.

Once it has been demystified and any claims to truth or objective renditions of reality have been relinquished, ethnography becomes nothing more than one among many methods for representing a culture. Its primary value to nonanthropologists is that it provides an outsider perspective. Bronislaw Malinowski argued that the goal of anthropology should be to see the world through the eyes of the native. If that were the only purpose of anthropology, Nichols would be correct. The future of ethnographic films would lie with films by woman/native/Other. I submit that the purpose of anthropology is to allow people to see the native through the eyes of the anthropologist. Films by woman/native/Other, documentaries that are cultural studies, feature fiction films, and ethnographic films all offer distinct ways of representing a culture. No one way has an inside track to the truth. All suffer the limitations of being from a particular point of view. To confuse one with the other inhibits critical discourse about all of them.

An ethnography can be distinguished from other forms of cultural analysis because it is intended to be an analytic or "thick" description of some aspect of a culture constructed to engage with and comment upon a particular tradition of anthropological thought (Geertz 1973). Tim Asch and Napoleon Chagnon's *The Feast* is a description of a Yanomamo sociopolitical-economic event and a comment upon Marcel Mauss's notion of reciprocity (1967). Ethnographies are more than "the representation, or self-representation, of one culture for another" (Nichols 1994:66). To reduce ethnography to such a common denominator is to render it indistinguishable from other cultural studies and rob it of its distinctive character. To belabor the obvious, to make an ethnography, one has to be familiar with anthropological thought and ethnographic practices. I do not understand why so many assume it is possible to produce a credible ethnographic film without being a knowledgeable ethnographer. As David Levinson pointed out in a *New York Times* letter to the editor, it is no longer possible for amateurs to contribute significantly to anthropological thought.[3]

Ethnographers assume they are producing for a professional audience to further or critique a tradition of anthropological thought. Nichols argues for a politically engaged purpose that would "alter the world itself" (1994:67).

From his perspective, ethnographic films must be interrogated to see whether or not they can "withstand the fundamental challenge of usefulness" (1994:66). Few ethnographies—written or filmic—are designed to change anything. I do not believe anthropology or film studies or most academic disciplines produce world-altering knowledge. Academic writing is too jargon-filled to be comprehensible to any but the most dedicated. Scholars mainly talk to other scholars. I find it ironic that Nichols, who writes in such a difficult style that it severely limits his audience to a tiny group of dedicated scholars, should claim that scholarship must have an impact on the world. Although most teachers would like to think they somehow enlighten their students, the world seems to be proceeding apace without the slightest trace of their impact. For all the thousands of students who have taken some cultural anthropology course, society is not appreciably less ethnocentric. There is a tradition of pretense among politically engaged documentarians. They argue that since mass media are very influential, their films have the potential to "alter the world." Since there are no reception studies of the documentary, the assumption must for now remain untested.

In recent years, most ethnographers have had to justify their work to the people they wish to study and attempt to compensate both individuals and the community. The need to justify is more commonly experienced by ethnographers than documentary filmmakers because ethnographers tend to stay in the field for prolonged periods and often wish to return for a restudy. They become temporary members of a community and, as such, assume certain obligations. Ethnographers have become increasingly aware that the people they study will read or see the finished product. This knowledge has to have a profound effect on how ethnographers characterize others. Most documentarians cannot afford to stay in the field very long, infrequently get to know the people they film very well, and almost never return to a site to make another film. It is becoming increasingly difficult for anyone to conduct any sort of field study anywhere in the world without justifying the work in terms that the people being studied understand. In that sense, ethnographies are becoming more "useful."

Questions of utility logically lead to considerations of audience, which, in turn, lead to a discussion of control of the production. For whom are these films made? Nichols suggests that they should "address an audience larger than anthropologists per se" (1994:66). For most anthropologists, their primary audience is other academics and then, in descending order of importance, graduate students, undergraduate students, and finally the educated general public.

For documentary/ethnographic film, the marketplace generally determines audience in that only certain projects get funded. It is assumed that because film is expensive and a mass medium, it must appeal to the largest possible audience. Currently available financing in the United States is largely confined to works that can be shown on public television with some secondary classroom use.

Most films labeled ethnographic are produced by independents—film-makers who operate outside of television stations, film studios, or the academic world (Nichols 1994:66). Nichols believes this is an advantage because the filmmakers are free of the restrictions of academia. I believe it is a deficit. Except for those of independent means, filmmakers must produce work that generates revenue and ensures their professional standing. They therefore strive to maintain certain production values because it is assumed that by so doing, they will attract a wide audience. With good ratings, the film will be deemed a success, making it possible to obtain funds for the next project. Consequently, documentary and ethnographic films are expensive and seldom experimental or risk-taking. Anthropologists associated with institutions are freed from these marketplace realities and could produce esoteric films designed to be understood by a small and select audience. They have not done so because they uncritically accept the professional limitations of the independent film community. Everyone seems to be striving to produce something the film industry calls "a good movie."

Ethnographic and documentary film in the United States has become dominated by public television. The possibility of a national television audience, together with the even greater potential of international broadcasting, has an enormous impact on how films are produced, from seemingly insignificant things like determining the length of a film (it must be must be thirty, sixty, or ninety minutes to be considered for television) to assumptions about an audience's ability to comprehend complex ideas that compete with their cultural predispositions. Virtually all research about television audiences in the United States suggests that viewers' motivation for watching television is the desire to be entertained. It is difficult to see anthropology's messages about the importance of culture in determining behavior or cultivating a nonjudge-mentalness about cultural difference as being entertaining. Anthropologists want to make people aware that difference can be appreciated without ethno-centric judgments. Viewers want to be amused by watching exotics doing strange things.

Whether independents can continue producing depends on their ability to sell their work—that is, they must conform to the values and suppositions of television and funding agencies. For example, television producers assume that their viewers will only have one chance to see a program. Audience profiles suggest that the people who watch PBS, and more specifically documentaries and ethnographic films, are urban, young middle-aged, well educated, primarily European American, with little or no knowledge of anthropology (Michael Ambrosino, personal communication, 1978). Audiences are motivated to watch these shows because they are curious about people and places exotic to their experience. They are not interested in anthropology per se. Although I have no empirical evidence to support it, I think that the audience for documentaries is composed primarily of people who also watch nature films and travelogues. Unlike psychological concepts, few anthropological concepts have entered common parlance—for every ten people who can explain what an Oedipus complex is, there is one who knows what patrilineality means. Logically, producers are loath to make any overly complex program that requires prior knowledge or is sufficiently difficult as to defy closure. It is assumed that successful programs end with a conclusion that gives the audience the comfort of knowing something clear and unproblematic. This assumption ensures that nothing very sophisticated will be aired.

The world of television programs seems at times to be fundamentally different from that of academic anthropology, in which most communications are tentative, even uncertain. Anthropological writings are designed for an esoteric audience of scholarly journals and university-press books in which a readership of students and fellow scholars seldom numbers more than a few thousand. Even "best-selling" authors like James Clifford are known to a relatively circumscribed circle of intellectuals and scholars. Few anthropologists before or after Margaret Mead have been interested in communicating to a mass audience or able to do so.

Whereas most ethnographic fieldwork is relatively inexpensive, a location documentary film typically costs in the hundreds of thousands of dollars. To gain approval from most funding agencies, the producers must demonstrate that there is a television market for the product with viewers who number in the hundreds of thousands if not millions. NEH and PBS are no different from corporate advertisers and commercial television networks. They want programs that will gain a substantial market share and seriously offend no one. I have personal knowledge of film projects that were turned down by NEH simply because the subject had been recently explored in another film—that is, the market had been saturated. When the educational film world was more lucrative, similar funding decisions were made based on the market need to develop certain curricula. This is not the way scholars make decisions about where to do research or what to study.

The intellectual curiosity that drives many anthropological research projects does not seem to be a dominant factor here. Seldom, if ever, do producers make esoteric ethnographic films designed to communicate to a select, sophisticated audience—the MacDougalls' Turkana Trilogy being an exception. Those independent documentary filmmakers outside the world of federal funds and public television tend to be motivated by a personal desire to explore social, political, and cultural issues that are parallel to, but separate from, the interests of most anthropologists. It is rare to find a film project ini-

tiated by an anthropologist who wishes to pictorially represent his or her research findings. The collaboration between Chagnon and Asch is an exception
(see chapter 4). The notion that film is a costly mass medium that can only justify itself if the work appeals to a mass audience dominates the thinking of
nearly everyone, scholar and producer alike.

No one makes a full-time living in ethnographic film production, even
though many try to. Only a few documentarians like Ken Burns, Errol Morris,
Les Blank, and Fred Wiseman survive on the income generated from their
work. What livelihood is created is the result of the production of marketable
films, not the study of anthropology. Since the profession with which one
identifies often determines one's loyalties, concept of success, and so on, the
fact that independent filmmakers control the production of ethnographic
films is significant. I am arguing that by training, interest, and temperament,
filmmakers who produce films labeled ethnographic look primarily to the
world of independent film and public television for validation and not to cultural anthropology.

There is a basic conflict between the conventions of successful television
documentary realism and an interpretive, reflexive, postcolonial, and critical
anthropology that has more to do with epistemological and economic differences than anything else. The former deals with packaging information in coherent units, whereas the latter sees knowledge as fragmentary, always
incomplete, and at times, contradictory.

Often filmmakers engage an anthropologist as a subject-matter specialist
but seldom as someone with authority equal to that of the producer. These
collaborations are rarely successful. Some are disastrous. They result in the
producer's needs always being foremost. Whether the film is good ethnography is secondary to whether it is "a good film." The point of this discussion is
not to denigrate the independent documentary filmmaking community but to
suggest that the purposes of ethnography cannot be served in that world. Nor
can its purposes be advanced by critiquing documentaries as ethnographies.
After decades of acting as a consultant for documentary and ethnographic
films, I am no longer willing to assume that role because it accomplishes little
in which I am interested.

Questions of utility, audience, and control of production are uncomfortable ones to seriously consider because addressing them reveals how little is
known about the reception of these films. Perhaps I am being overly harsh
about the potential of public television to communicate ethnography. At
present, we have so little information that it may be just a pessimistic assertion.
Along with a growing number of film and cultural-studies scholars, some anthropologists are beginning to recognize the need for ethnographic studies of
reception (Crawford and Hafsteinsson 1995). I explore these ideas more fully
in chapter 7. The only published work is most disturbing. Wilton Martinez's

(1992) research suggests that teachers of anthropology who use film may be perpetuating cultural stereotypes instead of challenging them. Fortunately, his findings are now being contested (Pack 1997), and the future may not be as bleak as it seemed. Nichols supports the need for studies of reception but suggests that "a visual anthropology devoted to the interpretation of texts" is needed because it "might raise from the anthropological unconscious questions regarding viewer and viewer response" (1994:80). Although I concur with the need for these studies, textual criticism is not adequate. The text needs to be contextualized, and therefore these studies must be ethnographic reception studies similar to those undertaken by Silverstone (1994). Nichols's suggestion merely reflects a lack of knowledge on the part of many film scholars about the abandonment of textual studies by many media scholars (Moores 1993).

I have argued that ethnographic film is most productively regarded as filmed ethnography, distinct from other filmic attempts to represent culture. It is to be critiqued in terms of how well it pictorially satisfies the requirements of ethnography. If anthropologists wish to move ethnographic film into the critical discourses within anthropology, they will have to gain control of its production and dissemination. None of these conditions currently exists. The future of ethnographic film as a significant contributor to anthropological discourse about the human condition lies in the development of critical expectations about how ethnographic knowledge can be transmitted pictorially. To explore this possibility, anthropologists must understand current thinking about the visible and pictorial world—both inside and outside of anthropology—and examine, critique, and borrow elements deemed usable in the creation of a theory and practice of film as ethnography.

Anthropologists also need to acquire a rudimentary understanding of video production and editing. The technology is relatively easy to master and inexpensive to acquire: everything necessary to record in the field costs about the same as the average computer. Simple editing facilities are becoming less and less expensive and more accessible. In this manner, field-workers can have a camera available throughout their fieldwork. They can grapple with questions about which aspects of culture are visible and how they might convey that knowledge and other fundamental questions about doing ethnography with a camera. How can you translate experience into images? Do images merely illustrate ideas, or are there "pictorial" ideas? Can you actually explore and discover with a camera, or must you wait until you know in order to film? When you are dealing with people whose sense of space, place, body movement, and event are different from your own, how do you know what you are looking at and when to turn the camera on or off?

It is only possible to explore these questions in the field when the ethnographer is freed from the economic restraints of professional filmmaking and the need to produce a marketable product. This approach does not involve the burden of raising hundreds of thousands of dollars, of transporting costly and delicate equipment, and of getting a crew used to the field situation, a particularly difficult task when they are seldom professionally trained or even committed to living through culture shock in order to accomplish their goals. The professional requirements of a filmmaker and the demands of public television for certain production values need not be a factor. Such a method would enable the anthropologist to show viewers what he or she "sees" and to edit the work as he or she sees fit regardless of the market potential of the final product.

Having access to the technology throughout the period of their fieldwork, anthropologists will be able to show the images they create to the people portrayed, enabling those depicted to actively engage in the creation of their image. They can develop their own critical relationship to the way in which they are represented, thus adding another layer of reflexivity to the work. In situations where people wish to produce their own tapes, it might be possible for multiple versions of the same event to appear in the same work, thus raising new questions about collaboration and multiple versions of actuality.

The uncritical acceptance of the conventions of broadcast journalism and mainstream documentary realism has not succeeded in creating filmed ethnography. Anthropologists incorrectly assumed that some cinematic styles are more "objective," more "scientific" than others. It is time to look at all forms of cinema for elements useful to the task. This approach will find allies among experimental and avant-garde producers. From Maya Deren (De Bouzek 1993) to Chick Strand (James n.d.), film artists have striven to make works that they regard as somehow "ethnographic." Unfortunately, they have done so with no support or commentary from the anthropological community. In addition, those dissonant elements from within the documentary community (works like *Silverlake Stories* [1993], *Daughter Rite* [1979], and *Far from Poland* [1984] come to mind) who play at the edges of the form could also become allies in this exploration.

Viewers will have to be cultivated and taught not to be passive. Their expectations about how a video should "look" will be violated. They will have to be taught that what they see in these new works is not a mistake or a sign of incompetence but rather the result of an authorial choice. They must accept the complexity of the work and actively view—stopping and rewinding the tape at passages unclear upon first glance. Viewers will have to learn to look at these videos not for the pleasure of the image but for the ethnographic knowledge and theoretical argument they contain. I am not making the old and tired argument that something called "ethnographic content" is more important than the cinematic form in which it is presented. I am arguing that the primary goal of an ethnographic film has to be communicating ethnographic knowledge, not producing something the industry calls "a good film." In a perfect world, all anthropological writers would produce compelling literature and all ethnographic filmmakers cinematic masterpieces. In reality, the professional consumers of anthropological knowledge "look through" or ignore the technical competence of anthropologists as writers to gain an understanding of the ideas contained in marginally competent writing. Why can't viewers of ethnographic film learn to do the same?

A final product could be designed for a tiny audience of specialists without violating funders' expectations or harming a filmmaker's reputation. It should be self-evident that from an economic standpoint, this activity would not be very rewarding. These "$1.98 videos" will have little commercial potential and lack the production values PBS deems necessary for broadcast. One cannot make a living from the kind of films I envision, but then the need to produce revenue from these activities inhibits the essential exploration of form.

As the cost of producing such work is minimal, once the anthropologist has secured funding for his or her fieldwork, the tapes could be sold at very modest prices. Probably no distribution company currently in existence would be able to accommodate this form of dissemination. Some sort of alternate distribution would have to be instituted. Deep Dish and Paper Tiger Television have created alternative systems of distribution for community and cable channels, which should be explored and possibly emulated.

Ethnographic film has been too long dominated by technical specialists and cinematic artists whose knowledge of the topic of their films is often limited to a few months of reading and scattered days of consulting with subject-matter specialists. To borrow a military cliché, ethnographic film is too serious a thing to be left to filmmakers.

Having introduced some of the problems associated with using film to communicate anthropology and proposed an alternative view and practice, I will now critically explore the works of several of the major U.S. filmmakers associated with ethnographic film—Flaherty, Gardner, and Asch—as well as the notion of research filming and indigenous media production. I will then proceed to discuss a number of issues fundamental to this subject, such as reflexivity, ethics, and reception. The book concludes with a view of pictorial ethnography and of film that provides the basis for an anthropological cinema to emerge.

Researching with a Camera:

The Anthropologist as Picture Taker

In October 1897 Messter's first German cinema catalogue appeared, illustrated with no less than 115 pages. . . . "By its means historical events can henceforth be preserved just as they happened and brought to view again not only now but also for the benefit of future generations . . . the lives and customs of the most distant primitives and tribes of savages." C. W. CERAM, *ARCHAEOLOGY OF THE CINEMA*

Now to be sure, to have "the actual facts" here we would have to have sound moving pictures which recorded not only everything which Navahos, interpreters and the investigator said, but also all their motor activities during the interviews.

CLYDE KLUCKHOLM, *NAVAHO WITCHCRAFT*

The Camera as a Positivist Dream Come True

One motivation for the creation of a motion-picture technology was to provide scientists with a mechanism to record and study human behavior (Musser 1990).[1] In fact, the tradition of research filming and the analysis of filmed behavior actually began prior to the invention of cinema with the work of people like E. Muybridge and E. Marey (Braun 1992). Their interest in animal and human locomotion motivated them to create protocinematic machines that would capture the subtleties and complexities of movement that were beyond the range of human vision. Although Muybridge's Zoopraxiscope and Marey's *chronophotographe* did not directly contribute to the technological breakthrough that signaled the beginning of the movies (Musser 1990), their work is an indication of the high level of interest in a technology that allowed humans to see behavior that occurred so rapidly as to be missed by the unaided eye.

The end of the nineteenth century was a period of optimism when it was widely believed that science would generate machines that would open up the mysteries of the universe and eventually provide an understanding of the laws of nature. Although the value of technology may be less certain today and the apparent indeterminacy of all things confuses and confounds more than enlightens, there is still a fascination with what the camera allows us to see, from the high-speed footage of a sprinter running the hundred-yard dash to the time-lapse sequences of the flowering of a desert plant.

The technology that aided vision held an additional attraction: information collected with these mechanical devices was regarded as being qualitatively and quantitatively superior to that obtained with the unaided eye.

[T]echniques of mechanical reproduction held out the promise of images uncontaminated by interpretation. . . . [T]he scientists' continuing claim to such judgment-free representation is testimony to the intensity of their longing for the perfect, "pure" image. In this context, the machine stood for authenticity; it was at once an observer and an artist, miraculously free from the inner temptation to theorize, anthropomorphize, beautify, or otherwise interpret nature. What the human observer could achieve only by iron self-discipline, the machine achieved willy-nilly—such, at least, was the hope, often expressed and just as often dashed. Here constitutive and symbolic functions of the machine blur, for the machine seemed at once a means to, and symbol of, mechanical objectivity. . . . One type of mechanical image, the photograph, became the emblem for all aspects of non-interventionist objectivity. . . . This was not because the photograph was necessarily truer to nature than hand-made images— many paintings bore a closer resemblance to their subject matter than early photographs, if only because they used color—but rather because the camera apparently eliminated human agency. Nonintervention, not verisimilitude, lay at the heart of mechanical objectivity, and this is why mechanically produced images captured its message best. (Daston and Galison 1992:81–128)

Cinema expands our vision in time as the microscope has expanded it in space. It permits us to see facts which escape our senses because they pass too quickly. It will become the instrument of the physiologist as the microscope has become that of the anatomist. Its importance is as great. . . . It [the cinema] provides exact and permanent documents to those who study movements. The film of a movement is better for research than the simple viewing of movement; it is superior, even if the movement is slow. Film decomposes movement in a series of images that one can examine at leisure while slowing the movement at will, while stopping it as necessary. Thus it eliminates the personal factor, whereas a movement, once it is finished, cannot be recalled except by memory, and this, even put in sequence, is not faithful. All in all, a film is superior to the best description. (Regnault 1922:65, translated by Rony 1996:46–47)

Motion-picture filming became regarded as a tool uniquely suited for certain scientific investigations. Gotthard Wolf, one of the founders of the *Encyclopedia Cinematographica* (EC) in Germany, has argued that

it is rarely possible to reconstruct a complicated movement from a verbal description without the aid of some visual method. The film makes it possible to record and to reproduce such transient phenomena. Furthermore movements can be studied by repeated viewing of the films as well as by measurement and analysis of the individual pictures, the results of which may frequently go beyond those obtainable with other methods. The film is thus a valuable tool in scientific research. (Wolf 1967:4)

Although the EC dealt with many scientific studies outside of human behavior, ethnology/sociocultural anthropology was one of its main divisions. The films about culture produced and accepted in the EC were treated in a fashion parallel to those in physics—that is, as scientifically obtained objective data. In a 1981 catalog from Pennsylvania State University, the U.S. repository for the EC collection, the basis for this collection was described as follows:[2]

Phenomena to be scientifically studied should be recorded on film because:
1. They cannot be observed by the unaided human eye and therefore demand the use of such film techniques as slow-motion or time-lapse cinematography.
2. They need to be compared with other phenomena—for which purpose verbal descriptions are inadequate.
3. They do not occur frequently; they are not readily available for observation by other individuals or students; or they are disappearing from the culture. (*Encyclopedia Cinematographica Catalog* 1981:i)

The EC collection was regarded as being sufficiently important to science that in 1975, a group of Nobel Prize recipients meeting in Lindau, Germany, passed a resolution endorsing its value.[3]

As point three in the EC list suggests, there was also some urgency to collect these data from certain parts of the world. By the end of the nineteenth century, Westerners were acutely aware of the rapid changes that they had wrought among non-Western cultures. World War II accelerated the pace of assumed "cultural loss" and change at an alarming rate. It was taken for granted that all that was unique and interesting about these "exotic Others" was being lost forever—that the cultures were "disappearing." There is, of course, great irony in this concern. As capitalism, colonial empires, and Christianity worked at a fever pitch to Westernize the world, scholars tried to preserve those very elements that the economic, political, and religious missionaries sought to destroy. A response to these perceived changes was to attempt to "salvage" and document as much exotica as possible and to reconstruct (some would argue construct) a precontact version of these cultures. This motivation fueled much exploration, anthropological and otherwise, for the past hundred and fifty years and remains until the present a motivation for much documentary and ethnographic filmmaking. In the popular imagination, it is one of the prime reasons for the existence of anthropology. It is also regarded by many of the cultures that were supposed to have "disappeared" by now as a profoundly offensive way of looking at their lifestyles.

Photographs and films of culture were thought to preserve reliable data for future generations. These photochemical records of human behavior were regarded as superior engines of description because they were believed to be objective—unimpeachable evidence. This assumption thus associated the filmed record of humanity with a nineteenth-century positivist science.

Only cinema provides objective documents in abundance; thanks to cinema, the anthropologist can, today, collect the life of all peoples; he will possess in his drawers all the special acts of different races. He will be able to thus have contact at the same time with a great number of peoples. He will study, when it pleases him, the series of movements that man executes for squatting, climbing trees, seizing and handling objects with his feet, etc. He will be present at feasts, at battles, at religious and civil ceremonies, at different ways of trading, eating, relaxing. (Regnault 1923:680–81, translated by Rony 1996:48)

In the seventy years since Regnault made that statement, the status of the idea of a positivist objectivity and its relationship to film and anthropology has become very complicated (see Rony 1996 for a critique of Regnault's work). In recent years, a number of scholars have questioned the validity of both positivism and objectivity. It may be that research film's association with these concepts has made it suspect for some. If objectivity and the philosophy underlying it—positivism—are discredited concepts, then the attraction of film as a superior form of recording is also in doubt. Therefore, to justify the use of film as a research tool, it becomes necessary to articulate a new rationale. Thus far, none has been forthcoming, and the idea of research film has languished.

To add to the reluctance of some to explore the scientific potential of film, the conflict over whether cinema (and indeed all forms of photochemical and electronic picture making) is an objective witness suitable for research purposes or an art form primarily useful as an expressive outlet has confused and perplexed many people. This apparent conundrum undoubtedly hampered a more extensive exploration of film as a social-science research tool (for an example of the dilemma, see the discussion between Mead and Bateson in Brand 1976). For example, Heider bases his analysis of ethnographic film on an assumed and unquestioned dichotomy between the "science" of anthropology and the "art" of film (1976). This dichotomy is simplistic and reflects an outmoded view of both art and science. In order to allow film to realize its potential in anthropology, these assumptions must be questioned. A theory of film and a theory of anthropology have to be constructed that will avoid this dead-ended distinction. I offer the beginning of a new approach in the concluding chapter.

Whatever the complexities, there is a long and rich history of efforts to use the technology of film to enhance our understanding of the world. In its fullest manifestation, film depicting human movement has been produced and analyzed for a large variety of purposes.[4] For example, the creation and analysis of film/video footage is now an integral part of the training of virtually all serious athletes—golfers, tennis and football players, gymnasts, and so on. In this instance, the analysis is completely pragmatic. There is no need to theorize about the activity. Its validity is tested in a relatively uncomplicated manner: does the golfer's swing improve after a careful examination of his or her behavior on film? Thousands of athletes and their coaches have spent untold hours learning how to become microanalysts of human movement. Their studies carry with them the burden of serious financial losses or rewards. One misstep by a quarterback can spell the difference between a sack and a touchdown or, worse, the end of a multimillion-dollar career.

The examination of filmed human behavior has fundamentally altered the way we see ourselves. This vast area deserves an amount of attention not possible in this study. Someone needs to do for film what William Ivins did for prints (1953) and Estelle Jussim did for photography (1983)—that is, explore the transformative potential of film on the human self-image. Now that human beings can see themselves in a way not possible with the unaided eye, what do they see and what are the consequences?

The Camera as an Anthropological Research Tool

Having claimed such general power for the motion picture, I will now return to a consideration of its role in cultural anthropological research. There is a tradition that stretches from the beginning of photography until the present day of anthropologists' attempting to use still- and moving-picture cameras to generate researchable data about culture. Developing a visual anthropology in which these tools become commonplace for the cultural anthropologist has been no easy task. Contradictory forces are at play. Although few would disagree with Margaret Mead's contention that "anthropology . . . has always been highly dependent upon photography" (1968:166), Mead has also pointed out that visual anthropology finds itself "in a discipline of words" (1975:1).

Recording cultural behavior on film has its origins in Europe with French physiologist and anthropologist Félix-Louis Regnault's study of Wolof pottery-making techniques and locomotion at a Paris exposition in 1896 (Rony 1996) and Alfred Cort Haddon's Torres Straits expedition in 1897. This formative period has been thoroughly examined by Alison Griffiths in "Origins of Ethnographic Film" (1998). From the 1950s onward, it blossomed in Europe and is most completely realized in Germany with *Encyclopedia Cinematographica* at the Institute for Scientific Film (*Insitut für den Wissenschaftlichen Film*) (Fuchs 1988; Taureg 1983).

In the United States, an interest in researching with a movie camera began as early as 1906 with people like Pliny Earl Goddard (Griffiths 1998). In the 1930s, Franz Boas attempted to finish his decades-long study of dance and body movement in Alaska by taking some film footage but died before he could reach any conclusions (Ruby 1980b). One of the first research-film projects completed in the United States was accomplished by Margaret Mead, Boas's student, and Gregory Bateson in Bali, also in the 1930s (Jacknis 1984). Influenced by Mead, Ray Birdwhistell developed a method for exploring the cultural basis of body movement called kinesics in the 1950s (1980), which was dependent on filmed records. In the 1960s and 1970s, Allison Jablonko (1968) and E. Richard Sorenson (1967), both students of Mead, conducted anthropological film research in New Guinea employing and embellishing upon Mead's ideas. Their studies are among the few in which film was actually submitted as an integral part of a dissertation in anthropology. During the 1960s and 1970s, the research-film idea reached an apex with a group of scholars and filmmakers associated with Sorenson (1967) and the Smithsonian Institution's Anthropological Film Archive. Alan Lomax's study of dance and culture (Choreometrics) and Edward Hall's proxemic investigations of space use as culturally symbolic behavior (1969) also involved the use of filmed data.

All of these scholars assumed that filmed records of human behavior would be of use to scholars other than the creators of the footage and that an archive of these materials would therefore be useful. This idea was first articulated in a resolution proposed by Félix-Louis Regnault and adopted by the 1900 International Ethnographic Congress of Paris. "All anthropological museums should add suitable film archives to their collections. The mere possession of a potter's wheel, a number of weapons or a primitive loom is not sufficient for a full understanding of their functional use; this can only be handed down to posterity by means of precise cinematographic records" (Regnault 1900:421, translated by Rony 1996:47). An archive was not realized in any systematic manner until the 1950s in Germany with the creation of the Institute for Scientific Film and in the United States at Pennsylvania State University, with the creation of the Psychological Cinema Register. The 1970s saw the development of the Anthropological Film Archive at the Smithsonian.

Although the idea of studying archived filmed information about culture obtained by another scholar remains theoretically possible, only a few anthropologists have actually conducted and published the results of such a study. Margaret Mead, a vocal advocate of field-research filming, was convinced that photographic and filmed records could be used for research purposes by scholars who had never been at the location of their filming; hence, her seminal role in the creation of the Smithsonian facility. Indeed, she was able to produce a study of child development with John McGregor in which McGregor used Mead's filmed data without ever actually setting foot in the field (1951). Apart from Alan Lomax's use of footage shot by numerous people for his study of dance as culture (1968), there is little evidence to support this potential value of a film archive. These institutions function more as sources for stock footage to be used for the production of compilation films and as places where scholars of film can study the behavior of the makers rather than as places to study the behavior of the filmed subjects. Some indigenous people have begun examining archived film footage of their culture's ceremonial life in hopes of revitalizing their own traditions (John Homiak, personal communication, 1997).

The U.S. field researchers just mentioned and indeed all anthropological scholars who studied human behavior with a camera share an interest in the cultural mechanics of body movement, locomotion, motor skills, gesture, posture, dance, the display of emotion, and space use. This interest developed quite independently of similar studies in France (Mauss 1939). Although Boas's notion of motor skills as culturally conditioned and Marcel Mauss's "Techniques of the Body" are similar, there is no evidence that either man was aware of the other's work. Movement, space, and time are the cultural variables for which the camera is best suited. The body is viewed as a means of cultural expression, or to use a contemporary phrase, the moving body embodies culture. Often the study of clothing and tattooing as bodily adornment is included. As the camera can only record bodies occupying space through time, it is these dimensions of culture that must be emphasized. At various times, this field has been called paralinguistics and nonverbal communication. It is sometimes included as an aspect of semiotics (Leeds-Hurwitz 1993). The emphasis was most often on the microlevel of movement as cultural behavior. The underlying assumption among these scholars of bodily detail was that whereas the range of potential body movements was biologically predetermined, actual movements—their sequence, duration, and meaning—were learned and cultural. The complexity of bodies moving through space and time is such that the unaided eye cannot take in all that is happening. So logically these scholars gravitated toward the camera as a means of recording data.

Although the idea of researching with a camera may be as old as anthropology itself, it remains a very minor tradition that has not produced results of sufficient consequence to attract many "mainstream" anthropologists—that is, anthropologists whose dominant area of interest is not nonverbal communication. Consequently, the literature about anthropological research film is filled with enthusiasm for its potential and calls for more anthropologists to join those who film in the field. What it seems to lack is a convincing theoretical basis, a well-developed set of methods, or much evidence that the technology produces analyzable data of a quantity and quality unique enough to support its use.

As early as 1900, Regnault argued that the technology would transform anthropology:

Thanks to [films and phonographs], the psychologist, the ethnographer, the sociologist, the linguist, and the folklorist will collect in their laboratories all the manners of numerous ethnicities and will be able to call up life at their will. In analyzing, in measuring these objective documents, in comparing them, in organizing them, they will fix the methods which make up their science, and know the laws of human mentality. The ethnographic museum with its collections of objects, films and phonographic records will become our laboratory and our center of teaching. (Regnault 1931:304–6, translated by Rony 1996:62)

This interest in film as a research tool is a logical extension of an earlier interest in still photography as a data-collecting device. In 1844, five years after the invention of the process, an anatomist, Antoine-Étienne-Renaud-Augustin Serres, displayed to the French Academy of Sciences daguerreotypes of a Botocudo man and woman taken in Paris by Adolf Thiesson, a photographer. Serres commented that a collection of daguerreotypes would be useful for the study of the human races (Serres 1844). Serres was sufficiently convinced of the validity of this idea to commission Thiesson to travel to several countries to produce more daguerreotypes of different "racial" types for a proposed "Musée Photographiques des Races Humaines." Serres (1845) thought that photography would provide the needed objective data base for making comparative anthropology a true science. As noted earlier, the advent of motion-picture technology merely extended this assumption of the great potential for photochemical recordings.

The hope for research film continued for decades. In 1949, Patrick O'Reilly complained that fifty years after the birth of the motion picture, research film had still not found its "rightful place" in anthropology. In the first overview of the role of research film in science in 1955, Anthony Michaelis confirmed O'Reilly's complaint. "It is more than disappointing to realize that only a limited number of them [anthropological films] can have been made from scientific research, and that so few anthropologists have followed Regnault's far-sighted precedent" (Michaelis 1955:188). In spite of these well-intended admonitions and E. Richard Sorenson's attempts to create a methodology and encourage more people to use film (1967), the possibility of generating researchable filmed materials is seldom even discussed anymore among anthropologists.[5]

The lack of a generally agreed upon justification and method for producing moving images and the insufficiency of analytic procedures have severely hampered this development. A loss of belief in the possibility of objectivity undermined the assumed unique potential of the medium. Only a few anthropologists currently employ the camera in a systematic manner to generate researchable data. The majority are primatologists. In spite of Steve Feld and Carroll Williams's attempt to articulate what constitutes a researchable film "language" (1975), anthropologists literally do not know where to point the camera, when to turn it on or off, and what to do with the film once it is generated. Moreover, they seem to be unwilling to question the conventions of other forms of cinema such as the documentary in order to discover an approach to filming uniquely suited to their purposes.

An interest in the cultural aspects of body movement and space use that necessitated the use of the camera was heavily invested in a structural model derived from the adaptation of structural linguistic paradigms to nonlinguistic forms of communication. The underlying assumption is that there are "languages of the body." Researchers searched for the bodily equivalent of the phoneme and morpheme and the grammar and syntax of movement. They failed to find them and were often reduced to making generalizations about "American" or "Indian" culture unsupported by published data (Birdwhistell 1980). Few ethnographies of body movement or space use that resulted from the analysis of filmed data were ever published. Lomax's approach to the anthropology of dance has found little support from other dance researchers who themselves seldom use film in their researches (Adrianne Kaeppler, personal communication, 1994).

Poststructuralist and postmodern critiques of structuralism succeeded in casting doubts on all nonlinguistic work modeled after linguistic paradigms. Microanalytic studies of filmed behavior, never very common even in their heyday, are seldom undertaken by anthropologists today but continue in disciplines like social psychology, where affect and interpersonal interaction studies have apparently benefited from use of this technology (Ekman 1982). Studies of the symbolic uses of space are more commonly conducted by architects and city planners than anthropologists, and even these researchers infrequently employ cameras.

An interesting dilemma can be seen here. It is self-evident that body movement and space use do vary among different cultures and are therefore legitimate areas of anthropological inquiry. Given the complexity and subtlety of the phenomena, recording data with a camera seems altogether logical. Anyone who spends any time in other cultures and is the slightest bit observant knows that people "sign" their culture with their bodies and the way they use space differs. From Boas's interest in motor skills onward, anthropologists have paid lip service to the need to study the anthropology of movement and space (Ruby 1983). Most introductory textbooks in cultural anthropology have sections that talk about proxemics and kinesics as if they were established fields of inquiry with a considerable literature. The term *body language* has been found in common parlance for several decades.

Yet little actual research about the body has been undertaken with a camera. Why? The problem may reach beyond the technical ignorance that inhibits many anthropologists from using cameras for any purpose. Margaret Lock has suggested that it is a generalized shortcoming of anthropology. "Since the body mediates all reflection and action upon the world, its centrality to the anthropological endeavor seems assured, but a perusal of the canon of social and cultural anthropology indicates that the body's explicit appearance has been sporadic throughout the history of the discipline" (1993:133). Ted Polhemus (1975) makes an argument that our cultural discomfort with the body has inhibited these explorations. Brenda Farnell expands upon these suggestions:

[T]he long-standing neglect of the body and human movement in the Western philosophical tradition, bolstered by the Christian disdain for the body as flesh, has in turn, deflected most social theorists from taking the embodiment of persons seriously. . . . Many investigators find it hard to imagine how body movement might "mean" at all beyond a kind of emotional incontinence, far less contribute anything to our understanding of social structure and cultural practices. . . . I am suggesting that detailed attention to the moving, visual component of human action and interaction in social events has been neglected in the social sciences to date because of fundamental philosophical difficulties inherent in the objectivist separation of mind from body, reason from imagination, cognition from emotion, and verbal from nonverbal, all of which have prevented modes of registration and specification for body movement becoming part of the conceptual resources, and therefore of the research practices of Western academics. (1994:35–36)

Wholstein (1977) has suggested that using the camera to generate accurate researchable data about spatial relations is extremely complicated and requires so much control over the setting in which the filming is to occur as to diminish the technology's potential. Even the briefest glance at Edward T. Hall's "Handbook for Proxemic Research" (1974) makes it clear that the study of space as symbolic behavior can easily drown even the best researcher in an unreasonably large amount of data. Although Hall spells out clearly how to do proxemic studies, I can find no publications that employed his methods. Others have argued that because film is "inherently" descriptive and can only display the particular in a minutely detailed fashion, it is unsuited to the cultural explorations of anthropology, which are generalizing and abstract in their construction (Asch et al. 1991).

There are other theoretical explanations. As Farnell has argued (1994), there has been a shift in interest away from the physical features of body movement to conceiving of the body as cultural symbol characterized by the term *the anthropology of the body*. It is now territory claimed by medical anthropologists, who explore the body in terms of social constructions of health and illness (Lock 1993) and social theorists like Michel Foucault (1977), who characterize the body as a site of contestation in which women, gays, and other oppressed people struggle to reclaim their identity and resist an image assumed to be designed by the culture industry to augment their oppression. Neither of these approaches creates an interest in the microanalytic or the mechanics of body movement. They do not seem to require the generation of researchable filmed data about movement, duration, or space. These scholars' only interest in the pictorial lies in the analysis of mass-mediated and medical images as sites of oppression (Cartwright 1995; Brownell 1995).

Perhaps all of these factors have contributed to a loss of whatever interest there was in the ethnographic study of cultural features of body movement and space use within anthropology and the need to film behavior in order to study it. The impact of this failure goes beyond the mere lack of use of this technology. The absence of a theoretical approach to the symbolic implications of bodies moving through time and space—culture as embodied knowledge—has also hampered the development of ethnographic film designed to be screened in public.

Although film may have been used by only a few anthropologists to generate data narrowly focused on the microanalytic study of body movement and space, there is a far more common research utilization of this medium. Countless anthropologists have taken ciné field notes since the advent of the 16mm camera in the 1920s. The practice continues until the present as low-cost hi-8mm video cameras are becoming as commonplace as the 35mm still camera in many cultural anthropologists' field kits. Ceremonies and rituals are often the subject of this filming because they have a clear cultural scenario—a definite beginning, middle, and end. Dance and the construction of material objects are also favorite subjects. As few anthropologists have formal training in film production, the quality of much of the work is technically marginal, often resembling the footage taken by tourists. As synchronous-sound film equipment is expensive and usually requires more than one person to operate, most of the footage shot before the advent of video is silent.[6]

This work is seldom edited into finished films and has gone largely unstudied even by the people who produced it. I recently discovered a cache of processed but unopened 16mm film boxes belonging to a deceased colleague that he shot in Africa in the 1950s. I have a strong hunch similar finds could be made in many departments of anthropology in the United States. Only a small percentage of this film has ended up in an archive. Little is known about this vast body of work. It is almost never presented in public as part of the field-worker's "publication." Moreover, the picture-taking habits of anthropologists in general have rarely been studied (see V. J. Caldarola's 1986 master's thesis as an exception). Like written notes and photographs, the film footage produced during fieldwork is a private document. Field-workers discover upon their return that it is unprofitable to subject the footage to close and detailed analysis or to edit it into a finished film.

At one time, it was thought possible for field-workers to produce footage that was both analyzable and usable for the production of a film. Boas unsuccessfully attempted to interest the motion-picture industry in a project in which anthropologists would work collaboratively with professional filmmakers to produce films about various cultures that would have box-office appeal as well as research value to the anthropologists (Jacknis 1987). Mead and Bateson's Balinese films exemplify the possibility of producing useful, researchable footage, but they are a rarity. Filmmaking conventions developed that tended to interfere with the assumed scholarly needs for researchable data. The perceived conflict between filmmaking's aesthetic conventions and positivism's scholarly requirements for researchable data caused film to be underutilized as an analytic technique. For example, filmmakers tend to fragment and reconstitute action into synthetic sequences that suggest time relationships sometimes at variance with the photographed action. Some anthropologists believe that only footage shot at eye level with a minimum of camera movement and with real-time coverage of the event are scientifically usable (Wolf 1967). Strategies appropriate to fiction were believed to create barriers between anthropologists and film professionals. These naive assumptions about the differences between the art of film and the science of anthropology are slowly being replaced by a conception of film as a culturally bound communication usable in a variety of discourses.

Based on an examination of the film work of a limited number of anthropologists, I contend that the majority of this footage would be difficult, if not impossible, to make into a film of interest to anyone except those with expert knowledge of the subject matter. Although such an endeavor would seem on the surface to be worthwhile—that is, producing a scholarly film of interest only to other scholars—anthropologists seem to have accepted the general cultural assumption that film must appeal to an audience larger than a few scholars. In addition, the marketplace governs decisions to distribute films. There is therefore little hope that a film made from footage shot by a nonfilmmaker could be edited into a marketable product.

There are certain parallels between the production of motion pictures and the production of still photographs in the field and their subsequent use for analysis. Although the subject of this book is not photography, it is a more commonplace field-media activity than film. Anthropologists' assumptions about photography undoubtedly inform their decisions about how moving pictures are employed. Therefore, some discussion of the role of still photography in cultural anthropological inquiry will be useful. For many years, the still camera has been a normal part of most cultural anthropologists' field equipment. A conservative estimate would place the number of photographs taken by anthropologists in the millions.

If "taking pictures" is an anthropological activity, it would seem quite reasonable to expect to find a body of literature that demonstrates that anthropological picture taking is somehow justifiable—supported by theory and methods and a tradition of proven results. In other words, if anthropologists spend their time, money, and energy taking pictures, they must do so because the unique qualities of this medium allow them to record, analyze, and present some visual manifestation of culture that could not be dealt with in any other way or that, at least, is dealt with better in this manner.

It was suggested earlier that these supports are missing for motion pictures. The situation is not appreciably better for photography. Both of these media were initially attractive to anthropologists because it was assumed that they had certain unique qualities that made them superior objective data-collecting devices. As the basis for this assumption has been successfully undermined, it has not been replaced with an alternative justification.

An examination of the traditional manuals for fieldwork, such as the Royal Anthropological Institute's *Notes and Queries on Anthropology* (1951), reveals a discussion about photography that is wholly technical—for example, which kind of film to use in the tropics. John Collier Jr.'s *Visual Anthropology* (1967), a canonical work, is equally deficient. Collier, a trained painter and photographer, was a pioneer in the effort to utilize photography in anthropological field research. However, a lack of formal training in anthropology and a naive belief in the objectivity of photographed evidence limited his contribution to technical suggestions about activities like photoelicitation interviewing. Margaret Mead and Gregory Bateson's *Balinese Character*, published in 1942, remains one of the few fully realized photographic ethnographies. I know of no scholarly literature dealing with the uses of image technology that does not suffer from a naive belief in the objective quality of photographed data or concentrate on the technical. We are therefore led to the somewhat confusing conclusion that although the proven anthropological relevance of photography is extremely limited, anthropologists continue to take a lot of pictures.

Looked at cynically, the still camera functions as an identity badge for field-workers. The act of picture taking helps to fulfill their image of a proper anthropologist. They take pictures in order to be good anthropologists and seldom in order to do anthropology. When they present themselves publicly or in writing, they perpetuate this image by including photographs in their lectures and books. However, to dismiss the activity on this basis alone would be a serious error. The lack of theoretical or methodological support does not mean that taking photographs is not an important component in the construction of an ethnography. It simply means that it is a practice without a theory.[7]

Although it may appear somewhat illogical, there can be little doubt that many anthropologists regard photographic field records as essential for writing their ethnographies. Making photographs remains a standard part of the behavior of most field researchers. The photographs are used, as Collier suggests (1967), as elicitation devices in interviews and as gifts for those people who allow themselves to be studied. As members of a culture that regularly uses photographs as a device for reclaiming experience (Musello 1980), anthropologists employ field photographs in the same way as they would use photographs of a wedding or a Fourth of July picnic—to recall experience. In the process of narrating the event surrounding the making of the photograph—a culturally common conversational trope—anthropologists reclaim their memories of the details of that event. The importance of this *aide de memoire* for the production of ethnographies should not be underestimated. Anthropologists may lack an explicit theory or method, but nonetheless, the thought of trying to write up their work without their photographs is daunting. One colleague told me that when his field photographs were stolen from his car on the way home from the field, the loss significantly delayed the completion of his ethnography.

Since using home movies to reconstruct experience is less common than employing still photographs in this manner, anthropologists do not have a similar cultural norm to appropriate. Moreover, the mechanics of retrieving and looking at photographs is relatively uncomplicated, whereas viewing film or even videotapes is less easy. One can search through many photographs in a relatively short period of time to locate the one image of interest. No such technology exists for film or videotapes.

However, a lack of theory and method has not prevented anthropologists from taking moving pictures in the field or from depositing them in places where others can view them. The question that comes to mind at this point is, would a theory of culture that logically generated a methodological necessity for gathering data with a camera create a situation in which camera-created information would illuminate a new understanding of culture?

I shall return to this possibility. At present, I wish to make concrete some of the abstract and generalized statements that I have made thus far by examining Franz Boas's experiment with the motion-picture camera.

Researching with a Camera

In 1930, Boas, one of the founding figures in U.S. anthropology, took a motion-picture camera and wax-cylinder sound-recording machine to the northwest coast. It was the seventy-year-old Boas's last field trip to the
Kwakwaka'wakw (Kwakiutl), a people he had studied for more than forty
years. He was accompanied by Julia Averkieva, a Russian anthropologist. During the field trip, Boas shot 16mm motion-picture footage of dances, games,
and some methods of manufacturing; recorded songs and music; and in general, sought to gain those bits of information he felt were missing from his
knowledge of the culture. Boas died in 1944, having neither completed the
analysis of the data he collected nor published the results. Some of his colleagues thought that the materials might have been stolen before Boas could
work on them. In describing the apparent loss, Ruth Benedict stated in a letter
to Margaret Mead that "Papa Franz takes it very hard that his pictures are
gone; he counted on them for a study of rhythm and he even says, 'I might as
well have stayed at home last winter'" (Mead 1959:405–6). Fortunately, the
films did survive. Franziska Boas, Franz Boas's daughter, states, "[T]he films
were not stolen. As I understand it, the wax cylinders [sound recordings] were
stolen out of Gladys Reichard's car trunk" (personal communication, 1978).
The point is worth making only because the idea that the loss of the films prevented Boas from doing research persists today (Jo-Ann Kealiinoh Omoku in
Hanna 1979:327).

I believe that Boas, like most anthropologists who have tried to use this
technology, simply could not find a way to profitably study the data he generated. Ray Birdwhistell concurs. He "was told by several [people] including
Margaret Mead and Jane Belo that there was no method available which suited
his [Boas's] interest in rhythm" (Birdwhistell, personal communication, 1975).

In any event, Boas asked his former student Gene Weltfish to study the
footage of games and technology because of her long-term interest in motor
habits. Her own research was sufficiently demanding at the time that she was
unable to complete the analysis (Weltfish, personal communication, 1976).
Boas also asked his daughter to study the dance footage. "The analysis of the
dance films was done by me [Franziska Boas] and was enlarged with material
from the 'Social Organization and Secret Societies of the Kwakiutl Indians'
[Boas 1897], and part of it was published as discussion after the Kwakwaka'wakw article by Boas in 'The Function of Dance in Human Society.'
The manuscript of that was sent to Erna Gunther along with the films"
(Franziska Boas, personal communication, 1975).

In the mid-1930s, Boas commissioned Stuyvesant Van Veen, a painter
working with David Efron on the study of gesture, to make some drawings
from the 1930 footage (Van Veen, personal communication, 1977). In 1961,

Researching with a Camera

Franziska Boas gave the footage, drawings, and manuscript to the Burke Museum of the University of Washington. Bill Holm of the Burke Museum edited the footage into a two-part film (Part I: *Games and Technology;* Part II: *Dances and Ceremonies*), annotated the footage with appropriate citations from Boas's publications, and attempted to locate the Kwakwaka'wakw in the film and ask them to describe what was depicted. The films, together with Holm's notes, are available from the University of Washington Press.

From the films, drawings, Boas's letters, publications, and the memories of people knowledgeable about the project, it is possible to partially reconstruct Boas's intentions, research plans, and ideas for the public presentation of the results. It provides a case study of the ways in which anthropologists have tried to use this medium in their research and publications. I am not claiming that Boas's work is somehow typical. He was one of the first anthropologists in the United States to use the motion-picture camera to generate data in natural settings (as opposed to a laboratory) in order to study gesture, motor habits, and dance as manifestations of culture. Although some anthropologists did take motion pictures in the field prior to Boas, they were more interested in exhibiting them to the public than in using them for scholarly purposes (Griffiths 1998). I believe that a systematic study of other anthropologists since Boas would reveal that although the technology has gotten more sophisticated, the problems remain the same—finding a productive method of data generation and analysis.

I have previously explored Boas's role in the development of a visual anthropology (Ruby 1983), as has Ira Jacknis (1984, 1987). Boas took a still camera with him on his first field trip in 1883. Dissatisfied with his own skills, he hired a professional in 1894. He is at least partially responsible for making picture taking a normative part of the anthropologist's field experience—a characteristic that has distinguished anthropologists from other students of the human condition. One can only speculate on the development of the general field of body-motion studies and visual anthropology had Boas completed his 1930 study and published the results. Would he have created an analytic method that produced the results he envisioned?

An examination of the footage together with references by Boas to the filming in his field letters (Rohner 1969) plus statements from his posthumously published article on dance (Boas 1944) and other publications provide an opportunity to reconstruct Boas's attitude toward filming as a research strategy and to speculate about how his ideas about body movement, dance, and culture became an ideology that caused him to construct the footage in a particular way. Blackman (1977) has previously examined Boas's potlatch photographs in a similar fashion. Boas's interest in body movements and dance brought together several lifelong themes in his work—the relationship of race and culture to behavior and the study of expressive and aesthetic forms of culture.

Whereas Boas had used still photography in the field since 1894, his interest in and use of the motion-picture camera was of much shorter duration. He wrote nothing about film as a scientific tool or even about his views on the role of the cinema in society. I have wondered for some time why Boas never reacted formally to Robert Flaherty's *Nanook of the North*—a popular film about people he had studied. Surely it must have been a topic of conversation among Boas's friends, colleagues, and students. The only connection I have uncovered is that Frances Flaherty, Robert's wife and collaborator, once visited Boas in 1914 to ask his support for her husband's work (see chapter 2). He declined.

I do not know whether Boas went to the movies or to travel and lecture films or whether he, like many of his contemporaries, saw all film as a vulgar perversion for the uneducated masses or, like Merian Cooper (1925), thought the medium had a great deal of educational potential. As Alison Griffiths (1998) has demonstrated, Boas undoubtedly participated in the various discussions the staff at the American Museum of Natural History in New York had about the role of films in anthropological and museum educational programs. After Boas's return from the field, he did engage in a discussion with Will Hays, head of the Motion Picture Producers and Distributors, regarding the possibility of anthropologists and professional filmmakers' working collaboratively (Jacknis 1987). Perhaps Boas's personal experience with filming in the field piqued his interest.

Boas certainly knew that some anthropologists, such as Regnault or Haddon in the 1897 Torres Straits expedition, had taken movie cameras into the field (Griffiths 1998). Many of these early attempts at making researchable film footage were frustrated by the bulkiness and costliness of 35mm-film equipment. Even when 16mm film did appear in 1923, it was marketed by Kodak as a strictly amateur film for making home movies—the moving-picture equivalent to the brownie snapshot. Professional filmmakers referred to 16mm as "substandard" to distinguish it from "real" film (that is, 35mm). For technological reasons, there was little chance for the use of field-research film to expand until the end of the 1920s.

Where Boas actually learned the mechanics of filmmaking is also unknown. Franziska Boas says her father "never had used a motion picture camera before. If he followed his usual pattern, he would have gotten instructions from a photographer and practiced with a camera before he left" (Franziska Boas, personal communication, 1976). It is interesting to speculate about whether his choice not to engage a professional filmmaker as collaborator was due to budgetary limitations or to a preference for shooting the footage himself. He had used a professional still photographer on earlier field trips (Jacknis 1984).

In screening his films on Kwakwaka'wakw dance, one notices the wax-cylinder sound recorder visible at times. Since the length of time the camera will run without rewinding the motor or replacing the film differs from the length of time the recorder will run, we can see Julia Averkieva, Boas's field assistant—a marvelous apparition with bobbed hair and a full-length leather coat—appear several times to change the wax cylinders. As Boas did not write about his field techniques, it is not certain what he was attempting. He could have been trying to record the dance and music at the same time for efficiency's sake, or he may have naively assumed that he could synchronously record sound and image. It was, of course, technically impossible to do field synchronous-sound filming in 1930, but perhaps he still wished to try. Boas espoused a theory of rhythm that encompassed dance, music, song, and many other aspects of culture, so it is quite possible the footage and sound recordings were made to study rhythm. Ruth Benedict, in a letter to Margaret Mead (1959:495–96) cited earlier, claims that that is indeed what he planned to do. Perhaps he simply did not have sufficient technical knowledge to realize that spring-wound camera motors run at erratic speeds and therefore produce footage that could not be used to study rhythm.

It is clear that this footage was shot primarily for research purposes. That is, Boas did not intend to use it for the production of a motion picture to be shown to the public. The viewer must ignore the sound-recording equipment (displaying the technology of filmmaking within the frame—showing equipment like the recorders, for example—only became acceptable as a sign of reflexive cinematic realism during the 1960s), the people standing around in the background, the exterior location of dances that are supposed to be conducted inside, and the telephone or electrical poles in the background. These images were not made to be seen by the lay public but by analysts who could "look the other way." One sees events that normally take place inside at night in front of an audience performed outside during the day in front of, and apparently solely for the benefit of, the researcher and his camera. The footage only makes sense if one believes that behavioral events removed from their normal social and physical context retain sufficient validity to reveal patterns of culture.

Boas felt an urgent need to salvage and, if necessary, reconstruct as much of the traditional culture of the Kwakwaka'wakw as possible. He subscribed to a theory of culture that allowed him to remove bits of behavior from their normal context for purposes of recording and analysis. This theory generated an approach to imaging. Boas filmed two Kwakwaka'wakw chiefs boasting—that is, making speeches. Normally, these speeches would have occurred inside at night within the context of a particular ceremony and in front of an audience. In the film, the two men are outside in the daylight with neither ceremony nor audience. For Boas, the performance retained those elements he wished to study and was therefore valid for his purposes. Mead and Bateson made similar assumptions when they asked the Balinese dancers to perform outside during the day so that the dance, normally performed at night inside a temple, could be filmed for *Trance and Dance in Bali*.

Today it is not hard to see how Boas's theory of culture became an ideological framework that caused him to take pictures in a particular way. The fact that few modern anthropologists subscribe to the "bits and pieces" approach to culture prevalent during Boas's time makes it easy to recognize the effect of his ideology on his photographs and films. If one were to attempt a similar analysis using contemporary photographs or films, it would be much more difficult, since the images would reflect current thinking, and the underlying ideology would consequently be much more transparent and elusive. I wish to make it very clear that by saying that Boas's view of culture caused him to generate data in a particular fashion, I am not implying that Boas was somehow different from other anthropologists. All theories of culture become ideological frameworks that shape and generate data. It is the nature of research design and anthropological knowledge.

In three letters written in the field to Ruth Benedict, Boas partially confirms these contentions. On November 9, 1930, he said, "The question of song and dance rhythm was not complicated. The feet and the hands move with the time-beating; but time-beating and singing are a tough problem." And again on November 13, 1930, "Julia [his field assistant] danced last night with the crowd and has her first formal dancing lesson tonight. . . . [T]he dance problem is difficult. *I hope that the films will give us adequate material for making a real study*" (emphasis added). And finally, on November 24, 1930, "I already have a good deal of materials for this style-motor question." On November 24, 1930, Boas wrote to his son, Ernst, "Julia is learning the dance, but I believe it is too difficult to learn quickly. At any rate, through the criticism she receives I learn what it is all about" (Rohner 1969:293–94).

Boas believed this footage would contain a more detailed and secure data base for his analysis. Since he had gathered data on Kwakwaka'wakw dance since 1888, it is interesting to speculate on why he thought the filmed data would provide him with "adequate material for making a real study" when his written observations would not. Franziska Boas suggests a tantalizing possibility. She feels that Boas filmed because he "wanted to know whether labanotation that was being expanded for wider use than just for dance [mostly ballet] could be used . . . but I did not know enough about it to make use of it myself. His pattern was to investigate any new channels that might be fruitful. He very probably would have used labanotation had he lived later into the 1940s" (Franziska Boas, personal communication, 1976).

If her conjecture is accurate, it means that Boas was among the earliest researchers to use a camera to study dance, to record dance on film for possible labanotation analysis, and to use labanotation for the study of non-Western dance and motor habits. Martha Davis (personal communication, 1977) informed me that Rudolf Laban had been working on his system as early as 1900, even though it was not published until 1927. According to Diane Freedman (personal communication, 1977), Laban was at this time thinking about expanding his system to include non-Western dance and broadening it to be a method for studying all forms of body movement. However, none of these ideas were published until long after Boas's death. Whether Boas knew Laban or discussed these ideas with him is not known. Boas's collected correspondence at the American Philosophical Society library in Philadelphia contains no letters between Boas and Laban. Nor is there any evidence that any of Laban's students, whom he had been training since 1915, ever had contact with Boas. In any event, Boas was an early proponent of the study of dance and body movement as culture and was noted for his catholic approach to the study of human beings: any human activity was automatically the subject matter of anthropology (Herskovits 1953:7).

In 1888, Boas published "On Certain Songs and Dances of the Kwakiutl of British Columbia" in the first volume of the *Journal of American Folklore*. The interest in Kwakwaka'wakw dance continued throughout his life. In his last published paper, Boas explained why it was so important to the understanding of that particular culture. "It will be seen from the foregoing that song and dance accompany all the events of Kwakiutl life, and that they are an essential part in the culture of the people. Song and dance are inseparable here. Although there are expert performers, everyone is obligated to take part in the singing and dancing, so that the separation between performer and audience that we find in our modern society does not occur in more primitive societies such as that represented by the Kwakiutl Indians" (Boas 1944:10).

Boas did not confine his interest in dance to the Kwakwaka'wakw but espoused the study of dance and indeed of all body movement in culture. In *Primitive Art* (1927), he articulated a theory of dance as emotional and symbolic expression as part of his theory of rhythm in art and culture. It is a reaction against the Marxist or economic-determinist arguments of Hans-Jurgen Bucher and others and at the same time avoids the obvious connection with Freud:

It is often assumed that regularity of musical rhythm, which is found in most primitive music, is due to the multiplicity of motor actions connected with music, particularly to the close relation between music and dance. It is true that primitive song is often accompanied by movements of the body,—a swinging of the whole trunk, movements of head, feet, and arms; hand clapping and stamping; but it is an error to assume that for these the same synchronism prevails to which we are accustomed. (1927:315)

On account of the physiologically determined emotional quality of rhythm it enters into all kinds of activities that are in any way related to emotional life. . . . The origin of rhythm must not be looked for in religious and social activities but the effect of rhythm is akin to the emotional states connected with them and, therefore, arouses them and is aroused by them. I believe the great variety of forms in which rhythmic repetition of the same or similar elements is used, in prose and in poetry as a rhythm of time, in decorative art as a rhythm of space, — shows that Bucher's theory according to which all rhythm is derived from the movements accompanying work cannot be maintained, certainly not in its totality. . . . There is no doubt that the feeling for rhythm is strengthened by dance and the movements required in the execution of work, not only in the common work of groups, of individuals who must try to keep time, but also in industrial work, such as basketry or pottery that require in their execution regularly repeated movements. The repetitions in prose narrative as well as the rhythms of decorative art, so far as they are not required by the technique, are proof of the inadequacy of the purely technical explanation. The pleasure given by regular repetition in embroidery, painting, and the stringing of beads cannot be explained as due to technically determined, regular movements, and there is no indication that would suggest that this kind of rhythm developed later than the one determined by motor habits. (1927:317)

Although Boas saw dance as an emotional and aesthetic outlet for the dancer, his interest was not in the rewards for the individual who engaged in the activity so much as in the social identity of the dance as an expression of culture. Movement, whether dance or merely walking, was a means of signing one's cultural identity and, as such, should be amenable to ethnographic description and analysis. In the published discussion following his paper on Kwakwaka'wakw dance, he articulates these ideas:

Q[UESTION]: What is the relation of ordinary movement in everyday activity to the movements of the dance? . . . This involves the relation between motor pattern and dance.

[FRANZ BOAS]: That is probably a very difficult question to answer. The relations between general motor habits and the dance is a complicated matter. I think that everyone will agree that when you see an Indian of one tribe walk, you realize it is an entirely different gait from that of another. Although I cannot prove it, I believe that the peculiar dancing movements have to do also with the general habit of walking. . . . The whole gesture habit cannot be easily reduced to outer conditions. Some people have free gesture-motions and others have restricted gestures, and these are generally determined by social environment in various ways; but the actual reason is very difficult to determine. We do not know whether we have any kind of detailed investigation which would make clear the sources. (Boas 1944:18)

His interest in the rhythms of dance and body movement was a complex one since it forced Boas the scientist and Boas the concerned citizen to coalesce. Boas was a fervent opponent of racial explanations of behavior. He sought to establish the primacy of culture over race as a means of understanding the differences between human groups (Stocking 1974:18–19; see Baker 1998 for an in-depth look at race and anthropology).

The interest was more than a mere involvement with a set of abstract ideas. It was personal and political. It was Boas's passion as a scientist, as a politically progressive individual, and as someone who engaged in a lifelong battle against racial discrimination. Boas left Germany because he felt he would have more opportunity in America. Ironically, he found anti-Semitism within his own profession. As a Jew, Boas all his life fought anti-Semitism (the dueling scar on his face displayed the depth of his convictions) and was an early champion of civil rights for black Americans (his friendship with W. E. B. Du Bois is something that needs further investigation). In the 1930s, Nazi social scientists began to publish their "scientific" explanations for the racial inferiority of non-Aryans. Boas now had an additional reason for advocating the primacy of culture for understanding human differences.

Boas combined his need to dispute the racists with his interest in gesture and motor habits in the work he directed by one of his last students, David Efron (1941). In the introduction to the published version of Efron's dissertation, Boas makes clear his interests:

The present publication deals with the problem of gesture habits from the point of view of their cultural or biological conditioning. The trend of this investigation as well as that of the other subjects investigated indicate that, as far as physiological and psychological functioning of the body is concerned, the environment has such fundamental influence that in larger groups, particularly in sub-divisions of the White race, the genetic element may be ruled out entirely or almost entirely as a determining factor. . . . The behavior of the individual depends upon his own anatomical and physiological make-up, over which is superimposed the important influence of [the] social and geographic environment in which he lives. (Boas in Efron 1941:ix–x)

Efron's work was among a number of studies being conducted under the guidance of Boas and other Columbia professors:

My research on race and gesture was indeed part of a more comprehensive investigation (to be exact, of a series of independent investigations) dealing with the question of the alleged racial determination of mental and bodily conduct. As far as I remember, in addition to "motor habits" (an expression coined by Boas himself and not by [Roman] Jakobson, as some people have suggested), the following aspects were also investigated: race and crime, race and mental disease, and race and intelligence. However, I do not think that the results of these studies have been made public. It is possible that part of the material concerning the study on race and intelligence was incorporated in some of Otto Klineberg's publications. (David Efron, personal communication, 1976)

Efron's study employed methods that remain unparalleled in their innovativeness. They included: "(1) direct observation of gestural behavior in natural situations, (2) sketches drawn from life by the American painter, Mr. Stuyvesant Van Veen of New York City under the same conditions, (3) rough counting, (4) motion pictures studied by (a) observations and judgments of naive observers, and (b) graphs and charts, together with measurements and tabulations of the same" (Efron 1941:41).

This is another indication of Boas's interest in film as a research tool. Paul Ekman, in his introduction to the new edition of Efron's book, has discussed the general importance of Efron's work to the development of the study of body movement. Two aspects of this work deserve more discussion. First, according to Efron (personal communication, 1977), "the idea of using film as a research device in the field of 'motor habits' originated entirely with 'Papa Franz' himself, who discussed with us at great length his ideas about photographs, motion pictures, and sketches as research tools. These ideas guided us continuously in the development of our techniques."

It would have been nice if Boas had articulated his interest in pictorial media as research tools in writing, but he did not. Among his students, Efron and Weltfish told me that Boas urged them to use all kinds of mechanical devices for recording in the field. In the late 1920s, Zora Neale Hurston, a student of Boas, was also encouraged to take motion pictures of African Americans as part of her folklore studies of Southern American culture. Hurston's contribution to visual anthropology has not been given the attention it deserves, although Elaine Charnov has begun this "rediscovery" of Hurston in her master's thesis (1991), as has Fatimah Rony (1996).

Mead did not recall discussing her interest in nonverbal communication or the use of cameras as research tools with Boas. In a March 29, 1938, letter from the field, Mead wrote to Boas, "When I said I was going to Bali, you said: 'If I were going to Bali I would study gesture'" (Mead 1977:212). And of course, she did. By the time Mead and Bateson returned from the field, Boas was not able to see their work or discuss it with them. "As to his [that is, Boas's] reaction to our Balinese films, I don't think he ever saw any. He died before *Balinese Character* was published, and during those last years, the war and his frailness interfered with many contacts" (Mead, personal communication, 1976).

As mentioned earlier, Efron employed the painter Stuyvesant Van Veen to make sketches of people engaged in public social interaction. He was to make quick sketches of the characteristic gestures they used. Van Veen became quite involved in the work: he began to talk to the people he sketched and ended up as a data source for Efron (Van Veen, personal communication, 1976). I believe Efron and Boas were among the few anthropologists who recognized that artists are also trained observers and that they have some significant insights into human behavior.

During the period when Van Veen was working with Efron, Boas, who had originally found Van Veen for Efron, asked him to make some drawings from the Kwakwaka'wakw dance footage. Someone selected a series of frames from the footage and had them enlarged into prints. Van Veen then blanked out the background in each frame (usually at least two sequential frames were made into enlargements). After he roughed out the features and costumes of the dancer, Van Veen produced a drawing that was a generalization based on the sketches. The finished drawing was of a Kwakwaka'wakw dancer in traditional costume with no background.

Why did Boas want these drawings? Van Veen (personal communication, 1976) does not remember why Boas asked him to make them. The only possible clue is a sketch apparently produced by some artist other than Van Veen that was found with these drawings. It resembles a preliminary sketch for a museum display. Above a rectangular shape that is undoubtedly a movie screen appear the words "The Movie of Man's Motor Habits." On either side of the screen are drawings of people with labels such as "Eastern European Jew" or "Italian American." Attached to all these drawings was a note that says, "Show this to Efron."

David Efron has no recollection of the drawings or the museum display. "I have no idea what the 'movie of man's motor habits' might be, unless it is a copy of my own films on the gestural behavior of traditional and assimilated Jews and Italians in New York City which became part of the archives of the Department of Anthropology of Columbia University" (Efron, personal communication, 1977).

There is no question that the drawings around the movie screen are from Efron's study of gesture. Since Efron had used film as one of his data bases, I suggest Boas was planning to construct a museum display showing the cultural basis of gesture, motor habits, and dance. He was planning to use Van Veen's drawings from Efron's study and the Kwakwaka'wakw dancers. The film footage of the Kwakwaka'wakw and Efron's footage would have been organized together for public display. Had Boas completed this display, it would have been at the very least controversial, considering the public attitude toward minorities at that time, and unusual for its time in Boas's use of film.

Boas was a researcher who never tired of trying new methods and techniques. His attempt to use the motion-picture camera to generate researchable data on body movement and dance was very advanced for its day. Most field-research film projects have failed to produce usable footage and suffered from a poorly designed schema for recording. Although Boas's technical naïveté prevented him from realizing his goals, he knew what he wanted. Had he lived long enough to work with the filmed data and been able to discuss the problems and promises of this technology for the study of human behavior, the development of the study of body movement and visual anthropology could have had a different history. Perhaps the field would not find itself having discarded research film as a data-generating device before its real potential has been explored.

Conclusion

Is it possible to use the technology of moving pictures to study cultural behavior? It is a tantalizing question, which, for the time being, remains unanswerable. There is no doubt that the ways in which humans use their bodies in time and space in everyday life and in special occasions like dance are only partially a result of biology and, in very important ways, a culturally learned phenomenon. The neglect of the body as a site for cultural analysis has been acknowledged for the past several decades. "[S]ocial anthropologists must give the facts of shifting somatic states and of their expression in bodily form increased importance in their efforts to understand the functioning of social structures and codes" (Beck 1975:486). John Blacking concurred and expressed the hope that "there can be some consensus about the need to study the biological and affective foundations of our social constructions of reality" (1977:1). As Farnell suggests:

Recent interest in the body centered on the physical body as cultural construct: on its regulation and restraint, as a metaphor represented by such topics as the medical body, the sexual body, the civilized body, the decorated body, the political body, and the body as social text. . . . However, in these developments there remains one major lacuna: the human body as a moving agent in a spatially organized world of meanings[;] . . . "the body" albeit a social and cultural one rather than a biological or mechanistic entity, nevertheless remains a static object. (1994:930)

The response to this lacuna, while interesting, has taken us away from looking at the visible aspects of body movement and from the need to discover the usefulness of the camera in these explorations.

For the moment, this exploration of the research potential of film must conclude on an indecisive note. The embodiment of culture needs to be rethought to make the moving body the locus of our attention. Then an interest in the technology of film might be rekindled.[8] We simply do not know enough about this possibility to reach any conclusions. Film will never be the "objective" recorder of reality for which the pioneers in this field had hoped. Like all other media of communication, film is a culturally constructed means of making statements about the world. It is neither better nor worse than other means of recording. Given those inherent limitations, new ways must be found to explore its potential. This problem is not confined to research film but applies to all possible uses of film within anthropology and is therefore the major focus of the conclusion of this book.

In the next chapters, I examine the work of some of the best-known U.S. ethnographic filmmakers. None were interested in doing research with a camera. They saw this medium as a means of expression. They wished to present empathetic portraits of people who lived in ways foreign to both the filmmakers and their intended audience. They wished to educate Westerners to respect and understand cultural difference. It is these endeavors that come first to mind when one thinks about anthropology and film.

The Aggie Must Come First:

Robert Flaherty's Place in Ethnographic

Film History

"Suppose we go," said I, "do you know that you and your men may have to give up making a kill, if it interferes with my film? Will you remember that it is the picture of you hunting the ivuik [walrus] that I want and not their meat?"

"Yes, yes, the aggie [movie] will come first," earnestly he assured me [emphasis added]. "Not a man will stir, not a harpoon will be thrown until you give the sign. It is my word." We shook hands and agreed to start the next day. CONVERSATION BETWEEN ROBERT FLAHERTY AND NANOOK, IN FLAHERTY'S "AN EARLY ACCOUNT OF THE FILM"

Robert J. Flaherty's *Nanook of the North* is considered by many to be the beginning of both documentary and ethnographic film. It is therefore essential to examine this film for its influence on subsequent films and the field in general. Recent scholarship makes that task easier. The late 1970s and 1980s saw a renewed interest in Flaherty as both photographer and filmmaker. A much more complete version of his seminal 1922 film *Nanook of the North* was released in 1976 by International Film Seminars (IFS) after years of painstaking archival research by David Shepard. Unfortunately, the IFS directors decided to commission a new score, even though the original produced by the 1920s distributor was available. The latest version of the film is best appreciated with the sound turned off. The new *Nanook* was followed by the 1976 publication of William Murphy's dissertation—an annotated guide to bibliographic resources pertaining to Flaherty and the "discovery" of Flaherty's Arctic photographs, together with new information about his 1916 pre-*Nanook* film and other gems derived from archival excavations.

By 1978, Jo-Anne Birnie Danzker was able to capitalize on these efforts and mount an exhibition of the forgotten Flaherty photographs at the Vancouver Art Gallery (Danzker 1979). In addition to traveling to the International Center for Photography, a New York City gallery, the photographs toured several Inuit communities, undoubtedly stirring a few old memories and creating much curiosity about the identity of the portrait subjects. Unfortunately, the attempts to discover the impact of the images on the descendants of the people portrayed were never realized, even though their circulation caused some Inuit to examine the identity of the actors in *Nanook* ("Search for Nanook" 1984).

In the process of preparing the original version of this chapter for Danzker's catalog,[1] I uncovered Paul Rotha and Basil Wright's seminal but unpublished study of Flaherty. They sold their original research notes and a partial draft of the book to Arthur Calder-Marshall, who produced his version in 1963 as *The Innocent Eye*—the first biography of Flaherty. As a consequence of Danzker's work, I edited an issue of *Studies in Visual Communication* (1980, vol. 6, no. 2) devoted to Flaherty's Arctic work that contained a chapter from Rotha and Wright's manuscript and other new materials relevant to Flaherty's early film work. In 1983, I edited Rotha and Wright's manuscript into *Robert Flaherty: A Biography*. Five years later, Richard Barsam published *The Vision of Robert Flaherty: The Artist as Myth and Filmmaker* (1988). Sadly, this renewed interest in Flaherty was short-lived. Currently, there is only one book about Flaherty in print—Helen Van Dongen's diary about the making of *Louisiana Story* (Orbanz and Bandy 1998).

The decade of publications about Flaherty reflected a new approach to scholarship countering the dominant paradigm in visual research of examining a film or photograph as object or text—divorced from any context. It was assumed that all important information was contained within the work itself and that only people interested in gleaning psychological tidbits about the author or constructing a hero would bother to look at the maker's life. As scholars examined the sociocultural processes involved in the making and using of these cultural artifacts, they saw the need to explore the relationship between the producer, the process of production, the product itself, and its consumption. As a result, other data became relevant. Consequently, scholarly interests have broadened from the text alone to the text in the contexts of its making and utilization. It is now recognized that it is important to understand not only the film or photograph but the maker, the conditions of production, and the conditions of consumption if the construction of meaning is to be comprehended.

The Aggie Must Come First

Examining the films of Robert J. Flaherty as if they were paintings is no longer sufficient, nor is the idolatry that has grown up around his persona very useful. Flaherty is a curious figure in film history. For generations, he was probably more revered than any other American filmmaker as a film artist who resisted the temptations of Hollywood. The construction, perpetuation, and attempts to destroy the "Flaherty myth" have been the subject of numerous articles (Barsam 1973; Corliss 1973; Griffith 1953; Van Dongen 1965). I had hoped that the renewed interest would place the personage of Flaherty within a context whereby neither hero worship nor iconoclasm was necessary or even very interesting. Sadly, that has not proved to be the case, as evidenced by the politically correct and superficial Flaherty bashing of Fatimah Rony (1996).[2]

The purpose of this chapter is to examine three aspects of the production of *Nanook of the North* as a way of critically assessing Flaherty's contribution to the development of ethnographic film: (1) his use of narrative form, (2) the relationship between art and commerce in Flaherty's career, and (3) his field-production methods. Whenever possible, I use Flaherty's own words, from his unpublished diaries and other writings, and his published work, since he wrote eloquently, as did Frances, his wife, in her unpublished diary, which I also quote extensively. Hopefully, someday their diaries will find a publisher.

Flaherty and Narrative Form

Flaherty's work, particularly in *Nanook*, has a peculiar place in the history of both the documentary and ethnographic film. The concept of a "documentary" film came into common usage in 1926, when John Grierson used it to discuss Flaherty's second film, *Moana* (Rotha 1983). So the term was applied to *Nanook* in retrospect. Although Flaherty is usually called the father of the documentary (Barnouw 1974), *Nanook* had little direct influence on subsequent documentaries. Similarly, *Nanook* is credited as being the first ethnographic film, and yet, until French anthropologist Jean Rouch acknowledged Flaherty's impact on his work in the late 1950s, the anthropological community virtually ignored the film and the man.

Nonetheless, it is essential to understand *Nanook of the North* if for no other reason than that it, along with John Marshall's *The Hunters* and Robert Gardner's *Dead Birds*, constitutes the most widely understood variety of ethnographic film—an epic-style narrative film that is a humanist portrayal of an exotic culture. These films are the pictorial equivalent of what James Clifford described as the "ethnographic pastoral" in his essays "Ethnographic Authority" and "Ethnographic Surrealism" in *The Predicament of Culture* (1988).

One of Flaherty's most significant and least understood contributions was his use of the narrative form. This accomplishment is usually described in one of two ways: either by assuming that he borrowed the idea from feature films ("Flaherty had apparently mastered—unlike the previous documentaries—the grammar of film as it had evolved in the fiction film" [Barnouw 1974:39]) or by simply touting his ability as a storyteller (Calder-Marshall 1963). Taken alone, these explanations are inadequate.

The role of narrative in both documentary and ethnographic film has not been clearly understood. Anthropologists who write have been reluctant to accept that they are storytellers (Clifford and Marcus 1986). Ethnographic filmmakers are even more resistant, as they associate films that tell stories with fiction. Writers about film share a common misunderstanding about the nature of narrative—a confusion that began at least with the first reviews of *Nanook*. For example, the reviewer for *Kinematograph Weekly* thought that "[t]here is no story in this picture—only life" ("Review of *Nanook of the North*" 1922).

Apparently, some people are under the impression that narrative means fiction alone; hence, the tradition among film scholars of using *narrative* as a synonym for *fiction*. This misconception may be one of the sources for the idea that *Nanook* was "staged" or not a "real" documentary. When critics recognized the narrative form of *Nanook*, they automatically assumed that they were watching a fiction film or a "faked" documentary. For example:

The first version of *Nanook* [which burned up accidentally] was a factual account of what he had seen. . . . It was the first time Flaherty had used a camera to record what he had experienced but it did not satisfy his imagination. . . . The second *Nanook* became a conflict between the explorer-scientist who had been disciplined into giving facts and figures and the story-teller-turned-film-director who left out certain facts and emphasized others. Facts and figures, useful as they are to the mine-owners and fur-traders, were not exciting to Flaherty whose nature leaned more toward the dramatic. Certainly Revillon Freres had no objections to the omission of steel traps. The ladies, enjoying the prowess of Nanook, might not feel so pleased if they saw how the foxes were caught whose pelts now adorned their shoulders. The story-teller won out over the scientist. (Van Dongen 1965:13)

This is an astonishing statement because the author is an experienced professional film editor who worked with Flaherty on *Louisiana Story* (Orbanz and Bandy 1998) as well as with many other documentarians. She must have known that Flaherty was not a scientist and never claimed to be and that until the 1960s, all documentaries contained "arranged" scenes. Everything in a documentary is a reflection of the maker's view of the subject. The idea that nonfiction film should not be narrative stems from the recognition that narrative is a structuring and interpretive device and from the naive assumption that nonfiction films should not be interpretive. Associating narrative form exclusively with fiction leads to misconceptions about the distinctions among narrative, fiction, and nonfiction. The development of ethnographic film has been hampered by this false assumption.

Nanook is a narrative film. The recognition of Flaherty's use of narrative in no way diminishes the film's value as a documentary about Inuit culture. Flaherty's penchant for telling stories to appreciative audiences was combined with a sophisticated understanding of narrative devices and a knowledge of the existing film styles and possibilities. Flaherty was not the innocent that his public was led to believe but someone with knowledge and forethought who used the narrative form in a very deliberate and intentional way. He says so in an early draft of an article that was to become "How I Filmed *Nanook of the North*" (Flaherty 1922). "I had planned to depict an ethnoligical [*sic*] film of life covering the various phases of their hunting, travel, domestic life, and religion in as much of a narrative form as is possible" (Flaherty n.d.).

It is the complex interweaving of a dramatic story with actuality that sets *Nanook* apart from the other films of its time. Flaherty elevated the nonfiction film from the often superficial dreariness of the travelogue and the adventure film to the documentary through the imposition of a narrative in order to cinematically tell dramatic and compelling stories of real people. As it is my contention that the future of ethnographic film lies in the discovery and exploration of the cultural scenarios that reside within the everyday life of ordinary people, Flaherty's use of narrative form takes on a contemporary interest.

Nanook becomes even more remarkable when it is compared to its contemporaries. In 1920, there were fiction feature films—melodramatic "photoplay" dramas from the dream factories; didactic educational films that usually employed an essay form; and the travelogue/adventure films—either the personal films of people like Osa and Martin Johnson, who were forever barely escaping the headhunters up the Zambezi, or scenics by people like Burton Holmes that had titles like *Bali—Land of Contrasts*. Flaherty had these models to which to look for guidance in his own work.

It is difficult to determine how familiar Flaherty was with the commercial films of his day, since he never wrote about their influence on him. However, we do know that he attended films. His wife, Frances Flaherty, said in a March 15, 1915, diary entry, "That evening we went to see the great film play, *The Birth of a Nation*—three hours of absorbing soul-wracking melodrama." Since the entry is rather matter-of-fact, one could suppose that going to the movies was at least not an unusual event.[3]

When searching for financial support, the Flahertys did approach several large commercial-film organizations such as Paramount. During the 1914–16 period, Frances's diary contains numerous references to appointments with film executives:

DECEMBER 11, 1915 [IN A DRAFT FRANCES WROTE OF A LETTER TO ROBERT]—That is the way I intend to try to handle this affair of the pictures. I wrote to the Paramount Co. that I was here [New York City] ready to take up negotiations where we left off last spring.

DECEMBER 29, 1915 —I think the Paramount Co. and the Scenograph Feature Film Co. are our only hope.

FEBRUARY 22, 1916 —I took the film to Pathe Freres yesterday.

These entries seem to indicate that the Flahertys were somewhat knowledgeable about the movie business.

Perhaps the strongest piece of evidence that Flaherty was familiar with and considered the conventions of photoplay narrative for his own work was the fact that he and Frances, on April 8, 1915, visited the New York office of Edward S. Curtis, a man known primarily for his monumental photographic work *The North American Indian* (1907). During their visit, they saw Curtis's photographs and his 1914 film *In the Land of the Headhunters*, a tale of love and conflict among the Kwakwaka'wakw (Kwakiutl) Indians of the northwest coast. In Curtis's film, one recognizes more readily than in *Nanook* the conventions of the Hollywood photoplay, with rivals fighting over the hand of a maiden.

Curtis made the film as a means of raising money for his lifelong photographic work among Native Americans. It failed to receive much acclaim or financial reward, although it was reviewed in the *New York Times* and mentioned by Vachel Lindsay in his book *The Art of the Moving Picture* (1915:114) as an important film. Curtis had high hopes, as he planned to produce a film about each culture he photographed as a means of financing his work. The film virtually disappeared until Bill Holm and George Quimby, of the University of Washington, found a print, restored it with the collaboration of the Kwakwaka'wakw, and released it under the title *In the Land of the War Canoes* along with a book about Curtis as a filmmaker (Holm and Quimby 1980). Curtis is finally receiving recognition for being a pioneer with Alison Griffiths's examination of his role in the history of ethnographic film (1998). Flaherty's knowledge of Curtis's film has been overlooked by his biographers and most scholars. Because Frances's diary entry describes the event, which gives so much insight into Flaherty, I include it here in its entirety:

APRIL 9, 1915, NEW YORK CITY—We decided to walk up the avenue and call upon Lee Keedick, Mawsons' agent; we were kept waiting in the outer office for some time, and when finally R. sent in his name and errand we were informed that Mr. K. was not interested. (It was undoubtedly our own fault, we should have written, enclosing press notices; this we subsequently did.)

Most crest-fallen, to console ourselves, we stopped in at Curtis's studio on the same floor. We were shown the portfolio of photogravures for the 10th volume of Mr. Curtis's colossal work on the North American Indian—500 sets at $4,200 and $3,500 per set—his life work and one to stir the imagination. The same thot crossed our minds at once: why not the same for the Eskimo! We learned that Mr. C. too had ventured into moving pictures and just put out an elaborate Indian Drama film,—the World Film Co., 50-50 royalty basis—26 copies routed.

From that moment Curtis became the man to be seen. Would he be interested in us? R. was sure of it. We made comparison between his portraits and ours:

Indian portraits,—flat, toneless quality of drawing, interest decorative, and dependent upon picturesque costumes and other details.

Eskimo portraits—depth and tone quality of painting, interest centering in personality independent of race, costume, or detail of any kind. On the whole the Eskimo portraits were "bigger"; the question in my mind was whether Curtis was a big enough man to interest himself in R's work.

TUESDAY, APRIL 13 [1915] —Surely our "stop in" at Mr. Curtis's studio was a lucky change. Yesterday Mr. C. saw R. by appointment and arranged to have the pictures shown this morning before an audience of experts, including besides the unapproachable Mr. Keedick, a Mr. Whitney, a broker for the European market, a Mr. Collier of the board of censors [author's note: "Mr. Collier" was John Collier Sr., whose son John Collier Jr. was a pioneering visual anthropologist], and several others. Cousin Julie and Molly came bringing Mrs. Damroschy; I rather took satisfaction when they came in turning a retaliatory back on Mr. K.

Mr. C. showed his own film first.—all taken in and about our old hunting ground that wonderful west coast of Vancouver's island,—vivid scenes that were like flashes of memory; and our old friends, Sulor's kinsmen, the Siwash Indians, were the actors. It was a story of the customs and ceremonies of the old head-hunting days a generation past with a thread of romance running through it.

It ran thro 6000 feet: by the time our pictures were called R. and I were prepared to see them fall perfectly flat on tired eyes and brains. They didn't,—everybody asked questions galore; and tho as R. said, it was an acid test for them, putting them with all their crudities in juxtaposition with an elaborately toned and perfected film such as Curtis's, it was a curiously happy one, in all their crudities they stood out human, real, convincing and big in contrast to the spectacular artificiality of Curtis's—wonderful as they were as a mere spectacle. As Mr. C. himself said of our pictures, there was an "intimacy" about them; but he also criticized them as "monotonous." Blood and thunder and the "punch" again: but it is my belief that the punch that the "yap" audience demands is not necessarily the blood and thunder for itself but the human appeal it has in it. And that is just where I think R's film would "get across" where C's wouldn't. Mr. C. told us how a little upstate NY town, a

Texas town, and Rochester NY itself had turned his film down as high-brow stuff. He had just been lunching with us here at the hotel. [B]een talking to us like a father, with such infinite tact, too,—giving us all the benefit of his own experience in the moving picture world; we swept it all, sweeping away kinds of illusions in so doing, and finally really getting down to what it would be best to do with our film. I am inclined to think he is right, absolutely.—to hold them over until expedition. The material with the real human punch in it. Sir Wm. would do it undoubtedly, has himself already suggested holding them over for a better market. The market at present is chaos, demoralized by over-speculation and the war; the whole business is a new, headlong, phenomenal thing, which nobody really knows anything about.

Flaherty chose not to employ the more overt, supposedly crowd-pleasing formula of sex and violence to which Curtis fell prey. Instead, Flaherty developed his "conflict and resolution"—an essential element in Western drama—into "human versus the environment." It is a drama of survival: Can the Inuit live in this place? The device was constructed to involve an audience in the Inuit's struggle against a harsh environment. The identification that is so essential in good drama is designed in *Nanook* to transform the audience's ethnocentrism into empathy for a people, a culture, and a hero.

Flaherty had another possible mode to emulate—the travel/adventure film. Given the popularity of this genre and the fact that Flaherty was a well-known explorer, why didn't he make a good scenic film? The answer is interesting historically, since Flaherty did indeed make such a film, but an accident prevented him from distributing it.

When Flaherty began to take motion pictures, he did so to have a record of his explorations of northern Canada for possible iron-ore deposits. During Flaherty's third (1913–14) and fourth (1915–16) expeditions, he shot about thirty thousand feet of motion-picture film in addition to the photographs he was already taking. At the conclusion of his third expedition, shortly after his marriage in 1914, Robert and Frances Flaherty began to examine the possibility of turning the footage into a film and of making Robert Flaherty into a full-time professional filmmaker, photographer, and lecturer. The transition between careers was rapid, since only two years before, he had barely thought about making motion pictures.

Frances Flaherty's diary during the 1914–16 period clearly indicates how important the films, the photographs, and the writings about Robert's work had become to her and how strongly she assumed that they would make this type of work their life's ambition. For example, on December 17, 1914, only a month after their marriage, she wrote, "We hope that they [the motion pictures] will attract a great deal of attention, be widely shown, and gain recognition for R. as an explorer, as an artist and interpreter of the Eskimo people, and consequently bring him greater opportunity." The Flahertys produced a travel/adventure film that would be accompanied by a lecture about Flaherty's exploration of the North. They contacted a variety of organizations, ranging from Paramount to Burton Holmes (the largest travelogue organization of the time), about purchasing their work.

A fire destroyed the negative of the 1914–16 film. With only a work print (sometimes referred to as the "Harvard print," since Flaherty apparently intended to show it at that institution), the Flahertys spent the next four years screening the film to raise money for another filming expedition. Finally, Flaherty convinced Thierry Mallet, of a French fur-trading company, Revillon Freres, to finance *Nanook*. Mallet and two other Revillon Freres employees accompanied Flaherty to the Arctic (Mallet 1926).

What is important about the oft-told story is that during this period, Flaherty discovered that his travel film was not very good. He became increasingly dissatisfied with it. *Nanook* was born out of that realization. Flaherty saw two essential flaws in the Harvard print—flaws that were endemic to the travelogue/adventure genre: (1) the lack of continuity: "It was a bad film: it was dull—it was little more than a travelogue. I had learned to explore, I had not learned to reveal. It was utterly inept, simply a scene of this and that, no relation, no thread of a story or continuity whatever. . . . Certainly it bored me" (Flaherty 1950:12); and (2) the emotional distance one feels from the subject in a typical adventure film, where the exotic natives are seen as curios for the outsider's amusement:

My wife and I thought it over for a long time. At last we realized why the film was bad, and we began to get a glimmer that perhaps if I went back to the North, where I had lived for eight years and knew the people intimately, I could make a film that this time would go. Why not take, we said to each other, a typical Eskimo and his family and make a biography of their lives through the year! What biography of any man could be more interesting? Here is a man who has less resources than any other man in the world. He lives in a desolation that no other race could possibly survive. His life is a constant fight against starvation. Nothing grows; he must depend utterly on what he can kill; and all of this against the most terrifying of tyrants—the bitter climate of the North, the bitterest climate in the world. Surely this story could be interesting! (Flaherty 1950:15)

Flaherty knew about travelogues. He had even tried to make one. He also knew the people who made adventure films, like Martin and Osa Johnson. He rejected these forms just as he had rejected the photoplay, not because he was an innocent who intuitively stumbled upon a narrative form that just happened to work—the genius of nonpreconception, as some would have us believe—but because he was sufficiently knowledgeable about the cinematic forms of his day to realize their inadequacies for his purposes. It could be argued that the accidental destruction of the Harvard print had as much to do with the creation of *Nanook* as did Flaherty's knowledge and intention, and in a superficial way, that would be correct. However, there was no reason why he could not have returned to the North, simply duplicated his earlier efforts, and brought back another travel film. Fortunately, he did not. When he did go back, Flaherty had something else in mind:

The urge that I had to make *Nanook* came from the way I felt about these people, my admiration for them; I wanted to tell others about them. This was my whole reason for making the film. In so many travelogues you see, the filmmaker looks down on and never up to his subject. He is always the big man from New York or from London.

But I had been dependent on these people, alone with them for months at a time, traveling with them and living with them. They had warmed my feet when they were cold, lit my cigarettes when my hands were too numb to do it myself; they had taken care of me on three or four expeditions over a period of eight years. My work had been built up along with them; I couldn't have done anything without them. In the end it is all a question of human relationships. (Flaherty 1950:16)

The World of Art and Commerce

Flaherty has for some time enjoyed a reputation as the prototypical independent film artist. The importance of the word *independent* cannot be overly stressed when one compares film to other media. Because of the technology and the cost of producing and distributing most films, filmmakers must effect some sort of working relationship with commerce in a way that marks them and separates them from other image makers. Until the recent years of foundation and government support, filmmakers had only three places to go: the commercial-film industry, wealthy patrons (who seldom saw film as an "art" worth supporting), and companies that might be cajoled into thinking that backing a film could be both profitable and *good* public relations. When Flaherty convinced Revillon Freres that producing *Nanook* would be worthwhile, he became a pioneer in persuading businesses to support the independent filmmaker.

As a consequence of the confluence of circumstances and his ability to be an excellent advertisement for himself, Flaherty is regarded as a paragon of artistic virtue and integrity—admired for his unswerving commitment to his own artistic values—someone unseduceable by the money sirens of Hollywood. Flaherty was an object of awe and reverence among the Hollywood and New York commercial, intellectual, and artistic circles. Actor-director John Houseman (whose own career spans from *Citizen Kane* to *The Paper Chase*) once wrote about Flaherty, "It is the measure of his greatness that after a quarter of a century, Flaherty's myth is today more valid, more universal, and more significant than ever before. And it is no wonder. For it is rooted in love. And what it tells is a story of the innate decency and fortitude and invincibility of the human spirit" (Taylor 1949:43).

It could be argued that if Flaherty hadn't existed, Hollywood industry and post–World War II New York intellectuals would have had to invent him. They needed a figure to whom to point as someone who had sufficient artistic integrity to resist the financial temptations of the commercial-film establishment. In his *New Yorker* profile of Flaherty written in 1949, Robert Lewis Taylor introduced Flaherty to that magazine's sophisticated readership:

His life to date has been a brilliant demonstration of the axiom that art doesn't pay. . . . From time to time he has been mixed up briefly in the production of a few other films, withdrawing in most cases after some truly memorable wrangles over commercialism vs. artistic integrity. . . . Though unopposed to earning an honest dollar, Flaherty was, and is today, re-pelled by the gross taint of commercialism; ignoring the Hollywood moneypots, he searched for a private patron[;] . . . he was wholly undismayed by the commercial failure of three movies he had made and the artistic collapse of a fourth, which he had worked on briefly. . . . Flaherty's case, with its slights, rebuffs, hardships, disasters and general lack of rewards, il-lustrates the depressing battle that faces an artist relentlessly dedicated to raising the stan-dard of a new cultural medium. (Taylor 11 June 1949:30)

Flaherty was accepted in the 1950s among the East Coast artistic and intel-lectual elite and in Hollywood as America's native son in a world of art film dominated by Italian neorealism and the newly discovered Russians, like pro-ducer Sergei Eisenstein. It must have made it easier for these people, who were convinced that all culture and art came from across the Atlantic, to accept the vulgar American Flaherty as their own homegrown genius when they discov-ered that Eisenstein had said, "We Russians learned more from *Nanook of the North* than from any other foreign film. We wore it out studying it. That was, in a way, our beginning" (cited in Taylor 25 June 1949:29).

There is, of course, some substance to the image. In addition to obtaining Revillon Freres' sponsorship for *Nanook*, Flaherty secured financial backing from Paramount Pictures (*Moana*), Standard Oil (*Louisiana Story*), and the United States government (*The Land*). In virtually every case, the relationship was mutually unsatisfying. He went over budget almost every time. He even walked out of several productions due to disputes with the management. Now, depending on one's point of view, either these were the actions of an artist who could not and should not have been burdened by the limitations of a commer-cial industry, or they were the unjustifiable actions of an unreasonable and undisciplined prima donna. The eye of the beholder is undoubtedly the crucial factor in this case.

The tensions and conflicts of the commercial and theatrical versus the artistic, educational, and socially concerned interests are certainly endemic to the cinema from the moment of its inception. In addition, there are the problems faced by any filmmaker who wishes to earn a living from his or her films but who needs or wishes to remain outside of the commercial industry. All of these tensions and problems are to be found within the career of Robert Flaherty. His solution is instructive.

In order to understand Flaherty's choices in these matters, one must first contextualize them in the world of film during the formative period of Flaherty's career—1914–20. There were virtually no nontheatrical film outlets of any consequence. A handful of people earned a living making travelogues. There was a smattering of screenings in schools, churches, union halls, and a few nascent film societies. Some museums, like the American Museum of Natural History in New York, occasionally showed films about exotic cultures (Griffiths 1998). However, 99 percent of the funds and activities were to be found in the commercial theatrical world. This situation remained virtually unchanged until the 1950s, when film societies such as Amos Vogel's Cinema 16 and the Museum of Modern Art in New York began to create alternative outlets.

It is quite clear that Flaherty was torn between his need to make a living; the seductive attraction of big money, with its promise of well-financed future projects; his desire to have his work seen; and other less commercial interests. Let me illustrate the ambivalence with some excerpts from Frances's diary from the 1914–16 period, when they were trying to sell the first footage and finance additional film expeditions. I cite the quotations in chronological order.

DECEMBER 21, 1914—It was Mr. Currelly [sic], curator of the Royal Ontario Museum. He has come in through a dark passage into a most interesting high studded room all wood paneled with a great open fire. After introducing his wife he immediately launched on the subject of the moving pictures and his plan to show them at Convocation Hall under the auspices of the University Archaeological Institute of America and with wide circulation of invitations and advertising[,] something that would give them a good send off.

Currelly did arrange a screening of the 1914 film. Afterward, Currelly wrote to Flaherty extolling the virtues of the film: "I cannot too strongly congratulate you on the moving pictures you exhibited in Convocation Hall. They are much the best I have ever seen. . . . I have never known anything received with greater enthusiasm."

FEBRUARY 7, 1915—The real intrinsic value of the pictures is of course scientific ethnological and geographical and the real place is with the schools and universities and scientific societies. I am not at all sure but that they should be exploited from that point of view alone.

The Aggie Must Come First

R. is full of the idea of the use of moving pictures in education in the teaching of geography and history. Someone might well make it a life work. Why not we?

MARCH 10, 1915—new york city—Today I sought out Dr. Grosvenor (brother of the head of the National Geographic) for possible light on the moving picture game. Finally reached him by telephone: How would we get our film before the market for open competitive bids? Suggested making arrangements with some theatre manager to run our film at a certain time and send a circular letter to M. P. Co. [motion-picture companies] inviting their inspection. Suggested also writing to Sir Douglas Mavson who was in "touch" with the N.Y. market for educational films.

APRIL 9, 1915—The Picture Playhouse people had estimated the film to be worth $50,000. This was far under R's own calculations and much figuring did we do.

The Flahertys failed to obtain the funds necessary to launch their lecture film from the 1914 expedition. Sir William MacKenzie was willing to fund another expedition, this time with an emphasis on filming more than exploring. At the time of this next entry, Robert was apparently not certain of MacKenzie's support.

MAY 16, 1915—Toronto—R., having reduced his estimate of cost to a minimum, cutting his own salaries, relinquishing past claims and with them all hope of paying his debts, is now turning every stone to get enough cash to get the expedition going. Wired to N.Y. offering the pictures [for example, the 1914 film] for cash: $5,000 was the most Paramount Co. would even consider paying outright. From $100,000 (dreams of an earlier day) to $5,000!

UNDATED DRAFT OF A LETTER TO SISTER "TOTTIE" FROM TORONTO [FROM ITS PLACEMENT IN THE DIARY, IT WAS WRITTEN IN MAY – JULY 1915—prior to the Flahertys' leaving for the fourth expedition]—Sir Wm. [William MacKenzie] gave R. $1,000 out of his own pocket for his photographic outfit. He seems keen about the moving pictures, holding onto them like a leech. I have given up the fight for the pictures on R's account: I was for basing his whole future on them, wrenching them free of Sir Bill somehow, and developing them by and for ourselves, gradually weaning ourselves away from this slavery to salary, MacKenzie and Mann, or anybody else; make the pictures pay for future expeditions of our own. But Sir Wm. won't give them up and he won't do anything with them, just sit upon them as though they were a mineral claim, while the reels reel on! Judge of his appreciation of R's work when he didn't even know it was R. himself who took the pictures.

FROM THE BRYN MAWR CLUB, NEW YORK CITY, DECEMBER 29, 1915 [ALSO TO SISTER TOTTIE]—just been reading the prospectus of the "Scenograph Feature Film Co." Percy A. McCord, Sec'y. and Treas. . . . Robt. Priest, Esq., Vice-Pres. and Gen'l. Mgr. Our old acquaintance, Mr. Hendricks has nothing to do with it: he fell down as Mr. McC. expressed it.

I had a talk with him yesterday morning in Boston at his office—a neat and unpretentious affair, the office.—and in spite of myself I was rather taken with the little man this time. His talk was straight forward and straight out, and I couldn't help admiring the stick-to-it-tiv-ness [sic] that after four months fooling with the picture corporations, and four more months wasted over Hendricks, kept him at it until he had formed a company of his own to handle his film and others like it on lines entirely outside the main movie system.

With the movies it's all drama this year, harder than ever, with one exception, the Paramount Co., and you see by the enclosed clipping what they are doing. Was much interested in that notice for the reason that Mr. Louis Francis Brown is the man I saw at the American Play Co. where I was recommended to go by Miss Anne Morgan thro' Molly. I found Mr. B on that occasion in the act of getting on his overcoat to catch a train to Phila and our whole interview [took] place in the elevator on the way down from the tenth story: but from it I gleaned the fact of his connection with Burton Holmes and on the strength of it went home and wrote him a letter giving all the explorational circumstances of the film. Then Mr. B. went and got sick like everybody else in this miserable pest-ridden city, and have not seen or heard from him since. It is no use bothering him again until the film comes anyway. Spent this afternoon at the customs, and delivery is promised for the first of the week. Then it's got to be cleaned up somehow before I show it.

I think that Paramount and the Scenograph feature film Co. are our only hope. Mr. McCord had the assurance to the MacKenzie expeditionary film in his Company's prospectus, so of course they are keen to get it. They would route it as a separate theatrical venture, like Mawson, Scott, Rainey, etc., putting out ten copies, each with a lecturer. I shall hear more about it when I see Mr. Priest, their theatrical manager. The plan is ideal; its working depends on the truth of that little statement [on] page four of the prospectus to the effect that a growing and eager public is waiting for just this sort of educational film food. No figures are given as to the "fortunes" so far made out of expeditionary films; we could name several that failed to make a red cent. They were attended in any case by a spasmodic public attracted thro special advertising means. The success of the Scenograph venture depends upon making of that spasmodic public a regular class of "better movie" patrons. I certainly do wish them well,—I certainly do believe in the idea and its eventual success; but that this particular company is destined to be the one to lead the way . . . neither its personnel, judging from my measure of Mr. McCord, nor its wares, judging from my view of the So. American Film, nor its backing, judging from the "names of interested Boston people" Mr. McCord gave me, are strong enough. Mr. McCord is, distinctly, uneducated, illiterate; the So. American film has no artistic or literary merit above the merest newspaper "copy"; the names given me as chief stock-holders and directors in the Scenograph Co. are not names known to "anybody one knows" in Boston. I'd rather [someone] with known reputation and weight in educational matters were chiefly concerned in the affair, together with some body else with the same sort of standing financially, and then a good business manager,—such as Mr. Priest may be.

The Paramount Co. then. They have signified their desire to see the film again. I'd give a good deal to know what arrangement Burton Holmes has made with them. I'd like to meet him personally. They would probably cut the film up, might probably not run it at all until they had your next-to-run-work in with it.

From my Line-a-Day Diary:

JAN. 11, Films received from Express Co. (after much fuss and fuming!)

JAN. 12 —Gave film to Joseph Fitterman to clean.

JAN. 17 —Burton Holmes lecture, —ran reel no. 1 for him to see, —very enthusiastic. This all happened at the Chandler Theatre as a result of dear Dr. Coggeshall's interest and effort in securing me an introduction to Mr. Holmes thro' his patient Mr. Kramer, Mr. Holmes' understudy. Showing the film was Mr. Brown's happy suggestion. Nothing came of it but a few minutes talk with Mr. H. on the subject of lecture films and lecturers.

JAN 18 —Pictures (4 reels) shown to Mr. Eaton, in charge of news and travel Dep't. of Paramount Co.

JAN 24 —Letter from Mr. Eaton. (They turned us down, gently, advising that the film would be just as valuable, "if not more so," six months or a year hence. The facts of the case are that they have under contract with Burton Holmes all the travel material they can use for more than a year to come. Mr. H. is supplying them with 1000 feet per week from his studio in Chicago.)

JAN 31, SUNDAY, 5.30 P.M. —pictures on at Globe Theatre (New Haven), audience of about 30. (I was visiting Jaynsie, the party was hers, and for fun.)

FEB. 20 —Interesting talk with "Brother Philip" about film. (Philip—Salisbury—is a wide-awake young business man employed in the advertising department of the Ingersoll Watch Co., in which capacity he has had to do with the Movie Companies, writing scenarios for animated cartoons (Edison Co.) and negotiating for a film of the plant in co[o]peration with some other company ($700 per 1000 ft.) for the Mutual Exchange. He thought the Pathe Co. Hearst-Vitagraph and Selig-Tribune the most likely people for us to deal with. But strongly advised against pushing this film now, in the interest of the next.

While Robert was in Toronto incorporating the 1915–16 footage into the 1914 film, Frances was in New York attempting to sell the 1914 version.

FEBRUARY 22, 1916 [ANOTHER OF FRANCES'S DRAFTS OF A LETTER TO ROBERT] —I took the film to Pathe Freres yesterday—my last move in the matter, because I have decided beyond doubt in my own mind that it would only hurt your next film to have this one out now. I regret nothing of the experience either in its main or its side issues, because in the main

I have acquired a few useful ideas and a certain philosophical point of view that may apply helpfully to the situation in the fall when you come down.

What these diary excerpts clearly demonstrate is the degree of ambivalence the Flahertys felt about the work: from delusions of grandeur in assuming that their footage was worth $100,000 to wanting to devote their lives to educational films.

When Flaherty's plans for an illustrated travel lecture film went up in smoke in Toronto, he went back to the North to film *Nanook*. He returned with a feature-length theatrical film with an investor looking to recoup the investment. Given his decision, he had only one possible outlet—the large theatrical distribution companies. He landed Pathé Pictures, which logically did what it knew how to do: promote *Nanook* as a movie that would be attractive to paying audiences.

If one examines from today's vantage point the *Campaign Book for Exhibitors* sent by Pathé to local exhibitors to promote *Nanook*, it looks like a tacky ad campaign pandering to the lowest common denominator in public taste. It should serve as a reminder of the socioeconomic factors facing Flaherty. It would be easy to use this booklet as evidence that Flaherty "sold out." Flaherty either actively participated in or was at least a passive supporter of promotional campaigns that were not exactly "uplifting" for several of his other films. Paramount released *Moana* as "The Love Story of a South Sea Siren." The Flaherty family appeared on stage at several screenings with their daughters performing in "native" dress. When *Man of Aran* was premiered in England and the United States, Flaherty paraded his "players" on stage as the first documentary pop stars. And finally, there is the unfortunate story of Sabu the Elephant Boy's road to fame and ruin, started when Flaherty "discovered" him in India (Edmund Carpenter, personal correspondence, 1979).

Before too facile a judgment about Flaherty's decisions to acquiesce to the commercial realities of theatrical cinema is made, the complexities of the situation must be understood. Flaherty had two viable options—theatrical release or the travelogue circuit. Both outlets promoted their wares in similar fashion—the only real difference being in the size of their budgets. It is quite clear from her diary that Frances scoured New York for backers. Short of refusing to release the film, Flaherty had little choice: either accept the commercial realities of the time or cease being a filmmaker.

It is clear that he did not care for these conditions. When they continued with *Moana*, he tried without success to create an alternative:

Paramount's head distribution executive told Flaherty that if he had had a series of good, modest-budget pictures, he could have built up the sort of specialized distribution Flaherty wanted. But economically it wasn't worthwhile to do it for a single picture. Appreciating that

The Aggie Must Come First

his problem concerned not merely Paramount, but the cinema industry as a whole, not merely himself, but other directors of "off-beat" films, Flaherty approached the Rockefeller Foundation with the suggestion that a special organization should be built up to draw the attention of the "latent audience" to unusual films from any part of the world. A meeting of their board was arranged to discuss the project and a representative of the Hays Organization was invited to attend. This representative agreed that the proposal was interesting, but its implementation ought to come within the province of the Hays Organization rather than a special foundation. (Calder-Marshall 1963:120)

Flaherty started the battle that is still being fought by independent filmmakers like those who wish to make ethnographic films. He wanted his work to be seen by large audiences, and he wanted to earn a living through his films. His decision was to continue to produce films by making the concessions that were necessary at the time, a decision that should be familiar to all filmmakers. Today, filmmakers try to sell their work to television—not a great change from the past, as television companies are very much like film companies. It is my contention that ethnographic film is not a field in which people can make a living. If the films are good ethnography, they will never appeal to a mass audience. Ethnographic film should be more like scholarly writing—an avocational pursuit of the academic who has the support of an institution and therefore need not produce a livable wage from the work.

Flaherty in the Field

The production methods Flaherty used in *Nanook* are strikingly different from those used by his contemporaries in both fiction and nonfiction. Moreover, they are amazingly similar to what is being advocated today by certain contemporary ethnographic filmmakers. He was a pioneer in participatory and reflexive cinema (see chapter 6). Flaherty is frequently called the first ethnographic filmmaker and *Nanook*, the beginning of ethnographic film. And yet Flaherty had no formal anthropological education, nor is there any evidence that he was self-trained or that he sought out the professional advice or assistance of any anthropologists. No evidence exists that he screened his films for anthropologists to get them to review or discuss them as serious attempts at doing anthropology on film.

There are only three known incidents in which anthropologists were even remotely associated with Flaherty's film work, and in none of these was Robert Flaherty directly involved. In 1915, when Frances Flaherty was in New York City trying to sell the 1913–14 travel/lecture film and raise funds for the fourth expedition (1915–16), she contacted several anthropologists. In the entry dated March 8, Frances describes the visit:

For the rest of the day R. and I parted company. I met Isabel who took me to Dr. Adler, who gave me a letter of introduction to Prof. Boas of Columbia University, "the foremost ethnologist and authority on the Eskimo in America." R. knew him immediately by reputation. Later in the afternoon I went to the Natural History Museum. . . . There I saw Mr. Sherwood and Dr. Whistler and the gist of the visit was that they would be glad to see a few reels of the picture run, that their lecture program for the year was filled but that Prof. Osborne on his return might consider a special lecture.

Later that week, Frances did see Franz Boas, and in an undated draft of a letter to her husband, she recounted the visit:

Late in the afternoon I reached Columbia for an appointment with Prof. Boas. I'd have given anything if you had been there in my stead, he would so gladly have talked with you, had read the article in the Times, — "very interesting" — and the portraits were "beautiful" — just where did you winter and how far had you penetrated—Amadjunk Lake, yes, it was he who had discovered it 30 years ago—and what could he do for us, I mentioned how anxious you were to go back to the islands;—yes, it has taken 20 years to get that same call out of his own blood—and how desirous it seemed to bring your work to the attention of interested people. Had I seen the Museum people?—yes, and I told him the result,—and did I know of Capt. Cromer and his work on Southampton Island—his own greatest interest lay in the region north of Southampton Island on the mainland. He thought it would be most advisable to get in touch with Capt. Cromer and his financial backer, Mr. Ellsworth,—thought that in conjunction with them and the Museum the chances for arranging an expedition for next year were excellent as next year the Museum would be "very rich." He gave me Capt. C's address.

Although the Flahertys were never able to convince Boas to become involved, Ira Jacknis has uncovered evidence that Boas did eventually see *Nanook* and thought it had possibilities for anthropologists. In a letter dated March 23, 1933, to Will Hays, the head of the Motion Picture Producers and Distributors, Boas suggested that it might be possible for anthropologists and filmmakers to make films collaboratively that would be both "scientifically" useful and popular at the box office. The venture never happened, but it is clear evidence that Boas believed that *Nanook* had some potential as an ethnographic film.

The subject matter of films like *Grass, Nanook, Moana, Chang,* and others [has] proved to me that there is an important field open to the Motion Picture industry that, up to this time has not been properly exploited. Excellent material is contained in these pictures; nevertheless they might have been made ever so much more interesting if a person had been consulted who knows the social life of the people intimately. Assuming for instance, that a man who knows Eskimo life in and out, had been at hand to direct a film like *Nanook*, many exceedingly picturesque and interesting features of native life might have been brought in which would not only have improved the quality of the film but would have also made it more attractive to the general audiences. I do not mean to imply that a film of this kind should be built up exclusively on scientific principles, but it ought to contain what is really fundamentally characteristic of each culture, bearing in view also what is picturesque and attractive to the public. (Cited in Jacknis 1987:606)

When *Nanook* was released in 1922, its distributor, Pathé Pictures, obtained a quotable blurb from a young anthropologist (who was later to become one of America's most prominent anthropologists) for its press release: "Ralph Linton, Assistant Curator of North American Ethnology (Chicago), 'It is the best show of the sort that I have ever seen. It is entertaining and at the same time has great scientific value.'" It would appear from the preceding that the extent of the Flahertys' involvement with anthropologists was to seek assistance for financing and promotion rather than ethnographic advice about the cultures they filmed.

Apart from the Linton quote, there is no evidence that anthropologists ever wrote about Flaherty's films as being anthropologically significant, even if they thought the films might be useful to them, as Margaret Mead suggested in a letter to me dated September 20, 1976:

I knew Flaherty's work from the time I went to Samoa (1928). I had seen *Nanook* before I went to Samoa, and an article by Flaherty which appeared in *Asia Magazine* provided me with pictures that I used in making a Samoan picture interpretation test. I met Flaherty for the first time in 1931, but I had always followed his work with interest. I should think that he kept up pretty well with anthropological works in areas where he worked, and that he undoubtedly had read Eskimo things. *Nanook, Moana,* and later *Man of Aran* were simply taken for granted as important documentary films. We didn't begin to formulate the defect of documentaries— which involve acting by "real people"—until much later. My Samoan Diorama in the Peoples of the Pacific Hall [in the American Museum of Natural History, New York], finished in 1972, is based upon a scene from *Moana*.

Whether or not anthropologists regarded Flaherty as being an anthropologist or his films as being ethnographically useful, the Flahertys certainly did and, so did many people who have written about the films since the 1920s. Virtually from the beginning of Flaherty's Inuit work (that is, from 1913 on), both Robert and Frances Flaherty saw his writings, still photographs, and films as having "ethnological import."

Since ethnology and anthropology were not professionalized at this time, Flaherty's lack of formal training or academic affiliation would not have prevented people from regarding him as an ethnologist or anthropologist. In a letter written to serve as an introduction to people in New York, a Canadian friend of the Flahertys wrote:

This will introduce Mr. Robert J. Flaherty of Toronto who has a most interesting series of ethnological moving pictures of Eskimo life which show the primitive existence of a people in the way they lived before being brought in contact with explorers. He is looking to bring them out in the best way. I know you are thoroughly in touch with the moving picture game from the inside and can at least give him some pointers. Do what you can. (Barnouw 1974:35)

Several reviewers of *Nanook* also made the same assumption. For example, Bruce Bliven said, in an August 8, 1922, review in the *New York Globe*, "It is, in the first place, a piece of ethnographic research of solid scientific value."

It would only be a slight exaggeration to suggest that everyone except professional anthropologists saw *Nanook*, and probably *Moana*, as being anthropologically significant and regarded Robert Flaherty as a gifted "amateur" (in the sense of lacking formal training) anthropologist.

In many important ways, Flaherty not only behaved like an anthropologist, but his field methods, his stated intentions, and his willingness to be methodologically explicit place him more solidly within orthodox anthropology than do the actions of most of the contemporary self-professed ethnographic filmmakers. Flaherty begins a tradition of filmmakers who produce films about culture that resemble what trained anthropologists do. The work of John Marshall and David MacDougall clearly carries on that tradition. The parallels between what Flaherty did and said and anthropological activities are striking. For example, Flaherty articulated a theory of ethnographic film—a theory that would find few supporters today but a theory nonetheless:

Films are a very simple form and a very narrow form in many ways. You can't say as much in a film as you can in writing, but what you can say, you can say with great conviction. For this reason, they are very well-suited to portraying the lives of primitive people whose lives are simply lived and who feel strongly, but whose activities are external and dramatic rather than internal and complicated. I don't think you could make a good film of the love affairs of an Eskimo because they never show much feeling in their faces but you can make a very good film of Eskimos spearing a walrus. (Flaherty 1949)

From the time of *Nanook*, Flaherty espoused a view of film as a medium for communicating ethnography that is very modern. In his 1922 review of *Nanook*, Bliven quoted Flaherty:

It seems to me that it is possible to record the life of primitive people in such a way as to preserve the scientific accuracy and yet make a picture which has vivid dramatic interest for the average man or woman. Plenty of pictures have been made of the life of savages in various parts of the world, especially the tropics. The difficulty is that such pictures are usually episodic, showing unrelated scenes with little to hold the wandering attention of one who has not a scientific interest in the lives of primitive people. In *Nanook of the North,* by taking a central character and portraying his exciting adventures and those of his family, in the effort to wrest a livelihood from the frigid arctic, we secure a dramatic value which is both legitimate and absorbing.

Flaherty's assumptions about the nature of "primitive" culture and cinema are, of course, subject to debate and rebuttal. Their validity is not important. What is important is the fact that he articulated his ideas so that they could be discussed. The explicit stating of the theoretical basis of one's work is the first premise of all scholarly investigation.

Furthermore, Flaherty was quite clear about his intentions in the making of *Nanook:* "I wanted to show the Inuit. And I wanted to show them, not from the civilized point of view, but as they saw themselves, as 'we, the people.' I realized then that I must go to work in an entirely different way" (cited in Griffith 1953:36).

To see how much Flaherty thought like an ethnographer, one has only to compare this statement with that of Bronislaw Malinowski, an anthropologist credited with the development of modern ethnographic field methods: "The final goal, of which an ethnographer should never lose sight[,] . . . is, briefly, to grasp the native's point of view, his relation to life, to realize his vision of his world" (Malinowski 1922:25).

Flaherty's assumption that the people in his film must be actively involved in the production also marks him as being ahead of his time. It is clear that Flaherty planned from the very beginning to have the Inuit participate in the making of the film. His contract with Revillon Freres stipulates "a $3,000 credit at Port Harrison for 'remuneration of natives'" (Barnouw 1974:36).

In the 1915–16 expedition, Flaherty began the process of asking the Inuit to be collaborators and sought feedback from them about his understanding of their way of life. He began revealing his methods as early as 1918, when he described showing footage to the Inuit:

During the winter, we compiled a series of motion pictures showing the primitive life, crafts, and modes of hunting and traveling of the islanders—an improved version of the film we had previously made on the Baffin Island expedition. With a portable projector bought for the purpose, we showed the islanders a copy of the Baffin Island film, purposing in this way to inspire them with that spirit of emulation so necessary to the success of our filming. Nor were we disappointed. Enthusiastic audiences crowded the hut. Their Ayee's and Ah's at the ways of these their kindred that were strange to them were such as none of the strange and wonderful ways of the kablunak (white man) even called forth. (Flaherty 1918:433)

Flaherty was quite explicit about his reasons for screening footage in the field:

It has always been most important for me to see my rushes—it is the only way I can make a film. But another reason for developing the film in the north was to project it to the Eskimos so that *they would accept and understand what I was doing and work together with me as partners* [emphasis added]. They were amazed when I first came with all this equipment, and they would ask me what I was going to do. When I told them that I had come to spend a year among them to make a film of them—pictures in which they moved—they roared with laughter. To begin with, some of my Eskimos could not even read a still-photograph. I made stills of several of them as preliminary tests. When I showed them the photograph as often as not they would look at it upside down, I'd have to take the photograph out of their hands and lead them to the mirror in my hut, then have them look at themselves and the photograph beside their heads before, suddenly with a smile that spread from ear to ear, they would understand. (Flaherty 1950:13–14)

Flaherty's participatory approach did indeed work. The Inuit themselves began to suggest scenes that Flaherty might include in his movie:

In the long evenings around the hut's crackling stove my Eskimos and I talked and speculated as to what scenes could be made. Said Wetallok one night: "Why not, when the ice breaks in spring, make the aggie (picture) of the big ivuik (walrus). There are small sea-swept islands some three sleeps north of here where the ivuik live I know, for I have killed them there. Twenty I killed during one short day.

"The walrus is bad when he is angry," Wetallok continued. "That same summer one Eskimo went out from shore with his kayak to hunt ducks. Though early in the morning there had been a walrus kill, there were no signs of walrus then. He did not come back. All that the people could find were pieces of kayak. The water was red, red, red.

"And you have heard of that kablunak (a member of the Northwest Mounted Police at Cape Fullerton). Their whale-boat was strong and big, but the walrus they had wounded with their gun but did not kill swam under the boat and up over the side. With his tusks he turned it over. Two of the kablunak swam in to shore, which was near, but the other one was frightened. He swam out. The two kablunak who swam in to shore saw the walrus charge the kablunak who was swimming. The walrus kept on charging him, even after he was dead. Then he went for the boat and smashed it to pieces with his tusks. And then he charged the pieces which floated on the sea.

"To come upon the walrus sleeping upon the shore will be surest way to make the aggie. I will crawl in among them and throw my harpoon. Quick they will all roll into the sea. Then will come the fight. It will take all of us to hold him with the line of my harpoon. You will see his mates close around him. They will all be very, very angry." Such was the beginning of the ivuik aggie. (Flaherty 1922:126–27)

The Inuit performed in front of the camera, reviewed and criticized their performance, and were able to offer suggestions for additional scenes in the film—a way of making films that, when tried today, is thought to be "innovative and original" and confounds the naive assumption that ethnographic films are merely a record of what happens in front of the camera.

As a further step in making *Nanook* a collaborative undertaking, Flaherty trained some Inuit to be technicians.

To "Harry Lauder" I deputed the care of my cameras. Bringing them from the cold outside into contact with the warm air of the base often frosted them inside and out, which necessitated taking them apart and carefully drying them piece by piece. With the motion picture cameras there was no difficulty, but with my Graflex I found to my sorrow such a complication of parts that I could not get it together again. For several days its "innards" lay strewn on my work table. "Harry Lauder" finally volunteered for the task of putting them together and through a long evening before a flickering candle and with a crowd of Eskimos around ejaculating their "ayee's" and "ah's," he managed to succeed where I had failed. (Flaherty 1922:140)

One of the oft-asked questions about *Nanook* and other ethnographic documentaries is, didn't the presence of the camera and crew alter the event being filmed? Although this question reveals a naive faith in the objectivity of the camera and reflects an outmoded theory of knowledge, I have heard and continue to hear it when people discuss documentary and ethnographic film. Flaherty was very aware of the fact that he was recreating the past in front of the camera and discussed it openly:

I am not going to make films about what the white man has made of primitive peoples. . . . What I want to show is the former majesty and character of these people, while it is still possible—before the white man has destroyed not only their character, but the people as well. The urge that I had to make *Nanook* came from the way I felt about these people, my admiration for them: I wanted to tell others about them. (Cited in Barnouw 1974:45)

Barnouw comments upon this aspect of the Flaherty method and its relationship to anthropology:

The urge to capture on film the nature of rapidly vanishing cultures had been pursued also by anthropologists, who have given it the name salvage ethnography. Flaherty was doing such work for deeply personal rather than scholarly reasons, but the outcome was similar. It has been called "romantic" in that Flaherty was not recording a current way of life but one filtered through memories of Nanook and his people. Unquestionably the film reflected their image of their traditional life. Yet a people's self-image may be a crucial ingredient in its culture, and worth recording. Anthropologists, while aware of the distorting lens, study it with care. In effect, so did Flaherty. (Barnouw 1974:45)

The idea of portraying native people as they see themselves, as Flaherty and Malinowski professed a wish to do, is made even more complicated when the self-image for which one is searching is not a contemporary one but that of the culture prior to the intervention of Westerners. Anthropologists call this time "the ethnographic present." In order to create this illusion, it is often necessary to rely on the oldest members of the culture to tell about the "good old days" (called memory culture or, as indicated in the preceding quotation from Barnouw, salvage ethnography). Both *Nanook* and written ethnographies of the time are "authentic reproductions." One is tempted to ask filmmakers and others who reconstruct to place some sort of disclaimer at the beginning of their work, much like the one in John Huston's film *The Life and Times of Judge Roy Bean*, which says: "If this ain't the way it was, it's the way it should have been." Although constructing the ethnographic present is no longer considered a viable idea, the notion of asking people to create an image of their lives that represents their view of themselves is very much a part of contemporary practice.

Flaherty has repeatedly been criticized for reconstructing Inuit culture in *Nanook* (Calder-Marshall 1963:85; Van Dongen 1965:13). It is somewhat ironic that he has been taken to task for doing something that anthropologists did with virtual impunity. The difference is even more striking when you realize that few anthropologists fulfill their scientific responsibilities of being methodologically explicit (see chapter 6). That is, anthropologists' writings and films tend to conceal the reconstructions and alterations that are necessary in order to provide the illusion of an ethnographic present. *Nanook* also conceals or avoids the contemporary cultural and political realities of Inuit life (for example, the trader and trading post are shown as benign rather than as exploitative agents of culture change). However, in Flaherty's writings, he was quite open about how much of *Nanook* was constructed. Barnouw discusses one of the most famous illusions—"the big aggie igloo":

The building of an igloo became one of the most celebrated sequences in the film. But interior photography presented a problem: the igloo was too small. So Nanook and others undertook to build an outsized "aggie igloo." During the first attempts the domes collapsed—as the builders roared with laughter. Finally they succeeded, but the interior was found too dark for photography. So half the igloo was sheared away. For the camera Nanook and his family went to sleep and awoke "with all the cold of out-of-doors pouring in." Daylight lit the scene. Flaherty was intent on authentically reproducing the event. That this might call for ingenious means did not disturb him. Film itself, and all its technology, were products of ingenuity. (Barnouw 1974:38)

The illusion is not exactly perfect. Even a casual viewer of the film can see shadows where they shouldn't be. Moreover, Flaherty does not hide the illusion; he describes it as an accomplishment:

One of Nanook's problems was to construct an igloo large enough for the filming of interior scenes. The average Eskimo igloo, about twelve feet in diameter, was much too small. On the dimensions I laid out for him, a diameter of twenty-five feet, Nanook and his companions started in to build the biggest igloo of their lives. For two days they worked. The women and children helping them. Then came the hard part—to cut inserts for five large slab-ice windows without weakening the dome. They had hardly begun when the dome fell in pieces to the ground. "Never mind," said Nanook, "I can do it next time."

For two days more they worked, but again with the same result, as soon as they began setting in the ice windows, their structure fell to the ground. It was a huge joke this time, and holding their sides, they laughed their misfortune away. Again Nanook began on the big aggie igloo but this time the women and children hauled barrels of water on sledges from the waterhole and iced the walls as fast as they went up. Finally, the igloo was finished and they stood eyeing it satisfied as so many children over a house of blocks. The light from the ice windows proved inadequate, however, and when the interiors were finally filmed the dome's half just over the camera had to be cut away, so Nanook and his family went to sleep and awakened with all the cold of out-of-doors pouring in. (Flaherty 1922:139–40)

Flaherty began a tradition of participatory filmmaking that continues today. The Netsilik Eskimo Film Project under the anthropological direction of Asen Balikci (Balikci and Brown 1966) and Jean Rouch's films *Jaguar*, *Petit à Petit*, and *Cocorico*, *Monsieur Poulet* are clear examples of films that employ Flaherty's participatory method or "shared anthropology," as Rouch (1974) calls it (Stoller 1992). Every time filmmakers show their rushes to the subjects of their films and ask for their comments and approval, every time filmmakers ask people to self-consciously portray themselves and the events of their lives in front of the camera, every time filmmakers try to mesh their interpretations with those of their subjects—the filmmakers are continuing to build "big aggie igloos" for their audience.

Conclusion

Flaherty's contribution to a dialogue about film and anthropology is uncertain. It is only in the past twenty years or so, when his work became reevaluated, that it was "discovered" that the problems with which Flaherty grappled are the problems of today's image makers and that his solutions are illuminating and worth considering. Historically, he was virtually overlooked by most filmmakers—both documentary and ethnographic, Jean Rouch being an important exception. His work reflects a set of assumptions about ethnographic films that until recently, were held in common by both audiences and makers. It was taken for granted that the proper subject for these films was the unsullied "primitive." In that sense, the early work of John Marshall and the entirety of Robert Gardner's films can be seen as being in the tradition of Flaherty's romantic attachment to an imagined primitive world.

There can be little doubt that Robert Flaherty is a seminal figure in cinema in general and ethnographic film in particular. He was a complex man who consciously sought to create an approach to the production of film that would be an alternative to Hollywood and to produce a new cinematic form. He was interested in finding a way to collaborate with the people he filmed so that his need to tell interesting and dramatic stories that would hold an audience could be interwoven with the image the people had of themselves. In doing so, he was able to synthesize the two dominant tendencies of the cinema of his time—the episodic "slices of life" travelogues, which espoused the "outsider's" view of the exotic world, and the dramatic fiction stories. Flaherty told stories about real people living out the drama of their lives. John Grierson summed it up well in his analysis of *Nanook:*

Nanook was the simple story of an Eskimo family and its fight for food, but in its approach to the whole question of film making was something entirely novel at the time it was made. It was a record of everyday life so selective in its detail and sequence, so intimate in its shots, and so appreciative of the nuances of common feeling, that it was a drama in many ways more telling than anything that had come out of the manufactured sets of Hollywood. . . . Without actors, almost without acting he built up in his camera what he considered the essential story of their lives. (Cited in Hardy 1979:124)

I began this chapter with a conversation between Flaherty and Nanook in which Flaherty explains to Nanook the difference between real life and the movies. Because Flaherty understood that "the aggie must come first," cinema was never the same after *Nanook.* Although *Nanook* did not have an immediate effect on ethnographic film, the importance of Flaherty's contributions are now being realized, due in no small measure to Rouch's acknowledgment of his debt to this man (Rouch, personal communication, 1978).

Nanook is now part of yet another chapter in the development of ethnographic film—the reevaluation and utilization of films by the people portrayed. On April 26, 1979, the Inuit Tapirisat of Canada (the Eskimo Brotherhood of Canada) requested screening rights for *Nanook of the North* to be used in its Anik B Satellite project.

Inukshuk Inuit Tapirisat of Canada is the National Inuit Brotherhood representing all 22,000 Inuit in Canada. The staff of *Inukshuk* saw *Nanook of the North* at a training workshop in November. It was the first time that most of them had seen the film and they were very excited by it and anxious for other Inuit to have the opportunity to see it. . . . I don't know if there is anything else I can add other than to emphasize the hopes that our staff have pinned on being able to screen this film in the communities with their families and friends. *The film excited*

great pride in the strength and dignity of their ancestors and they want to share this with their
elders and their children [emphasis added]. (Excerpt from a letter from Lyndsay Green, opera-
tions manager, *Inukshuk,* to Barbara Van Dyke, executive director, International Film Seminars)

So in June of 1979, Nanook's aggie was sent back home, this time to be seen on
a television set and not on the wall of the house. Since that time, several Inuit
filmmakers, such as Zacharias Kunuk, have striven to create a native cinema
that celebrates their cultural identity, and various Inuit television broadcasting
systems are attempting to discover how best to serve their communities. Although some Inuit find *Nanook* to be a positive part of their history and others
decry its romanticism, none can ignore its impact, thus ensuring that *Nanook
of the North* will continue to be an active part of the culture Flaherty portrayed
and well as the subject of debate and discussion among those in the ethnographic film community.

Robert Gardner and Anthropological Cinema

Robert Gardner is well-known for his deeply evocative films on exotic cultures. His film on ritual warfare, Dead Birds *(shot among the Dani tribes of New Guinea) created a huge controversy. . . . Equally controversial is the style of his films which don't pretend for a moment to be scientific but instead place before us the images of his dreams (or even nightmares) of what he has witnessed. In the North American, Anglo-Saxon rush towards pragmatic cinema, he has stayed aloof, to one side, continuing his highly professional work.* COLIN YOUNG'S INTRODUCTION TO GARDNER'S "THE FICTION OF NON-FICTION FILM"

Robert Gardner's are among the best-known ethnographic films. From *Dead Birds* in the early 1960s to *Ika Hands* in the late 1980s, he has produced an extensive body of work about the cultures of non-Western people. It would be no exaggeration to suggest that he is one of the most highly regarded "ethnographic" filmmakers in the United States, if not the world. It is therefore essential that a critical examination of his work be undertaken. I find his work problematic. This chapter began as a polemical retort to Gardner's response to Alexander Moore's (1988) and Jonathan Parry's (1988) critiques of his film *Forest of Bliss* (Ruby 1989c). Like many filmmakers in this field, Gardner has received little scholarly attention apart from reviews of his films. Trickster Verlag tried to correct that lacuna by organizing a Gardner retrospective with an accompanying volume of essays

(Kapfer, Petermann, and Thoms 1989). I expanded my polemical remarks into what I regarded as a more scholarly critique for that collection and then revised it for a film studies journal (Ruby 1989c). That essay, substantially revised and rewritten, served as the basis for this chapter.

Initially, I wrote out of a frustration with some anthropologists' seemingly uncritical acceptance of Gardner's films. What I had to say in those preliminary statements had already been said privately by a number of my colleagues. I thought it was time to deal with the issues in a public manner. I hoped that my work would have been taken in the spirit intended. It was not meant as a personal attack on Gardner but rather as the beginning of a long-overdue self-critical process within the field of ethnographic film. All of the criticisms I leveled at Gardner could have applied, in one form or other, to many of the "leading lights" in ethnographic film. The private response I received from some anthropologists, like Peter Loizos, was that I was merely a polemicist and probably had a personal grudge against Gardner. It is unfortunate that some academics cannot distinguish between vigorous debate and ad hominem attacks.

In brief, here is the viewpoint of this chapter: I believe Robert Gardner made a major contribution to ethnographic film during the 1950s and 1960s. However, since *Dead Birds*, his films have drifted away from the theoretical concerns of mainstream cultural anthropology. This movement is the result of two factors: (1) Gardner's dependence on an outmoded and inadequate theoretical perspective and (2) his failure to utilize anthropological knowledge derived from ethnographic fieldwork to organize his films. Gardner's adequacy as a film artist, a persona attached to him by some like Loizos (1993), must also be questioned when the aesthetic underlying his art has become morally and politically suspect. The remainder of the chapter explores and elaborates on these points.

Gardner's Legacy to Ethnographic Film

Robert Gardner's involvement with ethnographic film began at a time when few considered film a serious medium for anthropologists. From 1956 until today, Gardner has been attached to Harvard University's Film Study Center and well as the Carpenter Center for the Visual Arts. During the first decade of the Film Study Center's activities, Gardner assisted in the completion of *The Hunters*, produced *Dead Birds*, taught production courses, provided completion assistance for other filmmakers, and conceived a scheme for filming so-called disappearing cultures. With Karl Heider and Asen Balikci, he founded Program in Ethnographic Film, the first North American organization to deal with film and anthropology. For these efforts alone, he deserves recognition as a founding father of U.S. ethnographic film.

Gardner's ideas about filming other cultures were first articulated in 1957 as follows: "Cinematic recordings of human life are unchanging documents providing detailed and focused information on the behavioral characteristics of man. . . . The most significant advantages of cinematic documentation are that evidence provided is available to the view of many individuals both immediately and for a period" (Gardner 1957:345–46). In addition, he posited that evidence collected with a cine camera is "of a direct and unambiguous kind, being reality instantaneously captured and suffering no distortion due to faults of sight, memory, or semantic interpretation" (Gardner 1957:346). Once pictorial documentation was gathered, he argued that films should be made: "[A]fter [the center] has had the opportunity to document various wide contexts of human life, it can proceed to make from such documentation visual expressions of the meaningful parts of it to be seen and shared by as many people as can be reached" (Gardner 1957:349). Ultimately, the justification for this work went beyond anthropological goals to the humanistic assumption that "creating a careful and sensitive visual account of an unknown society was ample justification in itself" (Gardner and Heider 1968:xi). As Margaret Mead had been a vocal advocate of this position, it is reasonable to assume that Gardner was at the very least influenced by her ideas. Rather than critique the adequacy of this point of view from a contemporary perspective, I will point the reader to chapter 1 in this book, where the notion of film as evidence and the archive are examined.

Gardner had a marvelously grand plan: to produce films about cultures that represent basic ecological adaptations—a world sample based on an economic model. In describing the development of the idea for *Dead Birds*, Gardner articulated his plan:

With a film on a primitive hunting society already available [*The Hunters*], it seemed appropriate to think in terms of one about an agricultural group. Then at least two of the three basic ecological patterns of human society would have been documented. Materials I gathered on three pastoral societies in Ethiopia will be released as three full-length films early in 1970. [He is speaking about Hillary Harris's *The Nuer* and his *Deep Hearts* and *Rivers of Sand*.] With their appearance the third basic pattern of human adaptation will be represented. (Gardner 1969:25)

This model for mapping the cultures of the world in ecological/economic terms was much in vogue at this time and served as the basis for organizing many introductory cultural anthropology courses in the United States. It is reflected in the work of two other Boston-area filmmakers—Timothy Asch and John Marshall. They all felt the urge to filmicly salvage some of the cultures that were presumed to be disappearing (an assumption that, of course, proved false and deeply offensive to those cultures that survived in spite of having been salvaged). Although Gardner has never been overtly concerned with the uses of his films in the teaching of anthropology, both Asch and Marshall saw the model as primarily a pedagogical one. As readers will see in chapter 4, Asch tried to construct a film-based introduction to cultural anthropology around the model.

The Harvard-Peabody Expedition to New Guinea—*Dead Birds*

In 1961, Gardner organized the Harvard-Peabody expedition among the horticultural Dani of the highlands of New Guinea (today called Irian Jaya) with funds from the National Science Foundation as well as the government of Netherlands New Guinea and the Peabody Museum of Harvard University (Heider 1970:x). He spent six months doing ethnography and filming in collaboration with anthropologists Jan Brukhuijse and Karl Heider for what became his most widely acclaimed film, *Dead Birds*. The project, organized like a nineteenth-century natural historical and scientific expedition with a number of people each conducting their own research, was primarily a salvage ethnography project. The highlands of New Guinea were, at that point, one of the largest areas in the world not thoroughly explored and colonized by Westerners.

The work was also fueled by an interest in ritual warfare:

Hence it was partially in the spirit of conservators of a passing age that we planned the Harvard-Peabody New Guinea Expedition. . . . It was my hope to make a study of a society still practicing what in anthropological annals is known as "ritual warfare" that turned our attention to Melanesia. . . . The overall aim of the expedition was to make a comprehensive study of a single community of Neolithic warrior farmers. We intended to document verbally and visually the whole social and cultural fabric of this community. We were interested in its natural history and were equipped to scrutinize it from the standpoint of behavioral scientists, naturalists, photographers and filmmakers. (Gardner and Heider 1968:xii–xv)

The debate about U.S. military involvement in Southeast Asia was heating up at this time, and a discussion about the place of war in civilized society occupied many people's minds. In several screenings, I heard Gardner state that he hoped *Dead Birds* would contribute to the dialogue Americans were having about the Vietnam conflict, if not war in general.

According to Heider, Gardner conceived the expedition to produce materials "from different points of view, and give somewhat different pictures of the Dugum Dani . . . which would have important implications for anthropological methodology quite apart from its value as an intensive, multidimensional portrayal of a single group of Papuans" (Heider 1972:2–3). An account of Peter Matthiessen's encounter with the Dani (1962), ethnomusicological studies by Michael Rockefeller (never finished because he died in the field), as well as written ethnographic work by Karl Heider (1970) and Jan Brukhuijse were all produced for comparison and contrast with the film. Heider authored an exemplary study guide for the film, which contains a brief ethnographic description of the Dani, Gardner's discussion of the making of the film, and the script (1972). Unfortunately, the most intriguing aspect of the expedition—a comparison of the various versions of this culture—never received the attention it deserves. No one, neither a member of the original expedition nor any other scholar, has critically examined or compared the written and pictorial materials produced by the expedition. Jeff Ruoff is in the process of making these comparisons. Regardless of its shortcomings, *Dead Birds* caught the attention of the anthropological community as no film had done before.

A Critique of *Dead Birds*

There can be no question that *Dead Birds* is an important film that has been used successfully in many classrooms. I never taught an introductory course in cultural anthropology during the 1960s and 1970s without it. The film deals with a question that must vex all thinking human beings—the presence of violence in human society. As the film came out when the United States was involved in a tragic war in Southeast Asia, its relevance for the teaching of undergraduates during that period cannot be overestimated.

It is also a stylistic tour de force. The opening sequence in which Gardner visually describes the natural and cultural environment of the Dani—the location of the villages, gardens, the paths between them, the battlefields, and the natural barriers of the hills and mountains that comprise the limits of these features—is brilliant, never equaled before or after. It is one of the best uses of montage in an ethnographic film. As observational-style cinema became the vogue soon after the release of *Dead Birds*, montage became déclassé before many people had explored its potential. As a technique for juxtaposing seemingly disparate elements, it seems to me that montage deserves more attention than it has gotten among anthropologists wishing to make analytic statements in a film.

The flaws and shortcomings of *Dead Birds* are also quite visible to contemporary eyes, particularly given the vantage point of time. For some, the problems make the film almost worthless. "My judgment is that *Dead Birds* has been colored by so many subtle fictional pretensions and artistic ornamentations that it has surrendered most of its usefulness as a socially scientific document" (Mischler 1985:669). To suggest that this film would be more useful if it were an "astylistic" document seems to me to suggest that film's purpose is to produce primary research materials—documents—a strange assumption indeed and certainly one not shared by Gardner.

The film's inadequacies are best understood as the result of the choices the filmmaker made to follow certain cinematic customs of the time. *Dead Birds* employs the conventions of commercial feature fiction to achieve an illusion of actuality. The conventions are designed to make the illusion seamless. The film is the "story" of two people, Weyak and Pua—that is, like Nanook or the quartet of San hunters in *The Hunters*, the life of the culture is unfolded through the lives of the two individuals. The film is unlike John Marshall's *N!ai*, which chronicles the life of a San woman as a means of exploring her culture. Instead, *Dead Birds* has a story line contrived so that the principals just happen to be present at events the filmmaker wishes to use to reveal his point of view. Thus, warfare and events associated with it are revealed through Weyak's participation, while Pua serves as the marginal observer of his own culture. At times, the device becomes less than transparent—for example, when Pua *just happens* to visit Weyak when he is completing the weaving of a cowrie-shell band. It has been my experience as someone who uses the film in classroom teaching that students often become distanced from the artificiality of the narrative structure and begin to disbelieve it. Given the style of films today, Gardner's attempt at making the narrative structure seem natural is problematic.

Dead Birds is constructed so as to create a seamless illusion that is narratively compelling—a comprehensive story evolving naturally and chronologically. The voice of the narration is third-person passive, or what is known among filmmakers as "the voice of God." The film begins with "There is a tale told by a mountain people . . . " Neither the anonymous Dani author of the tale nor the film narrator has an identity. Even if one argues that cinema requires such artifices, the fact remains that the illusion is false and questionable if one purports to be doing anthropology, at least in contemporary terms. To give two obvious examples, the film concentrates on the role of ritual warfare, and yet we never see an actual battle but rather a composite one constructed from the footage of several battles: "The major battle sequence in *Dead Birds* is put together from shots of different battles at different locations" (Heider 1976:67). Similarly, the sound track is constructed to make you believe you are hearing synchronized sound when, in fact, "All the sound in *Dead Birds* is postsynchronized" (Heider 1976:70). Weyak's "voice" is a creation in a sound studio. It is actually the voice of Karl Heider speaking Dani.

Whether you find such an approach to anthropological cinema offensive depends on whether you believe that films should be made out of what is filmable or that what is deemed necessary should be constructed in order to have the film's thesis look convincing. Gardner believed that the footage he had of any one battle was inadequate to make the statement he wished to make about Dani warfare. So he constructed a "cine battle" containing all the elements he considered important. The notion of typicality that underlies the choice to construct a cine battle is but one example of the nineteenth-century scientific ideology found in Gardner's work. I am not arguing that the use of a narrative structure is inappropriate in ethnographic film. On the contrary, I believe it is essential. My dissatisfaction is with Gardener's need to erase the author and make the narrative structure seamless—that is, his lack of reflexivity. Ethnographic filmmakers are telling stories of their experience in their films. But because of audiences' tendency to believe in certain kinds of stories as being objective and true, filmmakers must remind viewers that they are telling them their stories, not revealing the truth. Gardner does not do this in *Dead Birds* or any of his films.

Like Marshall in *The Hunters*, Gardner created and narrated interior monologues for some of the principals. We are told Weyak's thoughts when he looks at a sunset. At another place in the film, we are told that a warrior recently wounded in battle is recalling how the enemy would take no chances in battles fought in the past. The scene of the warrior "recalling" is followed by a flashback of a battle scene. These fiction tactics provide continuity between sequences and act as a lead-in to a sequence that would otherwise be missing a smooth transition. I assume that most anthropologists then would have objected to attributing thoughts to the subjects of their studies, as would most anthropologists today. To argue that the nature of film requires that certain liberties be taken with knowledge is to suggest a serious lack of fit between film and anthropology.

From the opening narration of the fable about the race to determine the fate of humankind to the narrator's closing thoughts about our mortality, audiences are made aware that they are viewing a dramatically structured film designed to be a moral tale in the guise of an ethnographic film. "I seized the opportunity of speaking to certain fundamental issues in human life. The Dani were then less important to me than those issues. . . . My responsibility was as much to my own situation as a thinking person as to the Dani as also thinking people. I never thought this reflective or value-oriented approach was inconsistent either with my training as a social scientist or [with] my goals as the author of a film. . . . The film attempts to say something about how we all, as humans, meet our animal fate" (Gardner in Heider 1972:2–35).

Gardner's humanist desire to provide a meditation about morality took precedence over the need to articulate the details of Dani culture or to adhere to what was actually knowable about the people. Gardner is telling viewers that he is more of an artist/humanist than an anthropologist. Although a humanistic approach to anthropology is certainly commendable, and having aesthetic aspirations that cause one to become craft-conscious about the medium employed is praiseworthy, humanism or the creation of art are not adequate as the primary theoretical justification for doing anthropology. An argument could be made that it is unfair or even futile to critique *Dead Birds* as anthropology. But it is a weak argument since Gardner himself received funds based on the assumption that the film was to further anthropological purposes. When he completed the film, he sought out the critical approval of anthropologists by allowing the film to be reviewed in anthropological journals, and he showed the film in anthropological venues. Gardner has continued to do so with all of his films. Given his actions, I think it only reasonable to critique his work as if it were a serious attempt to make ethnographic films that advance the purposes of anthropology.

Dead Birds raises some fundamental methodological and moral questions that continue to be raised by Gardner's later work. They concern the issue of consent and the knowledge the subjects should have about a filmmaker's intention. Gardner believes that his work would have been hampered if the subjects had understood what was going on. In other words, he believes that providing the people in his films with sufficient knowledge to enable them to give informed consent would destroy his ability to make the kind of films in which he is interested. "My job was made easier because no one knew what I was doing" (Gardner in Heider 1972:2–34). "As far as my film was concerned, one essential advantage lay in the fact that the Dugum Dani did not know what a camera was. I decided to protect this innocence by keeping all photographs and magazines hidden. . . . I wanted above all to photograph *authentic* [emphasis added] Dani behavior" (Gardner 1969:30).

Given the agonizing debate over informed consent and the rights of subjects that has raged during the past twenty-plus years among North American anthropologists and other researchers who employ human subjects, Gardner's assumption that only naive subjects are worth filming at best is out of touch with contemporary ethical thinking and at worst reflects a naive assumption about what one can and should film (Gross, Katz, and Ruby 1988). Although it can be argued that in 1961, these issues were not in the forefront of the field, they certainly are now, and Gardner appears to be as unconcerned with them when discussing *Forest of Bliss*, a film made in the 1980s (Larson 1987), as he was in New Guinea.

The idea that you must conceal your intentions from people in order to get useful footage stands in direct opposition to Jean Rouch's notion of a shared anthropology—a concept he explored in a number of films prior to Gardner's work with the Dani (for example, *The Human Pyramid* [1958] and *Les Maitres Fous* [1957]). Rouch has said that the idea of a shared or collaborative anthropology was derived from Flaherty in the 1920s, when Flaherty showed Nanook the footage he shot in order to obtain his cooperation and collaboration (see chapter 2, on Flaherty). Gardner rejected the idea of a shared anthropology in which the participants in a film became collaborators with the director. With the exception of *Rivers of Sand*, Gardner seldom interviews the people in his films or in any other way shares authority with them. As Gardner knew Rouch and Rouch's films, it is evident that he chose to approach the Dani as naive subjects when he knew alternatives were available.[1] He apparently believed that only "authentic" behavior was worth filming—that is, behavior "unsullied" by Western influences and performed by people unaware of what was being done or of the long-term implications of being filmed. He appears to be more interested in his vision of a culture than that of the people he portrays.

In 1989, Gardner returned to the Baliem Valley and shot footage for an update on the Dani, an experience he describes in detail in his unpublished essay "The More Things Change." Ten years have passed since the filming, and no sequel has been released. Gardner's inability to finish this new film suggests that the highly acculturated Dani no longer hold his interest. Jeff Ruoff, who is in the midst of a major study of the *Dead Birds* expedition, offers additional evidence of how little Gardner's ideas have changed since the early 1960s:

Gardner returned to the Baliem River Valley in 1989 to track down his old acquaintances in the Dani neighborhood and to produce a sequel to *Dead Birds*. His twenty-four page account, "The More Things Change," reads like a parody of the salvage and redemptive modes of ethnographic writing described by [George] Marcus. In the fallen gardens of the Grand Valley, Gardner finds only the tattered remnants of a once vital, authentic, culture, now forever gone, beyond salvation. Pua, the young swineherd from *Dead Birds*, takes him to a model village, a sort of "Dani World" . . . , built for tourists who came in the wake of the 1961 expedition. Many come with photocopies of photographs from the Harvard-Peabody expedition—of Weyak, Um'ue, and Kurelu—looking for the warrior farmers of yesteryear. . . . Gardner chastises his former subjects[:] "Part of me felt they had shown themselves to be all too willing collaborators in the business of change. How could they tolerate so much compromise with what had been such a compelling life?" . . .

The filmmaker eventually finds Kurelu, once the most powerful leader in the highlands and an inspiration to Gardner[:] "From the very beginning I thought of him as the person who epitomized everything ancient and enduring about the Dani." . . . He projects *Dead Birds* for Kurelu, Um'ue, Pua, and Weyak only to recognize too late that they will not be able to comprehend his English-language narration, which he is incapable of translating. Since he cannot speak their language, Gardner fails to obtain their reactions to the screening (which he had hoped to integrate into his sequel). Unable to interact with his old Dani friends, Gardner understands only their repeated requests for material goods, a radio, a pair of pants . . . , requests which embarrass him. The deluge of modernization, anticipated in the publications of the Harvard-Peabody expedition, has run over the people of the Baliem River. Disappointed, Gardner's "melancholy encounter" ends. (Ruoff 1998:23–24; the quotations are from an unpublished version of Gardner's article "The More Things Change")

It could be argued that *Dead Birds* is a product of its time and that in 1961, there were no other models for making documentary or ethnographic films. Gardner was simply doing the best he could. The argument is not adequate. At the time Gardner was planning *Dead Birds*, a number of documentary and ethnographic filmmakers were voicing their discontent with the limitations imposed on them by their equipment and the dominant tradition of dramatic documentaries with "voice of God" narration that imitated Hollywood features. During 1960 and 1961, many experiments in sync-sound location shooting were being made—in Canada, by Michel Brault; in the United States, by Robert Drew, Richard Leacock, and D. A. Pennebaker, who produced *Primary* in 1960. When Jean Rouch and Edgar Morin released *Chronicle of a Summer* in 1961, it was regarded as a revolution in film. And as I suggested earlier, Rouch himself argued that the tradition of involving the subjects in the production of a film began in the 1920s with Robert Flaherty (see Barnouw 1974 for a history of this period in documentary film).

Direct cinema and *cinéma vérité* were being invented at the same time Robert Gardner chose to employ a traditional and, for some filmmakers, an outmoded approach to filming and documentary dramatic structure that deliberately ignored these innovations. The "look" of *Dead Birds* is no accident of technology or the time in which it was produced. It is the product of a certain approach to film and culture. Although his style has evolved somewhat—for example, there are more observational footage and sync-sound interviews in *Rivers of Sand* than in *Dead Birds*—Gardner has adhered to the theoretical stance that motivated *Dead Birds* in all of his subsequent work, and as can be seen in the quotation from Ruoff, he continues to see the Dani and, I would argue, all of the people in all of his films as remnants of an imagined past.

Robert Gardner as Anthropologist and Artist

Gardner's productions are understandable as enactments of the sentiments he first expressed in 1957—the assumption that salvage ethnographic film projects that produce visual records of the customs of "disappearing" cultures provide an invaluable resource for future generations as well as an opportunity to make films for the public. It was his stated desire to systematically record as many of the basic culture types as possible (Gardner 1957). The ideological underpinnings of his approach are found in nineteenth-century science, which sought to inductively describe phenomena, then produce a taxonomy. Once "all the data" were collected, a scientist could begin to make analyses and eventually draw conclusions. Natural history expeditions like the Harvard-Peabody expedition to New Guinea are expressions of these ideas. In anthropology, the paradigm manifested itself in the distinction between descriptive ethnography and ethnological analysis. To collect usable data, ethnographers sought out the least "disturbed" remnants of exotic cultures, or lacking any "survivals," they reconstructed the ethnographic present through the memories of the oldest members of the group. Only "authentic" culture was deemed appropriate to record. When photographed or filmed, natives were asked to remove any physical evidence of the actual circumstances—that is, Western clothing and ornaments—and "perform" authentic reproductions of their former lives. Dozens of books and numerous articles have been written critiquing the "vanishing culture" concept that underlies this approach.[2]

Altar of Fire (1975–76), a film Gardner was invited to direct by University of California scholar Fritz Staal, provides another example of the inadequacy of Gardner's paradigm. The film is a forty-five-minute condensation of what the promotional brochure from the distribution company modestly calls "the world's oldest surviving ceremony." In the brochure, Staal unselfconsciously explains that in order to "preserve" a ritual that had not been performed for some time, the filmmakers had to pay for the cost of the ceremony. Because of the somewhat unusual nature of this "media event," as Edmund Carpenter called it on the film's sound track, a number of spectators gathered. Staal and Gardner had to go to great pains to exclude the unreasonable "natives" who thought they might have some right to participate in their culture's ceremonial life. Despite their efforts, "Some film footage was spoiled or its use made impossible by these fully clothed people (that is, visitors from the outside who came to watch the ceremony), who contrasted sadly with the Nambudiris (Brahmin priests) in their white loincloths, themselves *disfigured* [emphasis added] only by an occasional wristwatch" (Staal 1976).

Although the "purity" of the media-generated ceremony was preserved, at least from the point of view of the filmmakers, the value of this "media event" seems in doubt. As Robert A. Paul suggested, "The only way this film could have worked, in both an ethical and a 'scientific' way, would have been for the makers to have been flexible and honest enough to record the media event which they themselves set in motion. Instead, they pretend to give us an authentic glimpse into ancient Vedic times, rendered hollow and ethically repugnant through the patronizing, rigid, antiquarian, and neo-colonialist attitudes it reveals" (Paul 1978:199).[3]

Staal's response to Paul's review implies that he failed to understand the criticism. He suggests that anyone reading the film's study guide would have known the circumstances of the filming and that those wishing to know something about the socioeconomic context could consult his written work (Staal 1979:346–47). The problem is that unless it is stated within the film, the information is nonexistent for most audiences. Staal and Gardner failed to see the implication of omitting these aspects of the event from the film. In his response to Staal, Paul says:

The filmmaker has certain responsibilities to the subjects of the film, to other local people whose lives are affected by the presence of a foreign-film crew, to the potential audience, and to the scholarly community. It was, and is, my opinion that *Altar of Fire* does not meet those responsibilities, sensitivity, or awareness of issues. With respect to the audience, lay and scholarly, it seems to me that the film is not sufficiently forthcoming about some of the circumstances surrounding the making of the film, knowledge of which would seriously affect what the viewer might suppose he were watching. (Paul 1979:348)

A proper critique of the intellectual, moral, and political implications of "salvaging authentic cultures" lies outside the limits of this chapter. Suffice it to say that the paradigm expressed by Staal—and I would argue, by Gardner in most of his films—systematically avoids the economic and political conditions of the people studied and filmed and is therefore easily criticized as romantic and supportive of political and economic neocolonialism and other forms of oppression. If one is able to deny the existence of political and economic inequality and oppression by causing people to perform some imagined version of their past lives, then the problems literally disappear before our eyes, together with whatever responsibility we may have for these conditions.

Gardner is certainly not the author of this concept, nor is he its only contemporary practitioner. However, his historical prominence makes his adherence to these ideas a stumbling block to the development of an anthropological cinema. A fondness for capturing the varieties of human experience in all their pristine and unsullied glory on film or in print has had a long history within anthropology as well as Western culture as a whole.[4] Although it is still possible to locate some proponents of the approach, North American anthropology has largely replaced this paradigm. Anthropologists more commonly assume that all behavior, Westernized or not, is authentic and that description that is not motivated by research questions and grounded in an articulated theory is virtually useless.[5] From the perspective of many current theoretical positions within anthropology (feminist, Marxist, Geertzian interpretive, and so forth), Robert Gardner's stated anthropological justification for his films is at best an anachronism.[6]

Although it could be argued that Gardner is entitled to his theoretical perspective no matter how out of touch it is with contemporary thinking, I assume that most anthropologists would agree that certain minimal methodological standards must be met if one is to call a film ethnographic. Early in his career, Gardner himself acknowledged that "for a film to be ethnographic, an ethnographer must make it, or at least be closely associated with its making" (Gardner 1958:66). Unfortunately, an examination of the fieldwork associated with Gardner's films often makes the anthropological/ethnographic designation questionable. To my knowledge, Gardner has never learned the language of any of the people he filmed, except for the Dani, nor has he stayed in the field in any of his filming expeditions long enough to do adequate ethnography.[7] He is sometimes credited with being an anthropologist and conducting ethnographic studies, but there is little evidence to support those assumptions.[8] Consequently, the only possibility his films have to express anthropological knowledge based on ethnographic research is through the anthropologists Gardner hires as subject-area specialists. Therefore, in order to critique the adequacy of Gardner's films as anthropology, we must examine his collaboration with anthropologists.

Collaborations between filmmakers and anthropologists are often problematic (see chapter 4 for a discussion of the Tim Asch–Napoleon Chagnon collaboration). If a survey were taken, I think most anthropologists would say that their experiences with professional filmmakers have been somewhat less than satisfying. Certainly that is my personal experience. I once had to threaten legal action to prevent my name from appearing in the credits of a film on which I had worked. Documentary and ethnographic filmmaking is often a collaborative effort in which the risk of disputes over credit is endemic. This is a problematic area, but nonetheless, it must be discussed. Some of Gardner's reputation appears to be built on what might generously be called "confused credits." The role he played in *The Hunters* is uncertain, at least to me. The stylistic similarities between the narration in *The Hunters* and in *Dead Birds* suggest that Gardner had an important voice in both. On the other hand, John Marshall's name does not even appear in the 1957 article Gardner wrote discussing the activities of the Film Study Center. Unless you knew otherwise, the article would lead you to believe that Robert Gardner made *The Hunters* by himself.

Whereas some ethnographic filmmakers, like Karl Heider, have found Gardner to be someone who generously gives his time and expertise, others have (only privately) expressed dissatisfaction with the credit Gardner has received for their films. *The Nuer* is a clear-cut example. Gardner produced it as part of the pastoral nomad project that included *Rivers of Sand*. Certainly, raising the funds, conceiving of the idea, and so forth are important, but if the film has authors, they are Hillary Harris and George Breidenbech. Yet in two editions, the Pennsylvania State University audiovisual catalog has contained the following listing: "*The Nuer*, a film by Robert Gardner and Hillary Harris," and retrospectives of Gardner's work usually include this film. It is not easy to determine who caused these errors, but at the very least, Gardner appears to have done little to dispel the notion that he was responsible for *The Hunters* and *The Nuer*.

The credits for *Rivers of Sand* (1974) read: "Ethnographic advice and translations: Ivo Strecker, Jean Lydall (Strecker) and Eike Berinas" (Bender 1977:196). In a 1988 article, Strecker makes it clear that when he joined Gardner in the field, one season of filming had already been completed with no assistance from anyone who knew the culture. The casualness with which this supposedly anthropological work was undertaken, at least as Strecker reports it, is truly appalling. The artistic vision of Gardner as auteur dominated the project with little competent ethnographic assistance. "I was also frustrated because I remained barred from the process of conceptualizing the film as a whole. In 1971, Bob and I both knew very little about Hamar culture . . . and I found it extremely difficult to make any generalizations. I sensed that Bob was planning a grand and explanatory film about the Hamar" (Strecker 1988:372).

Lionel Bender, reviewer for *American Anthropologist*, has argued that "this is a great film. . . . For the present, *Rivers of Sand* is our best available source on the Hamer [*sic*] of Southern Ethiopia. Fortunately, it is a magnificent source" (1977:197). Lydall and Strecker answered Bender, labeling the film "an ethnographic farce" and pointing out that they were denied participation in "the decisive stages of filming. . . . The result is that the film is not a reliable source of information on the Hamar but it is a source for a study of . . . the social milieu of filmmakers and anthropologists who use ethnography to indulge in prejudiced visions that have little to do with the people under study" (Lydall and Strecker 1978:945). Ten years after they wrote this, Strecker's opinion of the film had changed very little: "In *Rivers of Sand* Hamar life is not allowed, as it were, to reconstitute itself on the screen. The constant cuts and counterpositioning of short sequences never allow an authentic view of Hamar life to emerge but lead to a complete distortion of time, space, and action as they are experienced by the Hamar" (Strecker 1988:373). In more recent personal conversations with both Strecker and Lydall, I can attest to their continued discomfort with the film and Gardner's methods.

The narrative spine of *Rivers of Sand* is an interview with a Hamar woman, Omalleidna, lamenting the role of women in her society. The theme of physical abuse dominates the interview and some of the intercut scenes. According to Strecker, "[I]nstead of recognizing that Omalleidna's account was a conventionalized story of womanhood, Gardner treated it as though it were a factual commentary. . . . Gardner, in his flat undialectical view of social life, did not recognize this irony" (Lydall and Strecker 1978:945). In other words, Gardner failed to realize what is an anthropological cliché: What people say about themselves is not the truth but data. "Interestingly, other critics have rarely mentioned this point (that is, the distortion of Hamar life in the film). Even David MacDougall accepts the film at face value and writes: '*Rivers of Sand* examines a socially regulated sexual exploitation through the toll it takes upon individuals'" (Strecker 1988:373).

Gardner employs slow-motion shots of women running up to men, thrusting their breasts toward their "oppressors," and apparently taunting the men to beat them. Omalleidna claims she and all women in her group are oppressed, yet they appear to provoke the beatings. What is the audience to make of this conflict between what she says and what Gardner shows us? Gardner offers his viewers no apparent direction. "The relationship between men and women in Hamar society appears more complex than Omalleidna's theory. Bob, however, preferred to edit his material to fit her theory and his own ideas about male domination, rather than to explore actual relationships between men and women. . . . That the whipping was ritualized and initiated by the girls themselves, is not made clear in the film" (Strecker 1988:373). There is a clear choice to be made with this film. Either the "artistic vision" of someone who spent a few months in the field and presents no evidence of competence in the language or culture can be accepted, or the opinion of an ethnographer who knows the culture and language and has produced several publications and films based on his experience with the Hamar can be assumed to be more authoritative. The film raises a point that is interesting and very complex and that must remain rhetorical for now: If someone's artistic vision is at odds with a body of ethnographically derived evidence, is it defensible to argue that the accuracy of information conveyed about a culture is less important than the artist's vision? Answering that question adequately would require a lengthy discussion of the role of the artist in the late twentieth century that would simply take us too far afield from our primary goal.

Two of Gardner's films list no credits for anthropologist or translator or ethnographic advisers: *Deep Hearts* (my source is Michael Lieber's 1980 review) and *Ika Hands* (my source is the 1988 Festival dei Popoli catalog). The enthusiastic review Lieber gave *Deep Hearts* is yet another example of an anthropologist's being content with the artistic vision of a filmmaker rather than questioning whether the film is supported by any ethnographic research. "As in *Dead Birds*, his major work, Gardner exhibits a strongly felt humanism, viewing cultural events and styles as illustrations of the human condition. This view of things is almost always conveyed by his narration and only weakly supported by his imagery, which is specific and parochial. But, criticisms aside, Gardner must be thanked for bringing back such spectacular images, so lovingly filmed" (Lieber 1980:225).

Deep Hearts is about a male beauty contest among the Bororo Fulani of Niger. The contest takes place over a several-week period. There is no evidence within the film to suggest Gardner stayed any longer than those days. I can discover little about the circumstances of filming *Deep Hearts*, but logically there are two possibilities: either the film was made without benefit of any anthropologically competent personnel, or those who participated did not wish to be associated with the film. Who spoke the language, who contacted the people portrayed, and a myriad of other reasonable questions remain unanswered.

During the screening of the film *Ika Hands* in a European film festival, serious ethical questions were raised by a South American anthropologist who was involved in the filming. Unfortunately, he wishes to remain anonymous and has never published these statements. The film portrays the Ika as if they lived in a political and cultural vacuum in what anthropologists used to call "the ethnographic present"—that is, an imagined time prior to European contact. At the very least, one has to question the apparent isolation of people living so close to one of the Colombian centers of coca production. Why are there no credits for the person with language competence and cultural knowledge who worked with Gardner in the field? There had to be such a person.

Forest of Bliss, a film about Benares, India, is quite another matter. Unlike *Rivers of Sand, Deep Hearts*, or even *Ika Hands*, the anthropologist and coproducer, Akos Ostör, states that the film is based on six months of ethnographic field research. When the film came under attack, Ostör came to its defense as a credible ethnographic work (Ostör 1989). In Great Britain, *Forest of Bliss* won a prize as the best ethnographic film of the past two years. In spite of its apparent credentials as an ethnographic film, Gardner has made it quite clear that he views it as "a personal film, not an ethnographic one" (Larson 1987:98).[9] The writers of two reviews conclude that the film cannot be fruitfully considered as anthropology (Parry 1988; Moore 1988). Since Gardner apparently agrees, I would prefer to use the film as a means to critique his work as art.

Forest of Bliss has been characterized as a haunting portrait of the city of death. Alexander Moore, along with a number of other people, regards it as "an aesthetic masterpiece" (1988:1). I disagree. I found it to be a jumble of incomprehensible vignettes that apparently are to be savored for their formal content and the juxtaposition of the images and sequences. The film, like Louis Malle's *Phantom India*, falsely mystifies. I do not know the language of the people in the film, and there are no subtitles. I rarely can figure out what the people portrayed are doing, or if I can, the significance of the action is lost on me. I attribute meaning that stands a good chance of being accidentally ethnocentric and incorrect because I cannot infer anything about the maker's intention beyond his aesthetics. As Parry (1988) has pointed out, the film easily misleads all but the most expert viewers. Since Gardner has indicated that what is said is not important enough to translate and that the vignettes of behavior are not consequential enough to present in such a way as to make them understandable, I am left with a kind of pure formalism.

I do not completely agree with Parry's (1988) and Moore's (1988) position that a film dealing with an experience exotic for most viewers must have subtitling and spoken narration. Since the invention of sound, film has relied far too much on words to explain. The possibility of visual explanations is still intriguing. For example, video artist Edin Velez's *MetaMaya II* (1980) and *Cuna* (1983) seem to me to accomplish what Gardner was trying to achieve—an artistic film about an exotic culture without narration or subtitles. I do not

Robert Gardner and Anthropological Cinema

condemn this film because Gardner tried to convey meaning visually. I criticize him for having failed to do so.

A defense offered by some anthropologists, like Peter Loizos (1993), for Robert Gardner's recent films, such as *Forest of Bliss*, may be summarized as follows: "Well, they may not be so great as ethnography, but they are wonderful art. Because these films are so moving, convey important things about the human condition, have such beauty, we will forgive them their anthropological shortcomings and accept them anyway." There are two serious problems with this justification. The first and most profound is the assumption that because all film is art, ethnographic film must somehow compromise itself in order to succeed. The notion that all film is art is as silly as the idea that all writing is literature. For a more extended refutation of this cliché, see Sol Worth's classic essay "Film as Non-art" (Worth 1966). A corollary to that assumption is the idea that films that are sensitive, empathetic portraits of a people do not require the services of an anthropologist to make them into ethnographic films. I presume that those who take this position argue that because "artistic vision" is as important as "ethnographically derived knowledge and insight," we should accept these films as if they were anthropology (or of equal importance anyway).

The logic of this argument carries us to the absurd position of having to accept virtually the whole of literature and film as anthropology and thereby obliterate whatever uniqueness anthropology has as a means of generating statements about the human condition. If Gardner's art can be included in the canon, why not everyone else's? There are literally hundreds of sensitively made, poetic documentaries about the human condition. Why not characterize all of them as ethnographic? On a formal level, Gardner's films are in the mainstream of the poetic documentary of people like Basil Wright, whose film *Song of Ceylon* (1934) Gardner admires so much. The logic of Loizos's argument would mean that virtually all films and all novels that purport to provide insight into the human condition—and don't forget poems, paintings, and even music—should be labeled ethnographic. Loizos's position mirrors the logically absurd quotation from Karl Heider (1974:1) cited in the introduction, in which Heider argues that all films are ethnographic.

The ethics and politics of Gardner's art as manifested in *Forest of Bliss* require further discussion. Gardner transformed the lives of the people of Benares into aesthetic objects that form the raw material for the creative process of his art. He did so with no apparent moral qualms. "I had no ethical embarrassment in making the film. I had my own feelings about what was going on . . . and they shaped the film and the shots. I wasn't trying to suppress my feelings. I needed them" (Larson 1987:98).

Part of the appeal of this film to a Western audience is the exotic quality of Indian life. There is a history to the idea of the "mysterious" East, perhaps best explored in Edward Said's book *Orientalism* (1978). Tom Waugh has suggested that *Forest of Bliss* "was simply one more *Mondo Cane India*, an ethnographic variant of the recent glut of Indian imagery in the Western media marketplace. Our reliance on colonialized images of India such as these in the past, has greatly hampered our knowledge of, and our solidarity with, this vital and changing society" (1988:13). Gardner mistakes ignorance for mystery. India is mysterious only to those too lazy to learn something about it.

The basis for Gardner's art is to be found in nineteenth-century romanticism, and his behavior as film artist is justified by the notion of "artistic license." Briefly stated, it is the assumption that because artists create beauty essential for society, they are allowed to behave differently from other people. Artists must be true to their vision no matter what! For many of us, that notion of art is morally and politically out of step with the times. Artists are a part of society and must answer for their behavior just as other people do. Making art out of the lives of people who are politically and economically disadvantaged, disenfranchised, oppressed, is increasingly difficult to justify, particularly when the artist comes from the most privileged class of the world's most powerful nation.

But even if one believes that artists do have this right and can treat their colleagues and the people they film any way they wish in the name of art, how can anthropologists justify these notions? Since the Vietnam War, U.S. anthropologists have been made acutely aware of the need to examine the political and moral implications of their own work and the complexities involved in using the Other as the subject of their research. Why should they embrace the "art" of someone who is so apparently uninterested in those questions?

Conclusion

Robert Gardner was a seminal figure in ethnographic film during the 1950s and 1960s. However, his public remarks, his writings, and his films since *Dead Birds* reflect no apparent interest in or knowledge of the issues that have occupied anthropology since the 1970s. He has chosen to remain outside of this discourse. Instead, he has stayed faithful to an outmoded and inadequate notion that anthropology's primary task is to salvage the last remnants of "authentic primitive" culture. There appears to be some uncertainty on Gardner's part as to whether he regards himself as an ethnographic filmmaker. When he showed *Rivers of Sand* at the Robert Flaherty Film Seminar in 1977, he was uninterested in discussing the film or any of his work as anthropology. His most recent published essay, "The Fiction of Non-fiction Film" (1986), suggests a lack of interest in ethnographic film. Yet he has consistently and actively cooperated with the British Royal Anthropological Institute's Ethnographic Film

Robert Gardner and Anthropological Cinema

Festival and reviewed two of William Geddes's films for *American Anthropologist* (Gardner 1987).

Rather than regard Gardner's films as ethnography or anthropology, I believe it is more productive to critique them as the work of a romantic artist who believes that the exotic Other provides him with a unique chance to explore his personal responses to humanistic questions such as death (*Forest of Bliss*), the role of women (*Rivers of Sand*), and gender identity (*Deep Hearts*). Because some are easily seduced by what they regard as Gardner's "artistic vision," certain members of the anthropological community continue to appreciate Gardner's films as ethnographically significant. They do so, I might add, with the active encouragement of Gardner.

Gardner's work represents what many people would assume to be the aspirations of anthropological cinema—to produce artistically competent films about exotic people. The inadequacy of this conception should be quite clear to my readers by now. Gardner deserves his place in the history of this genre. He was a pioneer, and without his early efforts, the exploration of film and anthropology would have suffered. His imaginative use of montage and narrative form in *Dead Birds* deserves recognition. However, his continued use of a discredited version of anthropology and his promotion of an approach to art that others find ethically questionable diminish the value of most of his work since *Dead Birds*.

Out of Sync:

The Cinema of Tim Asch

Bring your camera over here. It's going to start. CHAGNON TO ASCH AT THE
BEGINNING OF *THE AX FIGHT*

Tim Asch has a unique place in the development of ethnographic film.[1] Unlike most filmmakers, he was not primarily concerned with producing "memorable" films to
enhance his reputation as an "auteur" or to further some sociopolitical agenda. He was not an anthropologist who conducted field research, analyzed, and published the results. He
was not very concerned with large theoretical issues. In a re-
markably single-handed fashion, Asch devoted more than thirty
years of his life to discovering ways in which he could produce
films in collaboration with anthropologists. The primary purpose of his films is to teach cultural anthropology to university
undergraduates and to make the filmic materials accessible so
that other scholars and teachers could make use of them in ways
not imagined by him.

To accomplish this goal, Asch has:

· Explored the nature of collaboration between anthropologists and filmmakers with a number of anthropologists in several different field situations

- Sought to develop a sequential method of filming that resulted in footage that is researchable and that can be edited into either single-concept or sequence films as well as be combined with other sequences into a larger film
- Explored ways to combine the benefits of observational-style shooting with the didactic anthropological interpretation
- Worked with the anthropologists to produce study guides to package the films for classroom use
- Developed a course of study to train other ethnographic filmmakers at the University of Southern California

Asch's work is crucial to an understanding of film and anthropology because most anthropologists believe that film is primarily useful as an aid to teaching. He is one of the few ethnographic filmmakers to devote themselves to these problems.

This chapter critically explores some of these goals and the degree to which Asch has accomplished them by focusing on two films: *The Feast* (1970), the first of Asch's films to be produced collaboratively, and *The Ax Fight* (1971), arguably the most complex and significant of his works.[2] In doing so, I acknowledge my neglect of Asch's later work in Indonesia as well as his still-photographic work. Hopefully a book-length examination of all of Asch's work that is being prepared by Doug Lewis will offer a more complete examination.

The heart of this chapter is a series of interviews I conducted with Asch in October 1993 in a New York City hotel and later by phone. The interviews were edited and combined into their present form. All "constructed" quotations were approved by Asch as representing his point of view. In some cases, he added material and revised his own words.[3] The main purpose of this chapter is to allow Asch to speak for himself in a way that he never did in his own publications and for me to critically assess his views. Asch's collaborator in all of the Yanomami[4] films, anthropologist Napoleon Chagnon, was sent a draft of the chapter. I have attempted to incorporate his comments either into the text or as notes. Although the emphasis of the chapter is on Asch, I would remind readers that these films were only possible because of Chagnon's fieldwork and analysis and the rapport that he had established with the Yanomami. The readings of the two films invoked in the chapter are solely mine. They are based on repeated screenings of both films in undergraduate and graduate courses, and observations of academics' reactions at professional meetings since the films were released. The title of the chapter should not be seen as a critical comment about Asch's work. His consistent lack of interest in pursuing current fashion, as well as his lack of synchronicity with the received wisdom of the film world and anthropology, have allowed him to make significant contributions to both.

Asch started his explorations of the pictorial world while attending The Putney School, a preparatory school in Vermont. With his roommate David Sapir (now anthropologist and current editor of *Visual Anthropology Review*), Tim taught himself the rudiments of still photography and was eventually able to apprentice himself as a fine-arts photographer to Edward Weston, Ansel Adams, and Minor White. Toward the end of his life, Asch returned to photography. Doug Harper published a monograph of Asch's last fieldwork photographs (1994).

In 1959, having just completed an undergraduate degree at Columbia, Asch was hired by Robert Gardner at Harvard's Film Study Center to assist in the editing of John Marshall's Bushman footage.[5] Marshall had released *The Hunters* and was looking for other ways in which he could utilize the vast amount of footage he had shot in southern Africa.

Dave Sapir phoned and told me that I had to go see *The Hunters*, which was playing at the American Film Festival. After I saw it, I wrote a letter to the Peabody Museum saying that I thought the film was wonderful. Apparently, Joe Brew filed the letter away. Some time later, when Gardner was looking for an editor, Brew showed him the letter. They contacted Margaret Mead, who recommended me. Gardner, Marshall, and Joe Brew, the director of the Peabody Museum, had gotten a large grant from the National Science Foundation to edit twenty films, and they were looking for an editor, particularly one that wasn't . . . that didn't have too much of their own will or mind of their own . . . to help edit their films. . . . When I annotated all 500,000 feet of John's Bushman footage, I discovered in all this footage these little sequences of social interaction that were shot in great detail because John's father (Laurence Marshall) said when you shoot something, shoot it in great detail. None of the rest of us ever had enough money to shoot this much film.

So instead of shooting little bits and pieces of an event the way Gardner might, John shot everything in detail. There was the *N/um Tchai* dance ceremony. . . . *An Argument about a Marriage* . . . *The Meat Fight.* [These titles are among the many single-concept films Asch helped edit.][6] And I saw in ten of these little sequences great material for teaching. I already suspected that because they were short, you could use them much more easily with the literature in short class periods. There wasn't a heavy voice to tell you what to look for and how to interpret what you saw. You could manipulate the film to suit your own curriculum. And I convinced John that it was OK that he wasn't going to make another thematic narrative film right now like *The Hunters*. He didn't have to make another long narrative film[;] . . . he could edit these films first . . . and then he could take bits and pieces of these and make a bigger film, which was done with *N!ai*. So we put all our energies into editing these short films. Gardner thought we were crazy. Joe Brew . . . thought that we were out of our minds. Both Gardner and Brew were worried because they were responsible to NSF (National Science Foundation) for meeting the conditions of the grant. But Brew supported us because I made such a strong case for it educationally.

As a consequence of his editing of the Bushman films, Asch began work with Jerome Bruner, then a Harvard educational psychologist, and others at the Educational Development Center (EDC) on the now-infamous *Man: A Course of Study* (MACOS) project (see Dow 1991 for a discussion of the fight by conservative politicians to censure MACOS). His job was to produce short films from the Bushman film corpus to be packaged into an anthropological curriculum for fifth graders.[7] During this time (1962–64), Asch completed a graduate degree at Boston University in its African Studies Program (with an anthropology concentration at Harvard University). At the same time, Asch and Marshall conceived of a sequential style of covering events with a clear social scenario in great detail and editing those sequences in a straightforward chronological manner. The approach has informed the majority of Asch's film work since.[8]

This was a period when Drew Associates was inventing American direct cinema with such films as *Primary* (O'Connell 1992) and Jean Rouch and his collaborators, such as Canadian Michel Brault, were creating the technology and ideology for *cinéma vérité* with films like *Chronicle of a Summer* (see vol. 11, no. 1 [1985], of *Studies in Visual Communication* for an extended exploration of this film). The documentary film was in an extraordinary period of expansion and invention in which filmmakers, many trained as social scientists like the Maysles brothers and Rouch, were instrumental in creating the conventions of observational and participatory cinema (Mamber 1974). Lightweight, portable 16mm cameras and tape recorders made it possible for the first time to record actual sequences of behavior on location with sync sound in a manner far less intrusive than before. Advocates of a passive-observational style abandoned "voice of God" narration. It was replaced by long, narrationless sequences of "spontaneous activity," shot in a way that it was hoped would entice viewers to make their own interpretations as to the meaning of the behavior portrayed. At the same time, Rouch was provoking "ciné trances" in the people he filmed so that they would reveal their culture in unique ways. These documentarians were part of the movement that revolutionized both nonfiction and fiction film (for example, Rouch had a major influence on the New Wave via Jean-Luc Godard, and the "new" realism of films like John Casavettes's *Faces* can be attributed to the influence of direct cinema).[9] Asch was familiar with these changes; knew some of the filmmakers, like Ricky Leacock, associated with Drew Associates; and had seen some of Rouch's work. (See Barnouw 1974 for an extended discussion of this period of documentary film history.)[10]

At the same time, films of value for the teaching of anthropology were not numerous, and those available were in the grand-epic tradition of the "ethnographic pastoral" (Clifford 1988) of films like *Nanook of the North*, *The Hunters*, and *Dead Birds*. As Asch points out, "In 1960, when I began making ethnographic films through the Peabody Museum at Harvard University, our models were Robert Flaherty's *Nanook of the North* (1922), Merian Cooper and Ernest Schoedsack's *Grass* (1925) and Basil Wright's *Song of Ceylon* (1937)" (Asch 1992:196). He has, of course, forgotten the obvious: John Marshall's *The Hunters* (1957). Grand films have much to offer in their own right, but they are all too long to use in the classroom and, of course, suffer from being products of the technology and times that produced them. They did not offer much of a model for making ethnographic film for teaching anthropology in the 1960s.

Although there might have been a revolution afoot in the technology and approach to making documentaries, Asch, who had not been to film school, was never concerned with "cinema" per se but with film as a vehicle for teaching anthropology. He never subscribed to the orthodoxy of "no narration." Before many ethnographic filmmakers had even embraced observational style, Asch realized that the problem with narrationless observational films about cultural behavior exotic to Western audiences was that viewers simply lacked the knowledge necessary to understand what they were seeing and, without some assistance, were more likely to employ racist stereotypes. If the observed behavior of the Other was self-evident, why was anthropology even necessary?

Asch's interest in the pedagogical value of single-concept films for the teaching of anthropology was unique for its time. Most anthropologists received no formal training in teaching. Often they used films as a "substitute" teacher when they had to be away from their classes. Films were shown at the American Anthropological Association's (AAA) meetings as an evening's entertainment rather than as they are now—a regular part of the program. Although the AAA had published a monograph on *The Teaching of Anthropology* (Mandelbaum 1963), the profession was not putting much thought or energy into developing a sophisticated multimedia curriculum. Asch found himself more allied with psychologists of education like Jerome Bruner than with anthropologists.

When I showed them [the Bushman films that Asch had been editing with John Marshall] to Jerry Bruner, he thought . . . these short little open-concept films were the best way to teach any subject but certainly the subject of anthropology. So I took a lot of John's films, some of which I had edited myself in rough form, and brought them out to Brandeis and taught an introductory anthropology class, which was fantastic. I mean, people were really bowled over. I was young and enthusiastic, I suppose, but in a way, I almost never have taught as well, as effectively, as I did with those sequences. . . . And so it was really with Jerry Bruner's support and interest and knowledge and what I learned from him as an apprentice that I took it all the way with the rest of the Bushman films and the Yanomami films and had the courage to teach anthropology in a different way.[11]

After having taught with these short films, Asch was now ready to make his own—to actualize his idea in a field situation. In the following remarks, he mentions the concept of a research film, which consists of putting together all the footage in the order in which it was shot and then heavily annotating it prior to editing. (See Sorenson 1967 for a discussion of this idea.) It has served as the basis for the first anthropological film archive, established by Carleton Gadjusek and E. Richard Sorenson at one of the National Institutes of Health and later at the Smithsonian Institution.

Well you know, I had this plan by then (mid-1960s) that shooting sequences was the best way to go because I could use them for teaching. I initially thought of making film solely for my own purposes to use for teaching, but because of Gadjusek and Sorenson's research film idea, . . . I thought we should make a research film first before doing anything else. . . . I would come back from the Yanomami with maybe sixty one thousand–foot sequences, which is exactly what I came back with. It really made such good sense to—in terms of economy—to first make this huge research film out of which you can make a number of different kinds of films instead of just spending a lot of money, time, and effort going out and getting one film like *Dead Birds* out of thirty hours of footage. And so, my idea was to film discrete events in detail that the anthropologist thought were interesting or that I thought were interesting. . . .[12]

So I was ready to go out and make my own corpus of material. . . . I put the shingle out saying, "Ethnographic Filmmaker Will Travel." I asked Manners [Robert Manners, then chair of the Department of Anthropology at Brandeis University] if he would stake me to a ream of paper saying the "Center for Documentary Anthropology," and then I wrote letters on it. And he said he would[;] . . . he was wonderfully supportive. I didn't even have the stationery yet and Chagnon phoned.

In 1968, Asch began his first collaboration with an anthropologist, Napoleon Chagnon. Over the next decade, it resulted in thirty-nine films. The Yanomami, like the Bushmen, became the most filmed non-Western, nonindustrialized society in the world. Among the films are Asch's most influential works—*The Feast* and *The Ax Fight*. With Chagnon's Holt, Rinehart and Winston monograph designed for introductory cultural anthropology courses (1968), college teachers had, for the first time, the chance to integrate readings with a film. In addition, the book and the films appeared at a time when the United States was in turmoil about the Vietnam War and concerned with the role of violence and aggression in society. As a consequence of their timeliness, the Yanomami films became as commonly used to teach anthropology as *The Hunters* and *Dead Birds*. So many other filmmakers have followed in Asch's footsteps that in 1978, Jean Rouch was able to convene a conference in Paris solely devoted to the ways in which the Yanomami have been filmed.[13]

When John Boorman was looking for a model of "primitive savagery" for his fiction fantasy *The Emerald Forest*, he chose the Yanomami.[14] The work has attracted the film world as well. Asch—along with Marshall, Gardner, and David MacDougall—is among the few ethnographic filmmakers to have had their works screened at the Whitney Museum of American Art and reviewed in such nonanthropological publications as the *Village Voice*.[15] Although some would argue that the interest in the Yanomami is more racist than enlightened, it is the case that these films and Chagnon's writings fueled the debate about the nature of human aggression in a way seldom seen before or since in anthropological circles.

The Feast represents two innovations. First, there is the film's form. It begins with a series of still frames from the film depicting the "highlights" of the event, with an explanatory narration by Chagnon. The second section of the film is an observational representation of the feast with only subtitles. *The Feast* is an experiment in combining the didactics of anthropological explanation with an opportunity for audiences to concentrate on the filmmaker's pictorial representation of the event. This experimental form becomes elaborated upon with *The Ax Fight*. It flew in the face of the received wisdom of the time, which caused documentary and ethnographic filmmakers to avoid all narration and rely on the viewers' ability to make sense out of what they saw.[16] Second, *The Feast* is one of the few films produced to illustrate an anthropological idea—Marcel Mauss's concept of reciprocity (1967).

In 1968, Chagnon was a recent University of Michigan Ph.D. involved in a medical study of the Yanomami of Venezuela. After attempting to shoot a film himself, Chagnon went looking for a filmmaker. Both Robert Gardner and Asen Balikci suggested that he go to the National Film Board of Canada or to Timothy Asch. Asch recalls that an early discussion with Chagnon about Mauss motivated him to go film the Yanomami:

And then he [Chagnon] stopped, and he said, "By the way, have you ever read Marcel Mauss's book *The Gift*?" Now *The Gift* was one of my favorite books as an anthropology student. And Chagnon said it was his favorite book. In fact, he said, "I would like our first film to be of a feast for which Mauss has written the script in . . . *The Gift*." . . . I thought if I could take a piece of theoretical literature and illustrate it or describe it to some degree in film so students could get it both ways. . . . What a challenge!

Chagnon recalls the event of filming the feast thusly:

In 1968, I was, as a researcher in the Department of Human Genetics, University of Michigan Medical School, responsible for bringing James V. Neel and our Venezuelan medical collaborators into a series of Yanomami villages per usual during my long-term collaboration with the Neel team (1966–72). That year was also my first filming collaboration with Tim Asch. Our filming effort was funded by Neel's Atomic Energy Commission grant on the condition that we also make a film about "multidisciplinary studies," which we did, using also some of the film I had previously shot before meeting Tim Asch. I intended, with Asch, to film a feast that year and knew that the Patanowa-teri would be having one with one of its allies, not knowing which one. Patanowa-teri was also one of the big villages I wanted to bring Neel's medical group to, but they were not at their regular location when the medical researchers arrived. The Patanowa-teri were being harassed by many enemies—and in response had begun clearing new gardens in a more remote area between the headwaters of the upper Mavaca and the upper Shanishani Rivers—near a site at which they had earlier lived. This site was impossibly far from a walkable point for the medical work we planned. Since I was heavily involved in responsibilities to the medical researchers and had to take them to more immediately accessible villages so they could get maximum work done in minimum time, I asked Asch if he would like to accompany the Yanomami messengers I was sending [to] the Patanowa-teri asking them to return to their earlier location. He enthusiastically agreed, since there wasn't much he could film at that point. Neel had also hired a young missionary named Daniel Shaylor to help his medical people that year as a translator, and since Shaylor was fluent in Yanomami and had a portable shortwave radio, I also asked him to go on the trip to find the Patanowa-teri. I located several well-informed Yanomami guides for them, all familiar with that area. Thus, Asch, Shaylor, and three Yanomami guides set out to find the Patanowa-teri and ask them to return to their earlier location so the medical people could treat their sick and do their investigations. Shaylor and Asch kept in daily contact with us via shortwave radio.[17]

Well, the guides got confused and lost, and it took them several days longer than anticipated to find the Patanowa-teri, but they finally did. . . . The Patanowa-teri agreed to return to their earlier site, where I eventually took the medical workers for their research project. Asch filmed them at work, resulting in footage that went into the film *Yanomamo: A Multidisciplinary Study*—along with footage I had earlier shot.

When the medical people left, I remained in Patanowa-teri with Asch to shoot ethnographic footage per our previously discussed plan. I knew they would most likely have a feast during that time but was not sure who it would be with. They eventually held a feast for the Mahekodo-teri. I did not "stage" this—it happened naturally. They could not have cared less about our interests in filming and are the kind of people who would not do something this costly and time-consuming for two whole communities simply to accommodate the filming interests of outsiders. (Chagnon, personal communication, 1994)

During the academic year 1968–69, Asch returned to Brandeis to teach and edit the film. Chagnon went to the University of Michigan. In the process of completing their first film, Asch and Chagnon devised a method of collaborating that enabled them to produce thirty-nine films over the next seven years while both were teaching full-time. The collaboration is one of the earliest and undoubtedly the most productive between a U.S. anthropologist and a filmmaker. For anyone interested in how wordsmiths and image makers work together, it is a collaboration essential to understand.

As a way of exploring their collaboration, I asked Asch about Chagnon's role in the making of *The Feast*. His response evolved into a general discussion of the way they worked in the editing of all their films:

Well, he [Chagnon] had very little input in editing the films. It wasn't necessary, as the work was pretty straightforward. Much of the film had already been edited in the camera while I was shooting. However, when I asked for translations, he gave them. And when I got stuck and I asked for advice and whatnot, he was always helpful. He was a first-class professional. . . . He never really had much of a role in any of the editing because he never really wanted it. That is, he would have wanted it if he hadn't liked what I had done. I would ask him questions, and I would ask him to translate sync-sound conversations. . . . He never balked at any amount of work that I would assign. . . . I was very good about showing him what I was doing, and he was always very praiseworthy, and then we would go out and drink beer. But at heart, he wanted to make didactic, self-contained films with heavy, long narration. I mean, the first script of *The Feast* was something like thirty-five pages that I had to cut down to four pages.

You see, I am not an auteur because I never went to film school. So I don't have that precious background about having to do this work all by my creative self. You know, *I'm the filmmaker*. What do I know about film, really? I'm . . . sort of somebody who's really interested in the anthropology of a particular area and working with an anthropologist who is knowledgeable about the language and the culture. So I feel it is only decent to work with the anthropologist and let him know what I am doing. I didn't have to do that with Chag. He didn't care. He just wanted to see the films. We could have done all our work on the phone. . . . "You remember that film of so and so? Yeah. Well, I am going to edit [it] this way" . . . pretty much as we saw it for what it was, which is the way I did everything. And he would say, "Fine," because he is busy, he is really busy. He likes the idea that I am independent. But I go to Michigan with a complete editing studio in two suitcases anyway. And we look at the film, and we discuss it. And I tell him what I am going to do. We had complete trust of each other. I'd say, "You know, I need this translated." And he didn't cry or moan or say, "Oh, God, I got an article due next week." He'd just go and translate until he was done—anything I would ask him to do. He was great that way. . . . You have to take your ego and just put it in the wastebasket because it is not going to serve you very well in a collaboration. And that is probably why few of my students collaborate.

Asch's editing of *The Feast* was a direct consequence of the sequential way in which it was shot. The editing consisted of a tightening of the actual chronological sequences. Once he had a rough version, Asch began to show a cut of the film to his classes. In this form, the narration ran throughout the length of the film. Although "test screenings" and "sneak previews" of a fine cut have long been a tradition of filmmaking, taking an unfinished version of a film into a classroom, seeking students' reactions, and then recutting the film as a consequence of their response is a somewhat unusual way to edit a film. Most filmmakers do not have the luxury of sufficient time to have so many test viewings. The economic realities of the world of professional filmmaking—in which deadlines are always tight—and the intellectual world of anthropology are not always compatible.

I'd been showing it [a cut of *The Feast*] in a lot of different classes to finish it. It edited pretty much the way I shot it in the camera. Most of my films do. Well, some of the later films haven't, but basically, even now, I film and edit events chronologically. . . . I worked hard showing the film in class. And it seemed to me . . . it wasn't working right with Chagnon's heavy narration. And I didn't know what to do until the day before the Flaherty Film Seminar [where the film was first shown publicly in 1969], while I was mixing the film with Chagnon's voice-over. And I just didn't like the way his voice interrupted the indigenous action.

I attended the 1969 screening of *The Feast* at the Flaherty Film Seminar along with Sol Worth. Sol and I were extremely impressed with the potential of this as yet unfinished film. The two of us spent the better part of an evening with Asch discussing the film and the need to professionalize the relationship between film and anthropology. We decided to ask the American Anthropological Association to include film screenings in its regular programming schedule—a symbolic act that gave films the same status as "scientific" papers. Tim and I took turns programming films for the AAA for the next several years. They have remained a part of the AAA program ever since. It was also during this evening of conversation that the seeds were planted for the establishment of a professional society (at first called the Society for the Anthropology of Visual Communication and now the Society for Visual Anthropology) and a newsletter/journal. It was a place where I established a strong personal and professional relationship with both of them that lasted until they died.

During these test screenings at the Flaherty Seminar and elsewhere, Asch determined that "it was too difficult for students to see the moving images and hear the narration. So freeze frames from the actual film were made into a sequence with Chagnon's analytic description of the event. The purpose of this part of the film was to enable viewers to focus their attention on the narration and understand the event better" (Ennis and Asch 1993:75). He constructed a still-visual sequence to serve as the background for Chagnon's narration, and the form of *The Feast* was created. The film was released in 1970. Because it was funded through the University of Michigan's medical research grant from the Atomic Energy Commission, *The Feast* was initially distributed by the National Audio-Visual Center in Washington, D.C., and sold at cost for an amazingly low seventy-five dollars—not an insignificant factor in the wide use of the film in teaching. Immediately after completing *The Feast*, Asch began to fund-raise for a second filming season among the Yanomami.

The Ax Fight is unlike any other film, and its uniqueness can be off-putting. For many people, a moment of serious confusion or revelation in *The Ax Fight* occurs when the screen goes black after the "rushes" have been shown. On the sound track is heard the slightly less-than-clear voices of three confused, stressed-out men who are trying to figure out what they have just witnessed. It is a moment of Goffmanesque "backstage"[18] that exemplifies the reflexive, reconstructive nature of this film. After reading the study guide, one discovers that the voices belong to Craig Johnson, the soundperson, Napoleon Chagnon, and Tim Asch. Once you realize who these people are, the subversive nature of this film becomes all too apparent. Their lack of certainty contrasts so sharply with what follows as to leave a viewer with no sense of closure and with a great deal of doubt about the "explanations" that follow. In one film, the conventions of documentary/ethnographic realism and the "scientific" certainty of anthropological explanations are called into question.

JOHNSON: Sound reel 14; February 28, 1971; finish of wife-beating sequence.

ASCH: Did you get sync on that?

CHAGNON: Wife-beating sequence, my foot.

JOHNSON: OK, what is it?

CHAGNON: It was a club fight.

JOHNSON: What was first?

CHAGNON: Well, two women were in the garden, and one of them was seduced by her "son." It was an incestuous relationship, and the others found out about it, and that's what started the fight.

ASCH: No kidding!

JOHNSON: About 3:30 in the afternoon.

CHAGNON: No, about 3:00 it started. . . . One guy was hit on the back from behind with an ax and just about knocked unconscious with the blow.

ASCH: So this is just the beginning of lots more?

CHAGNON: Well, when you get a village this big, things like this are bound to happen at any—

ASCH: Did you figure out how many there were in the village?

CHAGNON: No. I haven't counted them yet—there are over 200 there. [He turns to talk to Moawa in Yanomami.] Aaah, that's about the tenth person today that's asked me for my soap.

ASCH: Tell him I'll give him my soap—

CHAGNON: No, you won't give him your soap!

ASCH: —when I go home.

CHAGNON: They're going to make damn sure we leave in a hurry if we keep promising them everything when we go home.

ASCH: Shotiwa [brother-in-law], living in your village is going to be tiresome.

The Ax Fight was made possible because Asch was able to secure a National Science Foundation grant for a second filming expedition to the Yanomami in 1971. It was one of the last grants NSF gave in its "fear of Sputnik" era of providing money to improve science education (Dow 1991). Chagnon was already in the field when Asch arrived with his agenda for shooting a large number of sequential films. The proposal makes it clear that Asch, with Chagnon's advice, had developed a rather complete agenda for the variety of short, open-ended films that he needed to enact the curriculum he envisioned. What started out as a collaboration between two equally interested partners became a project of a filmmaker/teacher asking his anthropological colleague and subject-matter specialist for some assistance.

Asch's plans were interrupted when the unexpected happened on the second day after his arrival. He describes the circumstances of the filming:

I was lying in my hammock, and the camera, as usual, was tied to a post on a special slipknot that I could quickly undo. . . . [O]therwise, the Yanomami would have kicked out the legs of the tripod, and it would have fallen. I mean the young ones (ages 14 to 21)[;] . . . there was always a group of young ones who were showing off. And so I heard some women crying—I mean they were really crying. And they were about 100, 125 feet away from me. And I got up on my own and pulled the slipknot. I started photographing them on my own. I said, "Craig, get your sound." Craig came over with sound a little after I was filming. And then after those first shots of the women crying and whatnot, Chagnon said, "Say, come on over and get your camera. It's going to start" . . . meaning it's over there . . . whatever it was. But whatever was happening was happening down there. So I took the camera off the tripod and left it [the tripod] there. And started to go with the camera, when the guy who goes likes this with his hand in the film . . . remember him? [Asch indicates it is the young man who puts his hand out, meaning stop, and smiles directly at the camera.] . . . And I take my eye away and smile at him, and he smiles and puts his hand down. . . . That same guy did the same thing when he saw me running down to where the fight was most intense. And I . . . these are the kinds of things you get to know pretty quickly . . . this gesture was saying, "Don't come down there. You can film on your tripod if you want here. But there is no way of telling what could happen down there. And you know, we are having a fight, and we don't also want to have to be responsible for you. So please don't." Nobody is ever in real physical danger who's out of the picture. If I were Ken Good and married to a Yanomami woman, you know, that might be something different.[19] But the anthropologist is never in physical danger of something like that. But except . . . you can get in the way, and just being there can heighten tension.

The ax fight lasted about eighteen minutes. Asch filmed eleven minutes, which meant that although he had unusually complete coverage of the event, he did not have sufficient footage to make a straightforward chronological film that would be comprehensible. In addition, the event involved a lot of people and was so complex as to necessitate an equally complex explanation. He therefore had to invent a form sufficient to the task. The solution was a radical departure from the existing models. He chose to show the viewer all of the unedited footage; then a didactic version with wall-to-wall voice-over narration, slow motion, and arrows identifying the principals; a third section with kinship charts that carried viewers through a structural-functional model employing alliance theory and notions of fission and fusion; and finally a "Final Edited Version"—a passively slick observational-style rendition of the event with no narration. Asch explains the creation of this form in a pragmatic rather than theoretical manner:

The first thing I did was to go over with Chagnon to look at the film. So we looked at the film on a projector once. And I said, "What are we going to make out of this?" And he said, "Let's look up the people first." So we looked up the people in his good genealogy that he had constructed with photographs he had taken of everyone in the village so that we could see who the people were. And then it was easy to see how they were related. Once we knew how they were related, we could explain why the ax fight happened. These discoveries all happened in about fifteen minutes. So it wasn't really but a few minutes after having discovered how people were related that we could easily make at least a structural-functional analysis of what happened in the ax fight. It took moments, and that was it. We knew. Well, we had one explanation in what was still an acceptable form—structural functionalism. In 1971, it was perfectly OK. And alliance theory worked out perfectly well with what else we knew about the culture.

It was so easy. It was a question of going through the thing frame by frame and figuring out how you would explain this most efficiently. And there were things that Nap [Chagnon] wanted to say. So I said, "OK, Nap, here is what's happening." And I gave him an outline. "Now, what do you want to say?" So he went off, and he wrote his script. And then we pared it down[;] . . . he was always writing an article . . . always too verbose, as most anthropologists are. And then I felt I had something that was short enough to work with. Then it was just a question of here's the script. I got him to record it.

The first thing that got constructed was the middle of the second section of the film. And when I got the narration, then I could structure the rest of the film. Well, right away I conceived of it as a four-part film. The original film [footage]; the slowed-down detail part of it, some of which I even enlarged on the Oxberry animation stand; the kinship chart; and always this last, fourth edited version, which . . . if I could have gotten Leni Riefenstahl to edit [it], I would have. I wanted somebody who was a real expert to edit that final section and, you know, distort it as much as possible but have it look smooth and slick—the way any good ethnographic film looks. Because what we usually see is that last section. And shorten it, you know, shorten it as much as you can. . . . In the end, I had to edit the final section myself, just doing a little bit of distortion. . . . I couldn't do a hell of a lot of distortion. But the little bit that I did do was obvious enough to any audience. . . .

The final structure of the film comes out of teaching. I mean, how am I going to teach kids with this film? . . . I show it to my Harvard students, and they only [understand] half of what they are supposed to. So then it is a problem. They don't tell me how to edit the film, but I get a feeling of what it is that they don't understand and why. So I start changing it. And I am really using film as if it were clay. It's very much like that. I've got a strand of film here. It's not working here in this section. Well, it's . . . a twenty-foot section, . . . so I break it up and decide I need a title in there. I've got to have an explanatory title with a still-shot slide as background for it. So I type it on the typewriter in as large letters as I can and film it with a Bolex. So I've got that, and I take it up to the lab. I'll need a dissolve here. So I take the two pieces of film and put them into my little duplicator and make a dissolve. So I have another strand. But I will need a slide. I will need a slide I've got which would work well here. And so I will film that. So I may have four or five new strands to this film on the synchronizer. And then it is a question of syncing them all up and putting them on reels with twenty feet of leader and making sure that everything is exact. Then give it to the lab, and they marry the five strands together into one strand. Then I just snip the old twenty feet out, put this new strand in, and I race off to another friend's class. It might be at Boston University. It might be at Wellesley. You know, wherever. I'm off. And I'm listening. I'm really attuned to what's going on. And it works. It's there[;] . . . you know it may not work with another audience, but I'm through with that one section of the film for a while. When I see that it's not working quite right with another audience, I change it a little bit.

Well, in the end, it turned out . . . I didn't always have the uncut section first. You show them the raw material, stop the projector, have them talk about it—what is going on and so forth. Show them the second piece, which is our explanation, but let them know that there are other explanations. I mean, in this film, we are really locked into a very tight, simplistic structural-functional explanation here. And then the kinship chart, because that is what anthropologists love to have. . . . We are dealing with models now, I'm building a model the way anthropologists build models, only I am doing it with film. I think one of the biggest contributions to anthropology is to show how film can be manipulated to be an effective model. And then show them what it would be like ordinarily, which is all they get ordinarily—the slick version that I show at the very end. . . . I changed *The Ax Fight* twenty-five times in the course of that semester.

You know the joy of *The Ax Fight* . . . is that because Chagnon was so stuck in simple theories[,] right away, the film became a real joke. It is funny with its simplistic, straitjacketed, one-sided explanation. . . . One of the things I liked about it was that it's a pretty funny film. And it's a very dated film if you are going to take it as a piece of serious work. It belongs in another era. But I think also that the film is a harbinger of postmodernism long before we get postmodernism[,] . . . and I was feeling, you know, halfway into making the film, this great suspicion of the whole field beginning to fall apart before my eyes as I was putting *The Ax Fight* together. I had a powerful piece of material, and it was suddenly looking kind of foolish. But it was kind of fun. Actually, I wanted to do something like that for a long time. And I realized that when I saw the Oxberry animation stand that I could do it. But now I would love to put on an introduction to it that says, "About Realism."

I was dealing with a document of great realism and certainty. As anthropologists, we assumed that we could make an accurate translation and representation of culture. It was the culmination of my work with Mead, Arensberg, and Freed, on the one hand, and Biedelman and Middleton on the other.[20] At one point, I thought I was making a perfect film, but when I asked Chagnon to do the kinship diagram (his only responsibility) for a third time to show the marriage alliances between the combatants—which somehow didn't get into the first two attempts—that was the whole point of the kinship chart. He had done it twice and would not do it a third time. I was flabbergasted. I couldn't believe it because, you know, I was making a "perfect" film. But then I thought, so much of our work as anthropologists is flawed, why should this be any different? Its flaws were instructive to students. I felt it was a little bit like a gargoyle at Chartres . . . one of those strange things that stick out and you say, "What's this?" This flaw is very instructive to students, so I convinced myself that it was OK. It's like making one of those great oriental carpets. You sit down and start weaving and think, "This is going to be perfect," and always a third of the way through, there are all these flaws. And so it is going to be the next one. So that is kind of the way I looked at it.

I might have still believed wholeheartedly in the structural-functional explanation during the first three to five showings. But after the tenth or twenty-fifth, I was pretty much jaded. So what I am trying to say is that I went into this fairly naively with my anthropology training, thinking that I was making a fascinating truthful translation or representation of culture. But a third of the way through it . . . because I had had to see it so often, I began to get jaded about the whole thing. I mean it almost became a joke. I wasn't aware of any postmodern critiques of representation. I hadn't really picked it up on my own until about five months later. I was with the Australian anthropologists John and Leslie Haviland, and this whole notion of truth and making an accurate representation blew up in my face because they had already gone through this in very practical ways with their fieldwork. That was when my whole life and commitment to anthropology got really shattered. I had really put myself out to make this film, and in so doing, it completely undercut years and years of training. It is kind of interesting. These insights didn't take place through my reading at the time. I did it the way I always have done things in my life, in a practical way, through my hands. At that moment, I saw *The Ax Fight* as a subtle commentary about the end of an era. But that didn't mean it still wasn't fun to do. That is where a lot of the irony is; I mean, that is why I didn't make things explicit about the way I felt, because I didn't really feel that way until I was a third of the way into it. And then I thought, let the others figure it out for themselves.

In writing about the "final" section of the film in the study guide, Asch and his coauthors state:

The final section is the edited version. By comparing this version to the first section, students discover how strongly intellectual models influence visual perception. A by-product could be some understanding of how filmmakers create finished film from raw footage and sound. . . . The final interpretation of the fight, the edited version, was included as a counterpoint to the first version. It is only one example of the many ways this footage could be edited. The viewer

can see that in making the footage flow more quickly and smoothly a great deal of the information is lost and the initial integrity of the event is damaged. The film editor noted that the final presentation of the fight was edited to fit into the context of the entire film. Since the
viewer has seen the unedited footage, he could and did take liberties with the footage that he
would not have taken were he editing the fight to stand on its own as a sequence. Asch adds,
though, that few filmmakers edit social events in such a way that the integrity of the event is
maintained. (Bugos, Carter, and Asch 1993:133)

The Ax Fight is a truly remarkable film for a number of reasons.[21] I know of
no other nonfiction film that not only displays all of the footage shot but shows
three different edited versions. There are several "editing-exercise" films in
which a scene from a fiction film or television series like *Gunsmoke* is given to
several editors to recut. These films are designed to be used in courses about
fiction-film editing. Chris Marker, in *A Letter from Siberia* (1958), repeats the
same footage twice with ideologically different voice-over narrations as an exercise in demystifying the documentary. The Public Broadcast Lab of PBL
(the precursor of PBS) did a show, *Mirror, Mirror on the World* (1967), in which
it analyzed media coverage of the march on Washington, D.C., of the Jeannette Rankin Brigade of Woman against the Vietnam War. In it, the producers
showed in *Rashomon* fashion how various news agencies represented the event
to suit their formats. *The Ax Fight* accomplishes what the editing-exercise
films do, in that it demonstrates how the same footage can be edited into very
different versions of the same event. But it differs from these films because it
deals with nonfiction, a genre popularly assumed not to distort the "facts" of
an event. Like *Mirror, Mirror on the World* and *A Letter from Siberia*, *The Ax
Fight* undermines the naive belief in the objectivity of the documentary/
ethnographic film. In addition, the film calls into question the adequacy of anthropological theory to explain complex human encounters. For example,
nowhere in the film or in Chagnon's writings is the political role of women discussed. In *The Ax Fight*, their visibility confounds their invisibility in the literature. As Asch suggests, because of its reconstructive nature, *The Ax Fight* is
prematurely postmodern.[22]

Viewers who have never made a film are sometimes perplexed when they
see "rushes." They are not used to seeing all the "mistakes" in focus and exposure, and the jerky movements of the camera as Asch tries to locate the center
of the action and compose his shot. To the untrained eye, it all looks so messy
and haphazard. Often my undergraduate students will argue that Asch is simply an incompetent cinematographer. The inclusion of that which is hidden
from the eyes of the normal viewer affords the teacher a rare opportunity to
expose students to the constructed nature of film. Because the pictorial world
is seldom a topic of discussion in our educational system, students are unpre-
pared to deal in a critical fashion with films or photographs (or television, for

that matter). The implicit proscenium arch that surrounds all films, coupled with the students' vast exposure to television, predisposes them to watch films passively, expecting to be entertained—not challenged. Contrary to Marshall McLuhan's fondly held fantasies, growing up watching television does not cause students to become critical of what they see. The adolescent cynicism of MTV's *Beavis and Butt-head* has not thus far produced a generation of critical viewers. In order to teach anthropology with film, teachers must first instruct their students on how to critically examine what they see. *The Ax Fight* is designed for that purpose.

The three edited versions of the event extend the alienating quality of this film. The didactic version, at this point in the history of anthropology and educational film, appears dated. As Asch suggests, it is almost funny; one could even see it as a parody of those long-dead days when the *Encyclopaedia Britannica* ruled educational films.[23] Even the initial thrust of the narration alienates us from the incredible scene to which we are witness. Chagnon begins the narration of this section as if he were talking about a movie and not real life: "The film opens as Sinabimi is comforted by her sister." Whether intentional or not, it distances the viewers even more from the immediacy of the event and reminds them again that they are witness to a representation filtered through a complex process of abstraction and thought.

The next section, titled "The Final Edited Version," is at once the easiest to view and the most confusing. In this version, the event is represented in a seamlessly edited, passively observational manner. All backstage moments, such as the footage of Chagnon's accidentally walking into camera range with pipe and camera or Asch's berating the soundman for being scared, have disappeared. There are no confused observers trying to figure out what happened. The event now seems comprehensible and contained. And yet if viewers look carefully, they notice that some of the scenes of the "haranguing" woman, who so magnificently taunts her enemies, have been moved out of their chronological order. You know that only because you have seen the rushes. Exactly what Asch intended with this section is a bit unclear. On the one hand, a viewer could see the section as a warning not to believe what you see in films because editors can easily create a chronology that did not exist. Because the section is entitled "The Final Edited Version," however, it is not impossible to assume that this version is the one the filmmakers approve of.

Although Asch suggests in the interview quotation cited earlier that his intention was to undermine the verisimilitude of ethnographic film, his editor (Paul Bugos) suggests a less than subversive intent. As reflexive as this section may be in intent, Asch was not willing to give up on all movie illusions. In the film's second section, as the action is slowed down so that viewers can be informed about who the principals are and their kin relations to each other, when the climactic moment comes, when a crunching blow is delivered with the ax, the sound has been "sweetened" in the studio so the audience will have the gut reaction Asch desires. Ultimately, it does not matter, because, whether intended or not, the impact of this film is to create doubt about the conventions of representation in ethnographic film and about the nature of anthropological explanations. Both are very much at the center of the concerns of the "postmodern" turn in anthropology.

Conclusion

The Ax Fight and *The Feast* may not be Asch's best work,[24] but there can be no question they are what he is best known for. Although Asch has subsequently worked with several other anthropologists and produced a number of films in Bali and other cultures in Indonesia, it is the experiences of the Yanomami project that have informed his subsequent endeavors. It is during the period from 1967 to 1972 that Asch's notions of collaboration and constructing films and accompanying written materials for teaching and research were formulated. As a way to conclude this chapter, I will comment upon these three concepts as articulated and practiced by Asch.

COLLABORATION. The question of collaboration between filmmakers and scholars is often a touchy one. Agencies like the National Endowment for the Humanities have institutionalized the idea of working together. All of its media projects require a panel of academic humanists. The British *Disappearing World* and Japanese Nippon TV series television programs are always based on collaborations. Although seldom the subject of much public debate, the idea of working together has been a source of displeasure and discomfort for many who have tried it (see Hoover 1992 for a description of one such venture). In some instances, collaboration has meant that the anthropologist is a glorified "Kelly girl" for a filmmaker who is really the author of the work; anthropologists are asked to provide field rapport, translations, and cultural context, while the filmmaker pursues his or her vision of what is important. At times, the final product can be positively embarrassing to the anthropologist.

The collaborative work of Asch and Chagnon would appear to be exemplary, in that they were able to produce a record number of important films together. A closer examination reveals a venture that was less than satisfying for both parties. Although initially Asch and Chagnon appeared to have been equally interested, Chagnon's involvement lessened by the time of the second filming expedition. Many of Asch's grand-scheme notions were never realized.[25] The study guides for all of the Yanomami films remain in draft form, with the still hopeful admonition, "These are preliminary study notes which will be replaced by a comprehensive study guide written by Napoleon Chagnon." I cannot imagine that a final version will ever appear.

There are two responses to the model of collaboration that Asch described in the interview quoted earlier—the ideal and the pragmatic. In the best of all possible worlds, one would wish for more active participation by an anthropologist—a collaboration in which filmmaker and scholar were equally involved in all phases of the work from inception to completion. Realistically, as Asch points out, anthropologists have their books and articles to write.[26] As much as some of us would like to see a visual anthropology coequal to written anthropology, few anthropological careers have been established through the production of films. Rouch's early admonition (1960s) that only anthropologists are qualified to make films about the people they study could finally become realized as low-budget video technology becomes more common. Ultimately, it may be that the product is more important than the process. Although the Asch-Chagnon model is far from ideal, it did produce a large number of significant films. So at least, in this instance, the collaboration proved fruitful.

RESEARCH FILMING AND ARCHIVES. Asch has been an early advocate of the notion of shooting footage in the field for the production of a research film as well as films to be released as teaching devices. As this notion has already been critiqued in chapter 1, I will confine my remarks here to Asch's ideas and involvement. Beginning with the first Yanomami footage, Asch was convinced that depositing the footage and/or research film in an archive was the only ethically defensible way to make films about people who are in a period of rapid culture change. The footage can be edited by the filmmaker into teaching films and possibly a feature-length film. The footage is carefully annotated and available to scholars to study for a variety of purposes unimagined by the original producer and to the people themselves as a resource in the construction of their own history. Asch was one of the founding members of the Smithsonian's anthropological film archive and was diligent in seeing that his footage was annotated and deposited. He also encouraged others to do the same thing. The Yanomami research footage remains ready to be used at the Smithsonian, but as yet no one appears interested. For reasons stated in chapter 1, it is unlikely that anyone will be. Given the time and expense involved in preparing footage to be deposited in an archive and the apparent lack of interest in this footage, perhaps the time has come to suggest that ethnographic film archiving needs to be rethought and reconceptualized.

TEACHING. According to Asch's National Science Foundation proposal, he wished to produce a body of work that could be packaged to teach all of the basic ideas in an introductory course in cultural anthropology. With the thirty-nine films and the study guides he envisioned, a teacher could occupy most of a semester course. It is an ambitious idea that has seldom been enacted by anyone except Asch.[27] For those who organize their cultural anthropology course around culture types, the Yanomami may serve as a typical example of a "horticultural" society and warrant two or three weeks of the semester. Asch's model assumes that teachers will become as interested in Yanomami society as he has become. It is an unrealistic assumption.

The subtext of both *The Ax Fight* and *The Feast* is one of cultural relativism. Asch wishes us to see the Yanomami world as one that is as ruleful and logical as the one in which Westerners live. *The Feast* is the Yanomami equivalent to the West's summit meetings, in which alliances for war and peace are forged. *The Ax Fight* helps us understand that even the violence of this alien society is rule-governed. Clearly, the intent of these films falls squarely into the best humanist anthropological tradition of seeking to foster tolerance and understanding for other cultures.

Anthropologists' ability to use films this way can come into question. In a study done by Wilton Martinez, one of Asch's own students, undergraduates taking a course in cultural anthropology at the University of Southern California were discovered to retain their ethnocentric and racist assumptions in spite of, and perhaps because of, the films they saw (1992). Although Martinez suggests that it is possible to counter students' ethnocentric predispositions, there is little evidence that anyone has been able to accomplish that goal. The logical conclusion one can draw from Martinez's oft-quoted study is that anthropology in general and ethnographic film in particular fail at their primary goal. A new study, as yet unpublished, conducted by Sam Pack at Temple University (1997), questions both Martinez's methods and his conclusions. Only time and more reception studies will reveal the usefulness of films for anthropological teaching.

The world has changed drastically since the early 1970s. The Yanomami have moved rapidly from the relative isolation of the rain forest to being involved in global battles to save their environment and themselves.[28] When Asch went back to the people he filmed twenty years ago, "They looked at the films attentively and said that while they thought that the films were quite accurate, it would be the 'kiss of death' for people to think that the Yanomami still live today the way they appear to in the films. They suggested that I make a film about the way they live today" (Asch et al. 1991:102). His solution to the Yanomami's anxiety about being known solely as the people of *The Ax Fight* was not to make another film but to train the Yanomami to image themselves. Ethnographic filmmakers like Asch find themselves in a peculiar dilemma. On the one hand, they are concerned with recording, preserving, and displaying the varieties of human culture. At the same time, the people they have recorded are trying to forge a new, more equitable cultural and political identity, and some aspects of their culture provide the ignorant with definite "proof" of their inferiority. Asch discussed this problem and, in doing so, commented on a fundamental reason for his film work:

So far, the Yanomami have looked at these old films as home movies and said, "This is the way we used to live," and they are fairly proud about it now.[29] But if they are going to come to my USC [University of Southern California] class, at the end, they are going to discover that these films are being used to reinforce the basic prejudices these students already have about "the Other," and then they may see this isn't fair. Then perhaps the films should be removed from circulation. The curriculum was designed to force the USC students out of their set ways, to see the way other cultures see the world on its different terms and to even accept Yanomami values in a cultural relativistic way as being OK for the Yanomami. The purpose was not to threaten the students' values but to interest them in values we might all share. But if the students' values that they live and grow by are so well established and intransigent or entrenched, then what students see on film may only strengthen their values. If that is the case, for the sake of these students and the Yanomami, these thirty-nine films should be removed to an archive and not used for teaching.

Basically, what I am saying is that the lesson of anthropology is that [in order] for every culture to survive, [it is necessary] to have a strong set of values that everyone shares in and that are inculcated into the youth. The problem is that these values have always been at the expense of, or in contradiction to, the values of every other society. Because it is necessary to feel this way about their own set of values in order to survive, it's very tricky. It is a hard nut for us to crack. And the students, because they are good, solid members of a particular society, have to hold and share these values very dearly. And what we are asking them as anthropologists is to give them up. Well, we aren't really, but many anthropology professors somehow teach in such a way that they are asking [students] to suspend their values for a time and think about Yanomami values. It's a question of learning something about other people slightly different . . . understanding them for what they are. It's a fascinating world out there—I mean, the most beautiful thing that humankind has created is culture. Then why the hell are we not learning more about other cultures and sharing them and enjoying them?

Tim Asch's contribution to the development of an anthropological cinema is twofold: (1) he provides us with an example of someone who could occupy a professional position outside the norms of professional filmmaking and still make credible and useful films; and (2) his concern with the potential of film for the teaching of cultural anthropology caused him to make two classically important films—*The Ax Fight* and *The Feast*—that remain as useful today as they were when they were first released. For me, these films remain among the best examples of what ethnographic filmmakers should strive for.

At the conclusion of Asch's life, he began to see the need to relinquish the authorship of his films to the people portrayed (Asch et al. 1991). Perhaps if he had lived longer, his new work would have explored a new role for the anthropologist interested in film—to facilitate the production of indigenous films—a topic to be discussed in chapters 8 and 9.

The Ethics of Image Making; or,

"They're Going to Put Me in the Movies.

They're Going to Make a Big Star Out

of Me."

The ethics and politics of ethnographic film have been a topic of considerable debate for the past several decades. The discussion began when the traditional supports for doing anthropology and documentary film became eroded. When people began to question the neutrality of science and the objectivity of photographic images, it was only natural that the moral underpinnings of ethnographic film would become challenged. In this chapter,[1] I contextualize the ethical issues surrounding the production of ethnographic film by discussing the larger moral questions that arise when one person produces and uses a recognizable image of another. It is a brief exploration of some of the ethical problems that stem from justifying the use of human beings in the pursuit of art, social science, news, or entertainment when those uses involve the production of realistic and recognizable images of people. The questions that could be raised in contemplating these matters are seemingly infinite, and many important issues can only be touched on here. (For a more elaborate discussion of these issues, see Gross, Katz, and Ruby 1988 as well as Gross, Katz, and Ruby n.d., a work in progress.)

Let me cite a few of the more obvious. What does "informed consent" mean when a family is asked by a television crew to have their lives recorded and packaged into a documentary series for national television? How does one balance the public's right to be informed with the individual's right to privacy? If objectivity and balance are no longer the primary obligations of the nonfiction image makers, what has replaced them? Do visual artists have a moral license to use people differently from the ways in which social scientists or reporters use them? How can the anthropologist justify his or her representation of another culture when that representation differs from the self-image of that group? These questions have no easy answers, and anyone who claims to have solutions to the problems being raised should probably not be trusted. The best one can hope for is that image makers should demonstrate that they are wrestling with the issues, as can be seen in K. Braun's film *passing girl/riverside an essay on camera work* (1998) or Jill Godmilow's *Far from Poland* (1984) or Susan Meiseles's *Pictures from a Revolution* (1991)—all these works and many others make the moral questions that arise when taking other people's picture their central concern.

A New Ethic?

I cannot discuss the legal, philosophical, or theological implications of these issues. I am an anthropologist, who, for the past thirty years, has been a participant observer in the production, consumption, and analysis of documentary and ethnographic photographs and films. I can therefore speak as both native and researcher. I am concerned about society's shifting moral expectations of the image maker and the consequent ambivalence some professionals feel about their own ethical base. This uneasiness bespeaks a deep-seated and widespread concern about the nature of images. At times, society seems more confused than informed by pictures. The traditional arguments used to justify the behavior of artists, journalists, and social scientists who make images have become increasingly inadequate, convincing neither the professionals involved nor the public as thoroughly as they once did.

We are in an era of global telecommunications in which image-producing, image-distributing, and image-consuming technologies are available to more and more people. Andy Warhol's idea that eventually everyone will be a star for fifteen minutes is no longer futurist thinking. Eighteen-year-old country music stars like LeAnn Rimes write their autobiographies, and people read them. In chapters 8 and 9, I discuss some of the implications of the broadening of the range of image authorship. The traditional moral base on which image producers have relied is shaky, if not crumbling. Before every city block has its own police surveillance camera, news service, visual ethnographer, and resident visual artist, it is essential that we have a better understanding of how the decision to use someone else's image is made and where responsibilities lie.

Ethnic minorities, women, gays, third- and fourth-world peoples, the very rich, and the very poor are telling the middle-class, middle-aged straight white males who dominate the industry that the mass-mediated pictures of the Other are false. Many wish to produce their own representations of themselves and control or at least monitor the ways in which they are imaged by others. The organized protests that began in the 1970s with heated debates over the Metropolitan Museum of Art's photographic exhibition Harlem on My Mind and the gays' rage against the film *Cruising* and the Puerto Rican community's displeasure over the film *Fort Apache, The Bronx* have been growing ever since. For example, the Gay and Lesbian Alliance against Defamation (GLAAD) now releases on a regular basis evidence of the media's homophobia, as do other organizations that attempt to make the public aware of the ethnic, class, and gender narrowness of the media industry. Although the lack of proper representation of women, gays, lesbians, and ethnic minorities may not be improving that much, the public is at least informed of the anger of these groups at their mass-mediated image.

The time when an image maker could take photographs of strangers, usually poor or in some other way removed from the mainstream of America, and justify the action as the inherent right of the artist or the documentarian or the ethnographer is, I believe, ending (Brian Winston in Gross, Katz, and Ruby 1988).

The time when one could reconstruct a historical event by creating composite, and therefore fictional, characters for the sake of plot and not be held legally and ethically responsible ended with the popularity of the television docudrama. Both Frank Sinatra and Elizabeth Taylor were able to stop the production of "unauthorized" biographical TV films by invoking the notion of the "right to publicity" (John David Viera in Gross, Katz, and Ruby 1988).

The time when a reporter could rely on the principle that the public's right to know is more important than the individual's right to privacy, when people believed that a journalist's primary ethical responsibility was to be objective, fair, and honest, is over.

The time when a social scientist could depend on the public's belief in the material benefits of scientific knowledge to justify the use of double-blind studies, often employing hidden cameras, ceased with Stanley Milgram's frightening explorations of people's willingness to obey authority (Milgram 1974). People intent on producing *National Geographic* voyeuristic pictures of tribal peoples now find themselves discussing permissions with tribal lawyers.

Examples are endless, and they signal the demise of a naive trust that since the camera never lies, an image maker must perforce be telling the truth. More and more people understand the technologically produced image as a construction—as the interpretive act of someone who has a culture, an ideology, who comes from a particular socioeconomic class, is identified with a gender, and often has a conscious point of view, all of which causes the image to convey a certain kind of knowledge in a particular way. Image makers display their view of the world whether they mean to or not. No matter how much people may feel the need for an objective witness of reality, image-producing technologies will not provide it.

The Ethics of Realism

I argue elsewhere (chapter 6) that the maker of images has the moral obligation to reveal the covert—never to appear to produce an objective mirror by which the world can see its "true" image. For in doing so, the status quo is strengthened, the repressive forces of this world are supported, and the very people about whom image makers claim to be concerned are alienated. So long as the dominant culture's images of the world continue to be sold to others as *the* image of the world, image makers are being unethical.

To pursue this argument efficiently, I must be specific, and so I confine myself to one variety of imaging. I will not try to separate assertion from supportable theses; I will simply state that the argument presented here is based on a combination of personal experience, research, and passionately held belief. I make no claim that all aspects of the argument are verifiable, only that all other points of view are much less convincing.

I use examples from the documentary/ethnographic tradition—still and motion pictures—because it is the topic of this book. A similar case could, of course, be made using fiction films or paintings, but since the documentary is such a marvelously confused genre, it allows me to deal with art, social science, reportage, and so forth, in a rather inclusive way. In addition, the production of documentary images and the production of anthropological knowledge are in fundamental ways parallel pursuits. The moral and ethical concerns of one can be applied to the other. Most documentarians would agree that the following quotation from anthropologist Dell Hymes could just as well apply to the documentary tradition: "The fundamental fact that shapes the future of anthropology is that it deals in knowledge of others. Such knowledge has always implied ethical and political responsibilities, and today the 'others' whom anthropologists have studied make those responsibilities explicit and unavoidable. One must consider the consequences for those among whom one works of simply being there, of learning about them, and what becomes of what is learned" (Hymes, ed., 1972:48).

For a variety of reasons, anthropologists have been conducting public discussions about their ethical responsibilities to the people they study longer than have many other people in the business of making representations. I believe that the experience anthropologists have had in grappling with these questions can provide others with usable insights into their own problems.

The production and use of images involve four separable yet related moral issues, which, when combined into a professional activity, become an ethical position:

1. The image maker's personal moral contract to produce an image that is somehow an accurate reflection of his or her intention in making the image in the first place—to use the cliché, it is being true to oneself
2. The producer's moral obligation to his or her subjects
3. The producer's moral obligation to the institutions that provide the funds to do the work—that is, paying the piper
4. The producer's moral obligation to his or her intended audience

There is no one position that can resolve all of these questions for all situations.

The third of these issues is undoubtedly the least complicated. Funders and institutions that grant permissions to do research often require the image maker to sign a legally binding document as to the parameters of the work. Although conflicts do arise, they are most often settled in the courts, where ethical considerations are secondary to legal ones.

It is generally accepted that images are polysemous—that is, photographs and films have a variety of potential socially generated meanings that become enhanced through the context in which they appear (Ruby 1976b). The cultural expectations that producers, subjects, and audiences have about the various communication events that transpire in the production and consumption of images predispose people to employ different interpretive strategies to derive signification and meaning from images (Worth and Gross 1981). These interpretive strategies are embedded within a larger body of cultural knowledge and competencies that encompass or are supported by a moral system. That is, systems of knowledge and epistemologies are attached to moral systems. As an anthropologist, I would argue that morals and ethics are only comprehensible in relation to other facets of a culture. In other words, I am a moral relativist.

The particular signification or meaning that is appended to an image emerges as a consequence of a variety of factors: (1) the label attached to the image—for example, photographs that are considered to be news photos are regarded differently from art photos; (2) the context in which the image appears—for example, news photos that are made into high-quality enlargements and placed in an art museum tend to be regarded primarily as art and not news; and (3) the audience's socially acquired expectations regarding certain types of images produced by certain types of image makers that tend to appear in certain types of settings.

An illustration will help make these abstractions less abstruse. At the beginning of the century, Lewis Hine, a sociologist turned social reformer, took a series of photographs, commissioned by the National Committee to Reform Child Labor Laws, of children working in factories (Alland 1974). The archetypal Hine image is that of a prepubescent child, quite small, often frail, and always dirty, standing in front of an enormous piece of machinery. The child is staring into the lens of the camera and consequently into the eyes of the viewer. The machines are black and dirty, and the factory so dark that the edges of the machines disappear into nothingness. These images were designed to appear in tracts and posters that detailed the social and psychological abuses of child labor. They were often printed on inexpensive, porous newsprint with a cheap halftone process. All of the subtlety of tone and detail present in the negatives disappears. These tracts were sent to legislators, the clergy, and prominent citizens and handed out at meetings. The intended message of these images in this context is a pragmatic one—a call to arms. One is to feel pity for the child and anger at the exploitation by the factory owner implied by the large, ominous machines. If the photographer is thought of at all, he or she is assumed to be on the side of truth and justice, providing irrefutable evidence of wrongdoing.

If a set of Hine's photographs were prepared for exhibition at the Museum of Modern Art in New York, enlargements of fine quality would be matted, framed, and hung with a brief but articulate and insightful explanatory text in a stark, off-white room with subdued lighting. The audience in this context becomes people whose primary interest lies in museum going, art, and photography, not in reforming labor laws. The photographs are now regarded chiefly for their syntactic elements—that is, formal and aesthetic qualities. The waifs are no longer pitiable examples of capitalistic exploitation but aesthetic objects with interesting, if not haunting, faces. The machines are now examined for their texture and lines as industrial art objects, not as symbols of oppression. A little girl's stare is now simply a sign of her willingness to be photographed, not an indictment of our economic system. It is unlikely that anyone seeing the exhibit would be motivated to do anything except admire and applaud the artistic accomplishments of Lewis Hine. I am virtually certain that no one would rush to West Virginia or even Chinatown in New York to see whether similar conditions might still exist. At the conclusion of such an exhibit, no charitable checks would be written or picket lines formed.

The photographs in these two scenarios are the same, but the cultural expectations created by the two contexts cause viewers to regard Hine and his works in different ways. I am not suggesting that Hine was never regarded as a photographic artist when his images were used in political tracts or that no one would ponder the political or economic implications of the photographs in the museum. I am suggesting that one interpretive strategy seems more appropriate to most people given a particular setting. It's hard to imagine people concerned with the plight of children in factories arguing about Hine's compositional style, or tuxedoed gentlemen and bejeweled ladies rushing out into the streets to picket a corporation thought to be exploiting children.

In fact, readings of most images vacillate between these two extremes (Sekula 1975). It is a case of the confusion to which I alluded earlier with regard to documentary images. We are often uncertain whether the image maker is an artist who is to be critiqued for his or her mastery of the form or a technician who holds a mirror to the world.

This lack of clarity confronts producers with a moral dilemma that can be traced back to the beginnings of the tradition. Robert Flaherty, an American pioneer of documentary/ethnographic film, was immediately accused by his critics of "faking" *Nanook of the North* (see chapter 2). The film confused many commentators. Some failed to see any coherent story, since the narrative line was not obvious; others accused Flaherty of using actors and staging the entire movie. Criticism of the documentary form has not progressed far since the 1923 reviews of *Nanook*, and as a consequence, theory, criticism, and even reviews often flounder on the question "Is the documentary art or reportage?" As a participant in the Robert Flaherty Film Seminars in the 1960s and 1970s, I cannot count the number of times discussions about a particular film became mired in this sort of issue.

A cultural confusion has so limited the semantic and syntactic possibilities that some leave the documentary tradition for the apparent freedom of fiction. And yet the moral obligations of the producers of fiction—written and visual—have also become unclear. Some court decisions (particularly the 1978 decision against Gwen Davis Mitchell for apparently basing one of the characters in her 1976 novel *Touching* on a California psychologist, Paul Bindrim) appear to greatly limit the artistic license of even fiction makers—but seldom do the producers of fiction get accused of faking or criticized for staging. More and more publishing houses are offering liability insurance to their writers of fiction and nonfiction alike.

Ethics, Documentaries, and Aesthetics

If documentarians choose to regard themselves as artists and are so received by the public, conventional wisdom argues that their primary ethical obligation is to be true to their personal visions of the world—to make artistically competent statements. In this way, artists are thought to fulfill their moral responsibilities to the subjects of their work and to their audiences.

The artist is often regarded as being somewhat outside the moral constraints that confine other people—as having license to transform people into aesthetic objects without their knowledge and sometimes against their will.

For a long time, few critics except perhaps Marxists and Frankfort school critics argued that art contains and espouses the ideology of the artist or that photography is not a universal language transcending cultural boundaries. Now, it is almost a cliché. The shift can be seen in the about-face of Susan Sontag, who at one time argued that art dwelled outside of politics and morality (1966) and then discovered that a Nazi film like *Triumph of the Will* was produced by a fascist filmmaker who must bear the moral responsibility of her art no matter how competent it might be (Sontag 1982). Some people argue that ethics should have priority over aesthetics or, perhaps more correctly, that a morally acceptable ethical position produces the foundation for a good aesthetic. I make that argument in my critique of Robert Gardner's films in chapter 3.

If one takes the everyday lives of people—a favorite subject matter of the documentarian and ethnographer—and uses them to construct an artistic statement, where is the line drawn between the actuality of the subjects' lives and the aesthetic needs of the artist? How much fiction or interpretation is possible before the subjects not only disagree but begin to be offended or even fail to recognize themselves at all? These questions were raised with great passion with reference to videotapes produced by video artists, people not from the documentary tradition but in the field of nonrepresentational video art. When Juan Downey produced tapes about the Yanomamo Indians of Venezuela, some audiences become quite upset about the "exploitation" of the subjects for the sake of art (Michaels 1982a). It would appear that documentarians who employ more subtle and less obvious techniques of construction are less likely to be criticized for being exploitative than are the video artists who employ overt techniques of aesthetic manipulation. Where does the documentary artist seek verification and justification for his or her work? Must the subject agree with the artist's interpretation? Or is it sufficient that the artist remain true to a personal vision regardless of how offensive it might be to others? I believe this question has no easy answer anymore.

Where does the documentary artist's responsibility to the audience lie? Most audiences believe documentary images to be accurate representations of reality, unless they are overtly altered, as in the case of the videotapes just mentioned. Given a common belief in the "truthfulness" of the image, should the documentary artist remind the audience of the interpretive and constructed nature of the documentary form—that is, demystify the construction and become reflexive, as I suggest in chapter 6? For example, is it important for people to know that Flaherty cast his films by looking for ideal types? "Family members" in *Nanook of the North, Man of Aran*, and *Louisiana Story* were not related to each other; they were selected because they suited Flaherty's conception of what makes a good Inuit, Aran Islander, or Cajun family. Is the documentary artist being more ethical if methods and techniques are revealed? Does that knowledge cause the audience to regard the film differently?

Traditionally, documentarians have not revealed these things within their films, and some have never discussed the mechanics of their construction anywhere. Obviously, Flaherty has, or we would not be able to contemplate the consequences of his revelation and actions (see Rotha 1983). To remind an audience of the constructive and interpretive nature of images is regarded by some as counterproductive, if not actually destructive, to the nature of the film experience—that is, to the creation of an illusion of reality. Moreover, some people regard such revelation as self-indulgent, in that it turns the audience's attention away from the film and toward the filmmaker. For many, effective art requires a suspension of disbelief; being reminded that the images have an author disrupts the fantasy.

It is commonly assumed that art should be a little mysterious to be successful. A reflexive art has never been very popular and, at least in film, has become confused with a kind of self-indulgent autobiographical film that was first popular in the 1970s, in which young filmmakers expose themselves, exploit their families, and use the camera as therapist. Amalie Rothschild's *Nana, Mom and Me* (1974) is an example of this sort of film. Reflexivity has gotten a bad name because of its mistaken association with narcissism, self-consciousness, and other forms of self-contemplation (Myerhoff and Ruby 1982). I believe, however, that an intelligently used reflexivity is an essential part of all ethically produced documentaries—a matter I discuss at some length in chapter 6.

The confusion about which moral guidelines should be used to judge a documentary is compounded by the fact that some documentarians respond to aesthetic and moral criticism of their art by suggesting that their works are mere reflections of the reality observed and that their role as producer was to faithfully record and transmit what they experienced. They are not really the authors of their works, nor are they responsible for any conclusions audiences might draw. If one sees someone in a documentary image who appears stupid or disgusting, the implication is that the person so imaged is in reality stupid or disgusting, since the camera merely recorded what was in front of it with no modification. This aesthetic and moral neutrality is to be found in Frederick Wiseman's defense of his film *High School* (1968) (Anderson and Benson 1988).

When the American direct cinema movement, founded by people like Robert Drew and Richard Leacock, used television as its primary outlet, it associated the documentary with the ethical canons of broadcast journalism (O'Connell 1992). Fairness, balance, and objectivity became paramount. In doing so, it brought the tradition full circle. As Dan Schiller has argued, objectivity became an ideal for journalism partly as a consequence of the photograph's being introduced into newspapers (1977). As newspapers capitalized on the public's belief in the objectivity of the photograph, print journalists sought to emulate this objectivity in their writing. Fifty years later, documentary film became concerned with being objective because of its association with broadcast journalism.

Documentarians-as-journalists logically assume the ethical codes of the latter profession. In doing so, they become virtually unassailable, for, unlike their printed-word colleagues, photo and film journalists are thought to be employing a medium that when used properly, is inherently objective. Thus, apart from the occasional accusation of the outright faking of a picture or the staging of a scene in a television program, documentary-broadcast journalism has not been subjected to much critical examination until very recently.

The arguments raised by Marxists, postmodernists, poststructuralists, and others about the relation between ideology on the one hand and the producer of images on the other have, however, caused some people to critique broadcast journalism in a fashion similar to that discussed earlier for art. Stuart Hall and other British scholars of mass communication are among these analysts (Morley and Chen 1996). Criticism of objectivity as the primary ethical responsibility of journalists has increased in the last several decades. As James Carey pointed out:

What are lamely called the conventions of objective reporting were developed to report another century and another society. They were designed to report a secure world . . . about which there was a rather broad consensus, . . . a settled mode of life: . . . which could be rendered in the straightforward "who says what to whom" manner. . . . Today no accepted system of interpretation exists and political values and purposes are very much in contention . . . and cannot be encased within traditional forms of understanding. Consequently, "objective reporting" does little more than convey this disorder in isolated, fragmented news stories. (1969:35)

Some print journalists have responded to this criticism by acknowledging the active role of the reporter in creating, not finding, news. The so-called New Journalism of Tom Wolfe and Hunter Thompson is written in the first person and employs narrative techniques of fiction. With Truman Capote and Norman Mailer writing fiction in the same style, it is often impossible to know from the text whether you are reading fiction or nonfiction, and often even then there is no easy answer. Is Wolfe's *The Right Stuff* (1979) or Mailer's *The Executioner's Song* (1979) fiction or not? How are we to understand the potboiler crime thrillers of people like Joseph Wambaugh (for example, *The Onion Field* [1973]) when they only claim to be "based" on a true story? What about the parts that are not based on a true story? Does it really matter? It is a fascinating legal and ethical question but too great a detour for now. A visual equivalent to New Journalism has yet to be invented. When Truman Capote's nonfiction novel *In Cold Blood* (1965)—whose full title is *In Cold Blood: A True Account of a Multiple Murder and Its Consequences*—was made into a movie, it became straightforward fiction. "New" Journalism is no longer new. It is simply a taken-for-granted journalistic style employed when deemed appropriate. What is interesting is that scholars and critics of journalism have not been able to develop canons of criticism to adequately deal with this hybrid form.

Many documentarians who consider themselves more journalists than artists are people interested in investigating rather than merely reporting. They are committed people motivated to make images of social or political concerns. Since Jacob Riis (Alland 1974) and John Grierson (Hardy 1979), many documentarians have been social reformers, and some, even radical revolutionaries who shared Lenin's belief in the power of the cinema to change the world. They produce images to inform audiences of injustices, corruption, and other societal ills, often to persuade people to act against these evils.

The ethical considerations of these image makers differ somewhat from those of the documentary artist. Grierson (Hardy 1979) and other radicals argued that art should also be in the service of political and social change. Since politically committed image makers have definite points of view, often prior to the production of any images, they approach the content of the images, the people imaged, and their audiences with a fairly clear agenda. Unlike the documentary as art, the pragmatic features of the images must dominate. The images must have their desired effect to be successful, and that effect is known in advance. People in these images are no longer aesthetic objects but rather symbols of some collective force. A poor person is often used to stand for poverty or an oppressed factory worker for the ills of capitalism. The question arises: Is it acceptable to use someone's life to illustrate a thesis? Are the considerations different when you are seeking to aid someone you regard as a victim by using that person in your film, as opposed to using a subject in order to expose him or her as a villain?

Let me use an example from one of the favorite themes of documentary images—housing conditions for the poor. Let us say you are making a documentary on slums for local television and you select a family who appears to have suffered directly because of an irresponsible landlord. How do you weigh the possible harm that might come to the family as a consequence of their public exposure in the film versus the possibility that the film may prompt city officials to crack down on slumlords and consequently improve the living conditions for a large number of people?

Is it justifiable to try to avoid explaining your motivation and point of view to the landlord in order to be able to interview him or her on film? To be blunt about it, is it ethical to lie to someone assumed to be evil in order to perform what you regard as a positive act? For example, a film like Robert Mugee's *Amateur Night in City Hall* (1977), an exposé of Frank Rizzo, then mayor of Philadelphia, could not have been made if many of the people in it had known the maker's intention.

Because of the economic realities of distribution, documentary images with a political intent are usually viewed by the already committed, people who immediately comprehend the films' thesis. However, some find their way into theatrical release or public television and hence to a more diverse audience. Should the makers reveal themselves, their methods, and their goals to their audiences, or are they justified in employing the techniques of advertising and other forms of propaganda and persuasion? Two examples illuminate the problem: Julia Reichert and Jim Klein's film *Union Maids* (1976), a skillfully edited set of interviews of women active in union organizing in the thirties, and Connie Field's *The Life and Times of Rosie the Riveter* (1987), an exploration of women who worked during World War II. The makers failed to mention that some of the women were members of leftist political organizations because they felt that some audiences would be alienated from the films' primary message—the unsung role of women as union organizers or exploited workers. The makers also erased themselves and their motives.

Does this sort of selection taint a film to such an extent that all of it becomes suspect? Are political documentary makers caught in the dilemma of having a responsibility to reveal methods and motives that might lessen the impact of their message? Can political image makers justify their sins of omission on the basis of the service they provide in helping to bring public attention to our social problems? I think not. I am skeptical of the motives and sophistication of many political image makers. Even though thousands of films and millions of photographs have been employed in political causes in the past fifty years, there is little empirical evidence to suggest that they are a significant means of influencing people.

If all the money expended on all the images of the plight of migrant laborers since Edward R. Murrow and Fred Friendly's *Harvest of Shame* (1960) television program had been used for day-care centers and the improvement of these workers' living conditions, their plight would be significantly improved. But instead, the migrant workers' camp in Belle Glade, Florida, which is shown in *Harvest of Shame*, has remained virtually unchanged since Murrow and Friendly filmed it. I doubt that the professional sympathizers who produced all this work can defend it with much tangible evidence. The vast majority spend a few weeks on location and then never see the people they film again. Few revolutions were won in a movie house, on a television screen, or on the six o'clock news.

Conclusion

I have barely touched on a large number of important questions concerning the ethical obligations of the professional image maker. Whether artist, journalist, or social documentarian, more image makers need to confront their responsibilities in a more reflective and reflexive way than they have so far. I argue elsewhere for the necessity of a reflexive documentary and anthropological cinema (see chapter 6). I would extend the argument to all image makers.

As I argue throughout this book, the filmic illusion of reality is an extremely dangerous one, for it gives the people who control the image industry too much power. The majority of Americans, if not the majority of the world's population, receive information about the outside world from the images produced by film, television, and photography. If the lie that pictures always tell the truth is perpetuated, together with the lie that some images are objective witnesses to reality, then an industry that has the potential to symbolically recreate the world in its own image continues to wield far too much power. Technology grows out of a particular ideology. The Western world created image-producing technologies out of a profound need to have an irrefutable witness—to control reality by capturing it on film.

The world is in the midst of the telecommunications revolution—a revolution potentially as profound and far-reaching as the agricultural and industrial revolutions. The one significant difference between the present and past changes is that the telecommunications revolution is happening so fast, we can actually be aware of it. It took five thousand years of gradual change from the first experiments in plant domestication until people were fully sedentary farmers. Today, there are people still active in television who contributed their talents at the very beginnings of the industry. We have the opportunity to make the revolution anything we want it to be. As privileged members of the segment of the world that manages, if not controls, the image empires, we have an obligation to pause and reflect on the past and contemplate the future. We should not let the rush of the marketplace destroy our responsibility to act intelligently. We must demystify these technologies so that we can cultivate a more critical and sophisticated audience. We need to make it possible to include a greater variety of human experience via these media—to give the many available voices access to this revolution. The human condition is too complex to be filtered through the eyes of a small group of people. We need to see the world from as many perspectives as possible. We have the means to do so now. As people whose profession it is to make representations of the human condition, anthropologists have a special obligation to thoughtfully explore ways in which their representations accurately reflect and attempt to satisfy the ethical issues raised in this chapter.

Exposing Yourself:

Reflexivity, Anthropology, and Film

Any scholar who recognizes that self-reflection, as mediated linguistically, is integral to the characterization of human social conduct, must acknowledge that such holds also for his/her own activities as a social analyst or researcher. ANTHONY GIDDENS, NEW RULES OF SOCIOLOGICAL METHOD

In this chapter, I explore the relationship among reflexivity, anthropology, and film.[1] To be more precise, I am interested in the implications of regarding these three terms in a particular way. I make no claim that the conceptualizations proposed are the only, or even the best, ones. Rather, I wish to argue that if one examines anthropology in terms of reflexivity, then film assumes a particular role in the communication of anthropology. The core of this chapter was written twenty years ago (Ruby 1980a). I have made some revisions to take into account attempts to be reflexive that were made in the 1980s and 1990s. It is my contention that the arguments I made twenty years ago are still valid, which means I see little progress toward a more reflexive anthropology. Even with all of the rhetoric about the need to be reflexive, it has not become a normative part of written or filmic anthropology. If anything, there is a backlash against reflexivity because of its perceived association with the postmodern and the perceived dangers of the relativism associated with it. Although marvelously reflexive films like Kwame Braun's *passing girl/riverside an essay on camera work* (1998) continue to appear, they do so in a serendipitous manner rather than as the result of a systematic and knowledgeable exploration of the concept.

Reflexivity is a multifaceted concept that has been used in a variety of ways for many purposes. In this chapter, I concentrate on one very specific manifestation. To be reflexive, in terms of a work of anthropology, is to insist that anthropologists systematically and rigorously reveal their methods and themselves as the instrument of data generation and reflect upon how the medium through which they transmit their work predisposes readers/viewers to construct the meaning of the work in certain ways.

To be logically consistent with the position I espouse, I should reveal myself as producer and the process I employed in the construction of this chapter and book; that is, I should be reflexive about my ideas on reflexivity. I have started that process in the preface and introduction. I continue it here. Readers may find what I do ironic because I have chosen to write about film and anthropology rather than, like Dziga Vertov, make a film that illustrates my ideas. For the moment, theorizing about film appears to be best accomplished in writing, at least for me.

My interest in reflexivity stems from what began as an elitist fascination with backstage (Goffman 1959). I was convinced that if I could understand how someone made something and who the "author" was, that knowledge would enable me to become an insider. In time, the interest broadened and became more sophisticated. It caused me to admire the novels of Kurt Vonnegut Jr. and Tom Robbins, the music of Frank Zappa, the photography of Lee Friedlander and Duane Michaels, the films of Jean-Luc Godard and Woody Allen, the paintings of René Magritte, and the comedy of the Firesign Theatre and Monty Python. Whatever else these people may be doing, they are trying to raise the critical consciousness of their audiences by being publicly, explicitly, and openly self-aware and reflexive.

There are two other factors. For more than thirty years, I have been engaged in exploring the theoretical possibility of an anthropological cinema, which forms the basis for this book. During this process, I discovered an apparent conflict between the scholarly necessity for the anthropologist to reveal his or her methods and the conventions of documentary film, which, until recently, have strongly discouraged such a revelation. In seeking a solution to this dilemma, I was drawn to the literature on reflexivity. In 1974, during the Conference on Visual Anthropology at Temple University in Philadelphia, I organized a series of film screenings and discussions on autobiographical, personal, and self-referential films,[2] and in 1982, I edited the book *A Crack in the Mirror: Reflexive Perspectives in Anthropology*. Through these activities, I began, in a more formal and systematic way, to explore the relationship between reflexive film and reflexive anthropology. I continue my interest and have become an advocate for a reflexive anthropology, particularly as it applies to ethnographic film.

In a larger arena, I have felt a progressively widening ethical, political, and conceptual gap between the anthropology that I learned in graduate school in the early 1960s and the world as I have come to know it since. Among the wedges, I would note the publication of Bronislaw Malinowski's diary (1969), the public disclosure of the clandestine use of social scientists by the U.S. government in Latin America and Southeast Asia, and the underlying cynical manipulation of public sentiment during the Gulf War. These revelations produced a crisis of conscience and loss of innocence for many people. The events placed the personal dilemma about the researcher's role in research into a moral and political perspective noted as early as 1972 by Dell Hymes and other authors in *Reinventing Anthropology*—a book often overlooked by the postmodern critics of anthropology. It should be difficult if not impossible now to continue to defend naive assumptions about the responsibilities of anthropologists toward the people they study and toward the intended audiences for their work. Anthropologists as well as others who make representations should stop being shamans of objectivity. After Vietnam and all that has followed, it is an obscene and dishonest position. Although anthropology may have been grappling with its own identity for decades, if a more reflexive image has been forged out of all the soul-searching, I fail to see it.

It should be obvious by now that I am partisan. I strongly believe that all serious filmmakers and anthropologists have ethical, aesthetic, and scholarly obligations to be reflexive and self-critical about their work. I would, in fact, expand that mandate to include any scholar or intellectual or artist with a serious intent. Lest readers be led to believe that what follows is some hackneyed political and moralizing sermon on the sins of objectivity and value-free science, I wish to reassure them that, having exposed myself sufficiently to make everyone aware of the motivation for this chapter, I will now attempt a more reasoned argument for a reflexive anthropology as the basis for an anthropological cinema.

One final point should be made in these introductory remarks: the ideas espoused in this chapter are clearly not idiosyncratic to me, nor for that matter to film or anthropology. The *appearance* of being reflexive or publicly self-aware has become almost commonplace in every communicative form in our society, from so-called high art to television commercials. Although this is neither the time nor the place to attempt a survey of the various manifestations of reflexivity within our society and to critique the faddishness of the concept, a brief mention of some of the more obvious examples might be in order.

I believe they are to be found in the growing realization that the world is not what it appears to be and that on a very serious and commonsense level, what you don't know will, and often does, hurt you. People now want to know who made it and what the ingredients are before they will buy anything—aspirin, cars, television news, or education. Consumers no longer trust the producers to be people of goodwill. Ralph Nader, the consumer-protection movement, financial and personal disclosures by political figures, and the truth in lending and truth in advertising laws are all part of this felt need. There is a growing interest in knowing something about backstage in almost every aspect of the lives of middle-class Americans. The naive empiricism that pervaded our society and dominated nineteenth-century social science is being eroded. Many people are moving away from the positivist notion that meaning resides in the world and that human beings should strive to discover the inherent, immutable, and objectively true reality (Stent 1975). They are beginning to assume that human beings construct and impose meaning on the world. We create order. We don't discover it.

Reflexivity

Before it is possible to discuss potential relationships among reflexivity and anthropology and cinema, it is essential that my use of the term *reflexivity* be precisely stated, particularly since it is used in a variety of contexts to mean different things. I find Johannes Fabian's notion of producer, process, and product useful (1971). By *producer*, I simply mean the sender of a message—the creator of the sign. By *process*, I mean the means, methods, channel, and so forth whereby the message is shaped, encoded, and sent. The *product* is, of course, the cultural artifact—what the receiver gains. I am deliberately using general terms because it serves as a reminder that the issues raised are not confined to the cinema or social sciences, even though this chapter may be. To be reflexive is to conceive of the production of communicative statements thusly:

Producer ⟶ Process ⟶ Product

and to suggest that some knowledge of all three components is essential for a critical and sophisticated understanding.

In retrospect, what was missing in the diagram I just presented and from my entire original article is a concern with audience. The diagram should have a fourth element:

Producer ⟶ Process ⟶ Product ⟶ Reader/Viewer

This oversight is corrected in chapter 7, where the role of the viewer and reception is explored.

It is further necessary to distinguish between reflexivity and several other terms that are sometimes used as synonyms—*autobiography, self-reference*, and *self-consciousness* (this discussion is developed in more depth in Myerhoff and Ruby 1982).

In an autobiographical work, although the producer—the self—is the center of the work, he or she can be unselfconscious in the presentation of the autobiography. The author clearly has had to be self-conscious in the process of making the autobiography, but it is possible for him or her to keep that knowledge private and simply follow the established conventions of the genre. To be reflexive is not only to be self-conscious but to be sufficiently self-conscious to know what aspects of the self must be revealed to an audience to enable them to understand the process employed, as well as the resultant product, and to know how much revelation is purposive, intentional, and when it becomes narcissistic or accidentally revealing. This knowledge—that is, knowing how much of the self it is necessary to reveal—is the most difficult aspect of being reflexive. When successfully mastered, it separates self-indulgence from revelation.

Self-reference, on the other hand, is not necessarily autobiographical or reflexive. It is the allegorical or metaphorical use of self—for example, François Truffaut's films *400 Blows* (1959) and *Day for Night* (1973), or Janis Ian's song "Stars." The maker's life in these works becomes symbolic of some sort of collective—all filmmakers, all pop stars, and sometimes, everyperson. It is popularly assumed that self-reference occurs in virtually all art forms: as the cliché goes, artists use their personal experience as the basis of their art. The critics, scholars, and devotees of an art form or a particular artist try to ferret out biographical tidbits so that they can discover the "hidden meaning" behind the artist's work. Again, there is the cultural fact that many people believe it is quite common for producers to be self-referential. Discussions of novels often center on discovering the hidden "autobiographical" elements. What I wish to stress is that this self-reference is distinct from reflexivity; one does not necessarily lead to the other.

Being self-conscious has become a full-time preoccupation, particularly among the upper middle class. However, it is possible, and indeed common, for this kind of awareness to remain private knowledge for the producer, or at least to be so detached from the product that all but the most devoted are discouraged from exploring the relationship between the maker and his or her work; furthermore, the producer often does nothing to encourage that exploration. In other words, one can be reflective without being reflexive. That is, one can become self-conscious without being conscious of that self-consciousness (Babcock 1977). Only if a producer decides to make his or her awareness of self a public matter and convey that knowledge to the audience is it then possible to regard the product as reflexive.

I have just suggested that it is possible to produce products that are autobiographical, self-referential, or self-conscious without having those products regarded as being reflexive. Let me attempt to clarify these distinctions. I am simply trying to say that if the work does not contain sufficient indications that the producer intends his or her product to be regarded as reflexive, the audience will be uncertain as to whether they are reading into the product more or other than what was meant. They will attribute to the work what they assume rather than infer what the maker intended from the work (Worth and Gross 1981).

In sum, to be reflexive is to structure a product in such a way that the audience assumes that the characteristics of the producer's life, the process of construction, and the product are a coherent whole. Not only is an audience made aware of these relationships, but it is made to realize the necessity of that knowledge. To be more formal, I would argue that being reflexive means that the producer deliberately, intentionally reveals to his or her audience the underlying epistemological assumptions that caused him or her to formulate a set of questions in a particular way, to seek answers to those questions in a particular way, and finally, to present his or her findings in a particular way. The formulation is, of course, an idealized one. A question that is central to this conception that continues to perplex and confound is, how much knowledge of the producer and process is sufficient? I cannot point to a single film that I would regard as having totally satisfied these requirements, but then only a few films have been *designed* to explore the concept or to integrate it into the film. Dziga Vertov's 1928 *Man with a Movie Camera* and Jean Rouch and Edgar Morin's 1962 *Chronicle of a Summer* have not been equaled in this exploration because they were designed to explore this concept. The myriad of reflexive films that have followed these seminal works are often reflexive by accident rather than design or only partially reflexive and fail in some major way to satisfy the model I just outlined.

Although being reflexive, or at least publicly self-aware, has become more acceptable, until recently it was more common for most people, filmmakers and anthropologists included, to present a communicative product that excludes information about the producer or process. The revelation of these two is often thought to be nonessential and even inappropriate. To reveal the producer was thought to be narcissistic, overly personal, subjective, and even unscientific. To reveal the process was deemed untidy, ugly, and confusing to an audience. To borrow Erving Goffman's concept (1959), audiences are not supposed to see backstage. It destroys the illusion and causes them to break their suspension of disbelief. The conflicts between those who regard reflexivity as necessary and those who view it as self-indulgent will remain unresolved in society at large. Within anthropology, I argue it is a necessity.

I now wish to explore an apparent paradox within anthropology that was alluded to in the last section. It can be expressed as follows: why do most anthropologists identify themselves as social scientists and their work as being in a social-scientific tradition and yet often fail to adequately describe the methods they employed in their research and to account for the possible effects that the researchers and the form selected to transmit their work might have on their research?[3] In other words, why isn't anthropology a reflexive social science?

The results of scientific research in any branch of learning ought to be presented in a manner absolutely candid and above board. No one would dream of making an experimental contribution to physical or chemical science, without giving a detailed account of all the arrangements of the experiments; an exact description of the apparatus used; of the manner in which the observations were conducted; of their number; of the length of time devoted to them; and of the degree of approximation with which each measurement was made[;] . . . in ethnography, where a candid account of such data is perhaps even more necessary, it has unfortunately in the past not always been supplied with sufficient generosity and many writers do not ply the full searchlight of methodic sincerity, as they move among their facts, but produce them before us out of complete obscurity. (Malinowski 1922:2–3)

Why is Malinowski's seventy-seven-year-old admonition so seldom heeded?

It is important at this juncture to point out that I am using the terms *science* and *scientific* in a particular way. For many people, *science* is synonymous with quantitative analyses employing an experimental model in which all variables can be controlled. The in situ study of human behavior can never employ such methods. Therefore, one is left with a choice: either characterize anthropology as something other than a science or define science in such a way as to include qualitatively derived knowledge and accept that some science is an interpretative rather than an "objective" endeavor. I choose to see anthropology as a social science that employs the scientific method but is also part of the humanities—a complexity that resides outside of this discussion.

An examination of ethnographic literature reveals a fairly consistent lack of systematic and rigorous statements about method and discussions of the relationship between the research and the researcher. Only in the past thirty years has this trend shifted slightly, beginning with the publication of Gerald Berreman's *Behind Many Masks* (1962) and followed in the 1970s by Jean Paul Dumont's *The Headman and I* (1978), Paul Rabinow's *Reflections on Fieldwork in Morocco* (1977), and Napoleon Chagnon's *Studying the Yanomamo* (1974). In the 1980s and 1990s, the work of Michael Jackson has been exemplary (1986, 1989, 1995). Although these and a number of other books (for example, Plattner 1996; Lavie 1990; Tsing 1993) mark an increase in reflexive work, Robert Bellah is unfortunately still accurate when he states that it is unusual to have anthropologists regard fieldwork as a serious object of study (Bellah in Rabinow 1977:ix). Even the interest in "ethnographies as texts" (Clifford and Marcus 1986) has concentrated on ethnographies as completed products and not on an exploration of the process of ethnographic investigation.

In an unpublished study of reflexive elements in written ethnography, Ben Miller (1977) has suggested that when methodological and personal statements are made, they are most likely to be found outside of the work—in introductory remarks or prefaces or postscripts. The tradition appears to have begun with Malinowski (1922). In spite of his admonition quoted earlier, Malinowski's own statements about his methods were rather perfunctory. How perfunctory Malinowski's remarks were only became clear when his diary was published in 1969. Another example is Gregory Bateson's 1936 seminal ethnography *Naven*, in which the work is bracketed with reflexive statements in the preface and postscript. Personal reflections are also found in traveloguelike, popularized autobiographical accounts of fieldwork that are clearly separated from the serious and scholarly ethnography. For example, David Maybury-Lewis, in his introduction to *The Savage and the Innocent*, states that "this book is an account of our experiences[;] . . . *it is not an essay in anthropology* [emphasis added]. Indeed I have tried to put down many of those things which never get told in technical anthropological writings—our impressions of Central Brazil, our personal reactions to the various situations in which we found ourselves, and above all, our feelings about the day-to-day business which is mysteriously known as 'doing fieldwork'" (Maybury-Lewis 1965:9). Other examples of this form of reflexivity would include Claude Lévi-Strauss's memoir *Tristes Tropiques* (1955); Alex Alland Jr.'s account of his fieldwork in Africa (1975); Hortense Powdermaker's professional autobiography, *Stranger and Friend* (1966); and Paul Rabinow's 1977 *Reflections on Fieldwork in Morocco*. Dell Hymes's comment on Robert Jay's article "Personal and Extrapersonal Vision in Anthropology" (1969) remains quite apt: "[S]till, these books are separate from the 'official' professional account of the work[;] . . . what is considered known and how it came to be known are still compartmentalized. We are not yet able, or willing, to explain the conditions of our knowledge, as is, say an experimenter in a laboratory. It is as if field work were two unrelated things—reportable knowledge and personal adventure—and to join the two consciously, let alone publicly, would damage both" (in Jay 1969:380).

This problem appears to plague ethnography whether accomplished by an anthropologist or a sociologist, as this quote from sociologist William Whyte points out:

There are now many good published studies of communities and organizations, but generally the published report gives little attention to the actual process whereby the research was carried out. There have also been some useful statements on methods of research, but, with few exceptions they place the discussion entirely on a logical-intellectual basis. They fail to note that the researcher, like his informant, is a social animal. He has a role to play, and he has his own personality needs that must be met in some degree if he is to function successfully. (1964:3)

Perhaps the most extreme form of separation of the reflexive elements from the ethnography is to be found in the writing of a novel about fieldwork under a pseudonym, as seen in Elenore Bowen's *Return to Laughter* (1954). In short, anthropologists who have wished to be reflexive and still report on their fieldwork in an acceptable manner have found it difficult to locate a form. Jules Henry decided to openly disregard these antinarrative conventions: "*The Jungle People* has a plot because the life of the Kaingang has one. Yet, since behavioral science views life as plotless, *The Jungle People* violates an underlying premise. Moreover, in the behavioral sciences, to state that life not only has a plot but must be described as if it did is like spitting in Church" (1964:xvii). Hymes has stated the conflict between the reporting of experience as a narrative ethnography and the scientifically acceptable communicative forms quite well: "There is an inescapable tension in ethnography between the forms, the rhetorical and literary forms, considered necessary for presentation (and persuasion of colleagues), and the narrative form natural to the experience of the work, and natural to the meaningful report of it in other than monographic contexts. I would even suggest that the scientific styles often imposed on ethnographic writing may produce, not objectivity, but distortion" (Hymes 1973:199–200).

In addition to an antinarrative tradition within the canons of a social-scientific communication discussed earlier, there are two additional strictures that further hinder any attempt to be reflexive. Social scientists are supposed to use the passive voice and the third person—for example, to say "Bows and arrows are made by the Bushmen" rather than "I saw some Bushmen make bows and arrows during the six months that I lived among them." The literary devices of the passive third person cause statements to appear to be authorless, authoritarian, objective, and hence in keeping with the prevailing positivist/empiricist philosophies of science. Despite the "literary turn" that some anthropologists have taken since the work of Clifford and Marcus (1986), first-person narrative ethnographies remain the exception rather than the rule.

The paradox that I have been discussing can be succinctly summarized as follows:

1. Most anthropologists consider themselves to be social scientists and therefore place their work within that tradition.

Exposing Yourself

2. To be scientific means that social scientists are obligated to systematically reveal their methods and any other factors that might affect the outcome of their research.
3. Most ethnographies lack an adequate and integrated statement of method.
4. Those statements of method that do exist are most frequently not attached to the ethnography.

Some social scientists do not see the situation as paradoxical. They feel that being reflexive about their methods is actually counterproductive to their goals. For example, John Honigmann advocates the acceptance of the "personal" approach in anthropological research but cautions:

Critics demanding a high degree of self-awareness of investigators using the personal approach are unrealistic. It is chimerical to expect that a person will be able to report the details of how he learned manifold types of information through various sensory channels and processed it through a brain that can typically bind many more associations far more rapidly than the most advanced, well-stocked computer. . . . Some of the individual factors operating in description can be brought into awareness and controlled, but a high degree of self-conscious attention to the process of description can only be maintained by scaling down the number and range of events that are to be studied, thereby possibly impoverishing the results while gaining a comparatively explicit account of how information was collected. (1976:243–46)

An excessive concern with either the producer or the process will obviously cause the focus of the product to turn inward. Total attention to the producer creates autobiography rather than ethnography. Such dangers of excess do not constitute an adequate argument against being reflexive. Anthropologists have spent most of their history denying the need for reflexivity and ignoring the scientific necessity for revealing their methods. As a consequence, a brief period of overcompensation is required. More extensive attempts to explore the implications of doing reflexive anthropology are necessary before conventions for "how much is enough" can be established. Questions of narcissism, of turning oneself into an object of contemplation, of becoming a character in your own ethnography are very fundamental and complex. Until there exists a tradition, albeit a minor one, of the ethnography of anthropology that Bob Scholte advocated in 1972, I think that it is premature to warn of the dangers and to caution against becoming excessive.

What anthropology has to offer society is primarily a systematic way of understanding the whole of humanity. Therefore, the processes that anthropologists evolve to accomplish that task may be their most significant contribution—teaching others to see human beings from an anthropological perspective. Anthropology has too long suffered from the popular assumption that it is "the study of oddments by eccentrics." As such, it is, at best, a source of trivial information and cocktail-party conversations like "Did Carlos Castenada really fabricate Don Juan?" or "Did Margaret Mead not understand the Samoans?" The concept of culture as a means of understanding our humanness is a powerful idea. Too bad anthropologists haven't conveyed it to more people in a way that they can apply to their lives. To hide the personas and the procedures of investigation from the public clearly lessens the impact. Regardless of whether one is convinced by arguments for or against the need for a full reflexive statement in every ethnography, there can be little argument about the fact that anthropologists tend to be remiss in fulfilling their social-scientific obligations to report on their methods.

I believe that the reason for this apparently self-contradictory behavior—that is, anthropologists' claiming to be social scientists and yet not behaving as if they were—is to be found in the implicit, taken-for-granted philosophical position of many U.S. anthropologists, which I would characterize as naive empiricism and/or positivism-pragmatism. By *naive empiricist*, I simply mean someone who "tends to believe that the world 'out there' is isomorphic in every respect with the image the detached observer will form of it" (Nash and Wintrob 1972:529). By *positivism*, I mean the idea "that, since experience is the sole source of knowledge, the methods of empirical science are the only means by which the world can be understood" (Stent 1975:1052). Or as Fabian has put it:

By positivist-pragmatist philosophy I mean a view of the social-scientific activity which acknowledges there are two criteria: a. Whatever truth may be found is equated with the *logical* flawlessness of theories generating testable propositions; b. The meaning of such knowledge is its success in "accounting for," "predicting," and generally giving evidence of the manipulability of data. What this orientation does not imply (at least not in any radical way) is a critique of the working of reason and of the factuality of facts. It is an approach in which methodology (the rules of correct and successful procedure) has taken the place of epistemology (reflection on the constitution of communicable knowledge). (1971:20)

These philosophies of science, which dominated the development of social science, cause social scientists to strive to be detached, neutral, unbiased, and objective toward the object of their study; to withhold value judgments; and to disavow political, economic, and even moral positions—in other words, to attempt to negate or lose all traces of their culture so that they can study someone else's culture. As Nash and Wintrob put it, the field-worker becomes "a self-effacing creature without any reactions other than those of a recording machine" (1972:527). Although postmodernism has had some impact on anthropology and thereby made positivism and a belief in objectivity less common, it has also created a backlash in which some now argue for a restoration of objectivity as a counter to the nihilism of cultural relativity (Megill 1994).

The problem is that the procedures developed to ensure the neutrality of the observer, and the control necessary for this type of research, were evolved in a science of subject/object relations, and not an anthropological science of subject/subject relations. In other words, setting aside any political or ethical considerations, it is simply not the case that one can make another human being into an object of study in the same way that one can control animals or inanimate objects.

I happen to believe that a positivist philosophy of science is a false one, but that is another matter that cannot be properly explored in this chapter. However, it should be stated that implicit in my position is that, at least for the social sciences, any philosophy of science that generates an objective/subjective dichotomy and that insists that scientists strive to be objective is producing a socially and scientifically dangerous false consciousness. This point of view, when attached to a naive empiricism and applied to pictorial representations, becomes perhaps the most powerful and dangerous political weapon of the twentieth century (Gross 1977). As Gunnar Myrdal suggested:

At this point of the argument it should be stated most emphatically that the fault in most contemporary as well as earlier social science research is not in its lack of "objectivity" in the conventional sense of independence from all valuations. On the contrary, every study of a social problem, however limited in scope, is and must be determined by valuations. A "disinterested" social science has never existed and, for logical reasons, can never exist. However, the value premises that actually and of necessity determine social science research are generally hidden. The student can even remain unaware of them. They are then left implicit and vague, leaving the door open to biases. (1969:55)

This conceptualization of science may be possible if one assumes that researchers exclusively use quantitative methods in controlled experimental settings. While anthropologists do employ quantitative methods, although seldom in labs, their chief claim to methodological fame and the primary method for doing ethnography is the most involved, nonstandardized, personal, attached version of qualitative methods—participant observation. Anthropologists recognized quite early that "the first means to the proper knowledge of the savages is to become after a fashion like one of them" (Degerando 1969 [1800]:70). Although anthropologists seldom talk about it publicly, all field-workers know that "in the field the researcher becomes trapped in the role of power broker, economic agent, status symbol, healer, voyeur, advocate of special interests, manipulator, critic, secret agent, friend or foe" (Konrad 1977:920).

Anthropologists who subscribe to a naive empiricist/positivist view of science and practice participant observation in their fieldwork find themselves in a double bind. Since participant observation causes the researcher to become the primary instrument of data generation, his or her own behavior and basic assumptions, the interactional settings where research is conducted, and so forth, all now become data to be analyzed and reported upon. One is almost forced to the conclusion that "an ethnography is the reflective product of an individual's extended experience in (usually) an exotic society mediated by other experiences, beliefs, theories, techniques (including objective procedures when they are used), personal ideology, and the historical moment in which the work was done" (Honigmann 1976:259).

The more ethnographers attempt to fulfill their scientific obligation to articulate their methods, the more they must acknowledge that their own behavior and persona in the field are data. Their methodological statements then begin to appear to be more and more personal, subjective, biased, involved, and culture-bound—in other words, *the more scientific anthropologists try to be by revealing their methods, the less scientific they appear to be.*

Given that dilemma, it is not too difficult to see why most anthropologists have been less than candid about their methods. They are justifiably concerned that their audience will realize that, as Sue-Ellen Jacobs has said, "perhaps the best thing we learn from anthropological writings is how people who call themselves anthropologists see the world of others, whoever the others may be" (quoted in Chinngu 1976:469). It is asking anthropologists to reverse their traditional assumption about the ultimate goals of anthropology and to suggest instead that what anthropology has to offer is a chance to see the native through the eyes of the anthropologist. Hence, most anthropologists would rather live with the dilemma than explore the implications of being reflexive.

When faced with this problem, some anthropologists simply retreat behind slogans like "Anthropology is a soft science" or "Anthropology is actually a humanities with scientific pretensions." Novelist Kurt Vonnegut Jr. has summed up that position nicely in a recollection of his own graduate-student days at the University of Chicago:

I began with physical anthropology. I was taught how to measure the size of the brain of a human being who had been dead a long time, who was all dried out. I bored a hole in his skull, and I filled it with grains of polished rice. Then I emptied the rice into a graduated cylinder. I found this tedious.

I switched to archaeology, and I learned something I already knew; that man had been a maker and smasher of crockery since the dawn of time. And I went to my faculty adviser, and I confessed that science did not charm me, that I longed for poetry instead. I was depressed. I knew my wife and my father would want to kill me, if I went into poetry.

My adviser smiled. "How would you like to study poetry which *pretends* to be scientific?" he asked me.

"Is such a thing possible?" I said.

He shook my hand. "Welcome to the field of social or cultural anthropology," he said. He told me that Ruth Benedict and Margaret Mead were already in it—and some sensitive gentlemen as well. (1974:176)

Some anthropologists have been seeking a solution to the problem (Honigmann 1976; Nash and Wintrob 1972). The reasons for this renewed interest (renewed in the sense that Mead, Bateson, and others actually started in the 1930s, but the interest died out) beginning in the 1970s and increasing ever since are complex and probably have their origins outside anthropology in the culture at large. Nash and Wintrob list four factors for the emergence of what they call "self-consciousness" in anthropology: (1) an increasing personal involvement of ethnographers with their subjects; (2) the "democratization" of anthropology (that is a polite way of saying that some lower-middle-class students who got Ph.D.'s in the 1960s didn't share some of the class assumptions of the older anthropologists); (3) multiple field studies of the same culture; and (4) assertions of independence by native peoples (1972:529).

To those factors, I would add: (1) the influence of other disciplines, particularly the effect of phenomenological and symbolic interactional sociology and ethnomethodology and the postmodern turn; (2) the development of Marxist criticism of anthropology in the United States—a criticism aimed at an examination of anthropology as an ideology; and (3) the rise of an urban anthropology concerned with doing ethnography in the United States—the complexity of the subject matter has caused some researchers to question such fundamental ideas as culture. These concerns became narrowly focused by some anthropologists who dwelled upon the "crisis of representation" and a literary analysis of ethnographies (Clifford and Marcus 1986). These scholars tended to ignore the history of self-critical and self-conscious tendencies within anthropology, the contribution of ethnographic filmmakers like Jean Rouch, and the broader picture as well. They also failed to deal with ethnography as a process of knowledge production. In the process, they have not addressed some of the core concerns voiced in this chapter.

The problem, stated in its simplest form, is to find a way to satisfy the demands of social science to be reflexive about the methods employed and do anthropology, or in other words, to resolve the conflict between what anthropologists say and what they do. A solution can be found within the already existing works of some philosophers of science and some anthropologists who began experimenting with these idea in the 1960s and 1970s. Since a full explication of these ideas would require a book-length treatment, they will only be superficially described here.

Thomas Kuhn's idea (1962) about the role of the paradigm in science is an excellent place to begin—that is, with the recognition that scientific knowledge is the product of the particular paradigm of the moment and that science changes through the process of discovering the inadequacy of the old paradigm and subsequently creating a new one. The argument presented here and elsewhere (for example, Fabian 1971) has suggested that the old paradigm of positivism and empiricism is insufficient as a means of dealing with some of the questions being asked in contemporary anthropology. We are in need of a new paradigm that is openly interpretative and admits to its own limitations.

Although the sources for this new paradigm are many and varied, I will mention only two of the most obvious—Clifford Geertz and Margaret Mead. From Geertz (1973) comes the notion of anthropology as an interpretative science, where ethnography is "thick description" or an analytic description in which data and theory cannot be separated, but rather the theory is regarded as the origin of data generation. In other words, one regards data not as a property of entities but rather as an artifact of the questions one is researching.

Anthropologists have not always been as aware as they might be of this fact that although culture exists in the trading post, the hill fort, or the sheep run, anthropology exists in the book, the article, the lecture, the museum display, *or sometimes nowadays, the film* [emphasis added]. To become aware of it is to realize that the line between mode of representation and substantive content is as undrawable in cultural analysis as it is in painting; and that fact in turn seems to threaten the objective status of anthropological knowledge by suggesting that its source is not social reality but scholarly artifice. It does threaten it, but the threat is hollow. The claim to attention of an ethnographic account does not rest on its author's ability to capture primitive facts in faraway places and carry them home like a mask or a carving, but on the degree to which he is able to clarify what goes on in such places, to reduce the puzzlement— what manner of men are these?—to which unfamiliar acts emerging out of unknown backgrounds naturally give rise. This raises some serious problems of verification, all right—or if "verification" is too strong a word for so soft a science (I, myself, would prefer "appraisal"), of how you can tell a better account from a worse one. But that is precisely the virtue of it. If ethnography is thick description and ethnographers those who are doing the describing, then the determining question for any given example of it, whether a field journal squib or a Malinowski-sized monograph, is whether it sorts winks from twitches and real winks from mimicked ones. It is not against a body of uninterpreted data, radically thinned descriptions, that we must measure the cogency of our explications, but against the power of the scientific imagination to bring us into touch with the lives of strangers. It is not worth it, as Thoreau said, to go round the world to count the cats in Zanzibar. (Geertz 1973:16)

Margaret Mead, in her 1976 presidential address to the American Association for the Advancement of Science, offers a resolution of the old apparent conflict between science and humanities through the development of a human science capable of justifying within science both quantitative and qualitative knowledge:

It is in the sciences of living things that we find the greatest confusion but also the clearest demonstrations of the ways in which the two kinds of observation—the observation of human beings by human beings and of physical nature by human beings—meet. One group of students of living beings have attempted to adopt as far as possible the methods of the physical sciences through the use of controlled experiments, the deliberate limitation of the number of variables to be considered, and the construction of theories based on the findings arrived at by these means. The other group, taking their cues from our human capacity to understand through the observation of natural situations, have developed their methods from a natural history approach in which the principal reliance is on the integrative powers of the observer of a complex, nonreplicable event and on the experiments that are provided by history and by animals living in a particular ecological setting. . . . I would argue that it is not by rejecting one or the other but by appropriately combining the several methods evolved from these different types of search for knowledge that we are most likely in the long run to achieve a kind of scientific activity that is dominated neither by the arrogance of physical scientists nor by the arrogance of humanists who claim that the activities which concerned them cannot meaningfully be subjected to scientific inquiry. (Mead 1976:908)

Both the methods of science and the conflict of views about their more general applicability were developed within Euro-American culture and it is never easy to break out of such deeply felt but culturally bound conceptions. Because of the clarity that now has been achieved I believe we can move from conflict toward a new kind of integration.

As a first step in this direction I suggest that it is necessary to recognize that our knowledge of ourselves and of the universe within which we live comes not from a single source but, instead from two sources—from our capacity to explore events in which we and others participate through introspection and empathy, as well as from our capacity to make defensible observations about physical and animate nature. (Mead 1976:905)

Looked at together, these ideas form themselves into a definition of science in general and, more specifically, of anthropology as a social science that can account for and accommodate what anthropologists actually do—that is, a humanistic and an interpretative science of humankind that acknowledges the necessity of quantitative and qualitative methods; a science that can accept the inherently reflexive relationship between the producer, process, and product and the active role the viewer/reader has in the construction of meaning; a science founded on the idea that facts do not organize themselves into concepts and theories just by being looked at; indeed, except within the framework of concepts and theories, there are no scientific facts but only chaos. There is an inescapable a priori element in all scientific work. Questions must be asked before answers can be given. The questions are all expressions of our interest in the world; they are, at bottom, valuations. Valuations are thus necessarily involved already at the stage when we observe facts and carry on theoretical analysis, and not only at the stage when we draw political inferences from facts and valuations (Myrdal 1953:ix–xvi). Science is reflexive in the sense that the facts it explains refer back to the system in which they are explained. "Science is not static. Its development is determined to a great extent by the body of science as it stands at any given moment. This determinism is not one of a natural progression to a greater and greater number of known facts built on those previously discovered. It is rather one in which the fundamental principles, the structures in a broad sense, determine the nature of [the] search for the facts and finally, to some extent, the facts themselves. So science, which describes the world, also determined the world which it described" (Labrot 1977:7).

Logically, this point of view causes anthropology to be regarded as "not only a general set of general statements about mankind, it is also the product of a particular culture with its history of ideas proper to itself; its formulations are culturally committed and in major part determined" (Krader 1968:885). Once it is recognized that anthropologists ask research questions about the cultural world based on their overt theoretical positions and less conscious cultural assumptions, and that once the questions are asked in a particular way, there is a logical way to generate data and an equally logical way to present the analytic descriptions called ethnographies, then the necessity of publicly disclosing the entire process just outlined becomes inescapable. As Anthony Wilden suggests, "[P]sychology, anthropology and the social sciences, in general, have repeatedly falsified their observations by *unrecognized* [emphasis added] epistemological and ideological closures imposed on the system under study" (1972:389). As I have stated before, a complete exploration of the relationships among reflexivity, science, and anthropology would require a book-length treatment, which hopefully someone will someday undertake. For the moment, I can only assert my belief that being reflexive is virtually synonymous with being a proper social scientist and doing proper anthropology. Such a position logically leads toward a productive attitude about film and anthropology.

Reflexivity and Anthropological Film

I will now explore the implications of reflexivity for an anthropological cinema. It is particularly important for the discussion that follows to remember that in this book, anthropology is viewed as an ideological system (ideological not in the Marxist sense but as a system of ideas) and film as a medium for communication that can be used to convey the knowledge created with that system. Film is not being regarded primarily as an art form (Worth 1966). Anthropology is a method of constructing knowledge, and film is a potential vehicle for conveying that knowledge. Although this discussion excludes the experimental, avant-garde, and art film to concentrate on the documentary/ethnographic film, I argue in the introduction and final chapter that the future of an anthropological cinema may lie with an eclectic borrowing from fiction and art films rather than a slavish adherence to the norms of the documentary. Ironically, it is the art film that has been reflexive since its inception and the documentary that has been associated with positivism. Yet anthropologists have always assumed that the latter was the appropriate form of cinema to use and that the former had no relevance for anthropology.

Cinema and anthropology have a parallel history and development. They came from the same nineteenth-century Euro-American intellectual and cultural foundations. The cinema has four conceptual origins: (1) it is a device to tell stories (that is, it performs a narrative function), as seen in the early films of Thomas Edison and Edwin S. Porter, such as *A Day in the Life of an American Fireman* (1903); (2) it is a device of fantasy and art, as seen in the works of the conjurer George Méliés—for example, *A Trip to the Moon* (1902); (3) it is a device to capture everyday events in the lives of people—some ordinary and some exotic—as seen in the works of Louis and Auguste Lumiéré, such as *The Workers Leaving the Lumiéré Factory* (1895–97); and (4) it is a device to study movement through space and time, as seen in the protocinematic works of Eadweard Muybridge and Félix-Louis Regnault (see chapter 1 for details).

It is from categories three and four that the documentary, the travelogue, and the ethnographic film emerged. These film genres and written ethnography are culturally related. They were founded upon the Western middle-class need to explore, document, explain, understand, and hence, symbolically control the world, or at least that part of the world the middle class regards as being exotic. Ethnography and the documentary film are what the West does to the rest of humanity. "The rest" in this case are frequently the poor, the powerless, the disadvantaged, and the politically and economically suppressed. An anthropology of the rich and the powerful or even the middle class is as sparse as documentary films that deal with this subject. The exotic and the pathological remain the focus of most social science and documentary film.

Not only are ethnography and documentary films similar in their origins and subject matter, but they have similar goals and methods. Robert Flaherty, the U.S. founder of the documentary, and Bronislaw Malinowski, the father of modern anthropological field methods, started using participant observation in their fieldwork at the same time and with no apparent knowledge of each other's work (see chapter 2 for details). What is interesting is that Edward Curtis, a man who devoted most of his life to photographing Native Americans, also appears to have discovered participant observation at about the same time as Flaherty and Malinowski. In his diary, Curtis wrote:

Any account of another people, their daily lives, beliefs and troubles is bound to some extent to be subjective, especially when one has shared that way of life. The value of my work, in great measure, will lie in the breadth of its treatment. . . . While primarily a photographer, I do not see or think photographically; instead I have sought to bring art and science together in an effort to reach beneath the surface of what appears to be. . . . What are these people? How shall I manage the portraits and the handling of life? Conditions cannot be changed. I must fit myself to them. It became clear to me that I couldn't make my pictures unless I entered into their inner life, and understood it from their standpoint, not merely as an outside specta-tor. . . . Without the knowledge of their political and religious life, however, one cannot do the picture work well.[4]

Moreover, all three expressed a concern that their work should somehow al-low the lives of the people they studied to shine through. Malinowski's *Arg-onauts of the Western Pacific* (1922) and Flaherty's *Nanook of the North* (1923) began a half-century of parallel development.

It is therefore not surprising that reflexive elements begin to appear in doc-umentary film about the same time as they do in written anthropology. Berre-man's *Behind Many Masks*, a work already mentioned as one of the first systematic attempts to deal reflexively with fieldwork, appeared in 1962. Jean Rouch and Edgar Morin's film *Chronicle of a Summer*, perhaps the first reflex-ive social-science film, was released in the same year. In fact, the parallel is even closer. Bateson and Mead's written and photographic work in the 1930s (Bateson 1936; Bateson and Mead 1942) is among the earliest methodologi-cally self-aware anthropology. By and large, it failed to have the influence that it should have had. It is paralleled in documentary film by the work of Dziga Vertov. His films of the 1920s and 1930s also failed to affect other documen-tarians until they were "rediscovered" along with Flaherty's *Nanook* by Jean Rouch in the 1960s.

I am excluding from consideration the thousands of adventure/travelogue films that have been produced from the beginning of the cinema to the present day. The makers of these films frequently employ first-person narrations to describe themselves as authors and the process they used to make the film. In many cases, these films are primarily about the making of the films and thereby cause the films themselves to become the object of the audience's at-tention. However, like fiction films about movies and moviemakers such as François Truffaut's *Day for Night* (1973) or Robert Altman's *The Player* (1992) or Mike Rubbo's documentaries *Waiting for Fidel* (1973) and *The Sad Song of Yellow Skin* (1970), the apparent reflexiveness of these films only serves to per-petuate the myths of the genre. That is, the audience's interest in these films is partially based on the assumed difficulties of production and the heroic acts performed by the makers in the process of getting the footage. These films do not lead an audience to a sophisticated understanding of film as communica-tion but rather cause them to continue to marvel at the autobiographical exploits of the intrepid adventurer-filmmakers as "cinema stars."

In the 1920s, Vertov developed a theory of film in opposition to that of

Sergi Eisenstein and the other proponents of fiction film. Vertov argued that the role of film in a revolutionary society should be to raise the consciousness of the audience by creating a film style that caused them to see the world in Marxist ways. The kino eye (the camera eye) would produce kino pravda (cine truth). For Vertov, the artifices of fiction only produced entertainment—escape and fantasies. True revolutionary filmmakers should take pictures of actuality—the everyday events of ordinary people. This raw stuff of life could then be transformed into meaningful statements. Although Vertov was not intentionally doing social science, his interests and procedures sound strikingly like those of the ethnographer.

In his film *A Man with a Movie Camera*, Vertov attempted to explicate his theory (Vertov 1972). He was more concerned with revealing process than with revealing the producer. Vertov wished the audience to understand how film works—in a mechanical, technical, methodological, as well as conceptual way, thereby demystifying the creative process. He also wanted audiences to know that filmmaking is work and the filmmaker, a worker—a very important justification for film and filmmakers in Leninist Russia. We see the filmmaker in the film, but he is more a part of the process than anything else. One of Vertov's major goals was to aid the audience in their understanding of the process of construction in film so that they could develop a sophisticated and critical attitude. Vertov saw this raising of audiences' visual consciousness as the way to bring Marxist truth to the masses. Like the French filmmaker Jean-Luc Godard (who at one point in his career formed a Dziga Vertov film collective), Vertov wished to make revolutionary films that intentionally taught audiences how to see the world in a different way. To locate this idea in contemporary terminology (after Worth and Gross 1981), Vertov is suggesting that in order to be able to make the assumption of intention and then to make inferences, viewers must have structural competence—that is, have knowledge of the sociocultural conventions related to making inferences of meaning in filmic sign events. In other words, Vertov was being reflexive. Scholars interested in ethnographic film ought to become familiar with Marxist film theorists like Sergi Eisenstein, Vsevolod Pudovkin, Dziga Vertov, and Jean-Luc Godard because of the parallel between the development of a Marxist cinema and the development of an anthropological cinema. Marxist thinkers have been the leaders in the study and uses of ideology in communicative form. For example, Eisenstein tried to transform the Hegelian dialectic into a rationalization for his montages. If one regards anthropology as an ideology that causes one to perceive the human condition in a particular way, then Godard's statement that he wishes to make revolutionary films, not films about revolution, can be easily transformed into a dictum for ethnographic filmmakers. I have argued elsewhere (Ruby 1975) that too often, ethnographic filmmakers make films about anthropology but not anthropological films.

Jean Rouch (1974) is one of the few visual anthropologists who is overtly concerned with creating a cinematic form that is peculiarly suited for anthropological expression. His film *Chronicle of a Summer,* produced in collaboration with Edgar Morin, a sociologist, and several professional filmmakers, like *A Man with a Movie Camera,* represents an attempt to give shape to an idea. Rouch was concerned primarily with the personal and philosophical problems of doing research and the possible effects of filming research. He is also interested in form. But questions about the formal aspects of structure come from his concern with the self more than from Vertov's concern with process. Not only has Rouch continued to explore the issues surrounding reflexivity in his later films, like *Madame l'Eau* (1992), but he has also been the subject of two films both dedicated to exploring his cinema—*Rouch's Gang* (1990) and *Jean Rouch with His Camera in the Heart of Africa* (1992).

Both *Chronicle* and *Man with a Movie Camera* were ahead of their time. Vertov had to wait for Rouch to come along almost a quarter of a century later before someone would pursue the questions raised by *A Man with a Movie Camera.* Rouch (1974) has said that he sees his own films as being an attempt to combine the personal and participatory concerns of Robert Flaherty with an interest in process derived from Vertov. Morin, Rouch's collaborator, once described *Chronicle of a Summer* as being *cinéma vérité* in emulation of Vertov's kino pravda.

Rouch's influence in France has been extensive. Chris Marker's *Le Joli Mai* (1964) is a direct response to *Chronicle.* Rouch has had an acknowledged impact on all of the New Wave directors. In the United States, only a few of his films are shown regularly, and some of his seminal work is almost never seen. His work is frequently confused with that of such American direct cinema people as Donn Pennebaker, Richard Leacock, and the Maysles brothers. The distinction between American direct cinema films like Ricky Leacock and Donn Pennebaker's *Salesman* (1969) and *cinéma vérité* films like *Chronicle of a Summer* is the difference between observational and participatory style, or to use the outmoded terms, objective versus subjective style.

It is interesting to note that some U.S. anthropologists who have seen Rouch's work seem to distrust it because he employs an overtly narrative form and disregards some of the conventions of documentary film and, undoubtedly, because urban anthropology was too exotic for most people in the early sixties. *Chronicle of a Summer* is about Paris, not some unclothed native exotics. The confusion over what might be called the "ethnographicness" of *Chronicle of a Summer* has continued to the present and can be found even among people who know ethnographic film well. For example, Karl Heider, in comparing *Chronicle* to Rouch's other films, raises doubts about its anthropological appropriateness: "Rouch himself made some dozen other more obviously ethnographic films" (1976:40); and yet elsewhere in his book, Heider praises the film: "*Chronicle of a Summer* is a richly provocative film in the extent to which it reveals the methodological mystery of ethnography, but as yet no other ethnographic films have risen to its challenge" (1976:60). What was true in 1976 sadly remains true today.

Since Rouch's experiment, few ethnographic filmmakers have pursued the questions raised in *Chronicle of a Summer*. Along with Gregory Bateson and Margaret Mead's photographic and film studies of Bali in the 1930s, which were structured in the form of a scientific research report with a bibliography at the end, these films represent the beginning of reflexive visual anthropology. Unfortunately, few U.S. anthropologists saw the implications of this work, and consequently few pursued it, although Kwame Braun's *passing girl/riverside an essay on camera work* (1996), a meditation on image making, does carry on some of Rouch's ideas. Until very recently, the development of a reflexive cinema has been solely the work of fiction and a few documentary filmmakers like Jill Godmillow in *Far from Poland* (Ruby 1977), even though Rouch, an anthropologist, pioneered the movement and even though ethnographic filmmakers had no means within their films to describe their methods.

In 1975, Tim Asch produced a post hoc reflexive film, *The Ax Fight*, which I discuss in some detail in chapter 4. I characterize it as being post hoc reflexive because it was not conceived of or shot as an experiment in reflexivity. It became transformed into a reflexive film when Asch discovered that he lacked sufficient footage to edit the film in the manner he wished. It is nonetheless one of the most remarkable reflexive ethnographic films. The two ethnographic films that Barbara Myerhoff made with filmmaker Lynn Littman, *Number Our Days* (1977) and *In Her Own Time* (1985), are excellent examples of the difference between films that reveal the ethnographer and the process of making an ethnography while remaining silent about the processes of production—that is, they are personal and autobiographical but not reflexive. Myerhoff never properly explored what I would regard as her romanticized attachment to the people she was studying in *Number Our Days* and only was able to begin the process of being reflexive in *In Her Own Time* when she was dying.

There is one interesting attempt that was designed to explore the parameters of filmic reflexivity—a rare instance, in fact. Hubert Smith, a documentary filmmaker whose earlier films on the Aymara attracted the attention of some anthropologists, obtained funds from the National Endowment for the Humanities in the late 1970s to make a series of documentaries for public television on a group of lowland Maya. In the process of making these films, he was also to explore the implications of reflexivity to enhance the value of such films. He hired an anthropologist familiar with the area and the Mayan language as a collaborator. He also put together a panel of Mayanists and people interested in the development of ethnographic film—Richard Sorenson, Margaret Mead, and myself among them. The panelists were to be active consultants during the preparation for the fieldwork and were to meet with the film team to look at and discuss some of the early footage at a midpoint in the fieldwork and then again after all of the film/fieldwork was completed. The panelists' meetings were filmed and were to be included in the final film. On paper, this sounded like an ideal situation in which to field-test some of the ideas I have espoused in this chapter. I believed the project had the potential to significantly advance the concept of reflexivity. It occurred at the time I was writing the original article that eventually became this chapter.

For a number of complicated reasons, the project never realized its potential. In fact, the opposite happened. Conflicts between the filmmaker and the anthropologist caused the situation to deteriorate rapidly. The anthropologist either resigned or was fired—depends on whom you talked to. He was replaced with a Mayan fluent in Spanish but untrained in anthropology. The filming was completed without the benefit of any trained anthropologists. In the editing, Smith made a decision that destroyed the possibility that this work would mark an advance in reflexivity. He decided to erase the anthropologist and the conflict that he had with him and chose not to address the issues raised by this turn of events. Instead of reflexively exploring the complexities of collaboration and conflict in the field, he created a fiction that his Mayan interpreter had been with him from the beginning instead of joining him during the last weeks of the work. He did so because of the possibility of the "fired" anthropologist's taking legal action if he appeared in the film, because he was uncomfortable about what had actually happened, and because he thought that the inclusion of this material would detract from the real subject of the film, the lowland Maya.

As the project progressed, it became clear to me that the motivation behind Smith's desire to film the Maya was an unsophisticated and romantic attachment to peasant life. Smith thought that by being open to the panelists at the two meetings and eventually to the viewers, his reflexivity would be rewarded and the quality of his film enhanced. The opposite happened: some panelists found Smith's romantic attachment to the joys of peasant life to be superficial. The footage of the panel meetings was never used. I continued to try to convince him that being open about the conflicts and difficulties would make the film richer and more complex. When Smith refused to deal with these complexities, I resigned as consultant and demanded that my name be removed from the credits. Other consultants did also, but for other reasons. In a cosmically ironic fashion, a project designed to push the limits of filmic reflexivity ended up producing a film in which the historical development of the work is denied through the creation of a fictive chronology that gives the viewer a false impression. The remaining moments of reflexivity, mainly images of the filmmaker, hide more than they reveal. It is a good example of how the appearance of being reflexive can deceive just as easily as "objective" style.

In an attempt to be reflexive about my reflexivity, I sent a draft of this chapter to Hubert Smith. I include most of his lengthy response because the lowland Maya film project remains one of the few designed to explore filmic reflexivity:

Jay Ruby remains disappointed with my project but has been both gracious and true to an intellectual ideal in offering me an opportunity to disagree with his opinions. I, too, was disappointed with aspects of the work but, in the service of reflexiveness, the reader should know the enterprise was not, as Jay recalls, "organized from the inception to explore the parameters of filmic reflexivity."

The brief history is as follows: While my films on the Aymara may have "attracted the attention of some anthropologists," my 1968 film on a handicapped black woman attracted Jay's attention—some seven years prior to the Aymara work. Jay told me I was behaving like an anthropologist and, through him, I began to affiliate with a field which had codified purposeful observation. Jay became a friend and something of a patron and mentor.

Between 1960 and 1968 I worked on a documentary technique which leaned heavily on long-term observation. In 1969 I had begun occasional study and filming in Yucatan. I concentrated on traditional economic and religious structures within a rapidly modernizing Mexico. In 1975 I submitted a proposal for a television documentary on culture change in the lowland Maya to the National Endowment for the Humanities. That proposal was rejected but NEH came back to me asking if I could and would incorporate reflexiveness in my film yet retain PBS broadcast as its ultimate goal.

If the Endowment's unusual proposition was not influenced by Jay's ideas, it certainly offered a happy conjunction of his concepts with a ready test vehicle. To be sure, I was eager to incorporate reflexiveness and the new proposal was funded. I also published papers and moderated forums on the reflexive idea.

It is important to note that my collaborator and the advisory panel had been established before the first proposal was made. But everyone willingly took up the notion of the reflexive component even if their ideas about it were indistinct. At that time even Jay will concede his concepts were in their infancy.

The type of filming I did and which NEH and its readers obviously liked was dynamic. That is, we observed subjects going about their lives and, as possible, positioned our cameras and recorders to construct pictures and sound good enough to be screened on national television. Integrating reflexive material would demand a high level of acuity and not a little risk. That we would spend long stretches in tropical heat just made the work more demanding.

But my filmmaking methodology isn't typical of anthropological methodology. Many anthropologists elicit data, often with interviews rather than observation. When there are language difficulties, as is often the case, what is missed may be hammered out or sought the next day with nothing lost. Too, they are accustomed to assembling their data and analyzing it in relative calm. They publish after due care and deliberation are applied.

During a month-long trial run in Yucatan it appeared to me we were in trouble. Some of it had to do with my collaborator's difficulty making necessary adjustments to the conventional

Exposing Yourself

anthropologist's role. There were other issues as well, separate but serious, which made for major complications in the programmed six months of shooting. Despite considerable effort I never resolved these problems.

Finally, with less than two of our six months remaining, I moved a native-born Yucateco translator on to the three-person filming team. My collaborator went to work on a backlog of project research he'd been asking me for time to complete. Our film work immediately improved and I began to see the possibility of delivering what I'd promised.

What Jay terms "firing" the collaborator was actually the man's resignation which, after some unfortunate incidents, I could not allow him to rescind. Jay regrets the filming being completed "without the benefit of a trained anthropologist." I regret not having footage of reflexive insight and power that would undoubtedly have made the series more precise and engrossing.

Why do I stress the critical nature of enacting reflexivity within the filmic context? The Maya were inherently "the topic," interesting by their very nature. Audiences would want [us] North Americans to justify our intrusions. Unless these were timely and artful, we would be "noise" and the audience would depart. I find Jay Ruby's ideas about reflexivity to be compelling. I don't think he presents adequate rubrics for making them available on a certain type of film.

Once out of the field my editor and I screened the entire film corpus including the panel meetings. The collaboration showed a lot of confusion and pointless jockeying but almost no reflexive insights about our work or the Maya. The footage of the advisory panel was often fascinating but it belonged in another film. I concluded that, if used, these elements would send audiences away with words on their lips on the order of, "What in the name of heaven were those people thinking of?"

Jay laments "erasing" the collaborator and creating a "fictive chronology." So do I, but I don't regret it.

In my final product, a four-part series titled "Living Maya," the filmmaking process is indeed documented. Moreover, the relationship between filmmakers and subjects is evident. To that extent I find the series valid and unique in terms of visible authorship. It is true, as Jay observes, my own perceptions and biases are not challenged. On the other hand they were examined by some original and some new panelists. (Besides Jay Ruby a couple of original panelists also quit, largely over conflict with me about re-hiring the collaborator.)

However, if Jay thinks challenges were raised in the field to good effect and then excised, I disagree. And in fact, all the material has been available to him or any scholar for more than a decade. Since he regrets my not "exploring the complexities of collaboration and conflict in the field," perhaps he will write a successful grant to make that *other* film.

My films remain singular documents about the lowland Maya. They were seen on PBS and, in a condensed form, by countless students in the anthropology telecourse, "Faces of Culture." It is 1998 and I still have a home in that same Maya community and continue to film there in occasional collaboration with an anthropologist. These later films join the original corpus in the Human Studies Film Archives of the Smithsonian Institution.

Jay observes "no ethnographic filmmaker since Smith has attempted to systematically explore reflexivity." When I saw that sentence in his text my first thought was, "I wonder why?" But in fact it is regrettable. The anthropological view is an inspired avenue to explaining humankind. Filmic reflexiveness is a thorny but valuable and entirely feasible enterprise. Perhaps this book will advance it. (Hubert Smith, personal communication, 1998)

As Smith states, no ethnographic filmmaker since him has attempted to systematically explore reflexivity. In fact, an examination of the majority of the research footage and publicly released films made by or in association with anthropologists reveals a consistent lack of statements of method within the films or footage. It would appear that the paradox noted earlier for written anthropology is also to be found in visual anthropology. In fact, the analogy is a very precise one. The reflexive/methodological statements that do exist are to be found *outside* the films in written articles such as Asen Balikci and Quentin Brown's description of the Netsilik Eskimo film project (1966) or in study guides that are supposed to be used in conjunction with a film; for example, Heider's study guide for the film *Dead Birds* (1972).

Ethnographic filmmakers have experienced this paradox for the same reasons that their print-oriented brethren did, and moreover, their taken-for-granted assumptions about image-producing technologies (which are a consequence of their positivist/empiricist views) help to reinforce the paradox. Or to put it another way, the prevailing notions about the role of image-producing technologies serve to extend the scientific dilemmas created by positivist/empiricist frameworks in anthropology.

Based on an examination of the films and written literature available, it would appear that, with the exception of Jean Rouch, many filmmakers who purport to be making ethnographic films are naive empiricists and positivists. Like journalists and documentary filmmakers, they seem concerned with discovering ways of objectively recording data, or "what happens," free from the distortions of personal bias, subjectivity, or theory. They believe that the camera, properly handled, is the best means of accomplishing this task. They subscribe to the unsubstantiated folk belief that cameras, when unmanipulated, can't lie. Although the number of filmmakers who subscribe to these ideas may have diminished since I wrote the original article, I contend that this point of view still dominates.

Margaret Mead has most clearly articulated the position that image-producing technologies, when handled in a certain manner, produce inherently more reliable, measurably superior, and more objective data than other techniques. In fact, Mead has stated that these technologies are the best means of establishing the human sciences as a science containing verifiable data (Mead 1976): "If tape recorder, camera, or video is set up and left in the same place, large batches of material can be collected without the intervention of the filmmaker or ethnographer and without the continuous self-consciousness of those who are being observed. The camera or tape recorder that stays in one spot, that is not tuned, wound, refocused, or visibly loaded, does become part of the background scene, and what it records did happen" (Mead 1975:10).

A static camera mounted on a tripod that does not tilt, pan, zoom, or in any way move is assumed to be the most "scientific" technique and one that is less distorting and more "truthful" in the recording of "natural" behavior than other camera techniques. Moreover, the camera must be allowed to run as long as possible and used in as unobtrusive a manner as possible so that it records unaffected streams of culturally significant behavior. It would appear that the majority of the authors in the first (1975) as well as the second edition (1995) of Paul Hockings's *Principles of Visual Anthropology* agree with Mead's position. I will give only a few examples from the first edition. As all of these essays except Alexei Peterson's are included in the 1995 edition, it can be assumed that Hockings believes they represent a contemporary position. John Collier Jr. stated that "camera observations offer accuracy of identification and objective detail upon which to base judgments" (1975:221). Joseph Schaeffer felt that "[a]lthough extensive audiovisual records are subject to scientific fashion their appropriate production can alleviate its effect. If such records include sufficient data, they can be analyzed by researchers with varied interests either at the same time or at different points in time" (1975:279). Peterson believed that "[t]he less interference on the part of the filming team the more natural is the process on film" (1975:197). And Mark McCarty, in describing an unobtrusive camera style that he was advocating, said, "But after a time, the rewards are gratifying—you begin to get material that is simple, natural, and unaffected by the camera's presence" (1975:50).

These assumptions about the use of the camera are valid from the positivist viewpoint. If one assumes that there is an objectively meaningful world that can be empirically verified and that meaning inherently resides in phenomena, then the role of scientists is to discover it, not impose their interpretation on it, or if they do, to clearly separate their interpretation from the data. Given those assumptions, the camera can record reality through truthful and meaningful images of the world.

However, this method of camera use produces the same dilemma as its print equivalent: it leaves no room for the producer or the process or the audience in the creation of meaning. To introduce any of these into the frame would detract from the purpose of using a camera in the first place—that is, to record reality unobtrusively. So the ethnographic filmmaker has not been able to explicate his or her methodology. To do so would "disrupt" the "natural" flow of cultural events that are supposed to be recorded. It would introduce the apparently "subjective" presence of the researcher into the "objective" recording of data.

The problem of being both a social scientist and a filmmaker is further complicated when we undertake an examination of what happens to the footage once it is shot. Many people in Western culture, anthropologists included, regard film—all genres, whether fictional or documentary—as basically an art form. Heider has expressed this sentiment: "Cinema has developed primarily as a medium for imaginative statements in which questions of scientific-type accuracy are often irrelevant. Much of what is taught in film schools is how to translate or distort reality for aesthetic effect" (1976:7). It is commonly believed that the "art" of filmmakers occurs when they "manipulate" reality to serve their own particular expressive ends. This "manipulation"—or distortion, as Heider calls it—can happen at three points in the process of making a film: (1) in front of the camera through the intrusion of the maker—either with scripts and actors, as in a fiction film, or through the participation of the maker in the cultural scene being recorded; (2) in the use of camera style and techniques to express the filmmaker's view and not to simply record; and (3) in the use of editing to further distort what has been recorded and subjectively and aesthetically express the view of the maker.

Mead and Heider have argued that "static" camera style—or as Feld and Williams (1975) call it, "locked-on-camera"—is a solution to the problem of aesthetic manipulation while recording. There is an editing style that logically fits with this approach to cinematography and is assumed to safeguard the scientific authenticity of the footage. If one does almost no editing except to splice rolls of film together in chronological order, then there is apparently little danger of introducing further distortion. To summarize this position: a positivist/empiricist scientific cinematic style consists of a camera on a tripod that is touched as infrequently as is technically possible and that produces as long takes as possible. These long sequences are spliced together in chronological order. Although stated here in a somewhat "purist" way, I believe that this naive viewpoint is still held by some ethnographic filmmakers and anthropologists.

Although it might be possible to produce research footage in this manner, I have never seen a film made in this fashion, even by those researchers, like Richard Sorenson, who advocate an observational approach. Moreover, if one is interested in producing an ethnographic film (as opposed to research footage), cultural and scientific conflicts arise. Footage shot as just described is virtually uneditable within the conventions of documentary film.

A quick glance at the films most commonly known as ethnographic clearly reveals that their makers have followed the aesthetic conventions of the documentary in their shooting and editing. As a result, many anthropologists regard film as an adjunct or a marginal activity to mainstream anthropology—documentary films that may be suitable for teaching. Heider expresses this viewpoint: "What is 'ethnographic film'? The term itself seems to embody an inherent tension or conflict between two ways of seeing and understanding, two strategies for bringing order to (or imposing [it] on) experience: the scientific and the aesthetic" (1976:ix).

I have presented a clearly biased description of what I consider to be the dominant view of film in anthropology. I have argued that its marginal role is a direct consequence of the most common philosophy of science among anthropologists and their folk attitudes toward image-producing technologies. Since these folk models are derived from a positivist/empiricist view of the world, as long as that paradigm is prevalent in anthropology, film will remain a minor activity. I have also suggested that reflexive statements or statements of method are lacking in ethnographic film for the same reasons that they are absent from written anthropology. There is a conflict between what anthropologists do and the philosophy of science they espouse.

A position counter to this one is possible. An anthropological cinema could be developed. To do so would require that anthropology become the reflexive and interpretive social science that I outlined earlier. If this paradigmatic shift is beginning to emerge within anthropology, as I have suggested that it is, then the emergence of a new paradigm should bring with it a corresponding shift in the role of image-producing technologies. It has not as yet happened. The postmodern turn has not had the impact expected—undoubtedly because anthropological conservatism intervened.

I am suggesting that there is a complex and causal set of relationships between U.S. culture's ideological system, the paradigms used in science, and attitudes, both general and scientific, about the various forms of visual communication. I am arguing that the general cultural values, as well as scientific conceptualizations about these forms, will have to be altered before a significant visual anthropology or anthropological cinema can emerge. In addition to those concepts discussed earlier that dealt directly with science and anthropology, it will be necessary to examine the adequacy of our notions of art and science, particularly as they affect our understanding of pictorial communication. I have argued elsewhere (Ruby 1976a) that Westerners popularly conceive of art as an interpretation of reality and science as a mirror for reality, and as a consequence, only two major schools of pictorial communication theories have developed—the formalist and the realist. Neither of these theories is useful for a visual anthropology. As this is the core of my argument about film and anthropology, it will be explored in the conclusion.

It is necessary, then, to construct a theory of pictorial communication that would suit the particular needs of anthropology. To do so requires a greater understanding of the process of communication in the pictorial mode than we have now. In other words, once we begin to reflect on the development of a visual anthropology, we begin to see a set of general questions that ultimately involves the entirety of how human beings make meaning out of the world.

Anthropological inquiries about the visible and pictorial aspects of culture are essential to the development of an anthropological cinema.

During the past 150 years, devices that can freeze time and memory and allow us to see things in a way that the unaided eye will never see have been invented—devices that allow us to tell each other stories about the world. Increasingly, human beings are coming to know the world through the symbolically mediated versions of it they make for each other. Our society is currently constructing the technology necessary to project our image of the world everywhere to everyone. Where will anthropology fit into this scheme?

[D]isciplined introspection and empathy are essential to the study of the unique characteristics of humankind. (Mead 1976:905)

The Viewer Viewed: The Reception

of Ethnographic Films

Literary culture was an establishment that dictated fashionable discourse. It favored opinions and ideology over empirical testing of ideas—commentary spiraling upon commentary. As a cultural force, it is a dead end. JOHN BROCKMAN, "AGENT OF THE THIRD CULTURE"

A s I suggest throughout this book, the current state of knowledge about how viewers respond to an ethnographic film (or any film, for that matter) is limited.[1] It seems only logical to suggest that if anthropologists wish to use film to convey their knowledge to others, they must learn more about the audience's construction of meaning—that is, conduct ethnographic studies of film reception. The audience's role in the construction of meaning in ethnographic film is a complex one. A proper exploration requires a thorough examination of many undertheorized and unspoken assumptions. On the one hand, there are the larger questions concerning the role of the reader/viewer in the construction of meaning. As the focus narrows, there are questions about the viewer in relationship to films in general, films viewed as television, and films as educational components in the classroom.

And then there are the questions that pertain to the peculiarities of an anthropological communication. An anthropological integration of the usefulness of the concepts of reader, viewer, or audience must also be undertaken, along with a careful examination of the very concept of reception (Abu-Lughod 1997). Although the reception of ethnographic films may be a somewhat parochial issue, research in this area will undoubtedly be relevant for larger issues—that is, when an understanding of the reception of ethnographic films has been gained, something about the nature of the reception of all films will have been revealed in the process.

Questions of author, text, and reader or viewer have preoccupied literary criticism and communication research for some time, but anthropologists have only considered them recently, perhaps because they traditionally dealt with nonliterate societies. In the initial studies, the assumed force of the author and/or the text dominated. It has only been in the last thirty years, when reception theories became popular, that the role of the reader/viewer was even considered worth investigating. Scholarly opinion about the importance of viewers has vacillated from seeing them as passive recipients—that is, victims of hegemonic messages designed to oppress and repress—to representing them as the sole entity responsible for the construction of meaning. Most studies hypothesize audiences in one of three contradictory ways: as an undifferentiated mass, as discrete psychological entities, or as oppressed communities who create or should create oppositional readings of texts in their struggle for empowerment. Quantitative methods and psychological paradigms have dominated the field. As V. J. Caldarola suggests, until the 1990s, studies have been "constrained by an inadequate model of cultural experience and by the presumed communicative power of mass media systems" (1990:1).

Since the 1980s, the trend has been partly reversed. A growing number of scholars now evince an interest in exploring the significance of the context of reception as well as the role that gender, age, and ethnicity of viewers might play. The recent qualitative and ethnographic work that has resulted in this paradigmatic shift was accomplished initially by cultural-studies scholars and focused almost exclusively on television (Ang 1990, 1991, 1996; Lull 1988, 1990, 1995; Lull, ed., 1976; Morley 1986, 1992). Roger Silverstone and others among these media- and cultural-studies scholars have criticized a lack of adequate knowledge of what constitutes ethnographic research in this new field (Silverstone and Hirsch 1992; Silverstone 1994). As Lila Abu-Lughod suggests, "[T]hey use a notion of ethnography that little resembles the anthropological ideal" (1997:111). The problem stems from the fact that few of these scholars have had any formal training in ethnography. Unfortunately, most visual anthropologists—and for that matter, cultural anthropologists—have been remiss in contributing to the debate by either critiquing cultural-studies ethnographies or producing their own ethnographies of media use as exemplars. As Wilton Martinez points out, the postmodern turn in anthropology has so far paid "little attention to their [ethnographic texts'] reception by the 'general public' or to their linkage with the larger process of the construction of cross-cultural knowledge and cultural identities" (1992:131).

Some promising anthropological work does exist. Richard Chalfen (1987) and Christopher Musello (1980) produced ethnographic studies of the reception of snapshots, and Catherine Lutz and Jane L. Collins explored the photographic representation of the Other in *National Geographic* (1993). Ethnographic studies by V. J. Caldarola (1990), Sara Dickey (1993), Susan Kent (1985), C. P. Kottak (1990), Brian Larkin (1997), A. P. Lyons (1990), H. D. Lyons (1990), Eric Michaels (1982a, 1987a), Holly Wardlow (1996), and Richard Wilk (1993) are only some of the new anthropological studies of television and film reception in the United States. In addition, there have been several edited collections that explore this approach—Peter Crawford and Sigurjon Hafsteinsson's *The Construction of the Viewer: Media Ethnography and the Anthropology of Audiences* (1995), a special issue of *Public Culture* edited by Lila Abu-Lughod (1994), and the special section of an issue of *Visual Anthropology Review* edited by Victor Caldarola entitled "Embracing the Media Simulacrum" (1994).

These works clearly mark a new beginning for an anthropology of mass media (Spitulnik 1993; Ginsburg 1998), which Margaret Mead, Gregory Bateson, Hortense Powdermaker, and others unsuccessfully attempted to initiate in the 1940s and 1950s (Mead and Metraux, eds., 1953; Powdermaker 1953a, 1953b). In England, an even earlier attempt at an anthropological study of the movie going by members of the Mass Observation Project of the 1930s has been virtually ignored in spite of Raymond Firth's 1939 review (Richards and Sheridan 1987; Stanton 1996; MacClancy 1995). After forty-plus years of struggling with the question of how anthropologists might profitably study film or television, they remain, as Abu-Lughod suggests, at "the beginning to find the right point of entry for the ethnographic work—in the field and in our studies—that it would take to draw out the significance of television's [and I would add, film's, photography's, and videos'] existence as a ubiquitous presence in the lives and imaginaries of people in the contemporary world" (1997:110). In spite of this new interest in reception studies, television programs produced for mass audiences dominate. Work by Wilton Martinez (1992), Jayasinhji Jhala (1994), and Sam Pack (1997) remains the sole published research on the reception of ethnographic media.

From an anthropological perspective, reception theory would appear to be a step in the right direction for studying the impact of pictorial media on its users because it "recognizes that messages are not inherently meaningful, and that that which is perceived or understood by media audiences depends largely on the characteristics of the audience, rather than the intentions of communicators or any intrinsic features of media programs" (Caldarola 1990:3–4). Although a critical review of the rapidly expanding literature on reader response, audience, spectatorship, reception, uses and gratification, and reception studies would be invaluable, it would take us too far from the topic of this chapter and easily become a book in and of itself. Several excellent critical surveys already exist (Ginsburg 1998; Caldarola 1990; Martinez 1990; Seiter, Borchers, Kreutzner, and Warth, eds., 1989; Moores 1993; Staiger 1992).

As an anthropologist, I am obviously drawn to any model that argues for the primacy of culture in the construction of meaning and suspicious of any study that isolates something as complex as the impact of television or film viewing from the remainder of a person's social life. This vantage point, a bias toward theory grounded in culture, eliminates most literary and media criticism, including much that has been written about reader response and reception, and questions the usefulness of concepts like audience and viewer, as they assume that sharing a viewing experience is all that is important.

Although some writers like Stanley Fish (1980) propose that readers should be understood as belonging to interpretative communities, few theorists outside of anthropology and cultural studies argue for field-testing their concepts—that is, doing ethnographies of reception. Most reception theories hypothetically construct the viewer and his or her role in the construction of meaning with no reference to the real world. Literary critics, including the postmodernists like Larry Grossberg (1988), apparently see no need to discover whether there are any actual readers who consciously or otherwise employ the proposed models. Readers are invented rather than discovered. Research in reception consists of sitting in one's study reading or viewing texts and fantasizing about viewers. These models lack the means of verification and instead rely on the elegance of the scholars' argument. As support for their contentions, they often cite other works that also lack empirical verification; for example, Michel Foucault or Jean François Lyotard are cited as authenticating sources when their work is completely conjectural. During the past decade, the advent of ethnographic studies of television reception discussed earlier suggests that an anthropology of media use may soon challenge the mainstream paradigms of communication research.

Symbolic Strategies and Cultural Receptions

As I have discussed elsewhere, an anthropology of visual communication model appears to me to be the most inclusive available for the study of culture and communication and would therefore be of use in the study of media reception. Known as "symbolic strategies," it is derived from the ethnographic semiotics of Sol Worth and Larry Gross (1981) and Dell Hymes's ethnography of communication (1967). A theory that combines these approaches assumes that pictures—all kinds of pictures—are culturally coded communicative events designed to function in a particular context. Producers employ various codes they deem culturally appropriate for the context in which they wish the film seen. They imply a particular meaning that they wish viewers to infer. The producers take it for granted that viewers share their competencies and assumptions and that the picture will therefore have its intended impact. Lacking a convenient or common means of feedback, producers must hypothesize their viewers' ability to understand with little hope of ever really knowing whether their assumptions are correct. In other words, producers make cultural assumptions about their viewers' cultural assumptions about codes and their contexts. They construct an ideal or implied reader/viewer without ever really knowing whether their assumptions are correct or whether the pictures they produce will be seen in their preferred contexts by their assumed viewers (Jhala 1994).

Viewers have an active, perhaps seminal, role in this process, in that they can both imply from and attribute to pictures—that is, they can attempt to comprehend the picture as a symbolic act designed by the producer to be understood in a particular way, or they can attribute meaning to, for example, a film's plot, characters, and narrative, based on their cultural assumptions. Implying from a picture or attempting to understand the motives and intentions of the maker appears to be an activity largely confined to specialized viewers like critics, scholars, students in film courses, and others esoterically involved in picture viewing. Most viewers simply attribute to a picture what they already know about the people, places, and events depicted regardless of what the producer intended. In other words, if viewers choose to attribute their cultural assumptions to the film, they are able to overlook, ignore, contradict, or even misunderstand the producer's implied meaning.

When the producer's intended message conflicts with the viewers' worldview, it is the viewers' attributions that will most likely dominate. Viewers therefore construct a meaning that may be contrary to the producer's intentions. Let me give a concrete, if not obvious, example. It is not very complicated to understand Leni Riefenstahl's intention in her 1936 film *Triumph of the Will*. It is also equally easy to subvert that intention by understanding and dismissing the film as Nazi propaganda. This oppositional reading is facilitated in two ways: gatekeepers such as film programmers or teachers can place the film in a context that encourages a reading contrary to the one intended by the producer (for example, a holocaust survivors' group can show *Triumph of the Will*), or the knowledge and values of the viewer may be sufficiently contrary to the producer's as to thwart the producer. It has been reported that rural southern audiences loved Peter Fonda and Dennis Hopper's love poem to hippiedom, *Easy Rider*, because the "dirty" hippies got killed at the end of the film.

Before proceeding further, I must point out what I regard as the most serious problem facing ethnographic filmmakers and anthropologists who wish to use film to teach when they contemplate audiences. There is an apparent chasm between the intentions of anyone who attempts to communicate anthropological knowledge and the interpretive folk models used to understand difference by people in the United States. One of the primary goals of an anthropological communication is to make viewers or readers aware of their ethnocentrism, self-conscious about it, and uncomfortable with it. In other words, the general purpose of an anthropological communication is to alter the relationship between Westerners and the Other.

Postmodernist critics like George Marcus and James Clifford wish to add another goal—to make viewers aware of the constructed and tentative nature of anthropological knowledge (Marcus and Fischer 1986; Clifford and Marcus 1986). This admonition logically leads us into a discussion of reflexivity— something I have dealt with elsewhere (see chapter 6). Martinez (1992) has argued that these two goals should be linked. If a film is reflexively open, less authoritative, and multivocal, viewers may be more able to overcome their ethnocentric tendencies and gain some empathetic feelings for the people portrayed in the film. Based on his research, Martinez advocates that ethnographic filmmakers emulate the reflexive style of Jean Rouch, Barbara Myerhoff and Lynn Littman, or David and Judith MacDougall. Although in part merely attracted by innovative forms of representation and/or responding to their need for the author's reflexive mediation to help bridge the cross-cultural gap, spectators seem to manifest more than facile engagement in these films. Students in Martinez's study appear to accept the invitation to participate actively in discerning the diverse layers of representation (1992:138).

Mainstream U.S. middle-class culture provides two folk models when contemplating exotic cultures—the noble savage and the ignoble savage. It is popularly assumed that the subject matter of anthropology is exclusively the exotic Other—that is, third- and fourth-world people. To put it a bit crudely, anthropologists study partially clothed brown and black people who live far away from their audiences. The noble-savage model suggests that the Other resides in a cultural paradise of stressless activities, sexual freedom, and ecological balance. If we, the nasty West, would only leave them alone, the natives could lead idyllic lives. It is a folk rendition and misreading of Jean-Jacques Rousseau—very popular in the 1960s and 1970s and seen most recently in the various "save the rain forest" campaigns and forever in *National Geographic*.

The opposite but coexisting folk model is the ignoble savage, in which the Other is viewed as a backward, barbaric simpleton in desperate need of things Western. Westerners will be the salvation of these people—physically and spiritually. It is the basis for the nineteenth century's belief in the "white man's burden" and the twentieth century's development of the Peace Corps. All missionaries—whether Christian, capitalist, or Marxist—are manifestations of the concept. They all know what is best for the Other.

Although there are no studies to provide supporting evidence for my contention, it does seem reasonable to suggest that viewers of ethnography on television or in the classroom would tend to employ folk models of the noble and ignoble savage rather than accept the culturally relativistic meaning implied by the programs.

The moral, political, and intellectual task of anthropologists is to somehow thwart or subvert these folk models and, if they are to follow the dicta of Clifford and Marcus, to alienate viewers from their suspension of disbelief so ingrained in the realism of cinema and television—not a simple task. To employ the jargon of the Sol Worth–Larry Gross model (1981), anthropological producers' implied meanings should be diametrically opposed to their readers' and viewers' attributions. The role of ethnographic filmmakers from this perspective is to produce programs subversive to their audiences' view of the world and of the media. In its most radical formulation, anthropology's public message should be designed to alter the West's conceptualization of the Other and invalidate the assumption that knowledge is found, not constructed. Viewed from this perspective, ethnographic filmmakers are not merely attempting to educate their viewers about the humanity of exotic people but to propagandize for a fundamental alteration of their audience's view of the world. Given the economic and political realities of funding and distribution, ethnographic film has a difficult battle to fight.

Ethnography as Television—The Ethnography of Television

Regardless of the clarity of intention, ethnographic television programs (television being the dominant source of funding in the United States) continue to be made and broadcast and appropriated for the classroom. To understand their reception, it is necessary to comprehend the way people make sense out of television in general and the television documentary as it appears on outlets like the U.S. Public Broadcasting Service, the venue aspired to by most producers. I am, of course, consciously excluding the undeniably important films made outside the television world, such as those by Timothy Asch, Jean Rouch, and David and Judith MacDougall. As significant as they may be, they do not constitute the majority. I am concentrating on the kinds of film one finds on a regular basis at the Margaret Mead Festival, at the annual Society for Visual Anthropology screenings, and those reviewed in *American Anthropologist*. As much as some of us would like to deny it, they represent the majority.

Ethnographic films are seen irregularly on U.S. television—occasionally on the popular science series *Nova* or a National Geographic Special and sometimes as a special series like *Millennium*. In the 1970s, a PBS series about anthropology, *Odyssey*, was launched. It failed after two seasons. The British series *Disappearing World* has been on the Discovery cable channel—where other ethnographic programs occasionally appear. With the proliferation of cable channels, I am certain there will be more venues. However, it is highly unlikely that a regular series on ethnographic film will be offered in the United States.

No specialized audience has been developed as a consequence of the irregular appearance of ethnographic television shows. That is, no one has become socialized in the comprehension of conventions unique to the genre, the way, for example, soap opera fans learn to understand the passage of time. In fact, there is no distinct ethnographic film genre on or off television. Television ethnographies have the look of other television documentaries, except they are usually subtitled and often the people portrayed do not look like Euro-Americans. Since viewers spend far more time watching television than they do watching films, it is safe to say that they evaluate all moving pictures in terms of the conventions and expectations they acquire watching television. So regardless of whether an understanding of the reception of ethnographic film on television or in the classroom is the research goal, how viewers receive and make sense out of television in general must be understood first.

Without detouring into a discussion of the complexities of conducting ethnographic studies of television viewing, I will generalize from the findings of researchers who have conducted participant-observational studies of "TV talk" in naturalistic settings—that is, researchers watching people watch television in their homes with their families (a partial list of these cultural-studies works was presented earlier in the chapter). It is clear that being able to talk about television is a requisite for full membership in many social groups both within and outside of the family. Americans spend a large portion of their leisure time watching television. The lives of the fictitious people who inhabit televisionland may be one of the "safe" topics of conversation in American social life (Caughey 1984).

How people talk about television and integrate the viewing experience into their lives is conditioned by several pretelevision contexts (Liebes 1984; Lull 1990; Morley 1986). The dynamics of family interaction seems to provide the basis from which an individual develops interpretative strategies. Position in a family unit, age, gender, socioeconomic class, ethnicity, and culture all serve to construct the norms for attending to a program, the content of discussion topics, and so on. It seems reasonable to assume that the need to maintain a status in these groups is more important than the need to establish the authority to offer alternative readings of the television shows people watch, and therefore, most people render the socially preferred reading of what they watch. I am not suggesting that people lockstep their way through life as automatons, parroting the same views about television. The role of some family members may be to always go against the grain with oppositional readings.

In addition, peer groups outside the family provide alternative possibilities. For example, a teenager can view a program about family life with his or her family and render a "family-approved" reading. The next day, with other teenagers, he or she may parody the same program, savaging the "official" adult reading. Office workers during a coffee break may offer oppositional readings of their viewing that differ from the one they offered to their spouses the evening before. The long and the short of it is that if anthropologists wish to comprehend how viewers understand ethnographic film, they are going to have to begin conducting ethnographic studies of how watching television fits into the social fabric of people's lives.

A collateral consequence of the television-reception studies conducted by cultural-studies scholars is that they seem to reaffirm what common sense tells us about the context of television viewing, which, in turn, supports the received wisdom of the television industry. Television viewing is fundamentally different from the viewing of a film in a theater or classroom. (Whether video watching constitutes a viewing context that differs from television remains to be seen.) Television viewers are seldom alone, and they almost never only watch television. In a theater or classroom, the room is darkened, and your attention is directed toward the film. Anything that might distract your viewing has been minimized. Rattling popcorn boxes or chatting during a movie is antisocial behavior. In the classroom, there are potential penalties for not paying attention: students might be tested on their understanding of the film. When people watch television, they eat; read; do schoolwork; have discussions, disagreements, even serious arguments; answer the phone; leave the room; and so on. In short, they are only paying slight attention. The television industry's assumptions about the level of complexity possible in a television program seem altogether logical. Given the apparent lack of concentration, any program that challenges the folk models of its viewers is unlikely to be successful because it requires that viewers pay careful attention.

There is a strange lack of fit between the time, skill, and money a professional producer puts into crafting the best program possible and the casualness with which it is received. The context of television viewing certainly should justify a skeptical attitude about the success of an ethnographically intended program, unless its makers are content with modest intentions or the producer sees television as the financial means that would enable him or her to produce a film meant for uses outside broadcast television.

When I think back
On all the crap I learned in high school
It's a wonder
I can think at all
And though my lack of education
Hasn't hurt me none
I can read the writing on the wall.
—Paul Simon, "Kodachrome"

Television is a viewing situation constrained by the norms of family, peer group interaction, and many other sociocultural factors. There are few incentives to pay careful attention to a program so that one can reconstruct and critique the form and content. The classroom is different. Teachers are gatekeepers. They set the stage for the screening and can hold students responsible for rendering a particular reading of a film. A teacher can provide interpretative strategies that vary from those students acquire elsewhere. A classroom constructs a very different social world than a living room. The teacher, not a parent, now has the power to establish agendas for conversation, topics for discussion, and the norms for paying attention. Although the consequences for inappropriate behavior in the classroom are far less significant than the consequences for asocial behavior among family members and peers, the immediacy of flunking a course undoubtedly constrains most students into adhering to the teacher-approved reading of the film within the classroom but, if we are to believe Martinez (1992), not outside of that environment.

This controlled environment is an ideal place to ethnographically explore the reception of films. Because the classroom is a highly controlled site of reception, designing research to determine the fit between the producers' intentions and the viewers' perceptions is relatively easy. In recent years, educators and anthropologists have produced a considerable ethnography of education literature. Unfortunately, none of it deals with the role of films in the classroom, nor has the university classroom been the subject of study until now.

To my knowledge, only four research projects have been pursued to explore the place of ethnographic film in a university setting. "In an unpublished study done in 1973, Thomas Hearne and Paul DeVore found that the use of Yanomamo films (Asch, Chagnon) in introductory anthropology was reinforcing students' negative preconceptions of the Yanomamo. After watching the films, students' views evolved from simple impressions and characterizations to well-informed and more complex stereotypes about the 'primitive'" (Martinez 1990:35).

Wilton Martinez has conducted the most extensive study of the reception of ethnographic film by college students at the University of Southern California in a course taught by Tim Asch in which Martinez was a teaching assistant. Although the sample of films he used was larger than the sample used by Hearne and DeVore, his conclusions were similarly depressing. He discovered that "most students decoded ethnographic films in an 'aberrant' way, with high levels of 'culture shock' and alienation, and with relatively low levels of understanding of both film and subject matter" (Martinez 1990:45). As of the writing of this book, Sam Pack is conducting an ethnographic study about ethnographic films in the classroom (1997), and Naomi Offler is conducting an ethnographic study about ethnographic films in undergraduate cultural anthropology courses at the University of Melbourne (1998). Their preliminary findings are critical of Martinez's work and seem to at least partly refute it.

Pack's position is critical of Martinez and suggestive of the causes of the problems Martinez discovered. According to Pack:

In a much discussed project, Wilton Martinez conducted a reception study of ethnographic films among undergraduate anthropology students at the University of Southern California and found that instead of challenging stereotypic perceptions, these films confirmed and reinforced prejudices which audience members held toward foreign cultures [Martinez 1990, 1992]. Martinez's study has sounded a panic alarm in anthropological circles because of its subversive implications. "These symptomatic readings indicate more than a pedagogical problem; they suggest that the use of film has powerfully catalyzed the crisis of representation in the classroom" [1992:132]. His conclusions suggest that anthropology instructors may be unintentionally perpetuating the devaluing of other cultures by screening ethnographic films to their students.

Martinez calls the interpretive gap between the intentions of the filmmakers and student responses "aberrant readings" [1992:132]. From my perspective, a serious weakness of Martinez's study is that he never addresses where these so-called "aberrant readings" come from and offers no explanations for their causes. In other words, why do these ethnographic film representations reinforce negative stereotypes?

I contend that negative stereotypes of the "primitive" are inherited by and perpetuated through popular media representations. After a lifetime of television programs, feature films, music videos, video games, etc., how can consumers of the electronic age view the "exotic other" in any other way? Based on the breadth and depth of this inculcation, there is nothing "aberrant" about these readings at all. They are, in fact, perfectly "normal "readings.

To explore these issues further, I conducted my own reception study with undergraduates in two introductory anthropology courses at Temple University. By attempting to investigate all the circumstances of engagement in the viewing process, this study was intended as a development towards an ethnography of the communication of ethnography. The research design differed from Martinez's study in several important respects. First, I targeted a diversified group of respondents in contrast to the white, upper middle class students who comprised Martinez's sample. In addition, I charted the variations of students' responses to ethnographic films over the duration of the course, something which Martinez failed to even acknowledge.

If students do not progress from their initial interpretive strategies, this should be attributed to poor instruction rather than poor viewing skills. Finally, and most significant, I account for the reasons underlying these so-called "aberrant readings." Martinez is content to leave this a mystery, thereby buttressing his own notion of an inexplicable and subversive phenomenon. I clearly demonstrate that ethnographic and popular constructions of the "exotic other" are not only inextricably linked but mutually reinforcing. (Personal communication, 1999)

Students come to ethnographic films with two somewhat unrelated sets of interpretative expectations—one concerned with understanding moving pictures and the other providing a way of dealing with cultural difference. The former is derived from the many hours they have spent passively watching television and the generally dulling effect of mediocre education media. The latter was already described earlier as the twin folk models that are the ethnocentric and racist basis of U.S. society. Anyone wishing to use ethnographic films successfully in the classroom must confront both expectations and attempt to frustrate them. I assume that most teachers of anthropology are aware of the need to deal with their students' ethnocentrism. I wonder how many see the need to deal with their visual naïveté as well. Many years ago, Marshall McLuhan (1964) predicted that the television generation would be a visually sophisticated one. If so, all those pictorially hip students decided to attend some other university than the one in which I teach.

It would be comforting to think that the findings of these studies simply reflect the generally poor quality of American university teaching and that if a teacher really spent time organizing a class in an imaginative way, the students would respond differently. Martinez disagrees. He believes that the students' response is not always positively affected by the design of the course and the context in which the films are shown. "I have observed that the tendencies, the patterns of response outlined here, do not change very much; they may in degree, but not very much in kind" (Martinez 1990:46).

Conclusion

I have employed Sol Worth and Larry Gross's reception model (1981) to examine how ethnographic films are understood. I have argued that although the producers' intentions and the way in which they construct the text are important, it is the conditions of exhibition and the viewers that ultimately determine the meaning of the film.

I further suggested that there is an inherent tension between the goals of

The Viewer Viewed

anthropologists, who wish to make viewers self-conscious about their ethno-centrism, and their uncritical acceptance of the authority of television produc-ers and the assumptions those producers make about what kinds of programs will be funded, broadcast, and therefore, succeed. Because producers and not anthropologists determine what audiences see, viewers are offered programs that are more concerned with presenting difference as somehow entertaining rather than with explicating anthropological knowledge. At best, one can say that ethnographic television programs present a diluted or an implicit anthro-pological message. Some producers would argue that the nature of television prevents more complex films from being broadcast—a simplistic assumption about television that remains untested.

Whether the conflict can be solved remains to be seen. Those who wish to produce ethnographic films for television need to confront the problem. Anthropologists need to learn more about television audiences. They must become more knowledgeable about film/video production so they will have the choice of producing on their own or collaborating with professional pro-ducers in a more sophisticated manner. Producers need to learn more about anthropology as a theoretical construct so they can understand why anthro-pologists wish to go beyond mere description. Anthropologists must refuse to be seduced by the siren song of television that something is better than nothing.

Some people, like Tim Asch, would argue that ethnographic films should be produced for the classroom and as esoteric communiqués between schol-ars—that is, be directed to the same audiences and contexts that written an-thropology is. Rather than making premature decisions about what is the proper venue for ethnographic films, anthropologists need to address the complexities of pictorial communication as a researchable question. Once more is known about the nature of film communication, an informed decision can be made about how these films are to be constructed if producers wish to have their anthropological intentions understood. Ethnographic filmmakers are logically required to conduct ethnographic studies of the reception of their films if they are going to behave like anthropologists and not professional filmmakers.

Speaking for, Speaking about,
Speaking with, or Speaking Alongside

As soon as he aims the camera, the ethnologist disturbs the life he is recording. In Moi, un Noir *[Rouch's film] the actors played their everyday existence in front of the camera. I did not hide in order to film them. We were partners.* **JEAN ROUCH IN AN INTERVIEW BY JEAN CARTA**

It would seem that [Bronislaw] Malinowski's stricture that the function of the ethnographer was to see the native's culture from the native's own point of view could at last be achieved—literally, and not metaphorically.

What would such a world be like, and more importantly, what problems have we to set before our students now that will, at the least, not hinder them from coming to an understanding of an age in which man presents himself not in person but through the mediation of visual symbolic forms. . . . It is now no longer possible for the student of culture to ignore the fact that people all over the world have learned, and will continue in great numbers to learn, how to use the visual symbolic mode. Anthropologists must begin to articulate the problems that will face us in trying to understand others when their point of view is known to us primarily through movies distributed by broadcast television and cable. **SOL WORTH, "TOWARD AN ANTHROPOLOGICAL POLITICS OF SYMBOLIC FORM"**

T*he Passenger,* Michelangelo Antonioni's 1975 film, is about a documentarian making a film about a national liberation front in an unspecified North African country. When Mr. Locke, played by Jack Nicholson, tries to interview a rebel leader, the following conversation ensues:

LOCKE: Yesterday when we filmed you at the village, I understood that you were brought up to be a witch doctor. Isn't that unusual for someone like you to have spent several years in France and Yugoslavia? Has that changed your attitude towards certain tribal customs? Don't they strike you as false now and wrong perhaps for the tribe?

NATIVE: Mr. Locke. There are perfectly satisfactory answers to all your questions. But I don't think you understand how little you can learn from them. Your questions are much more revealing about yourself than my answer would be about me.

LOCKE: I meant them quite sincerely.

NATIVE: Mr. Locke. *We can have a conversation, but only if it is not just what you think is sincere but also what I believe to be honest* [emphasis added].

LOCKE: Yes, of course, but . . .

[*The rebel leader now turns the camera around so that Locke is centered in the frame.*]

NATIVE: Now, we can have an interview. You can ask me the same questions as before.

Questions of voice, authority, and authorship have become a serious concern for all cultural anthropologists. Who can represent someone else, with what intention, in what "language," and in what environment is a conundrum that characterizes the postmodern era. In this chapter, I explore some of the responses to these problems by focusing on the relationship between ethnographic and documentary filmmakers and the people they film—in particular, the development of cooperative, collaborative, and subject-generated films as a response to a felt need to rethink authorship.[1] The social, political, and epistemological implications of ethnographic filmmakers' sharing or relinquishing their power is also discussed. Although I am primarily concerned with ethnographic film, my remarks apply equally to all forms of actuality representations of the human condition. This chapter presents a broad overview of the movement away from single-authored films. In the next chapter, I become more specific and explore the work of one of the pioneers in the facilitation and study of indigenously produced media, Eric Michaels.

Cooperatively produced and subject-generated films are significant because they represent an approach to documentary and ethnographic films dissimilar to the dominant practice. From an anthropological perspective, they offer the possibility of perceiving the world from the viewpoint of people who lead lives that are different from those traditionally in control of the means of imaging the world. Subject-generated films are a tool used by some disenfranchised people in their efforts to negotiate a new cultural identity. For other indigenous and minority producers, making movies and television is a way into the profits and power of the established order. These films challenge some basic assumptions about the authorship of ethnographic films and potentially offer insight into the importance of culture in the construction of a film. This shift in authority has the potential to permanently alter ethnographic film practice.

Ethnographic film, as well as all actuality film, is motivated by two fundamentally different conceptions of the relationship between the filmmaker and those who are filmed. These approaches can be located in the works of Dziga Vertov and Robert Flaherty. Although they did not invent the formulations, they were seminal to their development.

In his *Kinok* manifestos, Dziga Vertov said:

I am kino-eye, I am a mechanical eye. I, a machine, show you the world as only I can see it.

Now and forever, I free myself from human immobility, I am in constant motion, I draw near, then away from objects, I crawl under, I climb onto them. I move apace with the muzzle of a galloping horse. I plunge full speed into a crowd, I outstrip running soldiers, I fall on my back, I ascend with an airplane, I plunge and soar together with plunging and soaring bodies. Now, I, a camera, fling myself along their resultant, maneuvering in the chaos of movement composed of the most complex combinations.

Freed from the rule of sixteen – seventeen frames per second, free of the limits of time and space, I put together any given points in the universe, no matter where I've recorded them. My path leads to the creation of a fresh perception of the world. I decipher in a new way a world unknown to you. (Vertov 1923 [1984]:17)[2]

For Vertov and most filmmakers, film is a vehicle for the expression of their sensibilities, and the filmmaker's view is paramount, even when the film's goal is to present the actuality of other people's lives. The input of the subjects is "raw material" to be transformed in the process of making the film.

For some, like John Grierson, a prime mover in the development of the British documentary movement, actuality films that explored sociocultural issues assumed the political role of giving a "voice to the voiceless"—that is, portraying the political, social, and economic actualities of oppressed minorities and others who were denied access to the means of producing their own image and who lacked the skills necessary to make images (Hardy 1979). From this perspective, these films are not only an art form but a social service and a political act.

In contrast to Vertov and Grierson, Robert Flaherty, particularly during the filming of *Nanook of the North*, sought to replicate the view of the world held by the people he filmed by seeking the subjects' response to his vision. As discussed in chapter 2, Nanook and other Inuit were shown footage in the field and asked to comment on its accuracy as well as assist Flaherty in planning for the next day's filming. "But another reason for developing the film in the north was to project it to the Eskimos so that they would accept and understand what I was doing and work together with me as partners" (Flaherty 1950:13–14). Some Inuit were trained as technicians to maintain Flaherty's equipment. *Nanook of the North* represents what today would be called a collaborative film. One can trace a thin line of tradition from Flaherty's nascent efforts to share creative power in the 1920s to the present day. Whereas most filmmakers are Vertovian or Griersonian—that is, authors who present their vision[3]—some, like Flaherty, aspire to replicate the subject's view of the world. Their intention duplicates the traditional goal of ethnography: "to grasp a native's point of view, his relation to life, to realize his vision of his world" (Malinowski 1922:25).

Historically, aspiring Vertovians and Griersonians have always outnumbered the followers of Flaherty's approach. It is generally assumed that films about culture are best made by having professional filmmakers employ their technical skills, artistic sensitivity, and insight to reveal the "reality" of others. The subjects seldom have direct input. Image makers who follow the dictates of broadcast journalism argue that any personal relationship between the filmmakers and the filmed compromises their journalistic "objectivity." They believe their task is to report without making value judgments—an effort some contend is not only impossible but misleading and even dangerous (Gross, Katz, and Ruby 1988). The technical and aesthetic skills and knowledge necessary to make a "good film" are regarded as being beyond the knowledge and financial means of most people. The assumption is that it is in everyone's best interest to have films made by professionals.

This commonsense—taken-for-granted—assumption has been under attack for some time from within the independent documentary community, the people traditionally filmed, and some critics of mainstream anthropological practice. A review of the literature disputing traditional forms of authorship would fill a book. The protest literally stares back at viewers. At the end of John Marshall's 1979 film *N!ai, Portrait of a San Woman*, the story of a fourth-world woman and the destructive transformation of her culture by white South Africans, N!ai confronts the camera and sings, "Now people mock me and I cry. My people abuse me. The white people scorn me. Death mocks me. Death dances with me. Don't look at my face. Don't look at my face." The viewers' gaze is again indicted in Edin Velez's videotape *Meta-Maya II* (1980), as the eyes of an Indian woman reproach the intrusion of the camera into her life. The examples grow daily. The right to represent is assumed to be the right to control one's cultural identity in the world arena. Some people, traditionally film subjects, are demanding that filmmakers share the authority and, in some cases, relinquish it altogether. These demands call for profound changes in the way in which images are produced as well as the means by which knowledge is presented to the public. The subjects' demand for some control over how they are represented can be heard almost everywhere in the world.

At the same time as subjects are asserting their right to control their own image, there is a growing recognition on the part of the independent documentary community and among some anthropologists that it is difficult to justify making films about the private acts of the pathological, the socially disadvantaged, the politically disenfranchised, the economically oppressed, and the exotic Others who are about to "disappear" under the avalanche of Western influence—subjects that loom large in social-science research and documentary-film practice. As Brian Winston (1988) has suggested, documentarians and social scientists are becoming self-conscious about their "tradition of the victim." Until recently, most of these "victims" passively allowed themselves to be transformed into aesthetic creations, topics of scholarly interest, news items, and objects of pity and concern. Western society used to condone this approach because it was assumed that the act of investigating, researching, and filming would do some good—cause something to be done about the problems. It is the traditional justification for all journalistic exposés and one of which the public has grown increasingly weary and suspicious. A case in point can be found in Mary Ellen Mark's *Streetwise* (1984)—a film acclaimed publicly as an impassioned plea for homeless children and critiqued privately as a cynical, scripted, manipulative career enhancement of a professional sympathizer.

As discussed in chapter 5, Edward R. Murrow and Fred Friendly's landmark television documentary about the plight of immigrant workers, *Harvest of Shame* (1960), and the dozens of "hard-hitting" television reports that followed, accomplished little to relieve the deplorable conditions of the workers' lives. The funds spent on these productions were wasted, except perhaps to advance the careers of their makers. Furthermore, there seems to have been little progress in developing empirical verification of the impact of social and political films—that is, studies of the reception of these films. Socially concerned and politically committed filmmakers erroneously assume that a compelling film automatically produces a desired political action. Perhaps it is time to realize that the image by itself may be more impotent than powerful when it comes to changing the world and that a different justification for making these films is therefore needed. Regardless of Lenin's oft-quoted statement about the revolutionary potential of film, it may not be a cost-effective tool for social and political change. More bluntly stated, the argument goes as follows: power is not created with the lens of a camera; it comes from the end of a rifle barrel. Therefore, if you really wish to change the world, put down the camera and pick up a gun. This chapter is not the place to critically examine the romantic and often naive liberal and leftist politics of the independent film movement. Lindsey Anderson's slogan in his film *Oh, Lucky Man* (1973) sums up my position: "Revolution is the opiate of the intellectual."

It is interesting to note that although recent political and economic conditions have brought about a need to reexamine basic assumptions about the role of the subject in nonfiction film, neither the question nor some of the solutions are actually new. In an interview with Elizabeth Sussex in 1975, John Grierson characterized the history of the documentary as follows:

I always think of documentary as having certain fundamental chapters. The first chapter is of course the travelogue. . . . The second chapter is the discovery by Flaherty that you can make a film of people on the spot, that is, you can get an insight of a dramatic sort, a dramatic pattern, on the spot with living people. But of course he did that in respect to faraway peoples, and he was romantic in that sense. The third chapter is our chapter, which is the discovery of the working people, that is, the drama on the doorstep, the drama of the ordinary. But there is a fourth chapter that's very interesting, and that would be the chapter in which people began to talk not about making films about people but filming with people. . . . However, the next chapter, this making films with people—you've still got the problem that you're making films with people and then going away again. Well, I see the next chapter being making films really locally, and there I'm following [Cesare] Zavantini. Zavantini once made a funny speech in which he thought it would be wonderful if all the villages in Italy were armed with cameras so that they could make films by themselves and write film letters to each other, and it was all supposed to be a great joke. I was the person who didn't laugh, because I think it is the next stage—not the villagers making film letters and sending them to each other, *but the local film people making films to state their case politically or otherwise, to express themselves whether it's in journalistic or other terms* [emphasis added]. (Sussex 1975:29–30)

As mentioned earlier, Robert Flaherty actively sought the cooperation of his subjects in *Nanook of the North*. In the twenties and the early thirties in the Soviet Union, the cine-train project of Alexander Medvedkin, Dziga Vertov, and others produced films about local problems of bureaucracy, inefficiency, nepotism, and so forth, with the assistance of local political workers. In the remarkable 1935 British film *Housing Problems*, by Edgar Anstey and Arthur Elton, people speak for themselves on the screen, not in a studio but from their own homes, perhaps for the first time, directly confronting audiences with their plight. I am certain that an impressive list of similar efforts could be compiled—some motivated by intellectual and artistic curiosity, others for political purposes, and still others from a moral commitment to the subjects of the films. However numerous the attempts and interesting the results might have been, the idea of doing collaborative and subject-generated work was, by and large, ignored until the 1960s.

The Death of Objectivity

During the last thirty or so years, a paradigmatic shift has occurred in the relationship between the filmer and the filmed. Although some continue to produce images in a traditional manner, I would argue that these mainstream practitioners do so with less and less conviction and impact. Professional inertia and the marginal position of nonfiction films within the image industry en-

Speaking for, Speaking about, Speaking with, or Speaking Alongside

sure that many professional image makers maintain a conservative position to satisfy their funders and distributors.

Regardless of how powerful the forces of tradition may be, the intellectual and moral support for mainstream practice has been seriously eroded. These changes are part of a complex of intellectual, artistic, political, and ethical factors discussed throughout this book. They provide the impetus for a reevaluation of the place of ethnography within anthropology.

In an earlier time, documentaries and ethnographic films were understood as uncontested statements of facts—the official version of someone else's actuality. The people portrayed were regarded as incapable of speaking for themselves. Today, "widespread perceptions of a radically changing world order have fueled this challenge and undermined confidence in the adequacy of our means to describe social reality. . . . Thus, in every contemporary field whose subject is society, there are either attempts at reorienting the field in distinctly new directions or efforts at synthesizing new challenges to theory. . . . At the broadest level, the contemporary debate is about how an emergent postmodern world is to be represented as an object for social thought" (Marcus and Fischer 1986:vii).

An adequate explication of the origins of this so-called crisis of representation would take us too far afield; however, some contributing factors do seem most relevant. First, the end of the colonial era among people subjugated by capitalist and socialist empires caused the authority of a Western male, middle-class, heterosexual construction of actuality to be contested. People formerly the object of our gaze and dissident people from within the system challenged the right of authority figures to represent anyone but themselves. Among the many results of this upheaval was the realization that cultural identity is not eternally fixed but something that has to be regularly renegotiated.

Second, the recognition that scientific inquiry consists of hypothesis testing rather than the search for eternal truths caused some philosophers of science to argue that the progress of scientific knowledge can be understood as a dialectical process. The impact of Werner Heisenberg's principle of uncertainty (Price and Chissick 1977) and Thomas Kuhn's (1962) analysis of the role of the paradigm in science come to mind as exemplary of this trend. Among those factors directly contributing to undermining traditional assumptions about actuality filmmaking are the concept of cultural relativism and the acceptance of the idea that reality is a social construction and the impact of academic Marxism, especially in terms of the recognition of the ideological base of knowledge. At the same time as the theoretical foundations of science were being probed, some young scholars questioned the moral and political validity of so-called value-free science. Social scientists' involvement in covert activities in Vietnam and Chile brought this predicament to a head. Positivist models of knowledge were challenged by more interpretive and politically self-conscious approaches—a reflexive stance in which producers of knowledge, be it a treatise on subatomic particles or a documentary film about the peace movement, are responsible for the knowledge they construct (see chapter 6 for details).

And finally, there was the development in the 1960s and 1970s of literary journalism, or "New Journalism"; nonfiction novels; docudramas; and other genres that blurred distinctions between fiction and nonfiction. Models of criticism developed that regarded all communicative forms as "serious fiction"—that is, constructed according to culturally bounded conventions (Geertz 1973, 1988). The documentarian's claim to an inside track to the truth and reality of other people was therefore undermined, if not destroyed completely. Ethnographic and other actuality films are now recognized as an articulation of a point of view—not a window onto reality.

A Response

The reaction by the independent documentary community to the crisis of representation has been far-reaching and most instructive for those interested in ethnographic film. Some documentarians have questioned their ability to speak for anyone and began looking for ways to speak about or speak with (Nichols 1983, 1994). As notions of objectivity were challenged by more tentative attitudes toward the social construction of reality, some filmmakers openly acknowledged that their authority was circumscribed, even uncertain at times.

Stated in a more formal way, there has been a reassessment of the moral and intellectual implications of documentary authorship. The documentary, particularly its journalistic manifestations, stopped hiding behind the idea that images are merely recordings. Some image makers and theorists now acknowledge films, fiction and nonfiction, as articulations made by someone wishing other people to infer meaning in a specified way (Worth and Gross in Worth 1981). Lest I be accused of painting too rosy a picture, it should be stated that many documentarians, regardless of their political orientation, are very conservative about changes in the form and see this new direction as a threat, as witness the less than enthusiastic reception of mixed-genre films like Jill Godmilow's *Far from Poland* (1984), Errol Morris's *Thin Blue Line* (1988), or documentary parodies like Mitchell Block's *Speeding?* (1975) and *No Lies* (1975). At a Flaherty Film Seminar in the 1970s, Willard Van Dyke, a pioneer in the documentary and then curator of film at New York's Museum of Modern Art, stated that he saw the film *No Lies* as an effort by filmmaker Mitch Block to destroy the documentary. More recently, a session of the Margaret Mead Film Festival I helped organize devoted to "fake documentaries" left some of its audience more confused than enlightened. Although the new directions I discuss here are not supported by the majority, they do represent what I would regard as the wave of the future.

Since some of the public still believes that documentary filmmakers should strive to be objective, some documentarians believe that they have the obligation never to appear neutral—that is, to disabuse people of the fantasy that films are somehow privileged messages with an inside track to truth and reality. As the acknowledged authors of a film, documentarians assume responsibility for whatever meaning exists in the image and therefore are obligated to discover ways to make people aware of point of view, ideology, author biography, and anything else deemed relevant to an understanding of the film—that is, to become reflexive (see chapter 6). They abandon the idea that being moral means being objective and in its place openly acknowledge the ideological base of all human knowledge, including films. Ironically, the traditional form of the journalistic documentary denied a voice not only to subjects but to the filmmakers as well. "Objective" documentaries have no authors, only reporters who present the "who, what, when, where, and whys" of the "truth." So the move toward a multivocal documentary form has also involved a renewed and increased role for the filmmaker—an overt acceptance of authorial responsibility.

Acknowledging the documentary filmmaker as the author of a socially constructed message has a number of consequences. The image, demystified as truth bearer, becomes a vehicle for the transmission of a message constrained by the range of social expression possible within a society. Social knowledge is accepted as always tentative—the result of a negotiation between the seeker and the object of study. This repositioning of the work and the documentary author carries with it the necessity for reconstituting the relationship of the author to the subject and to the viewer and, ultimately, redefining documentary subject matter. It seems to me that these inquiries are the only defensible position for anyone claiming to do anthropology on film. If a filmmaker accepts a renewed sense of responsibility for the authorship of actuality films, the question then becomes how to offer the subjects of these films a more active role.

Cinéma Vérité—Power to the People?

The advent of portable synchronous-sound film technology associated with direct cinema and *cinéma vérité* offered the possibility of empowerment to subjects through the use of on-camera interviews. The invention of this technology was the consequence of filmmakers like Michel Brault, Jean Rouch, and Drew Associates seeking the means to express a new documentary consciousness. Direct cinema (observational style) and *cinéma vérité* (participatory style) held the promise that people could have the authority to represent themselves on screen and have their opinions respected. Unfortunately, the promise was seldom realized. Although "voice of God" narration was declared déclassé, often it was replaced by the talking-head "expert witnesses." The offscreen voice of authority simply moved into the frame. Subtitled with their pedigree, authorities continued to tell audiences the "truth." "Talking heads" became a documentary cliché—the boring mainstay of television news and television documentaries, thus dulling the impact of the method. In just a few years, the excitement of seeing slum dwellers in *Housing Problems* articulate their plight became transformed into the jaded, predictable performance of a victim of the "disaster of the day" who appears on cue for the six o'clock news.

Observational cinema developed partly as a response to the limited effectiveness of talking-heads cinema. Colin Young argues that the work of his former students at UCLA David Hancock and Herb Digioia, in their New England films, and David and Judith MacDougall's Turkana trilogy offer subjects a chance to be themselves without the restrictions of voice-over, on-camera experts interpreting their lives, or the artificiality of formal interviews. Thus, it provided audiences the chance to interpret the lives represented on the screen (Young 1976).

Being able to hear people tell their stories and observe their lives instead of being told what they think and the meaning of their behavior clearly offers subjects a greater say in the construction of their image. It represents a major shift in attitude about where one looks for authority and authenticity. It recognizes that the experts' opinions and the filmmakers' vision need to be tempered by the subjects' lived experience and their view of themselves. It is "speaking with" instead of "speaking for." However, editorial control still remains in the hands of the filmmaker. The empowerment of the subject is therefore more illusory than actual. Although new voices are heard, traditional forms of authorship have not been significantly altered.

In a well-intended attempt to compensate for the mistakes of the past, the pendulum has now swung a bit too far in the opposite direction. The success of PBS series like *Eyes on the Prize* or other documentaries, such as *Berkeley in the Sixties*, where no experts or analysts or historians are interviewed, may cause some image makers to abandon the notion that analysis has any merit. In *Eyes on the Prize*, the on-camera authorities are participants in the civil rights movement, recalling their experiences a quarter of a century later. The theory of history implicit in these documentaries is most troublesome. The body of *Eyes on the Prize* consists of selected and highly edited news footage. The criteria for selection and editing are never made available to the viewer. The veracity and point of view of the archival footage are never questioned or even treated as problematic. Nor are audiences privy to how the interviews were structured, who did the interviewing, and what questions were asked. For example, were the interviews conducted after a rough cut of the news footage was assembled so they were designed to complement the footage, or did the substance of the interviews cause the producers to search for footage to illustrate them?

Village Voice critic Amy Taubin calls this approach "If-You-Were-There-You-Must-Have-Something-to-Say." The move to give greater voice and authority to the subject has now reached a logical but extreme point. There is an unspoken assumption about the validity of interviews, particularly with those outside the mainstream. These films seem to suggest that what subjects say about themselves and their situation is to be taken at face value. Although it is clear that the balance needs redressing and that the victims of Western oppression should represent themselves, it should not be assumed that any one group has a privileged insight into its own history. People seldom understand their own motivation. No one person can represent his or her gender, class, or culture as a whole. No particular group of people has the corner on being self-serving or adjusting the past to fit the needs of the present.

Cooperative Cinema—Is Informed Consent Possible?

In Jeff Vaughn and John Schott's 1978 film *Deal*, a documentary about Monte Hall and the television program *Let's Make a Deal*, the subjects were given the right to view all footage and to veto any scenes they felt were inappropriate. It was a condition imposed by Hatos-Hall Productions. I assume the producers were sensitive to the bad press the program had received from intellectuals and other highbrows. They wanted to protect their public image. It was also a matter of ethical concern for Vaughn and Schott. They felt a moral obligation to obtain informed consent before they finished their film. In an interview by Lenny Rubenstein, John Schott explains their approach:

Because we have access to such intimate aspects of their lives, we allow our subjects the review of all the uncut raw footage in which their faces and voices appear. Since they know they will be allowed to screen and review this footage, it builds a bond of trust between us. This does two things: it serves a moral purpose, makes *cinéma vérité* fair since in documentary filming there is a certain invasion of privacy—you can nail someone's skin to the wall for public display—and the other thing is that it allows the person to be relatively unguarded, since he knows he can review the material with us and negotiate cuts.

At that time we sit down with the person and ask whether they feel their ideas have been fairly represented; in both our films we've never lost any footage we thought essential. What did get out were personal references to other performers, curse words, extraneous scenes and libelous statements—that kind of thing. Bear in mind that we had forty hours of footage

and most people are mainly interested in their individual material. We got to use 99.99 percent of our footage. And, of course, we have a final cut. In this film [that is, *Deal*] all the people
interviewed extensively are public personalities; they're used to the public eye. They've also
been beleaguered by criticism which they felt was unjust, so the challenge represented was to
film them in a relatively neutral fashion. (Schott in Rubenstein 1978:36)

Asking subjects to become cooperatively involved by seeking their advice
and consent seems quite sound at first glance, but laypeople tend to respond
uncritically when they see themselves on the silver screen. Most lack the sophistication to grasp the implications of camera angles, lighting, pacing, and
so forth. I am uncertain whether even media sophisticates are competent to
evaluate documentaries about themselves. Vaughn and Schott told me that
when Monte Hall was viewing the footage, there was a particular scene that
the filmmakers wanted but were anxious about because the shot was unflatter-
ing to Hall. After the viewing, Hall commented that it made him look fat, but
they could use it because, after all, it was a documentary! Hall restates his position in a voice-over in the film:

Show it as it is, and show me as I am. I don't want anyone to canonize me, but this is our statement. And of course, this is your statement. You will only glean from what you have shot, and
if it's a document after that, . . . what are you going to make, make an editorial comment after
the whole thing is in the can? Are we going to take a close-up of you saying, "What you have all
seen folks, . . . what I'm really going to tell you is the inside dope"? You're going to show it as
it is, and that's all we have ever really asked. (Monte Hall in *Deal*, a documentary by E. J.
Vaughn and John Schott, 1977)

Documentaries are often regarded as elaborate home movies by the people
in them. Subjects become "documentary pop stars" and realize their fifteen
minutes of fame rather than critically examine how their images are constructed and the potential impact on audiences. The complex reaction of the
Loud family to their public image in Craig Gilbert's PBS series *An American
Family* was explored in Pat Loud's own book (1974), Alan and Susan Raymond's film *An American Family Revisited* (1983), and most recently in Jeff
Ruoff's study (1995). It is the most extensively documented example of the
ambivalence documentary subjects feel about their moment of cine fame. The
pattern seems to be this: people are flattered when they see themselves and
later become disillusioned when the critics make negative comments about
the life they see portrayed on the screen. At events like the annual Flaherty
Film Seminar, documentarians often attempt to justify their films by saying
the subjects saw the film and loved it. As appealing as this validation may be, it
is hardly adequate.

Informed consent in documentary/ethnographic production is a thorny issue (Pryluck 1976; Anderson and Benson 1988). The concept was initially developed to protect subjects in medical experiments. Researchers are required to explain in advance the "risk to benefit" ratio for people volunteering for an experiment. Documentary filmmakers and most social scientists seldom know the potential problems people in their films or writings may face. Whereas a medical researcher has a reasonably clear idea of the potential risks to individuals and the possible benefits to society, how can filmmakers ever have such clarity? People tend to be flattered when asked whether they mind being filmed and do not consider the potential problems of ending up in a distributor's catalog, available to anyone for any purpose. Some image makers feel that asking consent prior to taking pictures is destructive of the moment that interested them in the first place. In cases in which the film is about a subject's unethical, immoral, or illegal activities, the maker could hardly be expected to ask permission or offer the subject a chance to view the footage prior to completion. In some extreme cases, the filmmaker must overtly lie to make a film. If the subject is considered sufficiently evil, few would fault a filmmaker for using devious means to gain access. I can find no criticisms of Marcel Ophuls's hidden cameras or the other deceptive practices he employed in his films *Shoah* (1985) or *Hotel Terminus* (1988), in which he clandestinely interviewed Nazis.

As paternalistic as it sounds, it may be only the makers themselves who are in a position to judge whether the people in their films might be adversely affected. If you apply Janet Malcolm's (1990) wholesale condemnation of journalism to include the documentary and all of social science, my assumption that the documentarian has a moral obligation to the subject may be naive. Malcolm claims that the act of journalistic investigation is an inherently exploitative one no matter how actively you engage the subject of inquiry in the representation. It has been suggested that this moral dilemma lies at the heart of all forms of representation of other people (Smith 1998). Unless one plans to spend the time and money training subjects to become filmmakers or even reasonably competent critics, subjects will continue to lack the skills necessary to give informed consent. I am not suggesting that filmmakers should stop asking for permission or soliciting subjects' opinions. I am arguing that most people lack the knowledge necessary to exonerate the producer. Advice, consent, and cooperation are necessary but not sufficient when dealing with the potential for exploitation. I am suggesting that even with cooperatively produced films, the moral burden of authorship still resides with the filmmaker (Geertz 1988). Although a multivocal approach to the documentary does empower subjects, it will not absolve the filmmaker from the ethical and intellectual responsibility for the film.

Allowing subjects to represent themselves on-screen and asking their approval after they have reviewed the footage represents a definite shift in voice and authority. The distance maintained by those favoring journalistic "objectivity" is abandoned in favor of a shared authority. The subjects' view of themselves is recognized as having merit—something that must be acknowledged and represented.

Sharing Authority: Cooperative, Community, and Collaborative Films

Asking people to actively cooperate in the making of a film about their lives naturally increases their power. It is a practice found among a number of filmmakers. Often individuals are asked to work with a filmmaker as representatives of some social collective—a community, an organization, or even a culture. Finding one person or even a small group of people to represent accurately or fairly a community or a culture is difficult, perhaps impossible. Cooperative ventures turn into collaborations when filmmakers and subjects mutually determine the content and shape of the film. Although the idea of a film in which the authority is shared might have a certain appeal, there are few documented cases. Films labeled in this fashion seldom contain descriptions of the interaction between the filmer and the filmed, nor have people associated with the production written about the complex mechanics of collaborations. The Australian film *Two Laws* (1979) is a rare example of a truly collaborative effort. According to James MacBean, "the traditional (or tribal) peoples themselves collectively controlled the decision-making processes of what to film and how to film it—even down to what lens to use on the camera" (1983:31). Sarah Elder, who with Leonard Kamerling, produced a number of collaborative films in Alaska, remains one of the only filmmakers involved in this work to openly discuss it in print (Elder 1995). Most of what I know about cooperative, community, and collaborative films is the result of personal contact with the makers or hearing them discuss their work at a festival or seminar. The essential information about the nature of the collaboration is almost never contained within the film.

For a production to be truly collaborative, the parties involved must be equal in their competencies or have achieved an equitable division of labor. Involvement in the decision-making process must occur at all significant junctures. Before a film can be judged as a successful collaboration, the mechanics of the production must be understood. Is the collaboration to be found at all stages of the production? Have the filmmakers trained the subjects in technical and artistic production skills, or are the subjects merely "subject-area specialists" who gauge the accuracy of the information and pass upon the political and moral correctness of the finished work? Who had the idea for the film in the first place? Who raised and controls the funds? Who operates the equipment? Who is professionally concerned with the completion of the film? Who organizes and controls the distribution? Who travels with the film to confer-

Speaking for, Speaking about, Speaking with, or Speaking Alongside

ences, festivals, and other such events? Because films of shared authority represent a fundamental repositioning of the filmer and the filmed, these films must be reflexive if they are to be understood as the radical departure implied by the term. I know of no films that meet these requirements of disclosure.

During the late sixties, Challenge for Change was created by the Canadian government to discover ways in which film, and later video, could act as a catalyst for social change through new forms of interaction between the government and its citizenry. In one of the earliest projects, filmmaker Colin Low

relinquished the artistic prerogatives of the documentary-maker in offering film as a tool for the people of Fogo Island. He worked in tandem with Newfoundland's Memorial University, community organizers, and the inhabitants of Fogo. Members of the island community helped select topics and sites. Subjects were filmed only with their permission, and were the first afforded an opportunity to view and edit the rushes. Their consent was also required before a film could be shown outside a village or outside the island itself. The process by which the films were made and screened was central to their impact on the lives of the islanders. Group viewings organized all over the island fostered dialogue within an isolated, divided population. The films and discussions heightened the awareness of the people that they shared common problems and strengthened their collective identity as Fogo Islanders. As a result, the planned relocation of the community of Fogo Island was abandoned. . . . A number of media historians and activists have traced a new concept of public access to mass communications media and the seeds of community television to the Fogo project of Challenge for Change. (Engleman 1990:8–10)

Following the success on Fogo, Challenge for Change introduced the then-new portapak technology to community activists. Bonnie Sher Klein's film *VTR: St. Jacques* (1969) documents this early effort at subject-generated video. There was also an attempt to train indigenous people to make their own films. An all–Native American crew produced *You Are on Indian Land* (1974). Challenge for Change ended when the Canadian government stopped its funding. George Stoney, Challenge for Change's executive director, continued his interest in community media by founding New York University's Alternative Media Center and has had a major impact on cable access and community television in the United States.

Although the results of this program were temporary, it became a model for other "shared-authority" media projects. In an unpublished version of a review of *You Are on Indian Land*, Sol Worth disputed the program's claims and in the process raised some fundamental questions about what happens when you teach the Other to make films:

Although the Film Board has made great efforts to involve the people in the films . . . and to teach community members how to make films themselves, they have not been able to divorce themselves from their own professional filmmaking and reportorial culture. They still look upon film with the professional eye of the middle-class TV producer—liberal, committed to change, and versed in the use of "art" and "persuasion." Teaching others to make and use film was essentially teaching white middle-class values of how information films brought about gradual and democratic change. *You Are on Indian Land* is a perfect example of a professional white liberal film made in "consultation" with Indians. . . . Even if this film were made by the Indians themselves, I would feel that it was a white man's film. I would have been sorry that once again we had used our culture as a power play to overcome another. But this wasn't made by them. It was made by us. Even with the best of intentions and the greatest filmmaking skills, it is only another television documentary—by us about them. Again. (Worth 1972:n.p.)

Appalshop, in Whitesburg, Kentucky, is one of the most widely known community media centers. Started by a Yale architecture student, Bill Richardson, in 1969, Appalshop produces films, radio shows, television, and concerts for, about, and by Appalachian people. Appalshop's 1990 interim report to funders explains the purpose of "Headwaters," its television service, as an organization that

continues to work with communities and grass-roots organizations in the experiment we are calling "community directed" media. We form a partnership with local organizations involved in change, and work together to produce relevant television which explores their issues and allows people to speak with their own voice and to tell their own story. Community groups have directed us during productions, set priorities in editing, and have been able to use clips of the raw footage and finished programs as organizing tools. ("Interim Report" 1990)

The intention of Appalshop is to give people some control over the construction of their media image. Dee Davis, director, says Headwaters is "an attempt to create 'television that makes sense for here,' that takes its pace and style from the way people in Appalachia express themselves" (Nold 1990:32).

From its beginning, Appalshop's staff has been a mixture of outsiders and locals. Davis is from the region, whereas Anne Johnson, chief producer for Headwaters, came into the area in 1973 with Barbara Kopple during the production of the film *Harlan County*. She married a miner from the film and became an "adopted" native. Appalshop productions raise a fundamental question about film as an expression of cultural identity: what difference does it make whether the filmmaker is from the same culture or community as the subjects?

The controversy about the cultural fit between director and community represented in a film spills over into fiction film, as evidenced by the conflicts about who should have directed *The Autobiography of Malcolm X* (1993). "I have a big problem with Norman Jewison directing *The Autobiography of Malcolm X*," Spike Lee fumed in an interview with the *New York Times*. "That disturbs me deeply, gravely. It's wrong with a capital 'W.' Blacks have to control these films" (*New York Times* Entertainment Section, Sunday, January 27, 1991, page 1). Did the fact that Spike Lee ended up directing *Malcolm X* make it a more authentic film? Can a person who is not from a culture learn enough about it to produce works that accurately represent its world? Are Tony Buba's documentaries *Voices from a Steeltown* (1993) and *Lightning over Braddock* (1988) somehow more authentic because Buba is a native of Braddock? Until someone undertakes an ethnographic study of the production and utilization of community-based films like those produced at Appalshop, these important questions will remain unanswered.

Many so-called collaborative film productions involve anthropologists, undoubtedly because anthropologists tend to spend long periods of time with their subjects, develop a rapport seldom possible with traditional documentary methods, and seek feedback as a means of verification. Since the 1950s, French anthropologist Jean Rouch has been making films with his West African associates, whom he taught to take sound and perform other technical duties in the field. Rouch is also a pioneer in the training of other African filmmakers, such as Mustapha Alaassane, Safi Faye, Oumarou Ganda, and Desire Ecare. During the making of *Petit à Petit* (1968) and *Cocorico, Monsieur Poulet* (1983), Damoure Zika, Lam Ibrahim Dia, and Rouch formed a production company, Film Dalarou.

As an early advocate of subject-generated media, in 1974 Rouch suggested:

And tomorrow? Tomorrow will be the time of color video portapacks, video editing, of instant replay ("instant feedback"). The dreams of Vertov and Flaherty will be combined into a mechanical "ciné-eye-ear" and of a camera that can so totally participate that it will pass automatically into the hands of those who were, always in front of the lens. At that point, anthropologists will no longer control the monopoly on observation; their culture and they themselves will be observed and recorded. And it is that way ethnographic film will help us "share" anthropology. (Rouch 1974:43–44)

Rouch has written prophetically about what he calls "shared anthropology" (*anthropologie partagée*). "It is this permanent 'ethno-dialogue' which appears to me to be one of the most interesting angles in the current progress of ethnography. Knowledge is no longer a stolen secret, devoured in the Western temples of knowledge; it is the result of an endless quest where ethnographers and those whom they study meet on a path which some of us now call 'shared anthropology'" (Rouch 1971 [1978]:7).

According to Rouch, the role of the documentarian and ethnographic filmmaker as a professional outsider making films about other people's lives will become unnecessary. Filmmakers will produce only autobiographical works—films about the world they inhabit.

Rouch pioneered a reflexive style in *Chronicle of a Summer* (1961), in which one sees subjects actively participating in the production. Unfortunately, he has never made explicit the extent of his collaborations. Instead, viewers are left to ponder marvelously complex films like *Jaguar* (1955), in which the participants speak about themselves in the third person.[4]

In discussing the work of anthropologist Barbara Myerhoff, Marc Kaminsky (in his introduction to Myerhoff 1992) articulated a concept that he claims underlay her written and filmic work among the elderly Jewish population in Venice, California, *Number Our Days* (1980). Myerhoff proposed that the researcher-filmmaker seek to locate a *third voice*—an amalgam of the maker's voice and the subject's voice, blended in such a manner as to make it impossible to discern which voice dominates the work—in other words, films in which outsider and insider visions coalesce into a new perspective. It is a variation on the notion of collaboration in which the authority for the creation of the blend remains in the hands of the researcher. Providing the researcher actively consults with the subjects during this process, third-voice ethnography can be considered a kind of collaboration.

Films of shared authority are a difficult matter. Collaboration requires the participants to have some sort of technical, intellectual, and cultural parity. If subjects become knowledgeable as filmmakers in order to be collaborators, why would they need the outsider? Wouldn't they want to make their own films? Without more concrete information, the notion of sharing authority remains more of a politically correct fantasy than a field-tested actuality.

Films by "the Other"

During the past few decades, film subjects have gained considerable power over the construction of their image and to a limited extent have had the chance to speak for themselves.[5] They are now asked, with increasing frequency, to give their opinion and consent and to cooperate actively and, at times, to become full collaborators. For some, that is not sufficient. They want more. They wish to represent themselves, and they wish to have themselves, their communities, and their stories presented in ways that differ from the ways in which the mass media have presented them. This is not a recent desire. It is at the core of the development of an independent cinema movement.[6] At political, artistic, and economic odds with the mainstream media industries, independents have been engaged in a seventy-year-old ideological struggle against Hollywood and commercial television's representations of the world. They fight against the industries' attempt to keep the means of production in the hands of straight white males and the industries' insistence that moving images reduce the complexities of the human condition to mindless entertainment.

Speaking for, Speaking about, Speaking with, or Speaking Alongside

Although only a small part of this movement is directly concerned with anthropological image making, the struggle in general is permanently altering the way ethnographic films are made. It is important to distinguish a shift in the kinds of people who gain access to the means to produce their own image, from the expansion of cable and satellite outlets to new markets, as evidenced by the rapid growth of ethnic programming, with television channels devoted to Spanish-, Korean-, Japanese-, and other "minority"-language programs. Hamid Naficy has discussed this issue in his exploration of the Iranian American community in Los Angeles (1993). Although the emergence of an ethnically diverse television within the existing systems of production and distribution is an intriguing subject and does often involve the employment of minorities in production positions, it is not of immediate relevance to the subject of this chapter and the next, which is an exploration of the challenge represented by the demands of film subjects to participate in the construction of their image. It is one thing to explore what happens when people who have traditionally been the subjects of film seek to represent themselves and quite another to examine how ethnic minorities become professional image makers and have their cultures and worldviews represented on commercial television and in film.

In the 1960s, during the New Left radicalization of the United States, there was a renewed call for the decentralization of access to the means of producing images. Organizations like New York Newsreel collectively produced political films such as *A Woman's Film* (1969) in an effort to democratize the authority of the director. Women, African Americans, Asian Americans, Native Americans, Hispanics, the poor and the homeless, gays and lesbians now struggle to find the means to represent themselves. The movement in the United States is part of a worldwide expansion of the power base of film production in African, Asian, Latin American, and third-world cinemas (Armes 1988). Indigenous people have more recently joined in this battle.

Within the United States, the motivation of some of these so-called new filmmakers is focused on career enhancement. They are interested in joining the media establishment, seeing their stories told, and creating a market for their products. These image makers are "independents" only until they can join the mainstream industry. They lobby for internships, affirmative action, funding specially earmarked for minorities, and other methods of increasing minority representation in the media industries. They are convinced that the assimilation of people of color and other outsiders into the media industries is a sign of progress. The so-called blaxploitation films of the 1970s like *Super Fly* or the television series *I Spy* (1965–68), in which Bill Cosby plays a CIA agent disguised as a professional tennis coach, and his hugely successful situation comedy *Cosby*, are examples of this variety of "minority" image making. These producers strive to become assimilated into the media mainstream. Learning methods of mainstream expression and finding a place within this establishment fit the liberal/social-reformist notion that society can accommodate everyone's voice within existing structures.

Those media scholars who take their cues from the Frankfort school and view the media as agents of hegemonic forces argue that the addition of new subject matter or the acceptance of producers from communities that have not traditionally been a part of the image empires is simply another example of how those in power co-opt people who are potentially disruptive without seriously altering anything (Katz 1977). Although it may be rhetorical, the question has to be asked: Did *Super Fly*, *I Spy*, and *Cosby* really mark a significant change in the place of African Americans in the media industries or society at large? Marlon Riggs, in his brilliantly analytic film *Color Adjustment* (1993), has explored this question.

A tradition of critical scholarship developed during the time new image makers were emerging in which mass-mediated systems of representation were examined for the inaccurate and distorted images they offered of people outside the mainstream, thus further justifying the need for films produced by "the natives" (Gross 1988). The right and ability of outsiders to depict minorities accurately has been repeatedly questioned. Some suggest that the "misrepresentation" is so entrenched that only members of the group can properly represent themselves (Waugh 1988). Thus, it has been argued that only women should make films about women, gays about gays, and so on.

As a consequence of factors too numerous to adequately review here, several community-based alternative cinemas emerged. As members of the community in which they film, these minority producers often learn firsthand what the subjects and the community think about the film, thus introducing a form of accountability often lacking when an outsider makes a film. For some, autobiography, personal films, and films about one's family became the only films that could be politically and morally justified. In films produced by community members about that community, the self and the Other become intertwined (Katz and Katz 1988). Trinh T. Minh-ha quotes Jacques Rabemananjara's definition of the role of the black poet that characterizes the notion of native authority: "He is more than their spokesman: he is their 'voice': his noble mission entitled him to be not only the messenger, but the very message of his people" (1989:13).

This approach may not be so radical as it appears if one considers it from the standpoint of the empowerment of the subject. The New Left cinema, and indeed the whole of independent film practice, can be seen as a substitution of a new official vision and version of actuality for an older one. It was simply the creation of new elites—a change in masters. The conventional radical ideology does not include asking the subjects to cooperate, collaborate, or produce their own films. One of the egotistical qualities of Marxists is their belief that

Speaking for, Speaking about, Speaking with, or Speaking Alongside

they possess the "truth" about social relations. In Julianne Burton's analysis of "liberating impulses" in Latin American documentaries, she cites Fernando Birri's 1966 statement that "[t]he revolutionary function of the social documentary in Latin America is to present an image of the people which rectifies the false image presented by traditional cinema. This documentary image offers reality just as it is[;] . . . it shows things as they are—not as we might like them to be or as others . . . would have us believe them to be" (Burton 1984:374). Marxists' "scientific" analysis of other peoples' lives is assumed to be the correct one. If the subjects disagree, they are regarded as having a "false consciousness" and their opinions discounted. Given this perspective, there is little need to offer subjects a greater voice. It may even be counterrevolutionary.

Regardless of its limitations, broadening the power base in image production does represent a significant democratizing change. The possibility of feedback did cause some makers to think about the community impact of their work. However, it did not necessarily indicate a significant alteration of the relationship between the filmmaker and the filmed. The directors may have come from the communities they filmed, but most continued the dominant pattern of maintaining control over the production of the film as the author. The subject remained passively cooperative. Again, the transfer of power to represent is more illusory than actual.

The use of image-producing technologies by those traditionally the subject of films has a shorter history among indigenous peoples. It began in a political climate far different from today. In 1966, anthropologist John Adair and communications scholar Sol Worth taught the technology of film production to a group of Navajo Indians in New Mexico without suggesting what the films should be about or how they should look. The purpose of the study was to discover whether the Navajo would create films unique to their view of the world. Would a discernible Navajo film style emerge? The researchers concentrated on semiotic questions about the production of the films and the ways in which the makers attempted to produce meaning. They were not concerned about the ways Navajo audiences responded to the films or the possibility of any long-term media production by the Navajos. No Navajo involved with the project sought to capitalize on their experience and continue media work after the research was completed. The results seemed to indicate that Navajos organized their films in keeping with other narrative forms in their culture (see Worth and Adair 1972 for details). In the 1980s, Eric Michaels attempted to replicate their study among an Australian Aboriginal group (see chapter 9).

During the last decade, indigenous media-production groups have emerged throughout the world (Browne 1996; Philipsen and Markussen 1995) and seem to be increasing by leaps and bounds, from the government-sponsored programs among the Inuit in Canada (Marks 1994) and Aboriginal television in Australia (Batty 1993; Ginsburg 1993, 1995, 1998) to those like Inuit maker Zackarias Kunuk and Hopi artist Victor Masayesva and Aboriginal multimedia artist Tracey Moffatt, who choose to remain outside of official funding sources. In South America, Vincente Carelli's Video in the Villages project (Aufderheide 1995) and Terry Turner's various Kayapo projects (1991, 1992) are exemplary of work assisted by anthropologists and image makers. Within the development community, there are social-action projects that involve the media, such as Martha Stuart Communications' U.S. Agency for International Development–funded work with Video SEWA, a group of self-employed Indian women who use video as an organizing tool (Martha Stuart, personal communication, 1989). The journal *Media Development* frequently has relevant materials about these projects, as seen in "Video for the People" (no. 36, 1989) and the Group Media issue, "Coming to Terms with the Video" (no. 6, 1987).

Although most anthropologists have ignored the growth of media production among indigenous peoples (Ginsburg 1998), those anthropologists interested in the production of ethnographic film must react to it and accommodate the challenge it represents. It seems altogether reasonable that some ethnographic filmmakers would wish to replicate the work of Vincente Carelli (Aufderheide 1995) and Terry Turner in South America (1992), and Eric Michaels in Australia (1987a), and provide technology and training and the funds necessary for indigenous people to produce and disseminate their own work—that is, act as cultural brokers and facilitators. Although these activities can be viewed as paternalistic, they are the only way most indigenous people will obtain the technology and gain the skill to use it. Few have the wealth or knowledge to do it on their own.

Eventually these facilitators may not be needed or wanted, although the prospect of a completely independent indigenous media movement seems very unlikely unless government funding becomes available, as in the case of Aboriginal television in Australia (Batty 1993; Ginsburg 1993, 1995, 1998) and Inuit television in Canada (Marks 1994). Historically, the life of innovative media projects among people who do not have a tradition of image making is not long: when the funds from outside dry up, so do the pictures. Given the economic situation of many indigenous groups, it seems unlikely that they will want to spend their own resources on video equipment.

Lest readers think I am suggesting some completely altruistic endeavor, the exchange between anthropologists and indigenous media makers is a reciprocal one. The anthropologists provide technical assistance and equipment and in return have the opportunity to ethnographically observe the process of creating and using the videos. Viewed in this light, anthropologically initiated media projects are similar to other development studies in which anthropologists participate in the introduction of a new technology, observing the cultural changes that transpire. The intention of the anthropologists remains the same—to gain an understanding of other cultures, which, in turn, enables Westerners to critique their own culture. What has changed are the assumptions about what can be known and how that knowledge can be gained. As these indigenously produced works require some cultural translation to be understandable to audiences outside the culture of the makers, the focus of the ethnographic filmmaker now becomes a filmic study of the production and uses of these films.

Anthropologists have been derelict in their study of the media. By overlooking this subject, they have ignored a tremendous opportunity to study a profound cultural change that has occurred throughout the world in the last thirty years—the introduction of film and television to geographically remote communities. There has been a recent attempt to develop an anthropology of the media, as noted in the reviews of this work by Debra Spitulnik (1993), Sara Dickey (1997), and Faye Ginsburg (1998). Within this body of work, there are a number of studies of the production and reception of indigenously produced media, the most noteworthy being those of Michaels (to be discussed in chapter 9), Ginsburg (1993, 1995, 1998), and Turner (1991). Michaels's (1987a) and Turner's (1992) work provide us a rare glimpse into how a culture accommodates a new technology. Through these ethnographies, we are privy to the invention of alternative production methods; the development of a social organization and a division of power necessary to complete the task; and the selection of subject matter, shooting, and editing styles.

Equally important to studies of production is the reception of indigenous work. How do the "native" viewers learn to understand this new means of communication? In what social situations does viewing occur? Are preexisting hierarchies involved, or are new ones created? For example, Michaels found that because most of what the Warlpiri watched was in English, young children comprehended the programs better than the older adults, thus upsetting the traditional hierarchy based on age (1987a). How do natively produced programs compete with programs available via video stores and satellites from the Western image empires (A. P. Lyons 1990; H. D. Lyons 1990; Sullivan 1993)?

Finally, there is visual text itself. What subjects are selected and for what purpose? What does it look like? Where do the makers obtain their ideas about structure? Are the rules of narrative employed in the tapes borrowed from other places in the culture? In short, these occasions present a living laboratory in which the researcher can observe the dynamics of culture change brought about when an indigenous producer seeks to modify for his or her own purposes a communications technology that was originally designed to meet a set of needs defined by the dominant culture.

It is easy to fall into several traps when viewing work made by indigenous peoples. The first is patronizing bemusement that these "simple people" could do it at all. The result of this attitude is to uncritically accept anything they produce as being the truth about their culture. The essentialist fallacy of discussing these productions as somehow speaking for the entire culture is just as dangerous as the fallacy of accepting traditionally produced ethnographic films as being an objective record of their cultural reality. Indigenous people are as complicated as Westerners are. They cannot speak for their culture any more than Westerners can. What people say about themselves is seldom the truth. It's data that requires analysis if it is to be comprehensible. To suggest otherwise is to deny the place of the unconscious in human existence. These videos do not make the ethnographer's role redundant; they simply alter the focus of study.

The second trap is the assumption that indigenous people will automatically wish to confine themselves to portraying their own culture in documentary form. Aboriginal artist Tracey Moffatt has been criticized because she produces video art and has begun exploring non-Aboriginal subjects. Her latest film, *Bedevil* (1993), was featured at the Cannes Film Festival. Does this mean she is no longer an "Aboriginal artist"? The desire to confine indigenous producers to certain subject matter and styles is simply a reflection of Westerners' assumptions about their limitations.

Finally, there is the question of the comprehensibility of the work. Some would argue that these tapes transcend their culture and are easily understood—the global village fantasy that Ginsburg speaks about (1991). They—that is, the natives—"speak" in the "universal language of images." As an anthropologist, I question that possibility. Indigenous media must be recontextualized if the works are to have meaning for Westerners. An anthropologist or a bicultural individual must act as intermediary. These tapes do not speak directly to us. They employ a complex of cultural conventions—some native, some invented, and others borrowed from the West. These works need to be understood in terms of the conditions of production and how the people who made them wished them to be used, as well as in terms of the conventions employed.

Conclusion

The variety of experiments in recentering the authority of documentary and ethnographic films is staggering. This chapter has barely touched the surface. Mainstream documentaries and traditionally made ethnographic films still dominate the centers of production. White, straight, middle-class Western males still construct a world consonant with their reality and control the means of distribution, but alternative voices are being heard, and with greater regularity. A mixture of theories, methods, techniques, and ideologies all compete with one another—none seeming to offer a definite answer to the question of how to open up these films about culture to provide the subjects with some say in the construction of their image.

I have suggested two alternative positions—the anthropologist as facilitator and analyst of indigenous production or as collaborator. In the former, the anthropological image maker relinquishes the right to make pictures about another culture and concentrates on producing films about indigenous people producing films—a narrowly defined topic. In the latter, the anthropologist must be willing to assist indigenous people in becoming fully functioning collaborators—not an easy task. As anthropology in general becomes increasingly concerned with giving voice to the people it studies, ethnographic filmmakers will have to relinquish their traditional role as image makers empowered to speak for or about others. They will have to learn how to speak with or alongside. In the next chapter, I explore the work of Eric Michaels, a pioneer in facilitating indigenous production—someone who attempted to speak only after those he studied had had their turn.

In the Belly of the Beast:

Eric Michaels and Indigenous Media

I got into media studies, as an anthropologist, because I believed the media were the belly of the beast, and because I thought television was central to the creation of the extraordinary contradictions that plagued the contemporary world. ERIC MICHAELS, PERSONAL COMMUNICATION

This chapter attempts to make concrete some of the ideas expressed more abstractly in the last chapter. It is an exploration of Eric Michaels's pioneering contributions to the anthropology of the media and to indigenous media studies. Michaels was not an ethnographic filmmaker but rather an anthropological analyst of the media and a facilitator for the production of images by Australian Aboriginals. Michaels's publications represent a significant step forward in the application of ethnographic methods to an understanding of the role that mass-mediated pictorial forms play in people's lives. His Australian studies are an exemplar of one of the directions in which visual anthropological fieldwork will go in the future as more and more researchers become facilitators for and collaborators with the people they study. It is time for ethnographic filmmakers to stop being so concerned with making "important" films and to become more interested in how their work affects the people they portray and those who view the images. In other words, more people need to follow Eric Michaels's example.

This chapter is a first-person celebration of the tragically short career of Eric Michaels. As such, it is more descriptive than critical. I will reflexively frame my remarks within the history of my own ideas as well as those of others who have had an impact on his work. I do so as someone involved in formulating the tradition that, for a time, had an influence on Eric's thinking. I knew Eric Michaels for almost twenty years, first as a student and then as a colleague and friend. I met him while organizing Temple University's Conferences on Visual Anthropology (1968–80). He had recently returned to his hometown, Philadelphia, from a hippie commune near Taos, New Mexico, where he had lived for several years. He wanted me to see a film the commune had made—*Love, Peace, Taos*—*1968*—for possible inclusion in the conference. The film was very much a reflection of the pretensions of the hippie movement. It must have gone on for hours with its home-movie exploration of the "folk." I don't think either of us was very impressed with the other. Within a year, Eric returned to Temple University to complete his undergraduate degree. His experience as a hippie now became transformed into an ethnographic analysis of the commune as a "deliberate society" in a chapter entitled "The Family" in *Communitarian Societies*, edited by John Hostetler (Michaels 1974).

Although an English major, Eric took several of my courses in the anthropology of visual communication. When he left Philadelphia to do graduate studies at the University of Texas, Austin, Eric had two main interests— ethnography and visual communication. He pursued both for the rest of his life. We stayed in touch by letter, phone, and the occasional visit and exchanged critiques of each other's work. As an editor, I published two of his papers. Just before he became ill, I unsuccessfully tried to locate an academic position for him in the states. After he died, I wrote a preliminary version of this chapter as an essay for an issue of the Australian journal *Continuum* (Ruby 1990) devoted to an exploration of Michaels's Australian work.

Prior to accepting a research position at the Australian Institute of Aboriginal Studies (AIAS) in Canberra in 1982 to study the effects of satellite television on remote Aboriginal communities, Eric undertook two research projects. He became involved with Juan Downey and other video artists as a result of his organizing a symposium and screening series at Temple University's Conference on Visual Anthropology. He was interested in discovering whether anthropologists could benefit from collaborations with video artists whose work might help avoid what he and I conceived as the fallacy of associating ethnographic film with documentary conventions—an idea that still bears more exploration. He coproduced a videotape, curated a show of video art in 1979 at the Long Beach Museum of Art entitled Videthos, and wrote an ethnography of his experience—"How to Look at Us Looking at the Yanomami Looking at Us" (Michaels 1982a). Although the results of this work are far from conclusive, the project established Eric as someone willing to take risks and play at the margins of several disciplines. It also served as a useful initiation into the world of avant-garde, nonstandard television that enabled him to understand Warlpiri television from a perspective lacking in other researchers (Michaels 1987a).

Between 1979 and 1982, Eric did ethnographic fieldwork in Amarillo, Texas, for his doctoral dissertation (Michaels 1982b). The theoretical problem he explored was, "Do relations between people change with respect to television's usage?" The research involved an exploration of an effort by fundamentalist Christians to influence a television station's programming through boycotts. Partially sponsored by the Southwest Educational Development Lab and under the guidance of his dissertation adviser, Horace Newcombe, the study was also an attempt to explore the relevance of anthropological concepts like culture and techniques like ethnography for the study of television. The research design, involving a restudy three years after the protest, did not yield sufficient data to enable Eric to complete the work as contemplated. It was what might be called "an interesting failure." The people in Texas had tried to gain some control over what values television presented to them. They failed, but it gave Eric a chance to consider issues that were to dominate the remainder of his career.

The study's value for Eric's development lies not so much in his conclusions as in the design. The "meaning" of television was sought in the social relationships of people who watch it, not in the "text" of the programs. It was a nascent attempt to develop an anthropological view of television as a culturally embedded communication form—an interest that occupied Eric until his death. He intended to eventually revisit this research and publish it. His premature death prevented him from doing so. I am in the process of making the dissertation available via the World Wide Web as an early example of an anthropological study of the media.

Eric defended his dissertation after he had accepted a post at the Australian Institute of Aboriginal Studies. In fact, the promise of that position was a major motivation for his completion of the degree. For the next six years, he conducted ethnographic field research and wrote an amazing number of papers and monographs before his premature death in 1988.

Michaels's Influences

Before attempting a critique of some of that work, it is necessary to explicate the larger historical and conceptual framework from which it was derived and upon which it comments. The anthropology of visual communication is a relatively new area of study, a field yet to "realize its potential"—a polite way of saying that only a few people are interested in it. It is three times marginal: it deviates from the mainstream of anthropology, of communication, and of visual studies. It is even of minor interest to many who call themselves visual anthropologists. It takes as its field of study all visible manifestations of culture. This is not the place to discuss the whole of the concept. I will therefore concentrate on those aspects most relevant to Michaels's work—the anthropological study of the media.

Anthropologists have traditionally studied the folkways of nonindustrial, kin-based societies. The initial concern was to salvage the remnants of the disappearing world of colonialized people: their languages, customs, and artifacts. Studies were located in a time and place conceived as "the ethnographic present"—that is, prior to significant European intervention. When it was no longer possible to "discover" any "undiscovered" people, the "ruined" savage was reluctantly acknowledged. It became acceptable to admit that the subjects of study were often economically disadvantaged and politically disenfranchised and that at times, they eagerly sought after those aspects of Western culture researchers found undesirable, if not disgusting. The appetite for acquiring certain technologies and skills is usually viewed as a sign that the cultures are unhealthy rather than as an adaptive mechanism that might ensure the survival of some aspects of traditional cultures. As Ginsburg (1994, 1995, 1998) has pointed out, an attachment to or involvement with technologically complex forms of European-mediated communication by "exotic Others" is still infrequently examined by anthropologists. They simply do not wish to explore the implications of Australian Aboriginal country-and-western bands playing reggae or Hopi artists making avant-garde animated films.

At the same time as anthropologists lost "the savage" as their traditional subject matter, some researchers were "rediscovering" ethnography as a means to study Western cultures. George Marcus and Michael Fischer have argued that more anthropologists should join sociological ethnographers and other cultural-studies researchers in ethnographic studies of Western communities or, in their words, "bring the insights gained on the periphery back to the center to raise havoc with our settled ways of thinking and conceptualization" (1986:24).

In spite of the "writing culture" advocates' admonitions, the application of ethnographic methods to the study of mass communication remains an infrequently employed technique sometimes misunderstood by scholars who want to use it because they lack formal training in anthropology. Among some communications scholars, it has become chic to talk about and employ "qualitative" methods. However, mass communications research remains dominated by quantitative methods that are culturally blind. Anthropology and communication studies have yet to establish the value of ethnography for gaining unique insights into Western cultures. As a consequence, those people empowered to make policy decisions about how television will be regulated rely on information designed to ignore cultural aspects of the question. This lacuna has partly been overcome in the 1990s with ethnographic work by some cultural-studies scholars like Ien Ang (1990), James Lull (1990), David Morley (1992), and Roger Silverstone (1994) and an increased anthropological interest in the study of media (Abu-Lughod 1994; Crawford and Hafsteinsson 1995; Dickey 1997; Ginsburg 1998; and Spitulnik 1993).

Ironically, an alternative to the dominant approaches to the study of media has been available since the late sixties, primarily as a result of the efforts of Sol Worth, his students, and associates like Larry Gross and myself to create an anthropology of visual communication (Worth 1981). Although this social theory of communication has been, by and large, ignored by others, it constituted a foundation for Michaels's work. Eric summarized the attitude in *The Aboriginal Invention of Television in Central Australia:*

Communication isn't some quantifiable thing like houses or water bores, where a demonstrated lack is solved by increased numbers. Communication is relational; it brings about relationships between people. . . . [C]ulture is itself information, and kinship and social structures are communication systems which bring certain people together, but exclude others, protecting communication pathways and the value of information they carry. This suggests a deeper and less obvious concern with media's effects than simply worrying about whether viewers might imitate anti-social or cultural destructive behavior they see on TV. (1986a:153)

The foundation of an anthropology of visual communication is the assumption that the unit of analysis should be the social relations within a community that result from the production and consumption of images and should not focus exclusively on the image as text or artifact. The goal is to discover how people become competent in and use visual and pictorial forms in their everyday lives as one means of maintaining their social identity. Social behaviors that surround the making and using of these "artifacts" are the key to understanding the visual/pictorial domain as communication. (See Worth and Ruby [1981] in Worth 1981 for an early explication of this approach.)

Michaels's Australian Work

With this paradigm in mind and with the knowledge that Sol Worth and John Adair had successfully completed a study in which Navajos invented their own movies (Worth and Adair 1972), Eric Michaels arrived in Australia. He was awarded a three-year fellowship in 1982 from the Social Anthropology Committee of the Australian Institute of Aboriginal Studies to "assess the impact of television on remote Aboriginal communities." The mandate was somewhat vague. It did not specify which groups other than those who would receive television once a new satellite was in place. The clear implication was that a researcher would conduct a study before and after the advent of television and therefore be able to assess the impact. Michaels quickly abandoned this passive model for one that assumed intervention would produce more interesting results and was a more politically correct course of action because it allowed the people to have some agency.

Michaels therefore entered the field assuming he would replicate the Worth and Adair study by having Australian Aborigines make videotapes. His mandate as well as the cultural actuality of the people he was to study and the politics of the 1980s were significantly different from the 1960s Navajo study, thus making his initial intentions impossible to fulfill. In "Television—Drawing the Line," an unpublished AIAS seminar report (21 April 1983) presented a few months into the project, Eric acknowledged the uniqueness of the opportunity, his theoretical stance, and at the same time how and why he had to modify his preliminary illusions:

I embark, therefore, with no direct precedent. The literature on television's introduction is only partially useful and it asks very different questions of very different circumstances than those before us now. I believed, and believe, that the subject can and should be addressed as an anthropological study, because it is human expression and human symbolization which are at stake here, and it is human relationships which are affected. . . . I realized early on that TV would be a great missionary of post industrial ideology, and that throughout my lifetime, the situation I am now commissioned to research in remote Australia, will reoccur. Less than a decade ago, the Christian Bible was shown to what was probably the last uncontacted society. The process took nearly two thousand years, required the invention of the printing press, the associated rise of Protestantism, capitalism, and the industrial empires. TV was aired commercially for the first time just about when I was born. By the time I die, barring Apocalypse, everyone will probably have seen TV, everyone in the world. I share, therefore, an imperative that each generation of anthropologists has identified; to grapple with the loss of one kind of life and to prepare people to encounter another. Typical change agents in the past were genocide, disease, literacy and technology. The contemporary world adds novel agents: in the form of electronic media. But there is a difference that I take to be significant; earlier anthropologists were well versed in the characteristics of the change agents, they knew diplomacy, medicine, reading, and writing, and how to use manufactured tools. But we really don't know much more about television than the people at Yuendumu do. We are all, as McLuhan pointed out, primitives in the electronic age. Where previous generations of anthropologists recognized that one of the priorities of research among exotics was to inquire into modern life as well as to document tradition, this point is highlighted in the case of television. Critical questions about that medium have failed to find answers in the context of Western research on western producers and users. The Aboriginal experience may therefore have a kind of immediate pertinence, be able to make a profound contribution, not only to our understanding of their situation but our own as well. . . . I had intended to introduce video in the Australian bush in a very similar fashion [to that of Worth and Adair], with the difference that I would document the process more thoroughly, by reference to the Navajo experiment. I would also be paying particular attention to categories of activity and behavior that one would expect to be affected by exposure to television[;] . . . these would have much to do with who watched television, when and with whom . . . and what immediate effects could be observed in conversation, play and other forms of expression. This would provide a kind of ethnography of viewing. . . . What appears to have happened in places like Yuendumu is that for the first time I've heard of, an absence of broadcasting resources, combined with the availability of videocassette players has produced a situation where the community can approximate a broadcasting schedule from videotape. The schedule is listed in the council building in the store, and a number of other public places. It announces not the programs, but the hours of viewing . . . and, significantly, hours when men view, hours when women view, and hours when teenagers can view. So it appears that the television in Yuendumu is being designed, at the reception end anyway, to conform with some of the principles of social organization in that community.

For three years (1983–86), with Eric's assistance, the Warlpiri people at Yuendumu in the Northern Territory of Australia learned the technology of video production, how to create and manage a "pirate" low-power transmission facility, and the economic and political realities of fighting the world of television broadcasting. They produced hundreds of hours of videotape productions, inventing ways to make and show their works that would not violate their own values. They established the Warlpiri Media Association so that their efforts could continue after the research project ended. After the study was concluded and Michaels left their community, they continued to produce new tapes and narrowcast their programs. To my knowledge, they do so now.

While in the field, Eric walked the tightrope on which many ethnographers find themselves. He was attempting to "serve" three "masters" at the same time. He was researcher and scholar reporting his findings to colleagues at conferences and in journals while he was also facilitator, advocate, and cultural broker attempting to assist the people who gave him access to their lives in their struggle to gain some control over their media fare. At the same time, he was "explaining" the implications of his study to broadcasting bureaucrats. *The Aboriginal Invention of Television*, a summary of the project, was prepared in 1986 to satisfy the terms of his contract. It had one of its intended effects, in that it annoyed and confused the establishment (see Willmot 1987 and Michaels's retort [1987b]). Michaels's most literary and generally useful statement about the work is to be found in his monograph *For a Cultural Future: Francis Jupurrurla Makes TV at Yuendumu* (1987a).

This project has significance for a number of academic disciplines as well as broader cultural implications. One could argue that Eric discovered little that was not already known or at least imagined to exist. The importance of his findings lies not so much in the uniqueness of the information but in the fact that prior to this work, many assumptions about media, information, culture, and television were suppositions or vaguely worded programmatic ideals supported by sparse empirical evidence. There is an unfortunate tendency among some advocates of postmodern theory and cultural studies to sit in the comfort of their offices imagining the world outside and inventing arcane prose to describe it. Eric field-tested concepts and consequently was able to argue his position from an actual case study. It is in this way that his work is important. We no longer have to imagine what things mean to other people. Through Eric's eyes, we can see the production and consumption of meaning in an actual situation.

Michaels's Contribution to Culture and Communication Studies

Eric's work comments on several areas within the amorphous field of culture and communication—a blanket rubric under which one finds anthropology and film:

· The utility of perceiving culture as communication and social systems as regulators of information, thereby dismissing the notion that information ever flows freely in any society
· The fundamental differences between oral and electronic information societies and the implications of those differences when considering the introduction of a new communications technology
· The ethnocentrism of Western/European notions of freedom of expression, the press, artistic license, the need to know, what constitutes privacy, and our facile dichotomy between fiction and nonfiction narratives
· The advantage of ethnography for communication studies
· The need for anthropologists to take an active role in communication and development studies
· The difficulty of any struggle against the image empires of the transnational media corporations

I will briefly comment on these ideas in reference to a general understanding of the place of television in society, the relationship between anthropology and television studies, indigenous media, and the implications of this work for the construction of a new relationship between film and anthropology.

The Warlpiri-speaking Australian Aboriginals that Michaels studied are mainly an oral, kin-based people who exchange information face-to-face. Although the contrast between "oral-tradition" societies and the West is in many ways obvious, Michaels's examination of these differences in relation to the introduction of television into the world of the Warlpiri was innovative. Information in Warlpiri society is owned, inherited, and regulated in complex ways. Knowledge is the social, economic, and political glue that holds societies together. Some people have the right to know, others may have the right to use, and still others have the right to hear or see or perform. From this perspective, cultures are viewed as systems of communication regulated through a social system. To put it another way, understand the flow of information and you have a key to understanding a culture. European cultures have been striving to invent more efficient ways to increase their capacity to "broadcast" as much information as possible to as many people as possible, whereas oral-tradition societies need to "narrowcast" information in a very controlled manner in order to survive.

Contrary to Marshall McLuhan's fantasies, there never was a place where information flowed freely (McLuhan and Fiore 1967). A preindustrial "global village" is simply another Western construction of the exotic Other. It is only with the advent of the "space age" technology of telecommunications that information can even be thought of as instantaneous. The Western notion of the cultural function of information stands in direct contrast to the concept of its function among all oral-tradition peoples. Westerners believe in the freedom of expression and the press, in the right of all people to have open access to information, and that disclosing as much information as possible about as many things as possible is the only way an open, democratic, and free society can function. The clear implication of the Warlpiri study is that some of the fondly held liberal notions about education, information, and so on, are ethnocentric and potentially dangerous to the cultural identity of people who do not share them. Their worldviews and those held in the West are dichotomous, and the differences are not easily resolved.

Oral societies are a kind of "information society" in which access to knowledge is of particular social and economic consequence, and typically highly regulated. The introduction of new information technology to traditional information societies poses fundamental challenges to the maintenance and legitimate evolution of these groups. To the extent that new technologies alter traditional means of access [to] and control of information, and to the extent that novel information (content) devalues traditional knowledge and the authority of its purveyors, the integrity of the society as a whole is at risk. . . . [T]he economics of satellite distribution are essentially the inverse of the information economics of oral, face-to-face society. If such societies intend to participate in new communication technology, complimentary and corrective technology on the ground, at the local level, is suggested as a first priority. (Michaels 1985b:69–70)

The conflict between oral and electronic traditions about the flow of information should cause a revision in Western thinking about the production of images of native peoples and the introduction of television, literacy, and other Western forms of information dispersal into oral societies and cause ethnographic filmmakers to consider what sorts of topics they can legitimately explore and in what manner.

Michaels articulated four areas in which the values of Australian Aboriginal society and European society clash as regards the rights of individuals to produce and use pictorial information:

1. Unauthorized display or transmission of otherwise restricted materials, such as stories, songs, dances, graphic designs, and even oblique references to secret knowledge encoded in the landscape.

2. Violation of mortuary restrictions which may prohibit reproduction of a deceased person's body or voice in the presence of their relatives. This restriction may include songs, dances, or objects associated with the deceased person.

3. Invasion of privacy may include spaces regarded by Europeans as public.

4. The transformation of Aborigines into exotic others. (Michaels 1989: 261)

The question of whether any group of people can assume that they have "the right" to be represented in a manner consonant with their self-image is something that until recently has seldom been considered (Gross, Katz, and Ruby 1988). The roots of a Western cultural insensitivity to this issue are complex. Briefly stated, they are to be found in a set of apparently contradictory assumptions: (1) a naïve hope about the objectivity of the image (and the associated corollary that images reveal the truth) and (2) the idea that film artists have artistic license to interpret the world as they please. Both the image maker as "objective" recorder of reality and the image maker as artist have had a kind of carte blanche. As a consequence, the issue of representation has not been considered to be problematic. Westerners believe strongly in notions of freedom of the press, freedom of expression, and the primacy of knowledge and therefore assume that image makers have license to represent others. To use a fiction-film example, Peter Weir saw no need to consult with the Amish before he transgressed upon their world in making the film *Witness*, nor was it of much concern that his representation of them was profoundly offensive. (See Hostetler and Kraybill in Gross, Katz, and Ruby 1988 for a discussion of the Amish point of view.) As the notion of objectivity became challenged and the political and moral assumptions of image makers were called into question, the need for a new way of thinking about and justifying the representation of Aboriginal life became apparent. It is not too much of a logical leap to suggest that this reformulation should be part of a general questioning of the right to represent (see chapter 5).

Michaels's solution to the potential conflicts just outlined was to suggest that professional image makers behave like ethnographers—that is, spend suf-

In the Belly of the Beast

ficient time with people prior to taking images to develop a collaboration that allows the image makers to take pictures that are not offensive to the people portrayed and still useful for the makers. Although the suggestion is in many ways self-evident, it is also deeply subversive to the model of work found among news-gathering and documentary producers, if not the whole of television and film production. Driven as they are by the need for more and more product in the fastest possible time, the idea of allocating months of field time to the production of a program about Aboriginal life is sadly unrealistic.

In addition to being concerned with how the Warlpiri were represented, Michaels also explored the potential impact that broadcast television would have on the community. Some Warlpiri, fearful of the destructive power of the broadcasting of mainstream television into their communities, saw the advent of their own broadcasting as a means to stem the tide of Western influence. Freda Glynn, director of an Australian Aboriginal media association, CAMMA, has stated the anxiety and the hope in this way:

TV is like an invasion. We have had grog, guns and diseases, but we have been really fortunate that people outside the major communities have had no communication like radio or TV. Language and culture have been protected by neglect. Now, they are not going to be. They need protection because TV will be going into these communities twenty-four hours a day in a foreign language—English. It only takes a few months and the kids start changing. . . . We're trying to teach kids you can be Aboriginal and keep your language and still mix in the wider community and have English as well. At least they will be seeing black faces on the magic box that sits in the corner, instead of seeing white faces all day long. (An interview with Faye Ginsburg, quoted in Ginsburg 1991:98)

Most "communication effects" research assumes one can examine the content of a television program and discern its potential impact. "Because people concerned with the introduction of television to traditional communities want to know what the eventual effect of this introduction will be on Aborigines and their traditions, there is a tendency to jump directly from Western evaluations of television content to effects on Aboriginal audiences. Usually, they employ simple cause-effect assumptions" (Michaels 1986b:45). Michaels's work suggests that it is not so much the content but the form and presentation of the programs that are potentially the most revolutionary and destructive challenge to the Warlpiri worldview. It is not a question of whether violence on television "causes" people to be violent in real life—a favorite topic for politicians—but, for example, what will the introduction of fictional narrative into the Warlpiri worldview do to their society?

[F]ictional genres in the European sense are not apparent in the Warlpiri repertoire; fictional framing, the willing suspension of disbelief, the elements required to negotiate the fictional collusion between storyteller and audience, is absent. For all Warlpiri, stories are true. A single word *jukurrpa,* stands for stories, and dreaming, but also "law." Observers have commented upon the particular difficulty Aborigines have in evaluating the reality of European stories in the form of movies and Hollywood videotapes, although the distinction is eventually realized. (Michaels and Kelly 1984:28)

Television programs produced outside of their community and viewed by the Warlpiri caused them to ask whether some stories are true or not—a query potentially subversive to the core of their worldview—but the impact did not stop there. The imposition of European concepts of time in the form of a program schedule clashed with the Warlpiri's seasonal divisions. Broadcast television's need to maintain a centrally controlled, inflexible temporal structure was in direct conflict with the Warlpiri's more flexible sense of when things are to be accomplished. In addition, the fact that most programs brought in from the outside were in English had the potential to radically undermine traditional patterns of authority and knowledge, because younger people had a greater understanding of English and would therefore own the knowledge television offered them, thereby reducing the elders to a lesser status. "Where Aboriginal information is broadcast, especially when it is broadcast in English, a truly subversive and potentially 'culturecidal' situation is created. Here the authority for 'blackfella business' is wrenched from the appropriate local elders and the information made freely available to the young" (Michaels 1986b:5).

When the Warlpiri became videotape producers, their culture did not emerge so much in a style peculiar to their productions as it did in the social organization of the production. Stylistically the tapes have the "look" of amateurish Western documentaries or Western film students' first efforts. In discussing one of the early Warlpiri videos, Eric said, "[T]he 'creation' of a videotape by directorial design was interpreted by Jupurrurla to require that the entire taping event be organized consistent with the rules for story performance in the more formal and ceremonial terms of Aboriginal traditions. . . . [W]e might see this [as] an experiment by Jupurrurla to embed the videomaking process in his own cultural forms and thereby create a tape which the community would agree was proper and authentic" (Michaels and Kelly 1984:32).

The clear implication is that schemes for training Aboriginal peoples modeled after European ideas in which one always tries to find the "best" person for the job regardless of his or her social identity are in direct competition with the Warlpiri's notions that kinship obligations supersede any other considerations. "The fundamental place of kinship rules will influence all media activities. Anything which is exempted from kinship will be assumed to be European in ownership and purpose" (Michaels 1986a:10).

Assuming that the illustrations just given are only the tip of a cultural iceberg, it should become clear that new communication technologies are never introduced into a vacuum but into a dynamic political, social, and economic environment. In other words, studies designed to achieve an understanding of what happens to a society when people gain access to a new means to communicate require an ethnographic approach to see the technology embedded in a sociocultural framework. "The discovery of what Aboriginal people want from the media emerges only out of a dialogue that takes place around the production, post-production, viewing and reviewing of these tapes as they insert themselves into the community's life, or fail to. And these interactions lead tangentially into related areas of Warlpiri life which impinge on the question of communication, graphic production and interpretation, and traditional law" (Michaels 1985a:50).

Eric argued that the only way in which the Warlpiri or any other people who are invaded by the West's image empires could survive the onslaught would be to wrest some control over the transmission of programs from the agencies that normally dominate it (Michaels 1985b:69–70). He argued that the Warlpiri must create their own TV world, mixing their productions with those from the outside. Michaels also demonstrated that with a little money, people with no background or particular Western technological competence could accomplish this task. The Warlpiri made their own programs and ran their own station without significant financial or technical assistance.

The implications of these ideas strike at the very heart of most anthropological fieldwork and the assumptions of many development programs. Too many researchers have gone blithely into the field assuming they have the right, privilege, and license to study others, often without much thought as to their impact on them. New technologies and ideas are introduced, from literacy and democracy to Western medicine, without much thought as to whether the ideologies that created these technologies are in destructive conflict with the world of the "beneficiaries."

The Future of Indigenous Media

When I first became interested in the issues raised by Michaels's work and indeed saw early evidence that indigenous communities were producing their own images, my response to the possibility of the perpetuation of indigenous media was pessimistic, if not completely negative. I was convinced by the doom-and-gloom predictions of scholars following the Frankfort school view that the culture industry makes victims of us all—especially indigenous people (Katz 1977). I believed that the conclusions to be drawn from Michaels's research provided additional support for a hypothesis about the relationship of television and culture advocated by media scholars such as George Gerbner

(Gerbner, Gross, Morgan, and Signorielli 1980) and Larry Gross (1977). The resistance of indigenous people to this media onslaught and the many examples of indigenous production have caused me to rethink this position. Before I suggest a less harsh conclusion, let me review my original position, because it still has much merit. This section is based on a set of assumptions about television's sociocultural function. The ideas are grounded more in my personal feelings and my observations as an ethnographer looking at his own behavior and culture rather than in any systematic research I have conducted. Support for the position comes from Michaels as well as the work of George Gerbner and Larry Gross and their long-term Cultural Indicators project (Gerbner and Gross 1976; Gerbner, Gross, Morgan, and Signorielli 1980, 1982).

Television, whether private or state-controlled, whether broadcast, cable, or satellite, has been by its economic and technological construction a force for cultural centralization. A few conceive, construct, and are empowered to transmit for the many. The sociocultural purpose of television is to reify, underwrite, support, and espouse the ideology of the status quo. Television functions the way religion and other supernatural systems used to—that is, as the underpinning of official culture. I am not suggesting that the people in charge of a television system conspire to oppress deviation or that they deliberately mean to support the status quo. Often, in the United States, television representatives espouse liberal sentiments about cultural diversity. I simply mean that those who are given the responsibility tend to come from a privileged upper-middle-class segment of society that has clearly benefited from the current structure of society and that those who join them from outside this world are socialized into its values regardless of their background or desire to be thus socialized. Without necessarily realizing it, they assume that the world they know is the only world possible and project that assumption into their work. Although one can find some exceptions within every television system, the overwhelming historical evidence suggests that television has been and generally continues to be a centralizing melting pot that opposes any sort of real programming diversity or willingness to share broadcast power with producers from outside the mainstream.

When faced with linguistic, religious, ethnic, or sexual minorities, the historical response of the television industry in the United States, and I assume elsewhere in the West, has been to symbolically annihilate the group—that is, not represent them at all. If it is true that 80 some percent of the television viewers in the United States obtain information about world events from TV news, then the fact that a group seldom appears on television becomes a serious issue. For example, if we are to believe U.S. television, there were no lesbians in the United States or anywhere else until the advent of the situation comedy series *Ellen*. A variation of symbolic annihilation is the perpetuation of the dominant culture's stereotypical view of the world. Gays are seen as limp-wristed interior decorators, while African Americans appear as servants, criminals, or preachers. Since the perpetuation of these clichés made the television industry susceptible to liberal criticism, a change in representation occurred that was designed to make that industry less vulnerable.

One can therefore note some "progress" in U.S. television over the past two decades: announcers are permitted to retain their regional accents, more African Americans, women, and Hispanics are to be found in front of and behind the camera. Cable and satellite systems make access to a wide range of "minority-language" channels relatively easy. It is important to note that diversity has been introduced in a way that does not seriously threaten either the power structure already in place or its profit margins.

Diversity is "mainstreamed"—that is, it gives the appearance of minority representation without challenging anything. For example, programs are aired in which minority characters are featured, but they don't speak their native language or dress in a way distinct to their group; in short, none of the characteristics that provide the group with an identity is allowed to appear. In the United States, African Americans often appear as characters who display nothing unique to the African American "experience." In *Out of the Silent Land* (1987), author Eric Willmot suggested that Aboriginal representation be "embedded" in regular Australian Broadcasting Commission programming. Thus, the representation of disenfranchised urban Aboriginal characters in regular programming could be regarded as a progressive sign.

A conclusion one can draw from Michaels's study as well as the work of people like George Gerbner and Larry Gross is that broadcast television, regardless of the system employed (that is, on the air, through the cable, or from the satellite), is fundamentally incompatible with notions of cultural autonomy and diversity. In the early 1970s, Edmund Carpenter studied the impact of new media among traditional people in New Guinea. His deeply pessimistic conclusions seem partly to support Michaels's work:

Western audiences delight in stories about natives who use modern media in curious ways, their errors being both humorous and profound, suddenly illuminating the very nature of the media themselves. . . . Even when these stories are true, I think their importance is exaggerated. Surely, the significant point is that media permit little experimentation and only a person of enormous power and sophistication is capable of escaping their binding power. A very naive person may stumble across some interesting technique, though I think such stories are told more frequently than documented. The trend is otherwise. (1974:188)

The question that must for the time being remain unanswered is, Can the many experiments in indigenous media production survive the onslaught of the media empires? Although I still believe that the same industries control most of the means to produce and disseminate images, the total control that existed during the time Michaels was conducting research—that is, the 1980s—has diminished in the 1990s.

Conclusion

These are the days of lasers in the jungle
Lasers in the jungle somewhere
Staccato signals and constant information
A loose affiliation of millionaires and billionaires.
These are the days of miracle and wonder
This is a long distance call
The way the camera follows us in slo-mo
The way we look to us all.
The way we look to a distant constellation
That's dying in the corner of the sky
—Paul Simon, "The Boy in the Bubble"

It should be clear by now that this chapter is not an overview of indigenous media. I have made no attempt to describe the plethora of activity in Australia and in many parts of the world by indigenous people since Michaels's pioneering explorations. (See Ginsburg 1998 for this overview.) I see merit in concentrating on his accomplishments, as they in some ways begin the process being followed today by other scholar-advocates. I also concur with Michaels's cautionary tales about the long-term impact of this new work. Michaels reached a conclusion concerning the relationship between "remote Aboriginal" communities and satellite television even before the fieldwork was completed. It was straightforward and quite clear:

The question "do people of different cultures see, and therefore represent the world differently through visual media" produces answers which can be offered as evidence to argue Aboriginals' rights to access the new media systems proposed for remote Australia. . . . That remote Aborigines are capable and motivated to produce media on their own terms, argues that they can be acknowledged as the experts in the matter and that training, production and distribution assistance by Europeans be reduced to an ancillary role. Schemes to achieve Aboriginal access to new media by importing European crews, or by training Aborigines in western production styles in urban institutions will inhibit the development of a truly Aboriginal media. (Michaels and Kelly 1984:34)

Whether Michaels's notions about how indigenous people were to be trained had any merit is historically beside the point. The majority of indigenous productions are made today in collaboration with nonnatives or by natives trained in the realities of mainstream Western film and television. Indigenous media reflect the complexity of indigenous cultures—a mixture of traditional and Western and newly invented forms. Anthropologists interested in attempting to pictorially represent indigenous people have no choice but to position their needs within a framework that is, by and large, defined by the needs of the community to become involved in their own representation.

Sol Worth and Eric Michaels both died before they had the chance to "finish their work." The studies they conducted about how native people can adapt new media technologies remain seminal. In Worth's case, he died at fifty-five, just as he was to write *The Principles of Visual Communication*, a book that would have summarized thirty years of exploration. And he was about to embark on an ethnographic study of visual communication in a rural U.S. community (Worth and Ruby in Worth 1981). The Worth and Adair Navajo project should have excited other scholars to replicate the study in other cultures in the 1970s and 1980s. It did not. Only in the 1990s are scholars paying attention to these questions, only now it is the natives who are initiating the productions and not the scholars.

Eric Michaels died at the age of forty. He had too little time even to begin to realize his potential, and yet his gift to us was great. Although it may be naive to think that we can ever win the battle against the destructive forces of our society, we are not without hope or courses of action. I don't think Eric ever really believed that Aboriginal peoples could conquer institutions as powerful as the Australian Broadcasting Commission. But that knowledge did not stop him from continuing to work. Nor should it stop us from encouraging, facilitating, collaborating, and studying these efforts.

We may not win the war against the multinational corporations that monopolize the making of images, but there are at least some battles in which victories are possible. Eric demonstrated that it is in the world of videotape and VCRs that one can hope for some real diversity in the production and consumption of images. The technology is relatively inexpensive, very decentralized, and almost impossible to control. Warlpiri people had no trouble mastering the technology and developing their own strategies for the use of their tapes. There is no question that the Kayapo Indians of Brazil used video technology as a political weapon to stop the Brazilian government (Turner 1990). Many other indigenous groups and ethnic minorities are discovering that they can also use this technology for their own purposes. As long as their successes escape the notice of those in charge of the media, indigenous media work stands a chance. If those in charge of the image empires decide that the "market" for this work is sufficient to warrant their attention, the makers and their work will be co-opted, and the work will lose its uniqueness.

Eric Michaels made us acutely aware of our responsibility and impotence.

In the Belly of the Beast

I believe he would have strongly supported Larry Gross's conclusion about our chances to have the image empires represent us fairly or their willingness to aid the oppressed in their attempt to maintain some cultural integrity:

History offers too many precedents of new technologies which did not live up to their advance billing; which ended up being part of the problem rather than part of the solution. There surely are opportunities in the new communications order for more equitable and morally justifiable structures and practices, but I am not sure we can get there from here. As Kafka once wrote in his notebooks, "In the fight between you and the world, bet on the world." (Gross 1988:201)

Toward an Anthropological Cinema:

Some Conclusions and a Possible Future

In November of 1968, I organized a group of papers on film and anthropology for the American Anthropological Association meetings—my first professional panel. In addition to contributions by Sol Worth and Tim Asch, I gave a paper later published in 1970 in *Film Comment* entitled "Towards an Anthropological Cinema." Depending on my mood, I view this writing as being very avant garde or as a sign that I have spent the last thirty years polishing and refining the same ideas. I suppose it was a little of both.

My position should be abundantly clear to anyone who has read this far. Ethnographic filmmaking should be the exclusive province of anthropologists interested in making pictorial ethnographies. Although this may appear to be relatively simple, the consequences would be for anthropologists to divorce themselves from the current world of documentary/ethnographic film practice and the traditional supports that have evolved for the making of an ethnographic film (that is, the idea that film is a useful teaching aid and/or that the film will reach a large audience) and to produce work that confounds the expectations of its audience. To go against received wisdom and to be able to make audiences understand that the choices made were deliberate and not the result of incompetence is no easy task. The films will have to be painfully obvious about the intention of the makers to deliberately deviate from that which is expected.

When French "New Wave" filmmaker Jean-Luc Godard decided in the late 1960s to make nonbourgeois films because he wished to radicalize his audience's vision of the world, critics assumed he had somehow lost his ability to produce comprehensible work. *Wind from the East* (1969) and *See You at Mao* (1970) are still considered "mistakes." Such a radical departure is only feasible or even understandable if there is a rationale to support a new practice—one that makes it possible to visualize culture and to see behavior as an embodiment of culture so that it can be filmed, and to create film styles that transmit anthropological knowledge to a desired audience while at the same time making the theoretical position of the maker clear and the methods employed explicit. To accomplish this task, it is necessary to locate an approach to culture as communication and an approach to film that will allow anthropologists to create an appropriate practice of film. In the remainder of this concluding chapter, I explore two avenues into this construction—viewing culture as performance and creating a trompe l'oeil form of film realism.[1] I do not promise a "how-to" formula but rather reasons "why to."

Culture as a Screenplay; or, Are They "Not Waving but Drowning"?

Nobody heard him, the dead man,
But still he lay moaning
I was much further out than you thought
And not waving but drowning.

Poor chap, he always loved larking
And now he's dead
It must have been too cold for him his heart gave way,
They said.

Oh, no no no, it was too cold always
(Still the dead one lay moaning)
I was much too far out all my life
And not waving but drowning.
—Stevie Smith, "Not Waving but Drowning"

To be able to take pictures of human activity that can be understood by viewers as manifesting culture, a materialist stance is essential. From this perspective, culture can be seen as enacted through visible symbols embedded in behavior—gestures, body movements, and space use situated in constructed

Toward an Anthropological Cinema

and natural environments. These elements are arranged into something resembling a film script, with a plot involving cultural actors and actresses who have lines to say, costumes to wear, props to employ, and settings in which to perform for an intended and sometimes an unintended audience. The sociocultural self is the sum of the scenarios in which one participates as a performer and as an audience member. A culture becomes enacted in the social life of its members. The role of the ethnographic filmmaker is to discover the scripts and discern which are the most useful and revealing of the aspect of culture under study, and to turn these performances into a film. This general vantage point is, of course, a foundation from which the ethnographer can then proceed to the specific theoretical questions that motivate the research.

This approach does not imply that human beings are robotlike creatures mindlessly lockstepping in some narrowly defined set of cultural programs or cynics who self-consciously construct a world they assume will play well to an intended audience. No one ever quite does what he or she is expected to do, even when the person knows how it should be done. Lines are forgotten or deliberately changed for effect. Costumes are mixed or matched and props misused or improvised. Although the templates may be known, there is always lots of room to fudge and still be an acceptable member of society. Social life consists of the interplay between what one is supposed to do and what one actually does. No one has ever participated in the "perfect" bar mitzvah, and yet everyone knows how it should be done and how far one can deviate and still have a success.

People know the idealized cultural templates but seldom follow them completely. Instead, they improvise to find a way of meeting their needs without appearing incomprehensible or offensive. For example, the participants in a wedding among upper-middle-class educated urban folks in the United States work long and hard to get everything right—their clothes, the lines, where they stand, the food, music, and so forth. They know how weddings are supposed to be. They have knowledge of prior successes and failures. They can talk self-consciously, if not reflexively, about weddings in which they participated. The event has formal preparations, rehearsals, and receptions in which participants regularly critique the successes and failures of this wedding and compare it to others. One could compile a list of cultural performances and social dramas that are revealing of culture, from elaborate and complex events like the inauguration of a president to going to see a doctor, that have filmable cultural scripts.

Although passive naturalistic observations of behavior, with or without a camera, yield a certain quality of information, these data are, in and of themselves, not sufficient. A passive camera used to create pure observational-style films does not reveal culture. The researcher must, in some fashion, extrapolate from the particulars of observable behavior to the generalities of culture.

Some of the necessary data must be induced from those studied as the ethnographer becomes a provocateur. Other information becomes embodied in the experience of the ethnographer as participant. The comments, opinions, and critiques of the performers and their audiences are essential in this endeavor, even if what they say is data subjected to additional analysis. It must be further assumed that there are situations in which people do talk or can be placed in a circumstance in which they will talk, as in an interview, about these gestures, objects, and activities. Some cultural events "naturally" lend themselves to moments of reflection, reflexivity, and critique. In other words, human beings both perform their culture and observe others performing it. They can and do talk about both. These are the basic building blocks that the ethnographic filmmaker has to work with—filmed behavior and participants' metacomments about that behavior. Add the analytic devices of organizing filmed elements and the communication of the analyst's experience in the field, methods employed, and his or her point of view and you have an ethnographic film.

Films fail most often because they neglect one of these elements. As I have suggested earlier, it is the theoretical and methodological elements that are most often neglected. Even as worthy a film as Tim Asch's *The Feast* (1970), based on Marcel Mauss's notion of reciprocity, contains no direct mention of these ideas. Viewers must already know the concept or have the ideas explained by an instructor in a class to see the connection.

Anthropologists have been exploring the cultural implications of behavior since there has been anthropology. The observation and analysis of the everyday social activities of ordinary people have been more, and sometimes less, interesting to ethnographers. For a long time, the focus was not so much on behavior per se but on the "rules" that underlie it. During the last several decades, there has been a shift away from a concern with competency and toward an interest in understanding actual behavior—that is, the study of human action as sociocultural performance (Geertz 1973).

As I have suggested earlier, ethnographic film should be grounded in the assumption that culture is created, maintained, and modified through social acts of communication. Dell Hymes's ethnography of communication (1967) and Sol Worth and Larry Gross's modification of that model called "symbolic strategies" (1981) can serve as an overall or a general theoretical basis from which to proceed. Communication is looked upon as a social process in which people construct sign events based on their assumptions that certain codes and conventions will be understood in a certain way. These sign events are located in social contexts that the senders (makers) also assume are appropriate for their purposes. Receivers (or readers or viewers) make the assumption that the sign events are in that place because someone wanted them to understand something. They assume that the maker was competent and that the intended message was like others located in this social context. They attempt to infer what they believe was implied. This approach does not suggest that the maker's implication will always be inferred correctly. It does assume that people create sign events because they want others to understand something and that receivers of these sign events assume they are supposed to infer some meaning. The model is useful as a way to look at how culture is communicated by visible and pictorial means and as a way to think about the making of an ethnographic film.

Clifford Geertz's view of ethnography as thick description (1973) provides a place to begin a discussion of how culture can be extracted from visible behavior. To make a thick description—that is, one interlaced with theory— Geertz suggests that "behavior must be attended to, and with some exactness, *because it is through the flow of behavior—or more precisely, social action—that cultural forms find articulation* [emphasis added]. They find it as well, of course, in various sorts of artifacts, and various states of consciousness; but these draw their meaning from the role they play . . . in an ongoing pattern of life, not from any intrinsic relationships they bear to one another" (Geertz 1973:17). The central issue for the ethnographic filmmaker is to be able to find culture in filmable behavior, and then to generalize from the specific, to make concrete the abstract, and yet to retain the humanity and individuality of those portrayed while still making a statement about culture. In other words, ethnographers should strive to make ethnographically thick films.

Geertz suggests that culture can be seen in visible behavior. It seems logical that he therefore would assume it is filmable. Yet he appears uncertain— even though the implication of the quotation cited above suggests otherwise. In his now-classic distinction between a twitch as an involuntary eye movement with no intended cultural meaning and a wink as a movement fraught with cultural meaning, Geertz suggests that "the difference, *however unphotographable* [emphasis added], between a twitch and a wink, is vast: as anyone unfortunate enough to have had the first taken for the second knows" (Geertz 1973:6).

In the case of even more nuanced behavior, Geertz regards the camera as virtually useless. "One can go further: uncertain of his mimicking abilities, the would-be satirist may practice at home before the mirror, in which case he is not twitching, winking, or parodying, but rehearsing; though so far as what a camera, a radical behaviorist, or a believer in protocol sentence would record he is just rapidly contracting his right eyelid like all the others" (Geertz 1973:7). In a footnote from the same article, Geertz apparently contradicts the statement he made three pages earlier that "anthropology exists . . . nowadays [in] the film" when he suggests that "most ethnography is in fact to be found in books and articles, rather than films" (Geertz 1973:19, n. 3).

Geertz is clearly ambivalent. Perhaps it is because he assumes that the camera is a device of neutral observation and does not understand that it can be used in other than "radical behaviorist" ways. Employed intelligently, the camera is guided by the intention of the operator, so that the transformation of observation into written notes is similar/analogous to the same transformation into film footage. In other words, the abstracting process of going from observation to the production of field notes to the construction of written thick description can be seen as parallel to the process of observation, filmed footage, and finished film.

Although Geertz's seemingly contradictory statements suggest that he lacks confidence in the capacity of cinema to express ethnography, his point of view remains useful for our purposes in that he articulates a crucial problem in a productively general manner: finding a way to construct a communication—written or pictorial—that enables readers and viewers to discern when they are looking at winks, which are to be understood as culturally meaningful signs, and when they are looking at twitches, which have no cultural significance. In addition, it is essential that viewers be able to discern the differences among cultural signs so that they can understand when someone is merely waving and when he or she is drowning and therefore gesturing for help. If the ethnographer who writes can discover a way to make those distinctions, then surely he or she can find a way to construct a film that also does the same for viewers.

Discovering a way to do this is, of course, the fundamental task of ethnographic filmmaking as an anthropological activity. If, after repeated attempts to produce films that explore these distinctions, it is discovered that such films do not work, then we will have learned something we currently do not know about the limits of film to reveal culture. Because the assumptions of professional filmmakers have been superimposed upon ethnographic film owing to its association with documentary film, such risk-taking experiments are rare. In their explorations, ethnographic filmmakers should ally themselves with experimental filmmakers, who are content to produce works with no commercial potential designed for a very small audience.

Geertz's ambivalence about the camera as a "naive observer" renders his position somewhat marginal. However, there is a body of work, beginning in the 1950s and continuing to the present, concerned with the ethnographic analysis of behavior recognized by Geertz (1988) as part of the "interpretative turn in anthropology" that seems altogether suitable. It has been variously called a dramatological model of culture (Erving Goffman, the Chicago school ethnographic sociologists, and the symbolic interactionists), culture as secular ritual (Barbara Myerhoff and Sally Falk Moore), culture as performance and social dramas (Victor and Edie Turner, Milton Singer, Dwight Conquergood, and Richard Schechner). The similarities between performance models of culture and Hymes's ethnography of communication are obvious. For Hymes, people enact their culture in conversations in which the parties involved perform their culture for each other (Hymes 1967). It is not my purpose to exhaustively summarize or critique the work of these scholars or the field of performance studies in general but rather to select those elements most useful for ethnographic filmmakers. My emphasis is on the initial formulation of these ideas because they serve as the basis for contemporary practice.

Schechner provides a concise overview of the early stages of performance studies:

Victor Turner analyzes "social dramas" using theatrical terminology to describe disharmonic or crisis situations. These situations—arguments, combats, rites of passage—are inherently dramatic because participants not only do things, they show to others what they are doing or have done; actions take on a "performed for an audience" aspect. Erving Goffman takes a more directly scenographic approach in using the theatrical paradigm. He believes that all social interaction is staged. People prepare in the backstage, confront others while wearing masks and playing roles, use the main stage area for the performance of routines, and so on. For both Turner and Goffman, the basic human plot is the same: someone begins to move to a new place in the social order; this move is accomplished through ritual, or blocked; in either case a crisis arises because any change in status involves a readjustment of the entire scheme; this readjustment is effected ceremonially—that is, by means of theater. (1977: 120–23)

Schechner's background in the theater predisposes him to see this approach as deriving from the intersection of studies of the theater/drama and anthropological analyses of ceremonies/rituals. His interest is in using anthropological concepts to study theatrical performance and to explore the possible historical relationship between religious rituals and the origin of the theater. As my concern is an anthropological one, my emphasis is on the utility of seeing culture as performance.

Looked at from the viewpoint of ethnographic film, these performance scholars seem to imply that cultural performances have a scenariolike structure that resembles a screenplay, even though, with the exception of Richard Schechner, they fail to explore the cinematic implications of the idea. Elizabeth Fine and Jean Speer provide a more recent, nicely condensed, and very anthropological view of the approach: "Studying performance . . . is a critical way for grasping how persons choose to present themselves, how they construct their identity, and ultimately how they embody, reflect, and construct their culture" (1992:10).

Anthropologists have long been interested in those events in which one's status in a community and the core values of the community are publicly enacted. From Arnold van Gennep's notion of *rites de passage* (1960) to Victor Turner's social dramas (1976), these events are seen as excellent field sites to explore culture. Participants in rituals, ceremonies, and performances are concerned with "doing it right"—that is, fulfilling their personal and cultural expectations about how things are to transpire. It is a place in which being reflexive is expected and everyone concerned is a cultural critic. An interest in these events has a long history, but only since the 1970s have some anthropologists recognized the dramatic qualities of these events and incorporated ideas from the theater and performance studies into their work.

Although Milton Singer was the first anthropologist to suggest that cultural performances were "the elementary constituents of a culture" and "the ultimate units of observation" for the ethnographer (1972:71), it was Victor Turner, followed by Barbara Myerhoff, who defined and popularized the concept and suggested it should become a primary concern of ethnographers. "Performance, whether as speech behavior, the presentation of self in everyday life, stage drama or social drama, would now move to the center of observation and hermeneutical attention" (Turner 1986:77). Today it is a taken-for-granted approach to the study of culture (Schieffelin 1998).

Anthropological performance scholars have concentrated their efforts on what they term social dramas, cultural performances, sacred and secular rituals, and rites of passage. These occasions appear to be self-consciously constructed dramatic social events that resemble a play and therefore could lend themselves to being converted into ethnographic "screenplays." I wish to make it clear that in talking about culture as consisting of a series of screenplays, I am not suggesting that these social events are screenplays in the sense of having a written text or even that entire cultures can be understood as a text. As popular as that metaphor may be, the concept of a text implies something fixed, as in a written document. Cultural performances are more like improvisational theater than a play with a strictly performed script. Although the notion of "culture as text" is a popular one, the reduction of culture to a text systematically excludes the embodied and other sensory knowledge that is at the core of culture. The written text of a performance contains only some of the event, as anyone knows who has read the published versions of a Spalding Gray (1985) or Laurie Anderson (1984) performance.

While recognizing that the concept of performance can cover a broad range of human social behavior, as seen in Goffman's interest in *The Presentation of Self in Everyday Life* (1959), Victor Turner and most of those associated with this idea wish to narrow the focus. "Social drama . . . [is] an objectively isolatable sequence of social interactions of a conflictive, competitive or agonistic type" (Turner 1986:33). These events are separable from the everyday flow of life. "For me the dramatological phase begins when crises arise in the daily flow of social interaction" (Turner 1986:76). Turner believes that these social dramas cause the participants to become reflexive—transformed into persons unlike their daily selves. It is in this state of heightened self-awareness that they become valuable participants in the study of their own culture.

Jean Rouch has discussed a similar transformation that occurs when he films people. Rouch's approach to the making of ethnographic films is to be a provocateur, not a passive observer. Whereas Turner wished to observe social dramas, Rouch creates them. *Chronicle of a Summer* (1961) is filled with moments in which Rouch brings people together to see what will transpire, as can be seen in the lunch scene in *Chronicle* when Rouch asks one of his African students if he knows what the tattooed numbers on his student Marcelene's arm represent. He knows his African student has little knowledge of the Holocaust. The provoked scene tells us something about both participants. Rouch calls these moments "ciné trance" and argues that the camera does not record actuality but transforms it in such a way as to be revealing of culture. In fact, Rouch argues that the entire act of filming transforms everyone involved, including the crew (Rouch 1971 [1978], 1974).

Barbara Myerhoff expanded upon Rouch's notion and suggested that all ethnographic research with and without a camera is transformative. She refers to life history as "third-voice" endeavor—a blending of the voice of the investigator with that of the person portrayed in such a manner as to make it impossible to know who is author. The process does not produce "objective truth" but rather is a dialectical transformation of the researcher and the subject: "[W]hen one takes a very long, careful life history of another person, complex changes occur between subject and object. Inventions and distortions emerge, neither party remains the same. A new creation is constituted when two points of view are engaged in examining one life. The new creation has its own integrity but should not be mistaken for the spontaneous, unframed life as-lived person who existed before the interview began. This could be called an 'ethnoperson,' the third person who is born by virtue of the collusion between the interlocutor and subject" (Myerhoff 1992:281).

One can look at Rouch's collaborations in films like *Jaguar* (1955) as having third-voice tendencies. The name of his production company, Delaru, exemplified this tendency. The name combines the first two initials of his two African collaborators with his. The notion that people can perform their lives in response to the requests of the researcher and that those performances can concern the people's entire lives or can be a comment upon a social drama seems to be yet another example of how a performance model can aid in the making of ethnographic film. When Lorang, in David and Judith MacDougall's film *Lorang's Way* (1980), takes them through his compound commenting on his property, wives, and the world in general, he is responding to their request to show his world. He is self-consciously performing his life for the camera. In John Marshall's masterful *N!ai: The Story of a San Woman* (1980), N!ai sings a metacommentary about her life as Marshall portrays it.

Third voice and ethnopersons are complex ideas that Myerhoff's premature death prevented her from pursuing to the extent they deserve. In fact, these concepts are most fully discussed by Marc Kaminsky in his reconstruction of the ideas in his introduction to a posthumous volume of Myerhoff's essays (Myerhoff 1992). Hopefully, another anthropologist will pick up the concepts and more fully explore them. On the surface, they appear to have potential for ethnographic film as collaborative life histories become attractive film subjects.

Performance scholars interested in studying social life have confined themselves to the extraordinary because they believe these events are most revealing. Turner once told Edward Bruner that he thought "that anthropologists usually study cultures in their duller, more habitual aspects" (Bruner 1986:13). Perhaps the everyday lives of ordinary people are too commonplace and slow-paced to be effectively studied or filmed. Documentary films that purport to be "a day in the life of" or "a slice of life" are seldom that. The day or the slice or the person selected to be filmed is almost never ordinary. Turner even argues that

> human sociocultural life certainly has long stretches of non-dramatic activity, even *to the point of tedium* [emphasis added]. By temperament and training many social scientists prefer these "harmonic" periods for the social interactions they contain. They provide misleading information that resembles natural phenomena which can be measured and quantified. But perhaps it is no less "distorting" to metaphorize human social processes as physical or biological rhythms and regularities than it is to recognize an affinity between spontaneous human disturbances, group life, and that genre of cultural performance which we call "drama." (Turner 1986:37)

If the ordinary and everyday lives of people are not a fruitful place to study culture, two questions—both rhetorical—arise: are the results of the studies of social dramas and performances useful in understanding the nondramatic moments in people's lives, and are the theories and methods that performance anthropologists employ called into question because of this situation? Moments of social drama are uncommon. What about the rest of people's lives? How do we understand them? Do they lend themselves to making a credible film about culture? Although Ray Birdwhistell's wonderful admonition that "nothing never happens" is undoubtedly true, those who represent other people's lives rely on a narrative structure that contains some dramatic elements and seldom just portray the normal and undoubtedly dull flow of everyday life.

The idea of capturing life as it is found and presenting it untouched has been the claim of some filmmakers since Dziga Vertov. Italian neorealist film theorist Cesare Zavattini argued that fiction film should assume "a direct approach to everyday reality . . . without the intervention of fantasy or artifice" (1953:64). He believed that these simple stories that were to be found in actuality would make great films. "No other medium of expression has the cinema's original and innate capacity for showing things, that we believe worth showing, as they happen by day—in what we call their 'dailiness,' their longest and truest duration" (1953:65). Yet in practice, I can find no film—ethnographic, documentary, or fiction—in which the dramatic is totally absent. The simplest material-culture film tells the story of the making of an artifact. The work of Harvey Pekar, discussed later in the chapter, chronicles his life in a series of comic books titled American Splendor (1991), in which little drama occurs. Harvey simply lives and portrays his "humdrum life" (his expression).

When the technology first allowed filmmakers to take long, uninterrupted sequences of behavior in virtually any location, observational-style cinema was invented. Perhaps the most famous documentary film produced in this manner was the twelve-part U.S. public television series An American Family, from the early 1970s. Margaret Mead thought it signaled the invention of a new form of representation. "It is, I believe, as new and significant as the invention of drama or the novel—a new way in which people can learn to look at life, by seeing the real life of others interpreted by the camera" (Mead 1973:A61). Filmed over an extended period of time, the series represented a longitudinal look at the everyday lives of an upper-middle-class Euro-American family, the Louds of Santa Barbara, California. Audiences followed the series—one episode per week—with rapt attention similar to the devotion that soap operas engender. On the surface, this would appear to suggest that films of the nondramatic are possible. Although the series did contain long sequences in which "nothing significant happened," it was organized around the social drama of the separation and divorce of Pat and Bill Loud and the impact it had on everyone in the family. It also had a very dramatic, and at the time (the early 1970s) unusual, subplot involving one of the sons—namely, Lance Loud's "coming out" and moving to New York City. Scholars and critics have argued that without these events, the series would have been too slow and boring to hold its audience (Ruoff 1998).

Contemporary technology offers the possibility of observing the everyday lives of people in many locales. The notion of a kind of Big Brother recording the tiniest details of our lives and then making the recording available for mass consumption both repels and fascinates us, as attested to by Albert Brooks's over-the-top parody of An American Family (1972), Real Life (1979), and the more recent films The Truman Show (1998) and EdTV (1999). The announcer in The Truman Show calls it "the longest-running documentary soap opera in history." In a New York Times review, Janet Maslin queries, "What if our taste for trivia and voyeurism led to the purgatory of a whole life lived as show-biz illusion? What if that life became not only the ultimate paranoid fantasy but also achieved pulse-quickening heights of narcissism?" (1998).

There seems to be some evidence that viewers are interested in the "boring" everyday features of the lives of very ordinary people, as the existence of Jennicam suggests. A young woman, Jennifer, has placed a video camera in her bedroom and work space that is turned on all the time. It produces several images per minute and makes them available via the Internet to the entire world. The existence of a Jennicam Society in Australia attests to the extent of her following. Are we sufficiently voyeuristic or curious about the everyday lives of other people to be interested in ethnographic films that chronicle the mundane and the everyday? Can anthropologists effectively study culture as it is located in the mundane?

As there are no examples that audiences can use to understand nonfiction drama such as *An American Family*, it is not surprising that soap opera is the model most often employed. Fans of the Jennicam exchange E-mail pondering Jennifer's future as they would do for an actress in a soap opera. Extending that assumption in a not illogical merchandising direction, *The Truman Show* contains "references to memorable episodes over the years, postcards of favorite moments in the show, obscure characters from the program's past years, various bits of Truman Trivia and a catalog of products featured on the show, offered for sale and snapped up by its loyal international audiences" (Paramount Pictures Press Kit for *The Truman Show*). Had *An American Family* been produced in the nineties, I'm certain that T-shirts, coffee mugs, and other tie-in products would have been available. So perhaps the question to be asked is not "Can anthropologists/filmmakers produce work about everyday life in a way that would interest an audience?" but rather "Can they prevent audiences from reducing the work to a kind of 'actuality soap opera'?" The question is part of a larger and quite serious query. How do ethnographic filmmakers prevent audiences from employing their cultural models obtained from fiction film to understand the behavior portrayed in an ethnographic film? The question is a crucial one for anthropology because many of these folk models run counter to the purposes of anthropology. Must anthropologists didactically instruct viewers about how to understand the cultural performances captured on film?

Some scholars have questioned the utility of performance theory and argued that scholars are "creating" drama where none exists. Turner has been criticized by Raymond Firth, Max Gluckman, Lucy Mair, and others because they feel that he is imposing a dramatological model on events that are not "naturally dramatic." Firth argues that Turner is "adopting as a model a stylized aesthetic construct, the drama," and voices a concern that it could "deliberately shape, distort, and contrive his data for didactic purposes, and desert the facts that are his duty to study" (1957:1). Turner responded that he believed that "the drama is rooted in social reality, not imposed upon it" (Turner 1986:37). I think it is difficult to obtain evidence to support or refute Turner's contention. I am less certain that "social facts" exist outside the researcher's explorations. I choose to avoid the line of argument made by Turner and suggest that all theoretical models are "imposed." They do not reside in the people studied; they are simply devices that assist in making the social lives of others comprehensible. Theories are neither true nor false; they are merely useful. Performance theories appear useful as a basis for organizing ethnographic films.

It should be obvious that the approach proposed here is not original or some grand theory of culture. I am merely tweaking an already existing body of work now commonplace within cultural anthropology to suit my purposes. From my point of view, I am simply making explicit that which has always been implicit in the work of performance scholars. My approach is avowedly incomplete and inadequate in the grand scheme of things. But haven't grand theories exhausted themselves long ago? My version of performance theory is merely one way of looking at one manifestation of culture. It is a response to the question "Can you see culture, and can you make a film about it?" Viewing culture as performance is one of several nonpositivist, nonobjective positions that Geertz has characterized as being part of the "interpretative" turn in anthropology currently in vogue (1988). It furnishes a vantage point for looking at certain aspects of human behavior, which, in turn, provides a way of filming culture.

Applying theories of performance to culture requires that we go beyond the obvious dramatic metaphor. To say that all the world's a stage and human beings actors is, of course, to invoke a worn-out cliché and hope that it has some merit. As Erving Goffman pointed out long ago, "All the world is not of course a stage: but the crucial ways in which it is not are hard to specify" (1959:3). Life is considerably more complex than a stage play. There must be a space for preparation, or backstage; a place for the audience; "schools" to train actors and actresses and a socioeconomic structure that provides funds and interests for leisure-time activities such as theatergoing; and so on. To take the metaphor literally, to have a stage, you need a theater and a large number of accompanying cultural institutions like newspapers in which to advertise before any performance can be presented on the stage. In short, there are a lot of nondramatic elements that go into a dramatic performance. The actual play is a short-lived event compared to the infrastructure necessary to accomplish it.

Perhaps the weakest part of the metaphor is that stage dramas have directors and producers—someone with some authority who tells the actors and actresses how to perform their parts and someone who sees to the organization and finances necessary to make a performance possible. Human social dramas often lack such centralized and absolute leadership and authority. People are socialized into culturally proper ways of behavior, not trained by a director or drama coach. Nonetheless, the observation that we, like J. Arthur Prufrock, "put on a face to meet the faces that we meet" and that one's life can be viewed as having a script has been made in a convincing manner for centuries by numerous philosophers, poets, novelists, critics, and other observers of the human condition, both before and after Shakespeare. Here are two examples—Jean-Paul Sartre and Joan Didion:

Let us consider this waiter in the cafe. His movement is quick and forward, a little too precise, a little too rapid. He comes toward the patrons with a step a little too quick. He bends forward a little too eagerly; his voice, his eyes express an interest a little too solicitous for the order of the customer. Finally there he returns, trying to imitate in his walk the inflexible stiffness of some kind of automaton while carrying his tray with the recklessness of a tightrope-walker by putting it in a perpetually unstable, perpetually broken equilibrium which he perpetually reestablishes by a light movement of the arm and hand. All his behavior seems to us a game. He applies himself to chaining his movements as if they were mechanisms, the one regulating the other; his gestures and even his voice seem to be mechanisms; he gives himself the quickness and pitiless rapidity of things. He is playing, he is amusing himself. But what is he playing? We need not watch long before we can explain it: he is playing at being a waiter in a cafe. There is nothing there to surprise us. The game is a kind of marking out and investigation. The child plays with his body in order to explore it, to take inventory of it; the waiter in the cafe plays with his condition in order to *realize* it. This obligation is not different from that which is imposed on all tradesmen. Their condition is wholly one of ceremony. The public demands of them that they realize it as a ceremony; there is the dance of the grocer, of the tailor, of the auctioneer, by which they endeavor to persuade their clientele that they are nothing but a grocer, an auctioneer, a tailor. A grocer who dreams is offensive to the buyer, because such a grocer is not wholly a grocer. Society demands that he limit himself to his function as a grocer, just as the soldier at attention makes himself into a soldier thing with a direct regard which does not see at all, which is no longer meant to see, since it is the rule and not the interest of the moment which determines the point he must fix his eyes on (the sight "fixed at ten paces"). There are indeed many precautions to imprison a man in what he is, as if we lived in perpetual fear that he might escape from it, that he might break away and suddenly elude his condition. (Sartre 1956:59)

I was supposed to have a script, and had mislaid it. I was supposed to hear clues, and no longer did. I was meant to know the plot, but all I knew was what I saw: flash pictures in variable sequence, images with no "meaning" beyond their temporary arrangement, not a movie but a cutting room experience. In what would probably be the middle of my life I wanted still to believe in the narrative and in the narrative's intelligibility, but to know that one could change the sense with every cut was to begin to perceive the experience as rather more electrical than ethical. (Didion 1979:12–13)

For some, viewing human behavior as some form of "acting" may appear to be overly facile, if not cynical. For anyone who believes that people have a "true" self that resides outside of social interaction, this vantage point is unbearable. Indeed, some of Erving Goffman's critics characterize him as profoundly jaded. It is hard to disagree when he reserves the term *sincere* "for individuals who believe in the impression fostered by their own performance" (Goffman 1959:17). As Goffman moved away from dramatological analogies to game theory, as can be seen in *Frame Analysis* (1974), the alienation and disillusionment of viewing life as "merely" a game could seem overwhelming. There is no denying Goffman's pessimism, but to dismiss his ideas simply because of his tendency to construct marvelously flippant expressions like "civil inattention" is shortsighted. As Geertz points out, "not all game-like conceptions of social life are quite so grim [referring to Goffman] and some are positively frolicsome. What connects them all is the view that human beings are less driven by forces than submissive to rules, that the rules are such as to suggest strategies, the strategies are such as to inspire actions, and the actions are such as to be self-rewarding—*pour le sport*. . . . Seeing society as a collection of games means seeing it as a grand plurality of accepted conventions and appropriate procedures" (Geertz 1973:25–26). If we set aside for the moment those behaviors that are deliberately constructed to lie or misrepresent—that is, what might be termed in street vernacular "running a game on someone"— then looking at human behavior as a series of performances that are culturally constructed seems nonjudgmental and productive.

Goffman was among the first to suggest this model. As he is also the one who advocated its application to the whole of life and not just the special moments of social drama, his ideas deserve some further attention. It is important to mention that he did not work collaboratively with scholars from the theater or performance studies, and consequently his model is the least dependent on a theatrical metaphor. As a sociologist, Goffman's interest in social life as performance revolves around "impression management"—the ways in which individuals successfully perform their social lives—and the creation of a manageable social world from the vantage point of the individual. He examined social life in the following manner: "[W]hen an individual plays a part he implicitly requests his observers to take seriously the impression that is fostered before them. They are asked to believe that the character they see actually possesses the attributes he appears to possess, that the task he performs will have the consequences that are implicitly claimed for it, and that, in general, matters are what they appear to be" (Goffman 1976:89). In other words, the purpose of performances is to both maintain and perpetuate the social worlds of the performers and their audiences. Although not stated in anthropological terms, Goffman's view clearly implies an ethnography of communication view of culture.

Goffman was a curious mixture—a Chicago school sociologist who never employed quantitative methods and who seemed unconcerned with sampling or the representativeness of his remarks. For example, in *Gender Advertise-*

ments (1979), his marvelously provocative exploration of the image of women in magazine advertisements, Goffman never articulates the techniques he employed in selecting the magazines, the advertisements from the magazines, or the time period. His qualitative or ethnographic approach never produced any full-blown ethnographies, except his unpublished dissertation. His field research appears to be confined to a series of astute but generalized passive, if not casual, observations about middle-class urban Euro-Americans. In short, Goffman was talking about the world in which he was a performer. It is not unreasonable to argue that his adult life was a prolonged field trip. As someone who knew him slightly, I can attest to the fact that going to a movie or out to dinner with him was frequently an event fraught with anxiety because he seemed to be engaged in social experiments that often were close to the edge of social acceptability so that he could passively watch the results. I often felt that I was an involuntary experimental subject. Although his approach to research contrasts with that of Turner (1974, 1976) and Myerhoff (1980, 1992), who support their models from their published ethnographic studies, this lack does not invalidate the brilliance of his observations; it simply makes them researchable assertions.

His work may also suffer because of the influence of a now-abandoned structural linguistic model of body movement advocated by Ray Birdwhistell (1980), which I already critiqued in chapter 1. Toward the end of his career, Goffman became enamored of the direct-observation field techniques of ethologists—methods flawed because they suggest that behavior can be comprehended through passive observation no matter how distant the observer is from the culture of the observed. This approach implies a universality to behavior that anthropologists reject. Nonetheless, with all its limitations, his notion of performance remains useful because of its breadth and because it suggests a nondramatic approach. Goffman employs a semiotic/communications point of view to search for a syntax of conduct in the world of everyday conduct and face-to-face interaction. His position remains the broadest articulation of everyday social behavior as performance: "I have been using the term 'performance' to refer to all the activity of an individual which occurs during a period marked by his continuous presence before a particular set of observers and which has some influence on the observers" (Goffman 1976:91).

Although he is less concerned with reaching a more generalized or abstract level of culture, I see no reason why his notion cannot be used to study culture. I cannot imagine a social interaction that could not be explored as performance. Culture can be viewed as the set of values that enable or underlie a performance. The self becomes the sum of all the performances and audience memberships. Turner points out that "as Goffman and others have shown, ordinary life in a social structure is itself a performance. We play roles, occupy statuses, play games with one another, don and doff many masks, each a 'typification'" (1986:107). It is from Goffman that we can borrow the notion that all human interaction can be profitably explored as performance. Although the drama of certain performances makes them excellent subjects for a film, an examination of everyday life through film remains the least explored aspect of the culture as performance and of film in general. Until some work studying this idea is completed, the questions raised about the value of examining everyday life as performance will remain unanswered.

It is remarkable that none of the anthropologists involved in exploring culture through performance ever pursued the cinematic implications of their ideas, since their emphasis was on visible manifestations of culture. They apparently have not considered the possibility that performance theory could be used as a theoretical justification for the making of ethnographic film—as a way to construct filmable cultural screenplays. Victor Turner's only discussion of film is about how film, like theater, is a performance (1986). Barbara Myerhoff, a pioneer in the exploration of secular rituals (Moore and Myerhoff 1977), was involved in the making of two films about her fieldwork among elderly Jews in Los Angeles. These films, albeit quite moving and revealing of how fieldwork is done, are relatively standard television documentaries that report on her fieldwork but do not concentrate on social dramas or secular rituals that she discussed in her writings (Myerhoff 1980). For example, the birthday and death of a ninety-year-old man at the Israel Levin Center, which figure so prominently in her book *Number Our Days* (1980) and were the subject of several essays (Myerhoff 1992), assume a relatively minor place in the film of the same name. The two films about Myerhoff's life and her research— *Number Our Days* (1980) and *In Her Own Time* (1985)—were designed for a mass audience, not as scholarly publications. Myerhoff viewed film solely as a medium useful to popularize via television and to educate students (Myerhoff, personal communication, 1980).

It is ironic that someone like Myerhoff—who was in so many ways part of an anthropological avant garde; an early postmodernist; a pioneer in producing multivocal, reflexive ethnographies about urban U.S. communities; and someone who fulfilled her moral and political obligations to the people she studied in an exemplary fashion—should be so conventional in her attitudes about the potential of film. It is important in the history of film and anthropology to realize that Myerhoff was instrumental in the founding of the University of Southern California's program in ethnographic film. Although the leadership of the program was assumed by Tim Asch, he shared Myerhoff's attitude toward film. Given their assumptions about the limitations of film for anthropology, it is not surprising that most of their graduates became filmmakers and not anthropologists.

Of the group of scholars most associated with performance studies,

Richard Schechner is alone in contemplating the possibility of the usefulness of performance studies for ethnographic film when he states that "first, by replacing the notebook with a tape recorder, the still camera with a movie camera, the monograph with the film, a shift occurs whereby we understand social life as a narrative, display behavior, and so on" (1982:79). Schechner has also explored units of behavior as if they were strips of film (1985). In this study, he talks about ethnographers as "theater directors," in that they often ask the people portrayed to reenact (1985:107). I am not aware that Schechner has ever pursued the potential of film for his own work beyond these statements or that he was ever involved collaboratively with ethnographers and filmmakers in the production of films that explore his ideas about performance and culture.

The field of performance studies has mushroomed since the initial work in the 1970s, as can be seen in Marvin Carlson's recent overview of the field (1996). Unfortunately for anthropology, anthropologists have seldom become involved with performance scholars. Dwight Conquergood is one of the few performance scholars who remains a productive ethnographer. Collaboration has unfortunately become all too rare. For example, theater director Eugenio Barba, with no training in anthropology, developed an "International School of Theatre Anthropology" (ISTA) in Norway, designed for performance and theater people. "In ISTA the distinction is repeatedly emphasized that the term 'anthropology' is not being used in the sense of cultural anthropology but that ISTA's work is a new field of study applied to the human being in an organized performance situation" (Barba 1991:n.p.). Barba did collaboratively produce a play, *Talabot*, based on the life of Danish anthropologist Kirsten Hastrup. She has written an interesting account about how it feels to see your life transformed into theater (1992).

My impression of the work of performance scholars who are not trained ethnographers is that it parallels the situation in ethnographic film, in which many people who lack any training in ethnography nonetheless feel comfortable calling their work anthropological or ethnographic. Both groups are sincere in their interests but lack sufficient knowledge to make any direct contribution to anthropology. At the same time, the idea of studying culture as performance in the tradition started by Turner is commonplace among anthropologists, to the point where some anthropologists have felt the need to reclaim the territory from cultural and performance studies (Hughes-Freeland 1998). Although performance scholars may not be aware of the potential of their work, it seems to me it provides a view of culture that can serve as a schema for the making of ethnographic film.

PERFORMING ETHNOGRAPHY. The scholars discussed in the preceding section have gone beyond an exploration of culture as performance and experimented with performing ethnography—a logical extension of their interest in performance. They produced dramatic readings and plays based on their ethnographic research (Turner 1986; Lazarski n.d.). In the early 1970s, Colin Turnbull worked with dramatist Peter Brook in turning his work about the Ik of Uganda into a series of dramatic episodes. While at George Washington University, Turnbull taught some ethnographic performance courses with Nathan Garner, who, in turn, worked with anthropologist Catherine Allen to produce an ethnographic play, *Condor Qatay* (1997). In the early 1980s, the Turners, with Schechner, produced several experimental ethnographic performances with graduate students and faculty at the University of Virginia as a way of critiquing and enlarging insights derived from written ethnography (Turner 1986:141). In 1988 and 1991, Dwight Conquergood and Howard Becker (Conquergood 1995; Becker, with McCall and Morris, 1989) cotaught a seminar titled Performance and Social Science. Becker went on to produce some performances of his research (McCall and Becker 1990; Becker, with McCall and Morris, 1989). Barbara Myerhoff's ethnography and film *Number Our Days* was transformed into a play at the Mark Taper Forum in Los Angeles in the 1980s. There was some discussion about converting the work into a feature-length fiction film (Myerhoff, personal communication, 1981) that never was pursued after her death.

These experiments concentrated on the conversion of ethnographic knowledge into theater performed by actors and actresses (sometimes professionals and sometimes anthropology and theater students) collaboratively trained by a dramatist or performance scholar and an ethnographer—a division of labor that parallels the collaboration of professional filmmakers and ethnographers. Turner's interest was in developing a critique of written ethnography by having the actor, critics, and scholars embody the ethnographic knowledge through performance and then reread the ethnography with "new eyes." Allen, Garner, Becker, Myerhoff, and Turnbull were interested in looking at the theater as an alternative means of communicating ethnographic knowledge to a wider audience than those who read monographs. "We wanted to see whether playwriting could provide a vehicle for ethnographic description, interpretation, and even analysis, and we were interested in the ways a dramatic performance may communicate ethnographic insights to both audience and actors" (Allen and Garner 1997:2). Turnbull was interested in exploring similarities between the theater and anthropology:

In field work the anthropologist is perhaps like the playwright as he observes human behaviour and looks for that which is significant either in itself or by comparison with other forms of behaviour. The field-worker is also like the actor in that he too is playing a role and if he uses the technique of participant/observation, has comparable problems of association and dissociation. How far does he "play" the role, consciously remaining on the outside and, in a sense, observing himself as well as others, and how far does he lose himself in the participation, becoming that which he plays? (Turnbull 1979:2)

Apparently, none of these experiments was filmed, and no one involved saw the possibility that the work might be useful for the development of ethnographic film. With the deaths of Turnbull, Turner, and Myerhoff—the core of the anthropologists concerned with performance as a nontraditional means of publishing—the ethnographer's involvement in performance waned except for the recent play *Condor Qatay*. Like ethnographic novels and poems, plays based on an ethnography remain undertheorized and consequently underutilized.

COMMUNICATING ETHNOGRAPHY IN A NONTRADITIONAL WAY. Experiments in performing ethnography are part of a larger movement among anthropologists to explore nontraditional ways to communicate ethnography—how to break out of conventional ethnographic writing styles—and as such, it is directly related to our quest to find a way to communicate anthropology through film. Breaking out of the restrictions of conventional ethnographic writing styles has become a preoccupation of many since George Marcus and Michael Fischer declared there was a "crisis of representation" within anthropology (1986). Turner and others have been joined by a growing number of anthropologists who have decried the limitations of normative scientific writing for expressing ethnographic knowledge and, in a larger arena, the logocentric bias of anthropological theory. As Edward Bruner has suggested, "Social scientists have long given too much weight to verbalizations at the expense of visualizations, to language at the expense of images. Lived experience, as thought and desire, as word and image, is the primary reality. . . . Every anthropological fieldworker would readily acknowledge that the accepted genres of anthropological expression—our fieldnotes, diaries, lectures, and professional publications—do not capture the richness or the complexity of our lived experience in the field" (Bruner 1986:5, 7).

Some critics of traditional methods of reporting are concerned with the effects of reducing the sensory experience of field research to words. They acknowledge the difficulties that anthropologists have had in discovering ways to make public their experiences in the field within the confines of traditional ethnographic reporting. "One of the most vexing (and interesting) of these problems (that human events are multi-faceted and should be represented that way) is the fact that the 'totality' of human events is difficult—perhaps impossible—to capture in writing, particularly in the academic discourse(s) of the social sciences" (Allen and Garner 1997:1). Becker argues that his "invention" of

Toward an Anthropological Cinema

[p]erformance science rests on some ideas now current in the sociological and rhetorical analyses of science and other academic writing; that modes of reporting social science results are conventional, that no one format (especially the standard journal article in its canonical *American Journal of Sociology* or *American Sociology Review* form) is privileged or intrinsically better than others, that every format makes it easy to say some things and hard to say others equally worth saying, and that it is therefore worth experimenting with modes of representation. (1989:94)

A volume edited by Kirsten Hastrup and Peter Hervik, *Social Experience and Anthropological Knowledge* (1994), explores this issue in some detail. Although all of the authors in this volume and other critics of the limits of traditional ethnographic writing bemoan the limitations of writing to convey embodied ethnographic knowledge, they continue to write about it in a relatively conventional way and are extremely timid about suggesting nonprint alternatives. Although the concern is widespread, the experiments to counter the limits are few and far between. The rhetoric of discontent has become commonplace.

One thing for sure is that the standard modes of realist narrative storytelling about the momentous present as it unfolds [are] not enough for historians, anthropologists, literary critics, film and videomakers, philosophers, and other scholars of the present. . . . Rather the new languages and vocabularies will remain for the foreseeable future embedded in and inextricable from the messy, contestory discussions that predominate in the wake of the widely acknowledged crisis of representation. . . . We merely claim that distanced expository discourse and representations—whether theoretical, descriptive, or media commonsensical—are inadequate without the collaboration and exposure of the discourse of situated persons, who become the subjects of the contributions of the various fin-de-siècle themes taken by this series." (Marcus 1996:2)

Marcus's solution was to edit a book of interviews—a timid and hardly innovative variation.

All of these critics ignore the potential of film, photography, and other pictorial means of expression to expand the way in which anthropologists might express that which is "beyond words." Apparently none of them has seen the relevance of Margaret Mead and Gregory Bateson's 1942 masterpiece *Balinese Character*, in which the authors grapple with a similar problem almost a half century before the current interest—"that words which one culture has invested with meaning are by the very accuracy of their cultural fit, singularly inappropriate as vehicles for precise comment upon another culture" (Bateson and Mead 1942:xi). They offered their work as one example of a way to deal with the problem: "In the monograph, we are attempting a new method of stating the intangible relationships among different types of culturally standardized behavior by placing side by side mutually relevant photographs"

(1941:xii). The sound ethnographies of Steve Feld (1991), the experiments with performing ethnography mentioned in the preceding subsection, poetry, nonfiction novels, painting, let alone digital multimedia in which the senses are stimulated in a variety of ways are almost never discussed. Anthropologists have been far too "modest" in the solutions they propose to escape the trap of "scientific" writing.

Dwight Conquergood has argued that performing ethnography might be one way out of the limitations of written ethnography. In his article "Rethinking Ethnography," he asks, "What are the rhetorical problematics of performance as a complementary or alternative form of 'publishing' research?" and concludes with the recommendation that the idea has great potential (1991:190). He cites Talal Asad (in Clifford and Marcus 1986) for support: "If [Walter] Benjamin was right in proposing that translation may require not a mechanical reproduction of the original but a harmonization with its *intentio*, it follows that there is no reason why this should be done only in the same mode. Indeed, it could be argued that 'translating' an alien form of life, another culture, is not always done best through the representational discourse of ethnography, that under certain conditions a dramatic performance, the execution of a dance, or the playing of a piece of music might be more apt" (Asad 1986:159).

Michael Jackson has also suggested that there is a need in anthropology to reestablish "the intimate connection between our bodily experience in the everyday life and our conceptual life" (Jackson 1989:18). He argues for a "radical empiricism" that "stresses the ethnographer's *interactions* [emphasis added] with the people he or she studies," while urging us "to clarify the ways in which our knowledge is grounded in our practical, personal, and participatory experience in the field as much as our detached observations" (Jackson 1989:3). Jackson is among the more adventurous anthropologists with his experimental multivocal, genre-bending ethnography *Bawara* (1986). Jackson is arguing for the kind of reflexive multivocal ethnography that filmmakers like Rouch have been practicing for some time.

Certainly Jackson and those mentioned earlier are not alone in their frustrations with the assumed limitations of ethnographic writing. The list of discontents is extensive. Why have none of them looked to film as an alternative means? It has to be the case that their culturally acquired notions about the capabilities of film make them assume it simply cannot express that which they wish to communicate. To make it worse, those involved in the making of ethnographic film seem uninterested in pointing out the potential of film to overcome some of these frustrations with the limits of print.

Experiments in the presentation of lived experience that combine reporting about experience (for example, the lived experience of doing ethnography) with a concern for larger issues (some theoretical or sociopolitical concern) are by no means confined to anthropologists. Although not stated in social-science terminology, combining the personal with the political/theoretical into a coherent public statement is a concern of many people. Performance artists such as Laurie Anderson, Spalding Gray (Richard Schechner worked with Gray in the Performance Group), Coco Fusco, and Guillermo Gómez-Peña are able to interweave the personal/autobiographical as description with the theoretical in a way that resembles Geertz's notion of thick description. Fusco and Gómez-Peña's *Couple in a Cage*—the performance, the videotape, and Fusco's articles (1995)—is among the more sophisticated critiques of anthropological and museum practices by performance artists. *Swimming to Cambodia* (1987) is about a moment in Gray's life when he was a bit player in a film, and at the same time, it is a critique of U.S. involvement in Southeast Asia. Both Anderson and Gray had their stage performances successfully converted to film. Anthropologists interested in discovering new ways to communicate ethnography would do well to consider their work as well as that of other performance artists and experimental theatrical work, as they are grappling with problems similar to those experienced by ethnographers. Both are observers of the human condition, and both have had experiences that they wish to convey in terms that exceed the limits of autobiography and self-portraiture.

The artist who comes the closest to performing ethnography on the stage is Anne Deavere Smith—a performer and professor of theater at Stanford. She has produced several incredible multivocal dramatic performances such as *Fires in the Mirror* (1993), a drama that centers on the 1991 Crown Heights killings of Gavin Cato and Yankel Rosenblaum, that are worthy of serious consideration by anthropologists. *Fires* consists of twenty-six monologues, each offering different perspectives of and on the Crown Heights community. The material for the performance was gathered by conducting extensive interviews with a number of participants in the event and then producing a stage persona for each person. According to Shayla Stein, Smith sometimes "begins each monologue with a brief description of the actual interview (i.e., where it took place, who else was present, what people were wearing), which is used as stage directions. Contained in the description is usually a reference to the date, time and sometimes even includes a description about the weather" (1996:n.p.). Smith "performs" all of the characters. The scenes are orchestrated together to present audiences with a conflicting and nonoverlapping recounting of the event by the participants and the moral tales woven by commentators. She resembles the ethnographer who strives to be multivocal by allowing those participants in the event to literally speak through her agency. One could fault her work because her perspective is too buried and implicit. It is unclear where Smith positions herself in relationship to the multiple points of view expressed in *Fires*. The only person who appears not to have an explicit voice in the performance is Smith. Nonetheless, she seems to be doing on the stage what Myerhoff strove to do in her writing—to create a third voice that combines the voice of the ethnographer/performance artist with the voices of those represented in such a way to as create something that is greater than the sum of the two alone (Myerhoff 1992).

Although there are lessons to be learned from these talented performance artists, they are limited by audience expectations and the difficulty of mastering two disciplines—academic anthropology and the technical skills and knowledge needed to produce a convincing public performance. These artists remind us that the theater, like film, can be used for purposes other than simpleminded entertainment. Realistically, few ethnographers will be willing to be trained to become effective performers, nor do they have the talent. Awkwardly produced amateur productions are unlikely to be an effective means of communicating anthropology unless the performance ethnographer is willing to retrain audiences into having appropriate expectations.

The parallel with ethnographic film should be apparent. When an ethnographer collaborates with a theater person, the problem of whose needs and assumptions are to be met must be addressed. Should the performance be primarily good anthropology or good theater, and how does one decide which expectations are paramount? As an anthropologist, my response should not be in doubt. Allen, an anthropologist, and Garner, a theater person, who collaborated to produce *Condor Qatay*, suggest that "[i]f a body of ethnographic drama is to be produced, it is going to be produced by those who study societies in the way anthropologists do and who also fully understand how a theater piece works and how to make it happen. It will also have to be performed by actors who are committed to cross-cultural exploration and are willing to immerse themselves in ethnographic-detail" (1997:12).

This idea can be expanded even further: asking people—both the ethnographer and those the ethnographer studies—to perform their lives on a stage or in front of the camera is something worth serious consideration. To succeed, one would have to overcome the severe limitations of a history of mediocre docudramas and reenacted documentaries that have established a tradition that assumes that real life is simply not interesting enough to hold an audience's attention. It must be "jazzed up" with fictitious characters and events.

There is one additional pictorial method of communicating the personal and the theoretical that seems worth considering when searching for new ways of communicating ethnography. It has the potential to expand the ways in which ethnography can be communicated pictorially. Since the 1960s in the United States, a number of graphic artists have created adult, serious works in comic book or graphic novel form. Marginalized by the public's assumption that comic books are for children, hippies, science fiction fanatics, and soft-core porn fans, these works are often overlooked and have never reached the general level of cultural acceptance that *mangas* have in Japan, where it is not unusual to see businessmen reading comic book treatises on economic theory on the subway. "Japan is the first nation to accord 'comic books' . . . nearly the same social status as novels and films" (Schodt 1996:19). Rius's *Marx for Beginners* (1979) started a slew of instructional graphic books that are part of many undergraduates' education. Art Spiegelman's *Maus* (1986) is perhaps the most widely known of serious comic books—an allegorical tale about the Holocaust in which Jews and Nazis are portrayed as animals.

It is the autobiographical work of Harvey Pekar that is most directly relevant. In a self-published series, American Splendor, Pekar chronicles his life. Pekar works collaboratively. He writes out the story and then finds a graphic artist such as Robert Crumb to draw it. As a consequence, American Splendor contains several graphic styles. Each issue tells "stories about his [Pekar's] own daily life, depicts anecdotes and conversations he has heard and overheard, dramatizes vignettes from his civil-service job in Cleveland and presents his often glum ruminations about his career and his life in general" (Witek 1989:121). Titles such as "More Depressing Stories from Harvey Pekar's Humdrum Life" or "Awaking to the Terror of the New Day" provide some indication of his approach. The ordinariness of Pekar's life as presented in these stories is in some ways reminiscent of Spalding Gray's work and defies the assumption that readers or viewers need high drama to hold their attention. For example, in "Grub Street, U.S.A.," there is no action; Pekar simply sits and reads and gets up and thinks about the parallels between his efforts to find an audience and Victorian novelist George Gissing's problems. "His writing style usually eschews the neat packaging of traditional plot, his stories often seem to be all middle and no ending" (Witek 1989:133). Pekar comes as close as any contemporary figure to presenting the everyday life of an ordinary person. Comic books are similar to the photographic essays and storyboards employed by fiction filmmakers. They represent a flow of behavior reduced to those elements essential for comprehension. It does not seem much of a stretch to suggest that like Pekar, ethnographers could produce word sketches that a graphic artist could draw into ethnographic comics. If Marx, Foucault, semiotics, and capitalism can be represented in a productive way in comic books, why not an ethnography? In fact, a relatively timid attempt already does exist, with Gillian Crowther's 1990 article "Fieldwork Cartoons."

As long as anthropologists continue to assume that they must be confined to conventional forms of writing to communicate ethnography, they will continue to be frustrated that their intended audiences are being denied access to some fundamentally important forms of knowledge that the ethnographers acquired. In a digitized multimedia world, it is positively embarrassing to think that anthropology remains bound by words. It is unfortunate that more anthropologists don't share Catherine Allen and Nathan Garner's assumption that "[w]riting plays or other kinds of fiction gives anthropologists a vehicle—a kind of thought experiment—with which to work out the relationship between the kinds of real people they know and the kinds of situations these people create in their societies" (Allen and Garner 1997:11).

Although I make no claims to have exhaustively explored the literature about the problem of finding alternatives to print and speech to represent the embodied and sensory experience of ethnographic research, those authors whose works I have examined ignored film. I believe that this is yet another example of how marginalized ethnographic film is from the mainstream of cultural anthropology. The ethnographic filmmakers fail to pursue the anthropological implications of their work, often because they seek their validation from the film world or the "ghetto" of ethnographic film festivals and not among cultural anthropologists. Mainstream cultural anthropologists see film as having value only as a teaching tool. It is quite telling that no author in *Writing Culture* (Clifford and Marcus 1986), the seminal exploration of how anthropology is communicated, explored film as a potential alternative to the limits of print. This situation can only be corrected when those who make ethnographic films are anthropologists who are primarily concerned with the reception of their work as a contribution to anthropological discourses.

In embracing performance theory as the basis of a theory of culture that makes it filmable, I acknowledge that I, like Goffman and perhaps Harvey Pekar, wish to broaden the notion of performance beyond that which Turner and others suggested. Anthropologists of performance tend to confine themselves to events that are inherently dramatic—those regular moments of religious ceremonies and rituals and those special and extraordinary moments in which the social fabric is rent and in need of repair. This is an important and useful concept and one that can be employed in the making of film, but I wish to broaden the concept of performance to include the nondramatic elements of the everyday lives of ordinary people to provide a larger theoretical underpinning for the filming of culture. Both dramatic and nondramatic performances share the purpose of maintaining society and assisting its members through the recurring and unusual crises that constitute a part of all human experience. I am dubious of a model of culture that confines itself to the study of the extraordinary for confirmation.

A justifiable criticism of my position is to ask for examples of films that successfully depict people's ordinary and everyday existence. My answer is an ambivalent one. With the exception of a few experimental films, all films, fiction or nonfiction, are narrative. It is difficult to tell a story without a plot, and the expected norm is to have one with conflict and resolution. Ethnographies have two plots: there is the story of the ethnographer's experience in the field—a tale too often untold except over a beer at the American Anthropological

Association meetings; and there are the stories of the lives of the people studied—tales all too often poorly told. As many critics have pointed out, anthropologists need to become better storytellers and find a way to tell about their experiences in the field as well as to tell convincing and moving tales of those they studied. From the perspective of performance studies, the task for ethnographic filmmakers becomes finding a way to tell the stories they discovered in the field and to make it clear why these stories are important. As Sally Ness has suggested, "As the interpretative camp in anthropology grows, and as interest in the way different peoples perform their culture increases, the importance of film as a tool in anthropological education expands as well. Film offers the sort of text most appropriate for the study of cultural performance; however, the use of film in anthropology generally fails to develop its full potential" (1988:135).

If performance provides ethnographic film with a way of considering culture that is filmable, is there an approach to film that will fit this view of culture? I use the term *approach* advisedly, in that I do not think that some grand theory of film is possible; just as the notion of culture as performance is at best a partial model, any usable and defensible theory of film cannot be all-inclusive.

Trompe l'Oeil Ethnographic Realism

[T]he instinct of imitation is implanted in man from childhood, one difference between him and other animals being that he is the most imitative of living creatures, and through imitation learns his earliest lessons; and no less universal is the pleasure felt in things imitated. . . . Thus the reason why men enjoy seeing a likeness is, that in contemplating it they find themselves learning or inferring, and saying perhaps, "Ah, that is me." . . . Imitation, then, is one instinct of our nature.
—ARISTOTLE, *Poetics*, Part IV

They're gonna put me in the movies.
They're gonna make a big star out of me.
We'll make a film about a man that's sad and lonely.
And all I got to do is act naturally.
—Johnny Russell and Vonie Morrison, "Act Naturally"

Locating a theoretical position about film that fits with a performative theory of culture may seem like a simple task. However, regarding culture as a series of improvised screenplays and therefore organizing an ethnographic film around one or more of these performances assumes that ethnographies are narrative and appear to resemble fictional forms more than scientific reports or a conventional documentary film—a radical proposition that requires elaboration and justification.

This book is not the place to present an extended argument for the need to make ethnographies narrative. Rather, I will simply accept Edward Bruner's assertion: "Our anthropological productions are our stories about their stories; we are interpreting the people as they are interpreting themselves" (1986:10). I will therefore take it for granted that ethnographic film must be narrative—a nonfiction narrative, but a narrative nonetheless. Conventional fictional narratives have a beginning, a middle, and an end, usually with a plot that has conflict and resolution. Narrative ethnographic filmmakers will have to develop an unconventional way to tell their stories, as observed human behavior seldom fits into the neat packages that are associated with fictional narratives. Adopting an overtly narrative style will confuse some viewers, as they might associate a narrative film with fiction. It will require the filmmaker to instruct viewers as to how to view the film. This need to educate virtually forces the visual ethnographer to be reflexive so as to assure the viewer that the choices made were deliberate and are not a sign of technical incompetence.

At this point, my formulation of an ethnographic film is almost complete. I have argued that these films should be produced by anthropologists as the result of a long-term, intensive field research project concerned with the visible manifestation of culture in performative events that lend themselves to being transformed into filmable scenarios. The film itself would be a reflexive narrative in which the anthropologist tells the story of his or her field experiences as a series of observed cultural performances that reveal some aspect of the culture studied. Within this tale, the methods employed, the underlying theoretical assumptions, and relevant components of the ethnographer's persona would need to be revealed. Such films would both confound and confront the conventions of documentary realism and the assumption that narrative is a fictional device. The means necessary to accomplish these tasks will have to be borrowed from the whole of cinema and, when not readily available, invented. Given the eclectic and experimental nature of this proposed approach, ethnographic filmmakers will find themselves allied with the avant-garde, experimental, art-film world in their quest for a cinema alternative to the mainstream of fiction and documentary.

It may appear that contradictory messages are being conveyed here. I am suggesting a model for ethnographic film that is at once rigid and open-ended. I see no conflict in doing so. I maintain that to do ethnography demands certain things, like an articulated theoretical position, a knowledge of the language of the people studied, and a long-term, intensive period of participant observation. Films made by people who have not observed these methods fail to qualify as ethnography. Once a study has been completed in this manner, then the form in which it is communicated can be as innovative as the subject matter requires. The process of doing ethnography is generally agreed upon by anthropologists. It is difficult to imagine a professionally trained ethnographer deviating from these expectations. It is in the reporting of ethnographic knowledge that I am advocating some experimentation.

I have argued that anthropologists need to take the control of ethnographic film production away from professional filmmakers if they wish ethnographic film to be other than a pedagogical or popularizing activity. They must gain sufficient technical skills so as to be able to produce their own work—a task no longer difficult or expensive with small-format video. They need to regulate and limit their collaboration with professional documentary filmmakers and broadcast journalists in the same way that anthropologists have limited their interaction with professional writers. They need to make modestly budgeted work so that they do not have to satisfy the reasonable demands of funding agencies that wish grantees to produce conventionally "good" films that are understandable to the general public and reflect well on the agencies.

Ethnographic filmmakers should secure inexpensive distribution outside of television and commercial companies so that their work can be easily accessible to scholars and anyone else interested. They need to create venues in which their films are screened, critiqued, and receive scholarly attention from the mainstream of cultural anthropology. Their primary intention must be to produce "good anthropology" and not necessarily "good films"—not a surprising requirement if one considers that few print-oriented anthropologists would argue that their primary intention is to produce "good books." I wish to emphasize here that when I speak of "good anthropology," I am not suggesting that ethnographic filmmakers seek to please the conservative elements of the mainstream in anthropology. I mean the exact opposite—that ethnographic filmmakers should be challenging the logocentric bias of the mainstream. This concern for doing "good anthropology" does not preclude the making of popular films for television that would undoubtedly involve collaborating with professional filmmakers and television producers. It is suggested that developing these popularizing works be regarded as an adjunct to the primary task of making anthropology on film.

As anthropologists, anthropological filmmakers must be methodologically explicit, explain their theoretical assumptions, and seek to make their films contribute to the scholarly dialogues that constitute professional anthropology. As politically and morally sensitive scholars, they must actively seek ways for the people portrayed to have an active voice in the construction of their image. The work must be returned to the people imaged, and an ongoing dialogue must ensue between image maker and those imaged.

There is one final piece to this puzzle—one assumed attribute of film that needs to be confronted: realism—a topic of some importance to the world of film studies. The association of film with realism has caused people to assume

Toward an Anthropological Cinema

that film is merely a window on the world, a transparent view of the actuality in front of the camera, a medium that is inherently descriptive and specific to the people, places, and events recorded. This association has caused many anthropologists to assume that pictures cannot produce abstract analytic messages, that only words can do that. Therefore, these conventional assumptions about film realism must be addressed in a manner that deviates from the approach historically characteristic of film studies.

In searching for a theoretical support for a filmic approach to culture as performance, it is tempting to ignore the entire field of film studies as not relevant because of its preoccupation with using literary models of textual analysis to make "close" readings of films and its tendency to subscribe to outmoded positivist notions of objectivity and reality. However, a wholesale dismissal could offer critics a chance to suggest that the construct is born out of ignorance. There has been an unfortunate tendency among anthropologists writing about ethnographic film to avoid the work of film scholars. Karl Heider's canonical *Ethnographic Film* (1976) never even mentions film theory or film studies. More recently, Peter Loizos offhandedly rejected the relevance of film studies for ethnographic film because it "is a highly theorized field, with its own radical agendas and special interests" (1993:193). He seems uninterested in commenting on the writing of people like Bill Nichols, a film scholar who speaks directly about ethnographic film (1981, 1994).

I can certainly commiserate with Loizos. For the past several decades, film studies has become engulfed in turgid postmodern prose borrowed from literary studies that can easily alienate the uninitiated. From my perspective, these scholars are far too enchanted with invoking Jacques Lacan, Jacques Derrida, and Michel Foucault as authorities for textual analyses based on literary models. They seem uninterested in validating their assertions beyond claiming that these authorities (who, in turn, have nothing to support their contentions beyond the logic of their arguments) have said it is so. The notion of testing their ideas among viewers with ethnographic studies of film reception, for example, seems unheard of. As a social scientist, I find their work tautological. However, to ignore or dismiss the field because of a personal antipathy is not defensible. Both Heider and Loizos imply a theory of film in their writing, as does anyone who writes about film. Their implicit models are naive about film's apparent verisimilitude, undoubtedly as a consequence of their lack of knowledge of film studies. To guard against making the same mistake, I will briefly critique the concept of film realism and its relevance for my approach to ethnographic film.

Until the 1970s, scholarly questions about film seemed to revolve around a single issue: its relationship to realism or, as Gerald Mast, Marshall Cohen, and Leo Braudy phrased it, "[I]s the filmed world realistic or artificial?" (1992:ix). The connection to ethnographic film should be obvious, in that ethnography, whether written or filmic, has been logically associated with realism. "The ethnographic genre developed in a general Western cultural reaction which cannot be understood apart from an historical dialectic rooted in the contemporaneous rise of both positivist science and realist fiction in the nineteenth century" (Webster 1980:53). The power of the concept can be seen even among those experimenting with innovative forms of ethnography. According to the authors of *Condor Qatay*, the ethnographic play mentioned in the preceding section that was based on the fieldwork of Catherine Allen, it "attempts to embody as much verisimilitude as possible with respect to the culture of this Andean community" and "strives to be emphatically realistic" (Allen and Garner 1997:6).

It is not surprising that the questions about film and realism should be so compelling, since photochemical and electronic media appear to have such verisimilitude that they fulfill Aristotle's notion that art should imitate nature (1968) and, at the same time, positivist science's need for objective data. It is this verisimilitude that first attracted anthropologists to the medium. Film is, without a doubt, the most realistic of all media. Its existence seems to support the possibility that true mimesis—an exact copy or true representation of reality—is achievable. Mimesis has been one of the central ideas of Western aesthetics from the Greeks through the Renaissance and the Enlightenment (Gebauer 1995). The mid-nineteenth-century French version, in which painters like Jean Courbet strove to create "objective representations of the external world based upon the impartial observation of contemporary life" (Nochlin 1971:24), is the immediate ancestor of cinematic realism. The relationship between photography and mimesis is also historically important, in that film shares with photography similar mimetic qualities and, at the same time, extends those properties because film's "copy of nature" moves and talks. The relationship between representation and the "real" remains a central issue in postmodernism.

If the purpose of art is to achieve mimesis or "to create an illusion of reality, the motion picture makes it possible to achieve this ideal in an unprecedented way" (Mast, Cohen, and Braudy 1992:3), or so it would seem. Argued in semiotic terms, realist film sign events appear to be isomorphic with their referent—that is, film is transparent. If that were so, it would seem to fulfill Bronislaw Malinowski's dictum that anthropology should strive to help us "see the world through the eyes of the native" (1922). If that were possible, then all that anthropologists would have to do is hand the camera to the "natives" and have them produce "an exact copy" of their world—a scenario that would make anthropology redundant.

Interestingly enough, the value of this assumed property of film has been contested since the inception of the medium. At the same time as the first realist nonfiction films were being made in the late 1890s, an antirealist tradition was emerging, partly as a reaction against film's overwhelming verisimilitude. Louis and Auguste Lumières' short films of unadorned everyday life such as *The Workers Leaving the Factory* (1895–97) competed for audiences with magician George Melies's cine fantasies like *A Trip to the Moon* (1902). The Lumières' "actualities" apparently did not hold audiences' interest for long and gave way to the Melies-like fantasies and fiction films' illusions of actuality (Musser 1990). Nonfiction realist films became relegated to a minor place in world cinema, ignored by critics and theorists alike.

Although film realism was established as the earliest film practice by the Lumière brothers, some critics believed that the mimetic "nature" of film was a detriment. Some early theorists sought ways to subvert its verisimilitude by arguing that films should not allude to nature at all. Vachel Lindsay (1915), for example, was reacting against filmmakers like "Lumière" who "were certain the cinema has no lasting value beyond the events it could record" (Andrews 1976:11). Rudolf Arnheim (1957) suggested that by keeping film silent and black-and-white, it would appear to be less realistic. These formalists believed that film's true potential lay in the manipulation of actuality to transform it into art—the tension between mimesis and poesis. Chief among the antirealist film techniques was montage—the creative juxtaposition of scenes that did not "naturally" go together chronologically (Eisenstein 1949).

Arguments about formalism (antirealism) versus realism are a subset of a larger debate in art and literature about the relative importance of form and content and the even larger issue of being "objective" versus being "subjective." Interpretative anthropologists like Victor Turner have argued for an antirealist approach to ethnography or, as he put it, "[p]oesis, rather than mimesis; making not faking" (1982b:93). I certainly support his position and argue that the danger of realism for anthropological communications is that it may confuse readers and viewers into thinking that an anthropological representation is merely a copy of nature.

French critic André Bazin, the dominant proponent of film realism, argued that film best realizes itself with deep-focused single takes in which the action unfolds within the frame, requiring as few cuts as possible, so that the "natural flow of events" appears to be preserved (Bazin 1967). He believed that certain film styles would cause audiences to suspend their disbelief. Writing as a critic and an editor of the influential *Cahiers du Cinéma* just after World War II, Bazin never organized his concepts into a coherent theory; it must be implied from his various essays. What is clear is that his film realism depended on a positivist conception of film. "The objective nature of photography confers on it a quality of credibility absent from all other picture-making. In spite of any objections our critical spirit may offer, we are forced to accept as real the existence of the object reproduced, actually re-presented, set before us, that is to say, in time and space. Photography enjoys a certain advantage in virtue of this transference of reality from the thing to its reproduction" (Bazin 1967:13–14).

Bazin's ultimate goal was to create "the myth of total cinema"—the illusion of a perfect copy of the world with no discernible interpretation by the filmmaker. "The guiding myth . . . inspiring the invention of cinema, is the accomplishment of that which dominated in more or less vague fashion all the techniques of the mechanical reproduction of reality in the nineteenth century, from photography to the phonograph, namely an integral realism, a recreation of the world in its own image, an image unburdened by the freedom of interpretation of the artist or the irreversibility of time" (Bazin 1967:21). Bazin looked to Orson Welles and Italian neorealists such as Vittorio DeSica as exemplars. The opening shot of Welles's *Touch of Evil* (1958)—in which the camera describes the town, the characters, and the premise of the plot in one incredible shot—fulfilled Bazin's notion of mise-en-scène.

Bazin and other film realists were applauding the artistic ability of filmmakers to create fictive illusions that could achieve a high level of verisimilitude in feature theatrical films and not filmmakers who recorded actuality as it happened in front of the camera in order to produce documentaries. In other words, theories of film realism were designed as a justification for a certain variety of fiction rather than nonfiction. According to Mast, Cohen, and Braudy, realist cinema "obscures the distinction between authentic and staged events, making us feel like eyewitnesses at what are in fact fictional events" (1992:6).

Nonetheless, the earliest documentary theorists, Dziga Vertov and John Grierson, conceived of the documentary within a realist framework—that is, they, like Bazin, thought there was an objective reality that cinema could record or simulate—and indeed, most documentarians, until today, have assumed that they are making films in the realist manner. Film's mimetic capacity gave the documentarian raw material to be molded into a film. Vertov and Grierson were committed to a documentary that interpreted and did not simply record actuality. Documentary realism is the antithesis of Bazin's notions of film realism. For Grierson and Vertov, the documentarian does not merely record a world; he or she creates one consonant with what the filmmaker regards as actuality.

Grierson argued that "you photograph the natural life, but you also, by your juxtaposition of detail, create an interpretation of it" (Grierson in Hardy 1979:22–23). He is famous for his description of the documentary as the "creative treatment of actuality" (Hardy 1979:35). Vertov argued that filmmakers should produce a kino pravda, or "cine truth," that was unique to the vision of the world offered by the camera. Rouch was later to adapt Vertov's kino pravda and call it *cinéma vérité*. Vertov's and Grierson's notion that the documentary film was an interpretation of the realistic scenes the camera captured makes their ideas parallel to those of film realists like Bazin. All three thought that cinema was a product of the creative abilities of the maker. For Bazin, it was the creation of an illusion of actuality, and for Vertov and Grierson, it was the creative interpretation of actuality.

Although many documentaries produced prior to the 1960s employed fictionlike techniques such as reenactments (*Salt of the Earth*, 1954), staging (*Night Mail*, 1936), and even sets (the igloo scenes in *Nanook of the North*, 1922), the realists ignored the similarities between realist fiction and the documentary and focused on the creation of a fictive illusion of reality as the aesthetic achievement that made film into an art. Documentarians were regarded as being severely limited because they had to be "true to life"—the "artless" recording of actuality requiring little of its makers other than an "objective fidelity" to what was in front of the camera. With some few exceptions, like the work of Robert Flaherty, documentaries were assumed to constitute a minor film genre of little importance except as propaganda or for educational purposes. Some documentary practitioners, such as Grierson, would accept such a characterization without regarding it as negative. His interest was education and persuasion. Only Dziga Vertov dared to argue that the mission of cinema was to capture life unawares and to present true-life dramas without resorting to the artifices of fiction (Vertov 1972, 1923 [1984]). For Vertov, cinema best realized itself in nonfiction. Most documentarians seem to have accepted their marginalized status as a minor form of cinema for specialized audiences. As someone who advocates transforming ethnographic film into a form for anthropological expression, I openly acknowledge that should my ideas become a practice, ethnographic film would have the same narrow audience as written ethnography and would be further marginalized from the already marginalized documentary-film world—from my point of view, a consequence to be sought after.

The exclusion of documentary theory in discussions of film realism is telling. Film studies has shown a consistent lack of interest in all forms of film outside of feature fiction until the last decade or so. Even today, articles about documentary or experimental film are only occasionally found in publications like *The Cinema Journal*. No writing about the documentary has ever appeared in any of the five editions of the standard reference work *Film Theory and Criticism*, which Gerald Mast, Marshall Cohen, and now, Leo Braudy have edited since 1974 (Mast and Cohen 1974, 1979, 1985; Mast, Cohen, and Braudy 1992; Braudy and Cohen 1998). In 1976, J. Dudley Andrews argued that "none of them [that is, writings about the documentary] is developed or elaborated sufficiently to be considered a theory in the sense of the theories we have looked at so far" (104). Apparently, the lack of a coherent theoretical statement by Bazin did not prevent him from being included. Although there have been two concerted efforts to argue that one can tease a consistent theory of the documentary out of Grierson's various writings (Corner 1996; Winston

1995), nonfiction-film theory remains outside the canon of film theory. And Vertov is most often associated with experimental filmmaking, which has a literature all its own. The canon for film studies remains dominated by commercial-release fiction films. Christian Metz, the father of film semiotics, even claimed that the documentary has no place in film studies. "In the realm of the cinema, all nonnarrative genres—the documentary, the technical films, etc.—have become marginal provinces, border regions so to speak, while the feature-length film of novelistic fiction, which is simply called a 'film,'—the usage is significant—has traced more and more clearly the king's highway of filmic expression" (quoted in Renov 1993:1).

This last decade has seen a virtual explosion of books about the documentary (Corner 1996; De Greef and Hesling 1988; Grant and Sloniowski 1998; Guynn 1990; MacDonald and Cousins 1998; Rabinowitz 1994; Renov 1993; and Warren 1996). Most are "close readings" of films or filmmakers employing film studies' theories derived from semiotics, Marxism, feminism, and psychoanalysis. Although not uninteresting, these works contribute little that is useful for this exploration.

The book that represents the most ambitious attempt to construct a theory of the documentary, Bill Nichols's *Representing Reality* (1991), assumes that all documentaries are politically motivated and that all documentarians employ "discourses of sobriety" in order to "change the world." In my critique of his article "The Ethnographer's Tale" (1994), found in the introduction, I have already articulated the limitations of his approach and indeed of Nichols's ideas about the documentary in general. His arguments are mired in outmoded positivist notions of objectivity and reality that reflect a lack of knowledge of contemporary research on the constructive nature of human visual perception (see below). He is not alone among film scholars in his belief in objectivity (see Carroll 1996 for another example). I find most of Nichols's arguments confusing, unconvincing, and not useful for my purposes. For example, he argues that the documentary is nonnarrative while at the same time listing all the narrative features to be found in the form (1991:chapter 1). His notion of "documentary realism" (1991:26, 28, 165–66) has as its foundation a positivism that finds little support outside the world of film studies and journalism.

Although many documentarians—theorists and producers alike—continue to seek an association with film realism, this affiliation is not in the best interests of ethnographic film. As important as it was in the development of fiction-film theory, realism now lacks some fundamentally important intellectual supports and is in need of being reconceptualized or even discarded altogether. The validity of traditional notions of film realism has been the focus of much of the writing about film over the last several decades. Marxists, feminists, and scholars concerned with the representation of minorities—sexual, ethnic, and political—argue that film realism is an ideological construction that benefited those with power by naturalizing the status quo while at the same time oppressing the subaltern and erasing difference and cultural contestations. It is certainly easy to see why gays, for example, who were invisible for a long time in the supposedly "realistic" world of the cinema, would see film realism as oppressive. A few literary theorists are also dubious of the concept. J. A. Cuddon suggests that literary realism is "an exceptionally elastic critical term, often ambivalent and equivocal, which has acquired too many qualifying (but seldom clarifying) adjectives, and is a term which many now feel we could do without" (1991:772).

The premise that underlies all realism is that reality exists independently of human perception of it and that there is something meaningful out there to copy. Realism depends on a positivist philosophy about the existence of objective reality. This is not the place to review the extensive literature in the humanities and sciences that deconstructs the shortcomings of this approach. It has been alluded to already several times in this book. The problems with realism in written ethnography have become a major preoccupation among a number of anthropologists—Clifford and Marcus's *Writing Culture* (1986) being the most obvious site of this contestation. It is convenient to use 1966—the year in which Peter L. Berger and Thomas Luckman's *The Social Construction of Reality* was published—as a marker for realism's demise as a useful concept in the study of human social behavior. The view shared by a growing number of social scientists is that the reality that can be studied and represented is created and social. If other forms of reality exist, they are the province of the philosopher or theologian. As an anthropologist, I can only study the consequences of a society's belief in an objective reality and not whether that reality actually exists outside of those beliefs.

Classic film theory, whether realist or formalist (antirealist), as well as more contemporary conceptualizations were also dependent on certain discredited notions about how human visual perception works and how human perception is similar to the way the camera records images. For mimesis to be possible, the camera must be able to record the world "as it really is"—a philosophically impossible task if one assumes that reality is socially constructed and because it assumes that the world has some sort of universal meaning. In addition, the concept requires the camera-created image of the world to be isomorphic with that which the eye constructs—a concept that Nichols invokes (1991). The problem with that notion is that it is the brain, not the eye, that constructs images. Given contemporary thinking and scientific studies of visual perception, these related concepts are naive and no longer supportable. The camera is not an eye. It does not record an image the way the eye does. Moreover, the nature of human visual perception is not one of recording the objective reality that exists independently of observation but rather of actively constructing an image of the world that is only partly based on retinal stimulation. Florian Rötzer has summarized the contemporary view:

But there are other reasons for rejecting the use of a camera to explain visual perception. These have to do with the fact that "judgment" and "the visual act," or observer and image can no longer be as strictly separated, as was traditionally the case, once the eye is understood as a part of the brain, and seeing as an act of orientation by an organism existing in a complex and changing environment. . . . Today it is assumed that the brain does not pay attention to most of the data received by the retina but rather replaces them by simulations, only registering what was not "expected." That is to say, it compares the simulation only with the simulations from outside. Not only does the brain form hypotheses in swift sequence, it also complements the image of the retina. . . . It constructs, sometimes false, spatial and size relationships, censors a lot of what is impressed on the retina, and sees much that is not "really" present. . . . In brief, today, seeing the world is no longer understood as a process of copying but of modeling, a rendering based on data. A person does not see the world out there, but only sees the model created by the brain and projected outwards. His situation is similar to that of a pilot locked in his cabin, who receives information from the outside world via screens connected to measuring instruments, without being in direct contact with that outside world. From the sensory point of view he is living in a virtual world, comparable to that world mediated by a tele-presence-system where it is not possible to decide whether the user, by means for example of a robot which he steers, actually intervenes in the real world or in a simulated scene. . . . It is not the task of the brain and the sense organs to copy the environment as exactly and completely as possible, or to recognize the world "as it is." . . . Rather, their task is to orient the organism in its environment for the purpose of survival and reproduction. In the era of biology, of optical machines and computers, the ideological importance of photographic realism is declining. (1996:17–18)

One need only consider that it is a human being with a socially constructed reality and point of view peering through the eyepiece of a device that further alters the recorded image as a consequence of the placement of the camera, the type of lens used, and so on, to realize how deficient film realism has become.

Without its traditional foundation, realism becomes a concept devoid of support. It is invalidated. Ethnographic filmmakers must disassociate themselves from this naive realism and produce films that will become viewed as the filmmakers' construction of the social construction of the actuality of the people portrayed—an interpretation of someone else's interpretation. Such a view denies the possibility that one film style is more or less close to actuality than any other or that "reality" can be understood apart from people's social construction of it. Such a position refutes the claims that observational-style films are more open to interpretation by audiences because the makers passively record events without interpreting them (Young 1976).

However shaky the foundations of film realism may be, its popular appeal cannot be dismissed completely. Regardless of what theorists may argue, the cinema's apparent verisimilitude cannot be denied. It must be confronted. Film, fiction or not, often appears to be highly realistic to audiences who apparently react to that realism as if film were transparent. Not to belabor the point, but I would remind readers that our knowledge about how people view and understand films is severely hampered because of a lack of ethnographic reception studies—an argument I made previously. So I must assert, rather than argue from a secure data base, that most audiences "believe" what they see in the movies. "'We accept the reality of the world with which we're presented; it's as simple as that,' intones Christof," director of the lifelong TV drama of *The Truman Show* (Maslin 1998). Audience reactions to so-called fake documentaries like Mitchell Block's *No Lies* (1973), Jim McBride's *David Holzman's Diary* (1968), and more recently, Marlon Fuentes's *Bontoc Eulogy* (1997) seem to provide some evidence that if a film has a certain look, people will assume it is a documentary and therefore believe in the realism of the images.

This response runs counter to the purposes of anthropology. It is therefore necessary to consider ways to subvert audiences' assumptions about film's mimetic capacities—an argument I made earlier when discussing the need for reflexivity. For ethnographic film to succeed, audiences must understand that they are looking at an interpretation—a thick description—by an ethnographer based on his or her experiences in trying to understand the social reality of those portrayed and not a "copy of nature." Film realism needs to be reframed for audiences as a social convention that occurs when the filmmaker's socially constructed version of reality overlaps with the viewers' socially constructed version of reality.

The moral and political implications of realism for fiction film as a discredited concept is, fortunately, outside the purview of this book. However, the demise of support for film realism also creates a need to redefine the differences between fiction and nonfiction film. Claims about nonfiction's ability to produce objective depictions of life lack support. Once that has been said, there is also no reason to go to the apparently logical extreme of arguing that fiction and nonfiction film differ only in the codes and conventions they employ. I am suggesting that the rules governing fiction are those of the imagination and certain narrative conventions, whereas ethnographic nonfiction is limited to making interpretations of observable human behavior that become constructed into a film as a consequence of the observations and theoretical perspective of the ethnographer. The distinction between fiction and nonfiction becomes a matter of framing or metacommunication—that is, devices that instruct viewers as to the nature of what they are seeing. Fiction and nonfiction can share certain techniques, codes, and conventions without jeopardizing the integrity of either. In its new form, fictional realism is still dependent on the illusion of verisimilitude, but now this "appearance of reality" refers not to an objective reality but to a socially constructed one. To succeed, realist film must conform to the viewers' notion of what constitutes reality.

So we are left with an apparently contradictory situation. On the one hand, intellectual support for the notion that the purpose of film is "to copy the world"—mimesis—is no longer defensible. And at the same time, audiences are "taken in" by the verisimilitude of the images. Given the long history of the West's attraction to mimesis, it would be foolhardy to think that a few scholars can turn the tide of popular opinion. There is an apt parallel with the concept of race. For a number of years, organizations like the American Anthropological Association and the American Association for the Advancement of Science published clear statements that race is a social and not a biological construct. Yet I see no change in popularly articulated notions of race as a biological entity. Therefore, whether realism has any intellectual support is beside the point. Ethnographic filmmakers will simply have to accept and accommodate their audiences' expectations and frame the realism in such a way as to render it useful rather than detrimental. In order to succeed, ethnographic filmmakers must oppose the common sense of their viewers—an audience's pleasure in suspending disbelief that allows it to enjoy film realism.

The solution is to create an ethnographic trompe l'oeil for film. Filmic codes and conventions must be developed to frame or contextualize the apparent realism of the cinema and cause audiences to understand the images as anthropological articulations. The structure of Tim Asch's *The Ax Fight*, discussed in chapter 4, is perhaps the best example of this idea.

I am obviously using the term *trompe l'oeil* metaphorically. According to *Webster's Third International Dictionary*, *trompe l'oeil* is the "deception of the eye, especially by a painting as . . . the intensification of the reality of component objects in an unnaturally arranged still life through the use of minute detail and the careful rendition of tactile and tonal values" (quoted in Masrai 1979:8–9). In a still life, the painter attempts to create a tension between the aesthetic or, as *Webster's* puts it, "unnatural" arrangements of the parts of the painting—that is, the spatial relationships among the fruit and between the fruit and the bowl—and the painter's ability to realistically portray the fruit and the bowl. The painter strives to produce a temporary illusion that the apples are so real we could pick one up and eat it, while at the same time displaying his or her compositional skills. Bateson said it well: "Conjurers and painters of the trompe l'oeil school concentrate upon acquiring a virtuosity whose only reward is reached after the viewer detects that he has been deceived and is forced to smile or marvel at the skill of the deceiver. Hollywood filmmakers spend millions of dollars to increase the realism of a shadow" (1972:182).

The parallel with the ethnographic filmmaker is striking. If we grant Susan Sontag's (1977) notion that the apparent realism of photographic reproduction is its greatest achievement and gravest danger, it can be argued that the ethnographic filmmaker has to contextualize the realistic effect of film as merely an illusion by making overt the theoretical basis of the construction of the image—by being reflexive. This is not an issue for fiction film. Audiences know they are in the land of make-believe when they are watching a movie, even one that claims to be "based on a true story." The tension between the indexical resemblance of an ethnographic film sign event to its referents that causes people to attribute meaning to the film and the ideological construction of the film that causes people to infer meaning from the film must be made overt, explicit, and unavoidable. Like Bateson's notion of a metacommunication (as in the example he gave of "This is play," in which participants are made to realize the behavior is not to be taken seriously), ethnographic filmmakers need to remind audiences that "This is a film," not substitute actuality.

Audiences can have the pleasure of the illusion in which they are participating so long as it is made very clear to them that they are seeing a representation constructed because the filmmakers were motivated to present them with a particular view of the world. In an ethnographic film, we never see the world through the eyes of the native, but if we are lucky, we can see the native through the eyes of the anthropologist. The beginnings of such a cinema can already be found in the films of the French anthropological filmmaker Jean Rouch, particularly in his African films—*Jaguar* (1956), *Petit à Petit* (1970), and *Cocorico, Monsieur Poulet* (1974)—in which anthropological interpretation is blended with folk explanations and fantasies in a way that defies the labels of fiction and documentary. On a broader scale, every reflexive move in ethnographic film—for example, when Lorang addresses the MacDougalls on camera in *Lorang's Way* (1980)—breaks the frame and subverts a naively realistic vision of the film.

If ethnographic filmmakers were to produce films that tell the story of their field research, and the story of the people they studied, in a reflexive manner that permitted audiences to enjoy the cinematic illusion of verisimilitude without causing them to think they were seeing reality, then an anthropological cinema would be born.

Anthropologists have been making images of the people they study since there has been an anthropology and the technology for making images. From the crude images of the Wolof potter in Paris at the turn of the century by Félix-Louis Regnault to the hesitant 1990s reflexive ponderings of Kwame Braun about what it means to videotape a child passing in the street, images of humans enacting their culture flood our imagination. I hope that some of them will further the discourses of anthropology in a challenging and thoughtful way. It was my intention that this book provoke a dialogue to further that exploration.

To end, I wish to repeat the fantasy with which I started the book—a moral tale for anthropologists. It is a fantasy in which an anthropological cinema exists—not documentaries about "anthropological" subjects but films designed by anthropologists to communicate anthropological insights. It is a well-articulated genre distinct from the conceptual limitations of realist documentary and broadcast journalism. It borrows conventions and techniques from the whole of cinema—fiction, documentary, animation, and experimental. A multitude of film styles vie for prominence—equal to the number of theoretical positions found in the field. There are general-audience films produced for television as well as highly sophisticated works designed for professionals. Although some films intended for a general audience are collaboratively made with professional filmmakers, most are produced by professional anthropologists alone, who use the medium to convey the results of their ethnographic studies and ethnological knowledge. University departments regularly teach the theory, history, practice, and criticism of anthropological communications—verbal, written, and pictorial—enabling scholars from senior professors to graduate students to select the most appropriate mode in which to publish their work. There are a variety of venues where these works are displayed regularly and serve as the basis for scholarly discussion. Canons of criticism exist that allow for a critical discourse about the ways in which anthropology is realized pictorially. A low-cost distribution system for all these anthropological products is firmly established. Videotapes, CD-ROMs, and DVDs are as common as books in the libraries of anthropologists, and the Internet/World Wide Web occupies a place of some prominence as an anthropological resource.

Notes

INTRODUCTION

1. Throughout this book, I am using the term *anthropologist* in a very precise and descriptive way. Anthropologists are academics who have received formal graduate training, usually concluding in a Ph.D. Having such a degree does not make you smart or even necessarily well read in the field. I am not making a value judgment that anthropologists are somehow better than filmmakers. I am suggesting that anthropologists are qualified to be ethnographers and filmmakers are not. In addition, having professional training and making your living in anthropology cause you to look for critical reception and validation of your work within the field of anthropology, not within the film world.

2. The impact of social science on American direct cinema has yet to be properly explored. The Maysles brothers were trained as psychologists, and Richard Leacock's wife, Eleanor, was a prominent anthropologist who accompanied him on some of his filming trips.

3. Levinson's letter, which appeared in the *New York Times* Book Review Section, October 9, 1994, is as follows:

Anthropology for the Anthropologists

To the Editor:

It has become fashionable for the author of popular books on social issues to claim the status of "amateur anthropologist." Upon reading your review of Julia Blackburn's "Daisy Bates in the Desert" (Aug. 14), in which Linda Simon called Bates "a self-taught anthropologist," my wife, a journalist, asked me, a professional anthropologist, just what an amateur anthropologist is. I wasn't sure. No one speaks of amateur doctors, amateur lawyers, and to call someone an amateur psychologist is vaguely insulting, not jacket copy.

I do, however, know what a professional anthropologist is. The 10,000 or so of us are professionals because our careers are focused on anthropological research, teaching, and writing. We share an understanding of the basic concepts and methods used in anthropology, we have conducted field research, we have credentials in the form of master's degrees and Ph.D.s and we are participants in the profession.

It seems to me that those who claim amateur status as anthropologists do so because they have traveled widely, because they are observers of the human scene, because they have an interest in non-Western cultures or because they have taken a class in anthropology at some time in their careers. Traveling widely generally makes one a tourist. An interest in non-Western cultures means that one is curious. Observing the human scene means that one is a normal human being, and taking courses makes one educated. While anthropologists are human, educated, and curious, and as a rule enjoy travel, that is only part of what makes us anthropologists.

While I am happy to see the words "anthropology" and "anthropologist" in print as often as possible, I am troubled by the misuse of the concepts and methods and terminology of the profession, creating a distorted image of the way anthropology increases our understanding of the human situation, past and present and across cultures. I would like to think that we professional anthropologists and professional writers could collaborate, sharing ideas and information.

Readers would be better served by writers who write—from their observations of the human condition, of course, as writers always have—leaving anthropology to those whose profession it is.

David Levinson NEW HAVEN

CHAPTER ONE

1. My article "Franz Boas and Early Camera Study of Behavior" (Ruby 1980b), substantially revised and rewritten, served as the basis for this chapter. The writing of this chapter was greatly enhanced by a conversation with John Homiak of the Smithsonian Institution.

Thom Anderson, in a talk at the Whitney Museum in the late 1970s entitled "Science and Ideology in the Origins of the Cinema: Chronophotography to Micromotion Studies," has traced some of these interrelationships in a most intriguing way (McDonald 1980:3).

2. The Psychological Cinema Register at Pennsylvania State University was a unique attempt to elevate film production to the status of an academic publication. Unfortunately, the person most responsible for this, Leslie Greenhill, died before anyone could explore his contribution to making film production into a respectable academic activity.

3. By the 1990s, the collection was retired at Pennsylvania State University because of an almost total lack of use.

4. The use of the motion-picture camera in science and industry also deserves a mention even if this vast area lies outside our inquiry.

5. It is unfortunate that Paul Hockings decided to include Sorenson's twenty-plus-year-old essay "Visual Records, Human Knowledge, and the Future" in the 1995 second edition of *Principles of Visual Anthropology*, as the decades since the article was written make it clear that Sorenson's idea has little to do with the future of any aspect of anthropology and most especially visual anthropology. Reprinting the article gives the illusion that research filming is still a viable idea of interest among visual anthropologists. It is not.

6. I base the preceding generalizations not on any systematic study but on several decades of anecdotes obtained from fieldworkers and archivists. For example, Colin Young and Edmund Carpenter (1966) told me that in their 1960's survey of U.S. anthropologists who worked in the Pacific, over 75 percent of those who filmed stated that they did little with the footage after they returned from the field.

7. This is not the first time that I have encountered this strange situation. While researching the role of photographs in grief therapy, I discovered that many patients dealing with the loss of a loved one either brought in photographs of the deceased on their own or were encouraged to so by their therapist. As commonplace as this practice may be, there is no theoretical or even methodological discussion of it (Ruby 1995c).

8. Farnell does not agree and suggests that developing a notation system such as labanotation would suffice. "Perhaps the most significant technological breakthrough towards a genuine anthropology of embodiment will turn out to be, not, as might be supposed, video and film technology (although they are important aids), but the invention of an adequate script for writing human actions" (Farnell 1994:937).

CHAPTER TWO

1. My article in that catalog, "The Aggie Will Come First: The Demystification of Robert Flaherty" (Ruby 1979a), substantially revised and rewritten, served as the basis for this chapter.

2. Rony's chapter on Flaherty and *Nanook* is filled with unsubstantiated assertions. Two examples will suffice. On page 120, she claims that "critics" treasure a particular anecdote about *Nanook* without naming a single critic or citing any sources. On page 115, she claims that several Inuit were camera operators for Flaherty. As someone who has read all of Flaherty's diaries and other published and unpublished materials pertaining to *Nanook*, I can find no evidence to support this assertion, and Rony cites none. Almost every page of this chapter contains these errors of scholarship, thereby undermining the credibility of her arguments. Nor is this chapter an isolated example. The rest of the book is filled with similar errors. Rony, like Bill Nichols and Trinh T. Minh-ha, attempts to be critical of anthropology and ethnographic film without having sufficient knowledge of either to make a credible argument. Claude Massot and Sebastien Regnier's 1990 film *Nanook Revisited* also promised "new" insights into the filmmaker

and film by taking it back to Port Harrision, where Flaherty originally filmed, and showing it to some Inuit. Unfortunately, the filmmakers rehash knowledge that was readily
available in print and try to pass it off as their discovery. For example, they "discover"
that Flaherty both recreated and staged several scenes in the film. The film was produced while Massot was doing research for his fictionalized version of the making of
Nanook, entitled *Kablonnak*.

3. A fragment of Frances Flaherty's typescript diary covering 1914 to 1916 (housed
in the Robert J. Flaherty Papers at Butler Library, Columbia University) provides an
important source for this chapter. The passages quoted herein will be seen to have occasional typographical errors (generally quite obvious) and shorthand forms ("thot" for
"thought," "thro" for "through"), which will not be cited beyond this point. The "R." to
whom Frances refers repeatedly will easily be recognized as her husband, Robert. Permission to quote from the diary and other unpublished materials from the Flaherty
Papers was secured from International Film Seminars, Inc.

CHAPTER THREE

1. In an article on a UNESCO conference (Gardner 1958), Gardner discusses
Rouch's films, thereby providing evidence that he knew about Rouch's ideas.

2. See chapter 1 for a discussion of Boas's use of the camera and for a further explication of these ideas.

3. Richard Schechner (1982) has also made a most revealing analysis of the paradigm
Staal and Gardner employed in making this film.

4. A number of people, from Stanley Diamond (1974) to Edward Said (1978), have
explored our construction of the primitive and the exotic Other.

5. Among the many anthropologists who have made this argument, the work of Clifford Geertz (1973) is perhaps the most widely read.

6. It could be argued that Gardner wrote the article cited as explicating his ideas in
1957 and that his position has evolved over the past forty years. However, nothing in his
films, writings, or public statements suggests a significant change, and *Ika Hands* (1988),
his latest film, is about yet another "cultural survival."

7. I am assuming here that there is common agreement among anthropologists that
ethnography can only be accomplished through a long-term, intensive period of participant observation governed by an articulated research problem.

8. Heider (1983) credits Gardner as being "anthropologist" for *Rivers of Sand* but is
unable to support this contention with any evidence.

9. The source of Gardner's quotations is unattributed in Larson's review.

CHAPTER FOUR

1. I wish to thank Denise O'Brien for her critical reading of this chapter, which is a
substantially revised and rewritten version of my article "Out of Sync: The Cinema of
Tim Asch" (Ruby 1995b).

Notes

2. It is assumed that readers have already seen these two films and are therefore familiar with their basic story lines and that they have read the study guides distributed with the films. For those who have not seen the films or read the guides, they are available from Documentary Educational Resources (DER), 101 Morse Street, Watertown, MA 02172 ([617] 926-0491).

3. Perhaps some readers will find my "confession" of manipulation unnecessary, while others will profess shock at the idea of creating quotations. After the legal and ethical discussions surrounding the Jeffery Masson/Janet Malcolm legal battle, it is definitely unclear what our society thinks about how interviews should appear in print (Malcolm 1990).

4. Asch and Chagnon disagreed about the spelling of the name of the people they filmed. "I find his 'new spelling' of 'Yanomamo' (that is, 'Yanomami') to be a political act and an acquiescence to PC [political correctness]" (Chagnon, personal communication, 1994). I use the spelling Asch preferred—"Yanomami"—in this chapter, since it concentrates on his work.

5. *Bushman* is not the preferred designation among the San peoples of southern Africa. I use it because, during the time period under discussion, it was the term most frequently employed.

6. Among the other films Asch helped edit are *A Rite of Passage, Bitter Melons, Dehe's Tantrum, Men Bathing,* and *A Group of Women.*

7. Patsy Asch remembers Tim's job a bit differently:

While it may have been Jerry Bruner's long-term intent to have Tim edit the "Bushman" films, Tim was hired to (a) videotape (using the first portable system—1965) all of the experimental classes for the first MACOS summer school. The machine was huge, constantly broke down, but Tim taped hours of classes; (b) develop curricula materials, in whatever media he wanted—he was to give free [rein] to his imagination. I was head of a unit on the Bushman and developed materials from Lorna Marshall's diaries and from the sequences John and Tim had edited for university instruction. I convinced EDC to drop the Bushman unit several years later when it became apparent to me that unless teachers were willing to confront race and class explicitly, looking at small Black people who appeared very poor to American kids tended to reinforce racial prejudice. (personal correspondence, November 3, 1994)

8. The concept of "sequence" filming has also had a major impact on Fred Wiseman, who learned to make films when he hired Marshall as primary cameraperson and Asch as second camera on *Titicut Follies.*

9. The influence was not one-sided. Asch recalls seeing Jean-Luc Godard's *Breathless* around the time he was working on Marshall's Bushman footage. It was a transformative experience for him. Afterward, he was "absolutely committed" to what he was doing.

10. Patsy Asch believes that Tim did not see *Chronicle of a Summer* until after he had finished *The Feast* (personal correspondence, November 3, 1994).

11. In writing about Marshall's influence elsewhere, Asch makes it clear that the idea of sequential films comes from John Marshall. "It was Marshall's model of sequence

films that influenced the style of Timothy Asch's filming" (Tim and Patsy Asch 1987, note 2:352).

12. Asch has also suggested that his lack of experience in making films made him too timid to try to produce a grand-epic film in the style of *The Hunters* or *Dead Birds*. "I lacked the confidence in my own ability to make complex, narrative films about the Yanomami that would represent *their cultural perspective* [Asch's emphasis] in any significant way" (Asch 1993:3).

13. Although Ramos (1987) has done an admirable job of comparing the different views of the Yanomami in print, no one has done a similar comparison with the films. For example, video artist Juan Downey has produced a number of videos that offer a view contrastive of Asch's (Michaels 1982a).

14. There can be no question about the Yanomami's being the "model" for the tribe in *The Emerald Forest*, but it is not clear how much research Boorman actually undertook. Tim recalls his only meeting with the director:

> The cinematographer for Boorman came to see me and said he had a friend who wanted to meet me who was very shy and so it had to be sort of secretive. Could I think of a place we could meet? I said, "Look, so many people have asked me for a consultation that I have to say no." A week later, this guy came back again, and he was almost in tears, and he said, "This guy really wants to meet you." So I said to myself, "Look, I am really tired at the end of the week, and I don't have anything to do on Friday. Why don't I just meet him at Margarita Jones and you can pay for some margaritas?" So that's what we did. And this rather secretive-looking guy came. He could never look at me straight in the face, and he asked a million questions. And as I got more and more sloshed, I told them a million tales. It turns out later that it was Boorman.

15. It is interesting to note that neither the *New York Times* reviewer, A. H. Weller (March 5, 1976), nor the person who wrote the program notes for the 1980 screening of *The Ax Fight* appears to see its value in commenting upon the conventions of documentary realism. Their apparent interest is in the life depicted, not the form of the film.

16. See Banks (1992:122) for a contemporary argument that observational film is "the preferred style of ethnographic filmmaking" because it is "mimetic of anthropological practice."

17. Asch's memory of this time differs. He recalls that they were basically out of touch, lost even, for several days, and only when they reached the high ground around the village of the Patanowa-teri were they able to use the radio.

18. In a recent conversation, Craig Johnson, the soundperson for *The Ax Fight*, told me that he deliberately recorded the conversation even though they were not filming at that time because he sensed that what was being said was significant.

19. Good is another U.S. anthropologist who works among the Yanomami (Good 1991).

20. Asch is referring to Margaret Mead, Conrad Arensburg, and Morton Freed, the cultural anthropologists with whom he studied as an undergraduate at Columbia University, as well as Tom Biedelman and John Middleton, the Africanists with whom he did graduate work.

21. In my discussion of *The Ax Fight*, I do not deal with the value of the film for understanding the complexities of the social and political life of the Yanomami. Asch points out that the film was originally designed to be shown with another film, *Tapir Distribution*, which deals with the resolution of the conflict that precipitated the fight. Peter Biella, Napoleon Chagnon, and Gary Seaman have produced *Yanomamo Interactive*, a CD-ROM that explores *The Ax Fight* in yet another fashion (1997).

22. Chagnon points out that "for all of Tim's repudiation of scientism, *The Ax Fight* could not have been a successful film without the scientific data that underlies it" (personal communication, 1994).

23. Chagnon disagrees and suggests that people should consult the study guide for this film (Bugos, Carter, and Asch 1993) for an additional interpretation of the kinship data on the fight (personal communication, 1994). The guide is available from Documentary Educational Resources (see note 2 for this chapter).

24. Asch's *A Man Called Bee* (1974) and *Magical Death* (1973) are also among the most commonly used Yanomami films.

25. For example, Asch wanted to make a feature-length film about one of the Yanomami shamans.

26. Chagnon points out that anthropologists also, and most important, have to collect field data, and filming can interfere with this work (personal communication, 1994).

27. Even Asch did not find all of the films equally usable. "I find twenty-four of the Yanomami films especially useful in teaching. These open-ended, short films can be used in a variety of ways" (Asch 1993:7).

28. Chagnon argues that these statements about how acculturated the Yanomami have become are an oversimplification. He claims that one can still find villagers as isolated as the ones portrayed in *The Ax Fight*. "He [Asch] naively assumes that contemporary Yanomami are all like the ones he has recently visited at Salasian missions and seems to be quite unaware that there are still lots of villages very much like the ones he filmed with me in 1968 and 1971, albeit individuals in most of these villages have now seen *nabas* [Europeans] by walking out to contact points. This is a misrepresentation" (Chagnon, personal communication, 1994).

29. Chagnon argues that only the Yanomami who live at missions would have this reaction to the films (personal communication, 1994).

CHAPTER FIVE

1. My article "The Ethics of Imagemaking" (Ruby 1988), substantially revised and rewritten, served as the basis for this chapter.

CHAPTER SIX

1. This chapter first appeared in a preliminary form as a paper delivered at the Department of Sociology, University of California, La Jolla; the Center for the Humanities, University of Southern California; the Department of Anthropology, University of

California, Los Angeles; and the Department of Anthropology, Wesleyan University. Each time I presented the paper, I benefited from the comments of the audiences and more intensive and informal discussions with friends and colleagues at each institution. I wish to acknowledge those institutions for that opportunity. I also received helpful criticisms and suggestions from Sol Worth, Hubert Smith, Howard Becker, Janis Essner, Ron Gottesman, and Denise O'Brien.

2. The session was entitled "Exposing Yourself." The panelists included Bob Scholte, Richard Chalfen, Gerry O'Grady, and Sol Worth. For a discussion of the films and of reflexivity and the documentary film, see Ruby 1977.

3. Without getting sidetracked into a lengthy discussion of the nature of science and its relationship to anthropology, I will assume that most anthropologists would agree with Mead that "I am here concerned with the form of knowing that we call science— that is, with knowledge that can be arrived at and communicated in such a way that it can be shared with other human beings, is subject to their independent verification, and is open to further exploration by investigation in accordance with agreed-upon rules" (1976:905–6). Further, I am assuming that most anthropologists would agree that the following should be contained in their presentations: (1) an explicit statement of the researcher's theoretical assumptions; (2) an exposition of the methods employed for generating data and the logic of the fit between the theory, data generation, and analysis; and (3) a description of the shape and nature of the data.

4. Excerpt from the film script *The Shadow Catcher: Edward S. Curtis and the North American Indian*, written by T. C. McLuhan and Dennis Wheeler, © T. C. McLuhan. Used with permission of the author.

CHAPTER SEVEN

1. My article "The Viewer Viewed: The Reception of Ethnographic Films" (Ruby 1995d), substantially revised and rewritten, served as the basis for this chapter.

CHAPTER EIGHT

1. This chapter was originally prepared as a talk given at the 1990 Flaherty Soviet-American Film Seminar in Riga, Latvia. A second version was presented at American University. It was published in a preliminary form in 1991 as "Speaking for, Speaking about, Speaking with, or Speaking Alongside: An Anthropological and Documentary Dilemma," in *Visual Anthropology Review* 7, no. 2:50–67, and was extensively revised and rewritten as this chapter. I wish to acknowledge the close reading of the paper by Peter Biella, a discussant on the panel. John Katz, Bruce Jackson, and especially Pat Aufderheide read drafts of the paper. I greatly benefited from discussions with Faye Ginsburg and from reading several of her works in progress. All of their critiques added significantly to my understanding.

The chapter's title has been appropriated from Trinh T. Minh-ha's film *Reassemblage* (1982)—and not without some irony. I regard her films as uninspired derivatives of sixties U.S. experimental film and her "criticisms" of documentary film and anthropology uninformed by the tradition of self-criticism easily located within both fields. Alexander Moore (1990) is one of the few writers to suggest that the empress may have no clothes.

2. I would be doing a disservice to Vertov if I did not admit that his views of cinema are more complex than I have presented.

3. Seth Feldman (1977) has critiqued the Bantu Kimena Educational Experiment, a mid-1930s colonial effort to make effective educational films by having native producers.

4. For additional information on Rouch, see *Studies in Visual Communication* 11, no. 1 (1985; the entire issue was devoted to *Chronicle of a Summer*) and *Visual Anthropology* 2, nos. 3–4 (1989).

5. This discussion of subject-generated films does not include an exploration of the film-production workshops in which schoolchildren, teenagers, mental patients, and others who would not otherwise make a film are taught some production skills. The impetus for these projects comes from educators, researchers, and politically concerned outsiders, but not from the people themselves. The results are temporary. When the funding goes away, so do the equipment, the teachers, and the fledgling filmmakers. See Chalfen 1972 and 1989 for a review of some of these projects.

6. The independent video movement in many ways parallels the independent film movement. It has established a number of alternative distribution outlets such as Paper Tiger Television and Deep-Dish TV. People who would not normally have produced shows now have access to an audience that was virtually nonexistent prior to the invention of these technologies. The advent of cable systems, satellites with public and community access, and VCRs has had a decentralizing impact. However, in order to keep this chapter within reasonable bounds, I will not attempt to discuss the significance of these developments.

CHAPTER TEN

1. My article "Ethnography as Trompe l'Oeil: Anthropology and Film" (Ruby 1982), substantially revised and rewritten, served as the basis for this chapter.

References

Abu-Lughod, Lila. 1997. "The Interpretation of Culture(s) after Television." *Representations* 59 (summer):109–34.

Abu-Lughod, Lila, ed. 1994. Special Issue on Media. *Public Culture* 5, no. 3 (fall).

Aibel, Robert. 1987. "Ethnographic Fiction as 'Data of' and 'Data about' Culture: George Rouquier's *Farrebique*." In *Visual Explorations of the World*, edited by Martin Taureg and Jay Ruby, 205–16. Aachen, Germany: Edition Herodot in Rader-Verlag.

Alland, Alexander, Jr. 1975. *When the Spider Danced: Notes from an African Village*. New York: Doubleday.

Alland, Alexander, Sr. 1974. *Jacob A. Riis: Photographer and Citizen*. Millerton, N.Y.: Aperture.

Allen, Catherine J., and Nathan Garner. 1997. *Condor Qatay: Anthropology in Performance*. Prospect Heights, Ill.: Waveland Press.

Anderson, Carolyn, and Thomas W. Benson. 1988. "Direct Cinema and the Myth of Informed Consent: The Case of *Titicut Follies*." In *Image Ethics*, edited by Larry Gross, John Katz, and Jay Ruby. New York: Oxford University Press.

Anderson, Laurie. 1984. *United States*. New York: Harper & Row.

Andrews, J. Dudley. 1976. *The Major Film Theories*. New York: Oxford University Press.

Ang, Ien. 1990. "Culture and Communication: Towards an Ethnographic Critique of Media Consumption in the Transnational Media System." *European Journal of Communication* 5:239–60.

———. 1991. *Desperately Seeking the Audience*. New York: Routledge.

———. 1996. *Living Room Wars: Rethinking Media Audiences for a Postmodern World.* New York: Routledge.

Aristotle. 1968. *Poetics*. Oxford, U.K.: Clarendon Press.

Armes, Roy. 1988. *Third World Film Making and the West*. Berkeley: University of California Press.

Arnheim, Rudolf. 1957. *Film as Art*. Berkeley: University of California Press.

Asad, Talad. 1986. "The Concept of Cultural Translation in British Social Anthropology." In *Writing Culture*, edited by James Clifford and George Marcus, 141–64. Berkeley: University of California Press.

Asch, Tim. 1992. "The Ethics of Ethnographic Film-making." In *Film as Ethnography*, edited by Peter Ian Crawford and David Turton. Manchester, U.K.: Manchester University Press in association with the Granada Centre for Visual Anthropology.

———. 1993. "Bias in Ethnographic Reporting and Using the Yanomamo Films in Teaching." In *Yanomamo Film Study Guide*, edited by Tim Asch and Gary Seaman. Los Angeles: Ethnographics Press.

Asch, Tim, and Patsy Asch. 1987. "Images That Represent Ideas: The Use of Films on the !Kung to Teach Anthropology." In *The Past and Future of !Kung Ethnography: Critical Reflections and Symbolic Perspectives*, edited by Megan Biesele, with Robert Gordon and Richard Lee, 327–58. Hamburg, Germany: Helmut Buske Verlag.

Asch, Tim, et al. 1991. "The Story We Now Want to Hear Is Not Ours to Tell." *Visual Anthropology Review* 7, no. 2:102–6.

Ascher, Robert. 1990. "Approach, Theory, and Techniques in the Making of *Bar Yohat*." *Visual Anthropology* 3, no. 1:111–18.

Aufderheide, Pat. 1995. "The Video in the Villages Project: Videomaking with and by Brazilian Indians." *Visual Anthropology Review* 11, no. 2:83–93.

Babcock, Barbara. 1977. "Reflexivity: Definitions and Discriminations." Paper presented at the American Anthropological Association meetings, Washington, D.C.

Baker, Lee D. 1998. *From Savage to Negro: Anthropology and the Construction of Race, 1896–1954*. Berkeley: University of California Press.

Balikci, Asen. 1970. *The Netsilik Eskimo*. Garden City, N.Y.: Natural History Press.

Balikci, Asen, and Quentin Brown. 1966. "Ethnographic Filming and the Netsilik Eskimos." *ESI Reports:* 19–33.

———. 1989. "Anthropology, Film and the Arctic Peoples." *Anthropology Today* 5, no. 2:4–10.

Banks, Marcus. 1992. "Which Films Are Ethnographic?" In *Film as Ethnography*, edited by Peter Ian Crawford and David Turton. Manchester, U.K.: Manchester University Press in association with the Granada Centre for Visual Anthropology.

Banks, Marcus, and Howard Morphy, eds. 1997. *Rethinking Visual Anthropology*. New Haven, Conn.: Yale University Press.

Barba, Eugenio. 1991. *The Dictionary of Theatre Anthropology: The Secret Art of the Performer*. New York: Routledge.

Barnouw, Erik. 1974. *Documentary: A History of the Non-fiction Film*. New York: Oxford University Press.

Barnouw, Erik, and Patricia Zimmerman, eds. 1995. "The Flaherty: Four Decades in the Cause of Independent Cinema." *Wide Angle* 17, nos. 1–4.

Barsam, Richard Meran. 1973. "The Humanistic Vision of Robert Flaherty." In *Nonfiction Film: A Critical History*, edited by Richard M. Barsam. New York: Dutton.

———. 1988. *The Vision of Robert Flaherty: The Artist as Myth and Filmmaker.* Bloomington: Indiana University Press.

Bateson, Gregory. 1936. *Naven.* Palo Alto, Calif.: Stanford University Press.

———. 1972. *Steps Towards an Ecology of Mind.* New York: Ballantine.

Bateson, Gregory, and Margaret Mead. 1942. *Balinese Character. Special Publications of the New York Academy of Sciences* 11.

Batty, Philip. 1993. "Singing the Electric: Aboriginal Television in Australia." In *Channels of Resistance: Global Television and Local Empowerment*, edited by Tony Dowmunt. London: British Film Institute.

Bazin, André. 1967. *What Is Cinema?* Vol. 1. Berkeley: University of California Press.

Beck, B. E. F. 1975. "The Anthropology of the Body." *Current Anthropology* 16, no. 5:486–87.

Becker, Howard. 1974. "Photography and Sociology." *Studies in the Anthropology of Visual Communication* 1, no. 1:3–26.

———. 1982. *Art Worlds.* Berkeley: University of California Press.

Becker, Howard, with Michael McCall and Lori Morris. 1989. "Theaters and Communities: Three Scenes." *Social Problems* 36, no. 2 (April):93–112.

Bender, Lionel. 1977. "Review of *Rivers of Sand.*" *American Anthropologist* 79:196–97.

Benson, Thomas W., and Carolyn Anderson. 1989. *Reality Fictions: The Films of Frederick Wiseman.* Carbondale: Southern Illinois University Press.

Berger, John. 1972. *Ways of Seeing.* New York: Penguin.

———. 1980. *About Looking.* New York: Pantheon.

Berger, Peter L., and Thomas Luckman. 1966. *The Social Construction of Reality: A Treatise in the Sociology of Knowledge.* Garden City, N.Y.: Doubleday.

Berreman, Gerald D. 1962. *Behind Many Masks.* Society for Applied Anthropology, monograph no. 4.

Biella, Peter, Napoleon Chagnon, and Gary Seaman. 1997. *Yanomamo Interactive.* CD-ROM. New York: Harcourt Brace and Company.

Birdwhistell, Ray L. 1980. *Kinesics and Context: Essays on Body Motion Communication.* Philadelphia: University of Pennsylvania Press.

Blacking, John. 1977. "Towards the Anthropology of the Body." In *The Anthropology of the Body*, edited by John Blacking, 1–28. New York: Academic Press.

Blackman, Margaret. 1977. "Blankets, Bracelets, and Boas: The Potlach in Photographs." *Anthropological Papers of the University of Alaska* 18, no. 2:53–67.

Blakeley, Thomas, and Joan Williams. 1995. *Anthropological Excellence in Film: Ten Years of Award Winners in the SVA/AAA Film and Video Festival.* Arlington, Va.: American Anthropological Association.

Boas, Franz. 1888. "On Certain Songs and Dances of the Kwakiutl of British Columbia." *Journal of American Folklore* 1:49–64.

———. 1897. "The Social Organization and Secret Societies of the Kwakiutl Indians." *Report of the U.S. National Museum for 1895*, 311–738.

———. 1927 (1955). *Primitive Art*. New York: Dover Publications.

———. 1944. "Dance and Music in the Life of the Northwest Coast Indians of North America (Kwakiutl)." In *The Function of Dance in Human Society*, edited by Franziska Boas. New York: Dance Horizons.

Bowen, Elenore. 1954. *Return to Laughter.* New York: Doubleday.

Brand, Steward. 1976. "For God's Sake, Margaret: Conversations with Margaret Mead and Gregory Bateson." *Co-Evolutionary Quarterly* 10, no. 21:32–44.

Braun, Marta. 1992. *Picturing Time: The Work of Etienne-Jules Marey (1830–1904)*. Chicago: University of Chicago Press.

Brockman, John. 1995. "Agent of the Third Culture." *Wired* 3, no. 8 (August).

Browne, Donald. 1996. *Electronic Media and Indigenous Media: A Voice of Our Own?* Ames: Iowa State University Press.

Brownell, Susan. 1995. *Training the Body for China.* Chicago: University of Chicago Press.

Bruner, Edward. 1986. Introduction to *The Anthropology of Experience*, edited by Victor Turner and Edward Bruner. Chicago: University of Illinois Press.

Bugos, Paul, John Carter, and Tim Asch. 1993. "*The Ax Fight:* A Study Guide." In *Yanomamo Film Study Guide*, edited by Tim Asch and Gary Seaman. Los Angeles: Ethnographics Press.

Burton, Julianne. 1984. "Democratizing Documentary: Modes of Address in the Latin American Cinema, 1958–1972." In *Show Us Life: Towards a History and Aesthetics of the Committed Documentary*, edited by Thomas Waugh. Metuchen, N.J.: Scarecrow Press.

Caldarola, V. J. 1986. "The Ethnographic Use of Still Photographs: A Comparative Analysis of Three Photographically Illustrated Texts." Master's thesis, Annenberg School for Communication, University of Pennsylvania.

———. 1990. "Reception as Cultural Experience: Visual Mass Media and Reception Practices in Outer Indonesia." Ph.D. diss., Annenberg School for Communication, University of Pennsylvania.

———, ed. 1994. "Embracing the Media Simulacrum." *Visual Anthropology Review* 10, no. 1.

Calder-Marshall, Arthur. 1963. *The Innocent Eye: The Life of Robert J. Flaherty.* London: W. H. Allen.

Capote, Truman. 1965. *In Cold Blood: A True Account of a Multiple Murder and Its Consequences.* New York: Random House.

Carey, James. 1969. "The Communications Revolution and the Professional Communicator." *Sociological Review Monographs* (January).

Carlson, Marvin. 1996. *Performance: A Critical Introduction.* New York: Routledge.

Carpenter, Edmund. 1974. *Oh, What a Blow That Phantom Gave Me!* New York: Holt, Rinehart and Winston.

Carroll, Noël. 1996. "Nonfiction Film and Postmodern Skepticism." In *Post-Theory: Reconstructing Film Studies*, edited by David Bordwell and Noël Carroll, 283–306. Madison: University of Wisconsin Press.

Cartwright, Lisa. 1995. *Screening the Body: Tracing Medicine's Visual Culture.* Minneapolis: University of Minnesota Press.

Caughey, John L. 1984. *Imaginary Social Worlds: A Cultural Approach*. Lincoln: University of Nebraska Press.

Ceram, C. W. 1965. *Archaeology of the Cinema*. New York: Harcourt, Brace and World.

Chagnon, Napoleon. 1968. *The Yanomamo: The Fierce People*. New York: Holt, Rinehart and Winston.

———. 1974. *Studying the Yanomamo*. New York: Holt, Rinehart and Winston.

Chalfen, Richard. 1972. "How Groups in Our Society Act When Taught to Use Movie Cameras." In *Through Navaho Eyes*, edited by Sol Worth and John Adair. Bloomington: Indiana University Press.

———. 1987. *Snapshot Versions of Life*. Bowling Green, Ohio: Bowling Green State University Popular Press.

———. 1989. "Native Participation in Visual Studies: From Pine Springs to Philadelphia." *Eyes across the Water*, edited by Robert M. Boonzajer Flaes. Amsterdam: Het Spinhuis.

Charnov, Elaine. 1991. "Zora Neale Hurston: A Pioneer in Visual Anthropology." Master's thesis, Department of Anthropology, New York University.

Chinngu, Simeon W. 1976. "Issues in the Ethics of Research Methods: An Interpretation of the Anglo-American Perspective." *Current Anthropology* 17, no. 3:457–82.

Chiozzi, Paulo. 1989. "Reflections on Ethnographic Film with a General Bibliography." *Visual Anthropology* 2, no. 1.

———. 1993. *1942–1992: Fifty Years after* Balinese Character. Yearbook of Visual Anthropology. Firenze, Italy: Angelo Pontecoboli Editore.

Clifford, James. 1986. Introduction to *Writing Culture: The Poetics and Politics of Ethnography*, edited by James Clifford and George Marcus. Berkeley: University of California Press.

———. 1988. "On Ethnographic Authority." In *The Predicament of Culture*, 21–54. Cambridge, Mass.: Harvard University Press.

Clifford, James, and George Marcus, eds. 1986. *Writing Culture: The Poetics and Politics of Ethnography*. Berkeley: University of California Press.

Collier, John, Jr. 1967. *Visual Anthropology*. New York: Holt, Rinehart and Winston.

———. 1975. "Photography and Visual Anthropology." In *Principles of Visual Anthropology*, edited by Paul Hockings. The Hague: Mouton.

Connelly, Bob, and Robin Anderson. 1988. *First Contact*. New York: Viking Penguin.

Conquergood, Dwight. 1991. "Rethinking Ethnography: Towards a Critical Cultural Politics." *Communication Monographs* 58:179–94.

———. 1995. "Performing as a Moral Act: Ethical Dimensions of the Ethnography of Performance." In *Literature in Performance* (April):5.

Cooper, Merian C. 1925. *Grass*. New York: Putnam.

Corliss, Richard. 1973. "Robert Flaherty: The Man in the Iron Myth." *Film Comment* 6, no. 3:38–42.

Corner, John. 1996. *The Art of the Record: A Critical Introduction to Documentary*. Manchester, U.K.: Manchester University Press.

Crawford, Peter, and Sigurjon Hafsteinsson, eds. 1995. *The Construction of the Viewer: Media Ethnography and the Anthropology of Audiences*. Hojbjerg, Denmark: Intervention Press.

Crawford, Peter, and Jan Simonsen, eds. 1991. *Ethnographic Film Aesthetics and Narrative Traditions*. Aarhus, Denmark: Intervention Press.

Crawford, Peter, and David Turton, eds. 1992. *Film as Ethnography*. Manchester, U.K.: Manchester University Press.

Crowther, Gillian. 1990. "Fieldwork Cartoons." *Cambridge Anthropology* 14, no. 2:57–68.

Cuddon, J. A. 1991. *A Dictionary of Literary Terms and Theory*. Cambridge, Mass.: Blackwell.

Curling, Chris. 1978. "Anthropology and the General Audience: The Disappearing World." *Educational Broadcast International* 11, no. 2:79–84.

Danzker, Jo-Anne Birnie, ed. 1979. *Robert J. Flaherty: Photographer/Filmmaker*. Vancouver: Vancouver Art Gallery.

Daston, Lorraine, and Peter Galison. 1992. "The Image of Objectivity." *Representations* 40 (fall):81–128.

De Bouzek, Jeanette. 1989. "The 'Ethnographic Surrealism' of Jean Rouch." *Visual Anthropology* 2, nos. 3–4:301–16.

———. 1993. "Maya Deren: A Portrait of the Artist as Ethnographer." *Women and Performance* 5, no. 2:7–28.

de Brigard, Emilie Rahman. 1968. "History of Ethnographic Film." Master's thesis, UCLA.

Degerando, Joseph-Marie. 1969 (1800). *The Observation of Savage People*, translated by F. C. T. Moore. Berkeley: University of California Press.

De Greef, Willem, and Willem Hesling, eds. 1988. *Image, Reality, Spectator: Essays on Documentary Film and Television*. Louvain, Belgium: Acco.

De Heusch, Luc. 1962 (1988). "The Cinema and Social Science." *Visual Anthropology* 1, no. 2:99–156.

Deng, Francis Mading. 1984. *The Dinka of the Sudan*. Prospect Heights, Ill.: Waveland Press.

Devereaux, Leslie, and Roger Hillman, eds. 1995. *Fields of Vision: Essays in Film Studies, Visual Anthropology, and Photography*. Berkeley: University of California Press.

Diamond, Stanley. 1974. *In Search of the Primitive: A Critique of Civilization*. New Brunswick, N.J.: Transaction Books.

Dickey, Sara. 1993. *Cinema and the Urban Poor in South India*. Cambridge, U.K.: Cambridge University Press.

———. 1997. "Anthropology and Its Contributions to Studies in Mass Media." *International Social Science Journal* 153 (September):413–27.

Didion, Joan. 1979. "The White Album." In *The White Album*. New York: Simon and Schuster.

Dodds, John W. 1973. *The Several Worlds of Paul Fejos*. New York: Wenner-Gren Foundation.

Dornfeld, Barry. 1989. "*Chronicle of a Summer* and the Editing of Cinéma Vérité." *Visual Anthropology* 2, nos. 3–4:317–32.

———. 1998. *Producing Public Television, Producing Public Culture*. Princeton, N.J.: Princeton University Press.

Dow, P. 1991. *Schoolhouse Politics: Lessons from the Sputnik Era*. Cambridge, Mass.: Harvard University Press.

Dowmunt, Tony, ed. 1993. *Channels of Resistance: Global Television and Local Empowerment*. London: BFI Publishing in association with Channel Four.

Dumont, Jean Paul. 1978. *The Headman and I: Ambiguity and Ambivalence in the Fieldworking Experience*. Austin: University of Texas Press.

Dunlop, Ian. 1983. "Ethnographic Filmmaking in Australia: The First Seventy Years (1898–1968)." *Studies in Visual Communication* 9, no. 1:11–18.

Editorial. 1989. *Media Development* 4 (April):1.

Efron, David. 1941. *Gesture and Environment*. New York: King's Crown Press.

Eisenstein, Sergei. 1949. *Film Form: Essays in Film Theory*. New York: Harcourt, Brace.

Ekman, Paul. 1982. *Emotion in the Human Face*. New York: Cambridge University Press.

Elder, Sarah. 1995. "Collaborative Filmmaking: An Open Space for Making Meaning, a Moral Ground for Ethnographic Film." *Visual Anthropology Review* 11, no. 2:94–101.

Encyclopedia Cinematographica Catalog. 1981. University Park: A-V Services, Pennsylvania State University.

Engleman, Ralph. 1990. "The Origins of Public Access Cable Television: 1966–1972." *Journalism Monographs*, no. 123. Columbia, N.C.: Association for Education in Journalism and Mass Communication.

Ennis, Scott, and Tim Asch. 1993. "*The Feast:* A Study Guide." In *Yanomamo Film Study Guide*, edited by Tim Asch and Gary Seaman. Los Angeles: Ethnographics Press.

Fabian, Johannes. 1971. "Language, History, and Anthropology." *Journal of the Philosophy of the Social Sciences* 1:19–47.

Farnell, Brenda. 1994. "Ethno-graphics and the Moving Body." *Man*, n.s., 29:929–74.

Feld, Steve. 1974. "Avant-Propos: Jean Rouch." *Studies in the Anthropology of Visual Communication* 1, no. 1:35–36.

———. 1990. "Themes in the Cinema of Jean Rouch." *Visual Anthropology* 2, nos. 3–4:223–47.

———. 1991. *Voices in the Rainforest*. Music CD. Salem, Mass.: Rykodisc.

Feld, Steve, and Carroll Williams. 1975. "Toward a Researchable Film Language." *Studies in the Anthropology of Visual Communication* 2, no. 1:25–32.

Feldman, Seth. 1977. "Viewer, Viewing, Viewed: A Critique of Subject-Generated Documentary." *Journal of the University Film Association* 29:23–26, 35–36.

Fine, Elizabeth, and Jean Speer, eds. 1992. *Performance, Culture and Identity*. Westport, Conn.: Praeger.

Firth, Raymond. 1939. "An Anthropologist's View of Mass Observation." *Sociological Review* 31:166–93.

———. 1957. "Society and Its Symbols." *Times Literary Supplement* 13 (September): 1–2.

Fish, S. 1980. *Is There a Text in the Class? The Authority of Interpretive Community*. Cambridge, Mass.: Harvard University Press.

Fiske, John. 1987. *Television Culture*. London: Methuen.

Flaherty, Frances. N.d. Unpublished fragments of her diary. New York: Butler Library, Columbia University.

Flaherty, Robert J. 1918. "The Belcher Islands of Hudson Bay: Their Discovery and Exploration." *Geographical Review* 5, no. 6:433–58.

———. 1922. "How I Filmed *Nanook of the North*." *The World's Work* (September):553–60.

———. 1949. Recorded BBC talks. London: 14 June, 25 July, 5 September.

———. 1950. "Robert Flaherty Talking." In *Cinema 1950*, edited by Roger Malin Manvell. London: Pelican.

———. N.d. "An Early Account of the Film." Manuscript in the Robert J. Flaherty Papers, box 24. New York: Butler Library, Columbia University.

Flaherty, Robert J., in collaboration with Frances Flaherty. 1924. *My Eskimo Friends*. New York: Doubleday.

Foucault, Michel. 1977. *Discipline and Punish: The Birth of the Prison*. Translated from the French by Alan Sheridan. 1st American edition. New York: Pantheon Books.

Fuchs, Peter, ed. 1988. Special Issue on Ethnographic Film in Germany. *Visual Anthropology* 1, no. 3.

Fulchignoni, Enrico. 1990. "Conversation with Rouch." *Visual Anthropology* 2, nos. 3–4:265–300.

Fusco, Coco. 1995. *English Is Broken Here: Notes on Cultural Fusion in the Americas*. New York: New Press.

Gardner, Robert. 1957. "Anthropology and Film." *Daedulus* 86:344–52.

———. 1958. "The Ethnographic Film." *Films in Review* 9:65–73.

———. 1969. "Chronicles of the Human Experience: *Dead Birds*." *Film Comment* 2, no. 1:25–34.

———. 1970. "Program in Ethnographic Film (PIEF): A Review of Its History." *PIEF Newsletter* 1, no. 1:3–5.

———. 1986. "The Fiction of Non-fiction Film." *Cilect Review* 2, no. 1:23–24.

———. 1987. "Reviews of *The Soul of the Rice* and *Brides of the Gods*." *American Anthropologist* 89:265–67.

Gardner, Robert, and Karl G. Heider. 1968. *Gardens of War*. New York: Random House.

Gebauer, Gunter. 1995. *Mimesis: Culture, Art, Society*. Berkeley: University of California Press.

Geertz, Clifford. 1973. "Thick Description: Toward an Interpretive Theory of Culture." In *The Interpretation of Cultures*, 3–32. New York: Basic Books.

———. 1988. *Works and Lives: The Anthropologist as Author*. Stanford, Calif.: Stanford University Press.

Gerbner, George. 1972. "Communication and Social Environment." In *Communication*, A Scientific American Book. San Francisco: Freeman.

———. 1973. "Cultural Indicators: The Third Voice." In *Communication Technology and Social Policy*. New York: Wiley.

Gerbner, George, and Larry Gross. 1976. "Living with Television: The Violence Profile." *Journal of Communication* 26, no. 2:173–99.

Gerbner, George, Larry Gross, Michael Morgan, and Nancy Signorielli. 1980. "The Mainstreaming of America." *Journal of Communication* 30, no. 3:10–29.

———. 1982. "Charting the Mainstream: Television and Political Orientations." *Journal of Communication* 32, no. 1:100–127.

Giddens, Anthony. 1976. *New Rules of Sociological Method*. New York: Basic Books.

Gilbertson, M. 1980. "Taking the Science Out of Education." *Fusion* 3, no. 5:52–60.

Ginsburg, Faye. 1988. "Ethnographies on the Airwaves: The Presentation of Anthropology on American, British, and Japanese Television." In *Cinematographic Theory and New Dimensions on Ethnographic Film*, edited by Paul Hockings and Yasuhiro Omori. Osaka, Japan: National Museum of Ethnology.

———. 1989. "In Whose Image? Indigenous Media from Aboriginal Central Australia." *Commission on Visual Anthropology Review* 6:16–20.

———. 1991. "Indigenous Media: Faustian Contract or Global Village?" *Cultural Anthropology* 6, no. 1:92–112.

———. 1993. "Aboriginal Media and the Australian Imaginary." *Public Culture* 5, no. 3:557–78.

———. 1994. "Culture and Media: A (Mild) Polemic." *Anthropology Today* 10, no. 2:5–15.

———. 1995. "Indigenous Media and the Rhetoric of Self-Determination." In *Rhetorics of Self-Making*, edited by Debbora Battaglia. Berkeley: University of California Press.

———. 1998. "Institutionalizing the Unruly: Charting a Future for Visual Anthropology." *Ethnos* 63, no. 2:173–201.

Goffman, Erving. 1959. *The Presentation of Self in Everyday Life*. New York: Doubleday.

———. 1974. *Frame Analysis: An Essay on the Organization of Experience*. Cambridge, Mass.: Harvard University Press.

———. 1976. "Performances." In *Ritual, Play, and Performance: Readings in the Social Sciences/Theatre*, edited by Richard Schechner and May Schuman. New York: Seabury Press.

———. 1979. *Gender Advertisements*. New York: Harper and Row.

Good, Kenneth. 1991. *Into the Heart: One Man's Pursuit of Love and Knowledge among the Yanomama*. New York: Simon and Schuster.

Grant, Barry Keith, and Jeannette Sloniowski, eds. 1998. *Documenting the Documentary: Close Readings of Documentary Film and Video*. Detroit: Wayne State University Press.

Gray, Spalding. 1985. *Swimming to Cambodia*. New York: Theatre Communications Group.

Griffith, Richard. 1953. *The World of Robert Flaherty*. New York: Duell, Sloan and Pearce.

Griffiths, Alison. 1998. "Origins of Ethnographic Film." Ph.D. diss., Cinema Studies, New York University.

Gross, Larry. 1977. "Television as a Trojan Horse." *School Media Quarterly* (spring):175–80.

———. 1988. "The Ethics of (Mis)Representation." In *Image Ethics*, edited by Larry Gross, John Katz, and Jay Ruby. New York: Oxford University Press.

Gross, Larry, John Katz, and Jay Ruby, eds. 1988. *Image Ethics: The Moral Rights of Subjects in Photographs, Film, and Television*. New York: Oxford University Press.

———. N.d. "Image Ethics in the Digital Age." Work in progress.

Grossberg, L. 1988. "Wandering Audiences, Nomadic Critics." *Cultural Studies* 2, no. 3:377–91.

Guynn, William. 1990. *A Cinema of Nonfiction*. Rutherford, N.J.: Fairleigh Dickinson University Press.

Hall, Edward T. 1969. "Proxemics." *Current Anthropology* 9:83–104.

———. 1974. "Handbook for Proxemic Research." *Studies in the Anthropology of Visual Communication, Special Publication*. Washington, D.C.: American Anthropological Association.

Hanna, Judith Lynne. 1979. "Movements toward Understanding Humans through the Anthropological Study of Dance." *Current Anthropology* 20:313–39.

Hardy, Forsyth. 1979. *Grierson on Documentary*. London: Faber.

Harper, Douglas. 1994. "Cape Breton 1952: The Photographic Vision of Timothy Asch." *Visual Sociology* 9, no. 2.

Hastrup, Kirsten. 1992. "Out of Anthropology: The Anthropologist as an Object of Dramatic Representation." *Cultural Anthropology* 7, no. 3:327–45.

Hastrup, Kirsten, and Peter Hervik, eds. 1994. *Social Experience and Anthropological Knowledge*. New York: Routledge.

Hearne, T., and P. DeVore. 1973. "The Yanomamo on Paper and on Film." Paper presented at the Anthropological Film Conference, Smithsonian Institution, Washington, D.C.

Heider, Karl. 1970. *The Dugum Dani: A Papuan Culture in the Highlands of West New Guinea*. Chicago: Aldine.

———. 1972. *The Dani of West Iran: An Ethnographic Companion to the Film* Dead Birds. New York: MSS Modular Publication.

———. 1974. "Ethnographic Film" In *Learning Two-74*, 1–5. Berkeley: University of California Extension Media Center.

———. 1976. *Ethnographic Film*. Austin: University of Texas Press.

———. 1983. *Films for Anthropological Teaching*. Washington, D.C.: American Anthropological Association.

Heider, Karl, and Carol Hermer. 1995. *Films for Anthropological Teaching*. Special publication 29. Washington, D.C.: American Anthropological Association.

Henry, Jules. 1964. *The Jungle People*. New York: Vintage, Random House.

Herskovits, Melville. 1953. "Franz Boas." In *The Science of Man in the Making*. New York: Scribners.

Hockings, Paul, ed. 1975. *Principles of Visual Anthropology*. The Hague: Mouton.

———. 1995. *Principles of Visual Anthropology*. 2d ed. The Hague: Mouton.

Holm, Bill, and George Quimby. 1980. *Edward S. Curtis in the Land of the War Canoes: A Pioneer Cinematographer in the Pacific Northwest*. Seattle: University of Washington Press.

Honigmann, John J. 1976. "The Personal Approach in Cultural Anthropological Research." *Current Anthropology* 17, no. 2:243–61.

Hoover, Dwight. 1992. *Middletown: The Making of a Documentary Film Series*. New York: Gordon and Breach.

Hostetler, John, and Donald Kraybill. 1988. "Hollywood Markets the Amish." In

Image Ethics, edited by Larry Gross, John Katz, and Jay Ruby, 220–35. New York: Oxford University Press.

Hughes-Freeland, Felicia, ed. 1998. *Ritual, Performance, Media.* ASA Monographs, no. 35. New York: Routledge.

Husmann, Rolf, Ingrid Wellinger, Johannes Rühl, and Martin Taureg. 1992. *A Bibliography of Ethnographic Film.* Göttingen, Germany: Lit Verlag.

Hymes, Dell. 1967. "The Anthropology of Communication." In *Human Communication Theory*, edited by F. E. X. Dance, 1–39. New York: Holt, Rinehart and Winston.

——. 1973. "An Ethnographic Perspective." *New Literary History* 5, no. 1:187–201.

——, ed. 1972. *Reinventing Anthropology.* New York: Pantheon Books.

"Interim Report." 1990. Appalshop/Headwaters Television, 8 May.

Intintoli, Michael. 1984. *Taking Soaps Seriously: The World of Guiding Light.* New York: Praeger.

Ivins, William Mills. 1953. *Prints and Visual Communication.* Cambridge, Mass.: Harvard University Press.

Jablonko, Allison. 1968. "Dance and Daily Activities among the Maring People of New Guinea." Ph.D. diss., anthropology, Columbia University.

Jacknis, Ira. 1984. "Franz Boas and Photography." *Studies in Visual Communication* 10, no. 1:2–60.

——. 1987. "The Picturesque and the Scientific: Franz Boas' Plan for Anthropological Filmmaking." *Visual Anthropology* 1, no. 1:59–64.

——. 1988. "Margaret Mead and Gregory Bateson in Bali: Their Use of Photography and Film." *Cultural Anthropology* 3, no. 2:160–77.

Jackson, Michael. 1986. *Barawa and the Ways Birds Fly in the Sky: An Ethnographic Novel.* Washington, D.C.: Smithsonian Institution Press.

——. 1989. *Paths toward a Clearing: Radical Empiricism and Ethnographic Inquiry.* Bloomington: Indiana University Press.

——. 1995. *At Home in the World.* Durham, N.C.: Duke University Press.

James, David. N.d. "Light and Lost Bells: Chick Strand." Unpublished manuscript.

Jarvie, Ian. 1975. "Epistle of the Anthropologists." *American Anthropologist* 77, no. 2:253–66.

Jay, Robert. 1969. "Personal and Extrapersonal Vision in Anthropology." In *Reinventing Anthropology*, edited by Dell Hymes, 367–81. New York: Random House.

Jensen, K. Bruhn. 1987. "Qualitative Audience Research: Toward an Interactive Approach to Reception." *Critical Studies in Mass Communication* 4:21–36.

Jhala, Jayasinhji. 1994. "The Unintended Audience." In *The Construction of the Viewer: Media Ethnography and the Anthropology of Audiences*, edited by Peter Crawford and Sigurjon Hafsteinsson. Hojbjerg, Denmark: Intervention Press.

Jussim, Estelle. 1983. *Visual Communication and the Graphic Arts: Photographic Technologies in the Nineteenth Century.* New York: Bowker.

Kapfer, R., W. Petermann, and R. Thoms. 1989. *Ritual von Leben und Tod: Robert Gardner und seine Filme.* Hrsg. Munich: Trickster Verlag.

Katz, Elihu. 1977. "Can Authentic Cultures Survive New Media?" *Journal of Communication* (spring):113–21.

Katz, John Stuart. 1978. *Autobiography: Film, Video, Photography.* Toronto: Art Gallery of Ontario.

Katz, John Stuart, and Judith Milstein Katz. 1988. "Ethics and the Perception of Ethics in Autobiographical Film." In *Image Ethics,* edited by Larry Gross, John Katz, and Jay Ruby. New York: Oxford University Press.

Kent, Susan. 1985. "The Effects of Television Viewing: A Cross-Cultural Perspective." *Current Anthropology* 26, no. 1:121–26.

Kleinhans, Chuck. 1984. "Forms, Politics, Makers, and Contexts: Basic Issues for a Theory of Radical Political Documentary." In *Show Us Life: Toward a History and Aesthetics on the Committed Documentary,* edited by Thomas Waugh. Metuchen, N.J.: Scarecrow Press.

Kluckholm, Clyde. 1944. *Navaho Witchcraft.* Cambridge, Mass.: The Museum.

Konrad, Herman. 1977. "Review of *Ethics and Anthropology,* by Rynkiewich and Spradley." *American Anthropologist* 79, no. 4:920.

Kottak, C. P. 1990. *Prime-Time Society: An Anthropological Analysis of Television and Culture.* Belmont, Calif.: Wadsworth.

Krader, Lawrence. 1968. "Person and Collectivity: A Problem in the Dialectic of Anthropology." *Transactions of the New York Academy of Sciences,* ser. 11, vol. 30, no. 6:856–62.

Kuhn, Thomas S. 1962. *The Structure of Scientific Revolutions.* Chicago: University of Chicago Press.

Laban, R. 1926. *Choreographic.* Jena, Germany: Eugen Diederichs.

Labrot, Sharon. 1977. "Two Types of Self-reflexiveness." Manuscript. Center for the Humanities, University of Southern California.

Larkin, Brian. 1997. "Indian Films and Nigerian Lovers: Media and the Creation of Parallel Modernities." *Africa* 67, no. 3:406–40.

Larson, Heidi. 1987. "Gardner's *Forest Fires:* Hindu Bliss." *Anthropology and Humanism Quarterly* 12, nos. 3–4:97–98.

Lathrop, George Parsons. 1891. "Edison's Kinetograph." *Harper's Bazaar.* Reprinted in *Presenting the Past: Essays on History and the Public,* edited by Susan Benson, Stephen Brier, and Roy Rosenzweig. Philadelphia: Temple University Press, 1986.

Lavie, Smadar. 1990. *The Poetics of Military Occupation: Mzeina Allegories of Bedouin Identity under Israeli and Egyptian Rule.* Berkeley: University of California Press.

Lazarski, Robert. N.d. "Performance." Seminar paper. Philadelphia: Temple University.

Leach, Jerry W. 1988. "Structure and Message in Trobriand Cricket." In *Anthropological Filmmaking,* edited by Jack Rollwagon, 237–51. Chur, Switzerland: Harwood.

Leeds-Hurwitz, Wendy. 1993. *Semiotics and Communication: Signs, Codes, Cultures.* Hillsdale, N.J.: Lawrence Erlbaum Associates.

Levi-Strauss, Claude. 1955. *Tristes Tropiques.* Paris: Plon.

Lieber, Michael. 1980. "Review of *Deep Hearts.*" *American Anthropologist* 82:224–25.

Liebes, T. 1984. "Ethnocriticism: Israelis of Moroccan Ethnicity Negotiate the Meaning of *Dallas.*" *Studies in Visual Communication* 5, no. 4:277–92.

Lindsay, Vachel. 1915. *The Art of the Motion Picture.* New York: Macmillan.

Lock, Margaret. 1993. "Cultivating the Body: Anthropology and Epistemology of Bodily Practice and Knowledge." *Annual Reviews in Anthropology* 22:133–55.

Loizos, Peter. 1993. *Innovation in Ethnographic Film: From Innocence to Self-consciousness*. Chicago: University of Chicago Press.

Lomax, Alan. 1968. *Folk Song Style and Culture*. Washington, D.C.: American Association for the Advancement of Science.

Loud, Pat, with Nora Johnson. 1974. *Pat Loud: A Woman's Story*. New York: Bantam Books.

Lull, James. 1976. "Mass Media and Family Communication: An Ethnography of Audience Behavior." Ph.D. diss., University of Wisconsin.

———. 1988. *World Families Watch Television*. Newbury Park, Calif.: Sage.

———. 1990. *Inside Family Viewing: Ethnographic Research on Television's Audience*. New York: Routledge.

———. 1995. *Media, Communication, Culture: A Global Approach*. Cambridge, U.K.: Polity Press in association with Blackwell Publishers.

Lutz, Catherine, and Jane L. Collins. 1993. *Reading* National Geographic. Chicago: University of Chicago Press.

Lydall, Jean, and Ivo Strecker. 1978. "A Critique of Lionel Bender's Review of *Rivers of Sand*." *American Anthropologist* 80:945–46.

Lyons, A. P. 1990. "The Television and the Shrine: Towards a Theoretical Model for the Study of Mass Communications in Nigeria." *Visual Anthropology* 3, no. 4:429–56.

Lyons, H. D. 1990. "Television in Contemporary Urban Life: Benin City, Nigeria." *Visual Anthropology* 3, no. 4:411–28.

MacBean, James Roy. 1983. "Review of *Two Laws*." *Film Quarterly* 36, no. 3:30–36.

MacClancy, Jeremy. 1995. "Brief Encounter: The Meeting of Mass-Observation, British Surrealism and Popular Anthropology." *Journal of the Royal Anthropological Institute* 1:495–512.

MacDonald, Kevin, and Mark Cousins. 1998. *Imagining Reality: The Faber Book of Documentary*. London: Faber and Faber.

MacDougall, David. 1975. "Beyond Observational Cinema." In *Principles of Visual Anthropology*, edited by Paul Hockings, 109–24. The Hague: Mouton.

———. 1978. "Ethnographic Film: Failure and Promise." *Annual Review of Anthropology* 7:405–25.

———. 1992a. "Complicities of Style." In *Film as Ethnography*, edited by P. Crawford and D. Turton, 90–98. Manchester, U.K.: Manchester University Press.

———. 1992b. "When Less Is Less." *Film Quarterly* 46, no. 2:36–46.

———. 1994. "Whose Story Is It?" In *Visualizing Theory*, edited by L. Taylor, 27–36. New York: Routledge.

———. 1995a. "The Subjective Voice in Ethnographic Film." In *Fields of Vision*, edited by L. Devereaux and R. Hillman. Berkeley: University of California Press.

———. 1995b. "Visual Anthropology and the Ways of Knowing." Manuscript.

———. 1998. *Transcultural Cinema*. Princeton, N.J.: Princeton University Press.

Mailer, Norman. 1979. *The Executioner's Song*. Boston: Little, Brown.

Mainardi, Patricia. 1987. *Art and Politics of the Second Empire: The Universal Expositions*. New Haven, Conn.: Yale University Press.

Malcolm, Janet. 1990. *The Journalist and the Murderer*. New York: Random House.

Malinowski, Bronislaw. 1922. *The Argonauts of the Western Pacific*. New York: Dutton.

———. 1969. *A Diary in the Strict Sense of the Term*, translated by N. Guterman. New York: Harcourt, Brace and World.

Mallet, Captain Thierry. 1926. *Plain Tales of the North*. New York: Putnam.

Mamber, Stephen. 1974. *Cinéma Vérité in America: Studies in Uncontrolled Documentary*. Cambridge, Mass.: MIT Press.

Mandelbaum, David. 1963. *The Teaching of Anthropology*. Berkeley: University of California Press.

Marcus, George, ed. 1996. Introduction to the volume and reintroduction to the series, *Connected: Engagements with Media*. Chicago: University of Chicago Press.

Marcus, George, and Michael Fischer, eds. 1986. *Anthropology as Cultural Critique: An Experimental Movement in the Human Sciences*. Chicago: University of Chicago Press.

Marks, Laura. 1994. "Reconfigured Nationhood: A Partisan History of the Inuit Broadcasting Corporation." *Afterimage* (March):4–8.

Martinez, Wilton. 1990. "Critical Studies and Visual Anthropology: Aberrant vs. Anticipated Readings of Ethnographic Film." *CVA Review* (spring):34–47.

———. 1992. "Who Constructs Anthropological Knowledge? Toward a Theory of Ethnographic Film Spectatorship." In *Film as Ethnography*, edited by Peter Crawford and David Turton, 131–61. Manchester, U.K.: Manchester University Press.

Maslin, Janet. 1998. "*The Truman Show:* So, What's Wrong with This Picture?" *New York Times*, 5 June.

Masrai, M. L. d'Orange. 1979. *Illusion in Art: Trompe l'Oeil as a History of Pictorial Illusionism*. New York: Abaris Books.

Mast, Gerald, Marshall Cohen, and Leo Braudy, eds. 1992. *Film Theory and Criticism*. New York: Oxford University Press.

Matthiessen, Peter. 1962. *Under the Mountain Wall: A Chronicle of Two Seasons in the Stone Age*. New York: Viking Press.

Mauss, Marcel. 1939. "Les Techniques du Corps." *Journal de la Psychologie* 32 (March–April). Translated as "Techniques of the Body," in *Economy and Society* 2, no. 1 (1973):70–88.

———. 1967. *The Gift, Forms and Functions of Exchange in Archaic Society*. New York: Norton.

Maybury-Lewis, David. 1965. *The Savage and the Innocent*. Boston: Beacon Press.

McCall, Michael, and Howard Becker. 1990. "Performance Science." *Social Problems* 37, no. 1 (February):117–35.

McCarty, Mark. 1975. "McCarty's Law and How to Break It." In *Principles of Visual Anthropology*, edited by Paul Hockings. The Hague: Mouton.

McDonald, Scott. 1980. "Whitney Film Conference: Back to the Beginning." *Afterimage* 7, no. 6:3.

McLuhan, Marshall. 1964. *Understanding Media: The Extensions of Man*. New York: New American Library.

McLuhan, Marshall, and Quentin Fiore. 1967. *The Medium Is the Message*. New York: Bantam Books.

Mead, Margaret. 1956. "Some Uses of Still Photography in Culture and Personality."

In *Personal Character and Cultural Milieu*, edited by D. G. Haring, 79–103. Syracuse, N.Y.: Syracuse University Press.

———. 1959. *An Anthropologist at Work: Writings of Ruth Benedict*. Boston: Houghton Mifflin.

———. 1968. "Anthropology and the Camera." In *The Encyclopedia of Photography*, edited by Willard Morgan, 166–85. Vol. 1. New York: Greystone Press.

———. 1973. "As Significant as the Invention of Drama or the Novel." *TV Guide*, 6 January, A61–63.

———. 1975. "Visual Anthropology in a Discipline of Words." In *Principles of Visual Anthropology*, edited by Paul Hockings. The Hague: Mouton.

———. 1976. "Towards a Human Science." *Science* 191:903–9.

———. 1977. *Letters from the Field, 1925–1975*. New York: Harper and Row.

Mead, Margaret, and Francis MacGregor. 1951. *Growth and Culture*. New York: Putnam.

Mead, Margaret, and Rhoda Metraux, eds. 1953. *The Study of Culture at a Distance*. Chicago: University of Chicago Press.

Megill, Allan, ed. 1994. *Rethinking Objectivity*. Durham, N.C.: Duke University.

Michaelis, Anthony R. 1955. *Research Films in Biology, Anthropology, Psychology, and Medicine*. New York: Academic Press.

Michaels, Eric. 1974. "The Family." In *Communitarian Societies*, edited by John Hostetler. New York: Holt, Rinehart and Winston.

———. 1982a. "How to Look at Us Looking at the Yanomami Looking at Us." In *A Crack in the Mirror: Reflexive Perspectives in Anthropology*, edited by Jay Ruby. Philadelphia: University of Pennsylvania Press.

———. 1982b. "TV Tribes." Ph.D. diss., Communications, University of Texas, Austin.

———. 1985a. "Ask a Foolish Question: On the Methodologies of Cross-Cultural Media Research." *Australian Journal of Cultural Studies* 3, no. 2:45–59.

———. 1985b. "New Technologies in the Outback and Their Implication." *Media Information Australia* 38:69–71.

———. 1986a. *The Aboriginal Invention of Television in Central Australia, 1982–1985*. Institute Report. Canberra: Australian Institute of Aboriginal Studies.

———. 1986b. "The Impact of Television, Videos, and Satellite on Remote Communities." In *Science and Technology for Aboriginal Development*, edited by B. Froan and B. Walker. Canberra, Australia: CSIRO.

———. 1987a. *For a Cultural Future: Francis Jupurrurla Makes TV at Yuendumu*. Art and Criticism Series, vol. 3. Sydney, Australia: Art Space.

———. 1987b. "Response to Eric Willmot's Review 'Aboriginal Broadcasting in Remote Australia.'" *Media Information Australia* 43:41–44.

———. 1989. "A Primer on Restrictions on Picture-Taking in Traditional Areas of Aboriginal Australia." *Visual Anthropology* 4, nos. 3–4:259–76.

Michaels, Eric, with Francis Jupurrurla Kelly. 1984. "The Social Organization of an Aboriginal Video Workplace." *Australian Aboriginal Studies* 3:26–34.

Milgram, Stanley. 1974. *Obedience to Authority: An Experimental View*. 1st ed. New York: Harper and Row.

Miller, Ben. 1977. "Reflexivity in Ethnography: An Annotated Bibliography." Manuscript. Philadelphia: Temple University.

Minh-ha, Trinh T. 1984. "Mechanical Eye, Electronic Ear." *Wide-Angle* 6, no. 2:58–62.

———. 1987. "Rethinking the Subject in Ethno-Documentary." Paper presented at the Visual Anthropology Conference in Jodhpur, India.

———. 1989. *Woman, Native, Other: Writing Postcoloniality and Feminism*. Bloomington: Indiana University Press.

Mischler, Craig. 1985. "Narrativity and Metaphor in Ethnographic Film: A Critique of Robert Gardner's *Dead Birds*." *American Anthropologist* 87:668–72.

Mitchell, Gwen Davis. 1976. *Touching*. New York: Morrow.

Mitchell, W. J. T. 1986. "What Is an Image?" In *Iconology*. Chicago: University of Chicago Press.

Moore, Alexander. 1988. "The Limitations of Imagist Documentary: A Review of Robert Gardner's *Forest of Bliss*." *SVA Newsletter* 4, no. 2:1–3.

———. 1990. "Performance Battles: Progress and Mis-steps of a Woman Warrior." *Society for Visual Anthropology Review* 6, no. 2:73–79.

Moore, Sally F., and Barbara Myerhoff, eds. 1977. *Secular Ritual*. Assen, Netherlands: Van Gorcum.

Moores, Shaun. 1993. *Interpreting Audiences: The Ethnography of Media Consumption*. London: Sage Publications.

Morley, David. 1986. *Family Television: Cultural Power and Domestic Leisure*. London: Routledge.

———. 1992. *Television, Audiences, and Cultural Studies*. New York: Routledge.

Morley, David, and Kuan-Hsing Chen, eds. 1996. *Stuart Hall: Critical Dialogues in Cultural Studies*. New York: Routledge.

Murphy, William Thomas. 1978. *Robert Flaherty: A Guide to References and Resources*. Boston: G. K. Hall.

Musello, Christopher. 1980. "Studying the Home Mode." *Studies in Visual Communication* 6, no. 1:23–42.

Musser, Charles. 1990. *The Emergence of Cinema: The American Screen to 1907*. New York: Scribner.

Myerhoff, Barbara G. 1980. *Number Our Days*. New York: Simon and Schuster.

———. 1992. *Remembered Lives: The Work of Ritual, Storytelling, and Growing Older*, edited and with an introduction by Marc Kaminsky. Ann Arbor: University of Michigan Press.

Myerhoff, Barbara, and Jay Ruby. 1982. Introduction to *A Crack in the Mirror: Reflexive Perspectives in Anthropology*, edited by Jay Ruby, 1–38. Philadelphia: University of Pennsylvania Press.

Myers, Fred. 1988. "From Ethnography to Metaphor: Recent Films from David and Judith MacDougall." *Cultural Anthropology* 3, no. 2:205–20.

Myrdal, Gunnar. 1953. *The Political Element in the Development of Economic Theory*, translated by Paul Streeten. London: Routledge and Kegan Paul.

———. 1969. *Objectivity in Social Research*. New York: Pantheon.

Naficy, Hamid. 1993. *The Making of Exile Cultures: Iranian Television in Los Angeles*. Minneapolis: University of Minnesota Press.

Naficy, Hamid, and Teshome Gabriel, eds. 1993. *Otherness and the Media: The Ethnography of the Imagined and the Imaged.* New York: Harwood.

Nash, Dennison, and Ronald Wintrob. 1972. "The Emergence of Self-consciousness in Ethnography." *Current Anthropology* 13, no. 5:527–42.

Ness, Sally Ann. 1988. "Understanding Cultural Performance: *Trobriand Cricket.*" *TDR* 32, no. 4:135–45.

Nichols, Bill. 1981. *Ideology and the Image.* Bloomington: Indiana University Press.

———. 1983. "The Voice of the Documentary." *Film Quarterly* 36, no. 3:17–29.

———. 1991. *Representing Reality: Issues and Concepts in Documentary.* Bloomington: Indiana University Press.

———. 1994. "The Ethnographer's Tale." In *Blurred Boundaries,* 63–91. Bloomington: Indiana University Press.

Nochlin, Linda. 1971. *Realism.* New York: Penguin Books.

Nold, James, Jr. 1990. "Television for the People." *Channels,* 22 October, 30–33.

O'Connell, P. J. 1992. *Robert Drew and the Development of Cinéma Vérité in America.* University Park: Pennsylvania State University Press.

Offler, Naomi. 1998. "Seeking 'Good' Communication: Examining Student Responses to Ethnographic Film." Paper presented at the Conference on the Future of the Anthropology of Visual Communication, Philadelphia.

Orbanz, Eva, and Mary Lea Bandy. 1998. *Filming Robert Flaherty's* Louisiana Story: *The Helen Van Dongen Diary.* New York: Abrams.

O'Reilly, Patrick. 1949. "Le Documentaire Ethnographique en Océanie." *Journal Société Océanist* 5, no. 5:117ff.

Ortiz, Alfonso. 1969. *The Tewa World: Space, Time, Being, and Becoming in a Pueblo Society.* Chicago: University of Chicago Press.

Ostör, Akos. 1989. "Is That What *Forest of Bliss* Is All About?" *SVA Newsletter* 5, no. 1:4–11.

Pack, Sam. 1997. "Beauty and the Beast: Imaging the 'Primitive' in Ethnographic Film and Indigenous Media." Manuscript.

Parry, Jonathan P. 1988. "Comment on Robert Gardner's *Forest of Bliss.*" *SVA Newsletter* 4, no. 2:4–7.

Paul, Robert A. 1978. "Review of *Altar of Fire.*" *American Anthropologist* 80:197–99.

———. 1979. "Reply to Staal's Comment." *American Anthropologist* 81:347–48.

Pekar, Harvey. 1991. *The New American Splendor Anthology.* New York: Four Walls Eight Windows.

Peterson, Alexei. 1975. "Some Methods of Ethnographic Filming." In *Principles of Visual Anthropology,* edited by Paul Hockings. The Hague: Mouton.

Philipsen, Hans Henrik, and Bridgitte Markussen, eds. 1995. *Advocacy and Indigenous Filmmaking.* Aarhus, Denmark: Intervention Press.

Plattner, Stuart. 1996. *High Art Down Home: An Economic Ethnography of a Local Art Market.* Chicago: University of Chicago Press.

Polhemus, Ted. 1975. "Social Bodies." In *The Body as a Medium of Expression,* edited by Jonathan Benthall and Ted Polhemus. New York: Dutton.

Powdermaker, Hortense. 1953a. *Hollywood, the Dream Factory: An Anthropologist Looks at the Movie-makers.* Boston: Little, Brown.

———. 1953b. *Mass Communication Seminar.* New York: Wenner-Gren Foundation.

———. 1966. *Stranger and Friend.* New York: Norton.

Price, William C., and Seymour S. Chissick, eds. 1977. *The Uncertainty Principle and Foundations of Quantum Mechanics: A Fifty Years' Survey.* New York: Wiley.

Pryluck, Calvin. 1976. "Ultimately We Are All Outsiders: The Ethics of Documentary Filming." *Journal of the University Film Association* 33:21–29.

Rabinow, Paul. 1977. *Reflections on Fieldwork in Morocco.* Berkeley: University of California Press.

Rabinowitz, Paula. 1994. *They Must Be Represented: The Politics of Documentary.* London and New York: Verso.

Ramos, Alcida. 1987. "Reflecting on the Yanomami: Ethnographic Images and the Pursuit of the Exotic." *Cultural Anthropology* 2, no. 3:284–304.

Regnault, Félix-Louis. 1900. "La chronophotographie dans l'ethnographie." *Bulletins et mémoires de la Société d'anthropologie de Paris,* 5th ser., 1st tome (4 October):421–22. Translated in Rony 1996:47.

———. 1922. "L'histoire du cinema: Son rôle en anthropologie." *Bulletins et mémoires de la Société d'anthropologie de Paris,* 7th ser., 3 (6 July):65. Translated in Rony 1996:46–47.

———. 1923. "Films et musées d'ethnographie." *Comptes rendu de l'Association française pour l'avancement des sciences* 2:680–81.

———. 1931. "Le Rôle du cinéma en ethnographie." *La Nature* 2866 (1 October):304–6. Translated in Rony 1996:48.

Renov, Michael, ed. 1993. *Theorizing Documentary.* New York: Routledge.

"Review of *Nanook of the North.*" 1922. London: *Kinematograph Weekly,* 14 September, 735.

Richards, Jeffrey, and Dorothy Sheridan, eds. 1987. *Mass Observation at the Movies.* New York: Routledge.

Rius. 1979. *Marx for Beginners.* New York: Pantheon Books.

Roberts, Martin. 1995. "The Self in the Other: Ethnographic Film, Surrealism, Politics." *Visual Anthropology* 8, no. 1:79–94.

Rohner, Ronald, ed. 1969. *The Ethnography of Franz Boas: Letters and Diaries of Franz Boas Written on the Northwest Coast from 1886 to 1931.* Chicago: University of Chicago Press.

Rollwagon, Jack, ed. 1988. "The Role of Anthropological Theory in Ethnographic Filmmaking." In *Anthropological Filmmaking,* 287–316. New York: Harwood Academic Publishers.

Rony, Fatimah Tobing. 1996. *The Third Eye: Race, Cinema, and Ethnographic Spectacle.* Durham, N.C.: Duke University Press.

Rosenstone, Robert. 1975. *Romantic Revolutionary: Biography of John Reed.* New York: Random House.

Rosler, Martha. 1981. "In, Around, and Afterthoughts (on Documentary Photography)." In *Three Works,* 71–86. Halifax: Press of Nova Scotia College of Art and Design.

Rotha, Paul. 1983. *Robert J. Flaherty: A Biography,* edited by Jay Ruby. Philadelphia: University of Pennsylvania Press.

Rötzer, Florian. 1996. "Re: Photography." In *Photography after Photography: Memory and Representation in the Digital Age,* edited by Hubertus V. Amelunxen, Stefan Iglhau, and Florian Rötzer, in collaboration with Alexis Cassel and Nikolaus G. Schneider. Amsterdam: G&B Arts.

Rouch, Jean. 1971 (1978). "On the Vicissitudes of the Self." *Studies in Visual Communication* 5, no. 1:2–7.

———. 1974. "The Camera and Man." *Studies in the Anthropology of Visual Communication* 1, no. 1:37–44.

———. 1975. "The Situation and Tendencies of the Cinema in Africa." *Studies in the Anthropology of Visual Communication* 2, no. 1:51–58.

———. 1988. "Our Totemic Ancestors and Crazed Masters." In *Cinematographic Theory and New Dimensions in Ethnographic Film,* edited by P. Hockings and Yasuhiro Omori, 225–38. Osaka, Japan: National Museum of Ethnology.

Royal Anthropological Institute of Great Britain and Ireland. 1951. *Notes and Queries on Anthropology.* 6th ed. Revised and rewritten by a committee of the Royal Anthropological Institute of Great Britain and Ireland. London: Routledge and Kegan Paul.

Rubenstein, Lenny. 1978. "*Deal:* Behind the Scenes on 'Let's Make a Deal.'" Interview with E. J. Vaughn and John Schott. *Cineaste* 9:36.

Ruby, Jay. 1969. "Visual Anthropology." *Journal of the University Film Association* 21, no. 3:68–71.

———. 1970. "Anthropological Film: Prospects and Promises." *Rural African* 12:13–17.

———. 1971. "Towards an Anthropological Cinema." *Film Comment* 7, no. 1:35–40.

———. 1973. "Up the Zambesi with Notebook and Camera; or, Being an Anthropologist without Doing Anthropology." In *Program in Ethnographic Film Newsletter* 4, no. 3:12–14.

———. 1975. "Is an Ethnographic Film a Filmic Ethnography?" *Studies in the Anthropology of Visual Communication* 2, no. 2:104–11.

———. 1976a. "Anthropology and Film: The Social Science Implications of Regarding Film as Communication." *Quarterly Review of Film Studies* 1, no. 4:436–45.

———. 1976b. "In a Pic's Eye: Interpretive Strategies for Deriving Significance and Meaning from Photographs." *Afterimage* 3, no. 9:5–7.

———. 1977. "The Image Mirrored: Reflexivity and the Documentary Film." *Journal of the University Film Association* 29, no. 4:3–13.

———. 1979a. "The Aggie Will Come First: The Demystification of Robert Flaherty." In *Robert J. Flaherty: Photographer/Filmmaker,* edited by Jo-Anne Birnie Danzker, 67–74, 94–96. Vancouver: Vancouver Art Gallery.

———. 1979b. "Philosophical Toys: A Theory of Anthropology and Film." *Proceedings of the International Visual Literacy Association Meetings,* Rochester, N.Y.

———. 1980a. "Exposing Yourself: Reflexivity, Anthropology and Film." *Semiotica* 3, nos. 1–2:153–79.

———. 1980b. "Franz Boas and Early Camera Study of Behavior." *Kinesis Reports* 3, no. 1:6–11.

———. 1981a. "Beyond Realism/Formalism: Toward a New Role for Film in Anthropology." *Journal of Visual/Verbal Languaging* 1, no. 1:49–60.

———. 1981b. "A Re-examination of the Early Career of Robert J. Flaherty." *Quarterly Review of Film Studies* 5, no. 4:431–57.

———. 1982. "Ethnography as Trompe l'Oeil: Anthropology and Film." In *A Crack in the Mirror,* edited by Jay Ruby, 121–32. Philadelphia: University of Pennsylvania Press.

———. 1983. "An Early Attempt at Studying Human Behavior with a Camera: Franz Boas and the Kwakiutl: 1930." In *Methodology in Anthropological Film Making,* edited by Nico C. R. Bogaart and Henk Ketelaar, 25–38. Gottingen, Germany: Edition Herodot.

———. 1986. "The Future of Anthropological Cinema: A Modest Polemic." *Visual Sociology Review* 1, no. 2:9–13.

———. 1988. "The Ethics of Imagemaking." In *New Challenges to Documentary,* edited by Alan Rosenthal. Berkeley: University of California Press.

———. 1989a. "The Emperor and His Clothes." *Society for Visual Anthropology Newsletter* 5, no. 1:9–11.

———. 1989b. "Ethnographic Film." *Encyclopedia of Communication,* edited by Erik Barnouw. New York: Oxford University Press.

———. 1989c. "Robert Gardner und der Anthropologische Film." In *Ritual von Leben und Tod: Robert Gardner und seine Filme,* edited by R. Kapfer, W. Petermann, and R. Thoms, Hrsg. Munich, Germany: Trickster Verlag. (Reprinted in a slightly revised form in 1991 as "An Anthropological Critique of the Films of Robert Gardner." *Journal of Film and Video* 43, no. 4:3–17.)

———. 1990. "The Belly of the Beast: Eric Michaels and the Anthropology of Visual Communication." In *Communication and Tradition: Essays after Eric Michaels,* edited by Tom O'Regan. *Continuum* 2, no. 3:53–98.

———. 1991. "Speaking for, Speaking about, Speaking with, or Speaking Alongside: An Anthropological and Documentary Dilemma." *Visual Anthropology Review* 7, no. 2:50–67.

———. 1995a. "The Moral Burden of Authorship in Ethnographic Film." *Visual Anthropology Review* 11, no. 2:1–6.

———. 1995b. "Out of Sync: The Cinema of Tim Asch." *Visual Anthropology Review* 11, no. 1:19–37.

———. 1995c. *Secure the Shadow: Death and Photography in America.* Cambridge, Mass.: MIT Press.

———. 1995d. "The Viewer Viewed: The Reception of Ethnographic Films." *Reader* 31:75–87.

———, ed. 1982. *A Crack in the Mirror: Reflexive Perspectives in Anthropology.* Philadelphia: University of Pennsylvania Press.

———, ed. 1992. *The Films of John Marshall.* New York: Gordon and Breach.

Ruby, Jay, with Barbara Myerhoff. 1982. Introduction to *A Crack in the Mirror: Reflexive Perspectives in Anthropology,* edited by Jay Ruby, 1–38. Philadelphia: University of Pennsylvania Press.

Ruoff, Jeffrey. 1995. "Family Programming, Television, and American Culture: A Case Study of an American Family." Ph.D. diss., Department of Communication Studies, University of Iowa, Iowa City.

———. 1998. "A Stone Age Anthropology: The 1961 Harvard-Peabody Expedition to New Guinea." Manuscript.

Russo, Vito. 1981. *The Celluloid Closet*. New York: Harper and Row.

Said, Edward. 1978. *Orientalism*. New York: Pantheon Books.

Sartre, Jean Paul. 1956. *Being and Nothingness: An Essay on Phenomenological Ontology*. New York: Philosophical Library.

Schaeffer, Joseph. 1975. "Videotape: New Techniques of Observation and Analysis in Anthropology." In *Principles of Visual Anthropology*, edited by Paul Hockings. The Hague: Mouton.

Schechner, Richard. 1977. "Towards a Poetics of Performance." In *Essays on Performance Theory, 1970–1976*. New York: Drama Book Specialists.

———. 1982. "Collective Reflexivity: Restoration of Behavior." In *A Crack in the Mirror: Reflexive Perspectives in Anthropology*, edited by Jay Ruby. Philadelphia: University of Pennsylvania Press.

———. 1985. *Between Theater and Anthropology*. Philadelphia: University of Pennsylvania Press.

Schieffelin, Edward, and Bambi Schieffelin. 1974. "Review of *Tidikawa and Friends*." *American Anthropologist* 76:710–14.

Schieffelin, Edward L. 1998. "Problematizing Performance." In *Ritual, Performance, Media*, edited by Felicia Hughes-Freeland, 194–207. ASA Monographs, no. 35. New York: Routledge.

Schiller, Dan. 1977. "Realism, Photography, and Journalistic Objectivity in Nineteenth-Century America." *Studies in the Anthropology of Visual Communication* 4, no. 2:86–98.

Schodt, Frederik L. 1996. *Dreamland Japan: Writings on Modern Manga*. Berkeley, Calif.: Stone Bridge Press.

Scholte, Bob. 1972. "On Defining Anthropological Traditions: An Exercise in the Ethnology of Ethnology." In *The Nature and Function of Anthropological Traditions*, edited by Stanley Diamond. Philadelphia: University of Pennsylvania Press.

"Search for Nanook." 1984. *Inuktitut* (Ottawa), Indian and Northern Affairs (winter).

Seiter, E., H. Borchers, G. Kreutzner, and E.-M. Warth, eds. 1989. *Remote Control: Television, Audiences, and Cultural Power*. New York: Routledge.

Sekula, Alan. 1975. "On the Invention of Meaning in Photographs." *Artforum* 13, no. 5:36–45.

———. 1985. *Photography against the Grain*. Halifax: Press of the Nova Scotia College of Art and Design.

Serres, Antoine-Étienne-Renaud-Augustin. 1844. "Présentation de cinq portraits représentant deux naturels de l'Amérique de Sud (Botocudes), et pris au daguerreotype par le procédé de M. Thiesson." *Comptes rundus hebdomadaires des séances de l'Académic des Sciences* (Paris) 29, 2me semestre, no. 10, séance du lundi, 2 septembre, 490.

———. 1845. "Observations sur l'application de la photographie a l'étude des races humaine." *Comptes rundus hebdomadaires des séances de l'Académic des Sciences* (Paris) 21, no. 3, séance du lundi, 21 juillet, 242–46.

Silverstone, Roger. 1985. *Framing Science: The Making of a BBC Documentary*. London: BFI Publishing.

———. 1994. *Television and Everyday Life*. New York: Routledge.

Silverstone, Roger, and Eric Hirsch, eds. 1992. *Consuming Technologies: Media and Information in Domestic Spaces*. New York: Routledge.

Silverstone, Roger, Eric Hirsch, and David Morley. 1991. "Listening to a Long Conversation: An Ethnographic Approach to the Study of Information and Communication Technologies in the Home." *Cultural Studies* 5, no. 2:204–27.

Singer, Andre, and Leslie Woodhead. 1988. *Disappearing World: Television and Anthropology*. London: Boxtree, in association with Granada Television.

Singer, Milton B. 1972. *When a Great Tradition Modernizes: An Anthropological Approach to Indian Civilization*. New York: Praeger.

Smith, Dinitia. 1998. "Writers as Plunderers: Why Do They Give Away People's Secrets?" *New York Times*, 24 October.

Smith, Stevie. 1976. *The Collected Poems of Stevie Smith*. New York: Oxford University Press.

Sontag, Susan. 1966. *Against Interpretation, and Other Essays*. New York: Farrar, Straus and Giroux.

———. 1977. *On Photography*. New York: Farrar, Straus, and Giroux.

———. 1982. *A Susan Sontag Reader*. New York: Farrar, Straus and Giroux.

Sorenson, E. Richard. 1967. "A Research Film Program in the Study of Changing Man." *Current Anthropology* 8, no. 5:443–69.

———. 1995 (1973). "Visual Records, Human Knowledge and the Future." In *Principles of Visual Anthropology*, edited by Paul Hockings, 493–506. The Hague: Mouton.

Spiegelman, A. 1986. *Maus*. New York: Random House.

Spitulnik, Debra. 1993. "Anthropology and Mass Media." *Annual Review of Anthropology 1993* 22:293–315.

Staal, Fritz. 1976. *Altar of Fire* promotional brochure. University of California Extension Media Center.

———. 1979. "Comment: *Altar of Fire*." *American Anthropologist* 81:346–47.

Staiger, J. 1992. *Interpreting Films: Studies in the Historical Reception of American Cinema*. Princeton, N.J.: Princeton University Press.

Stanton, Gareth. 1996. "Ethnography, Anthropology and Cultural Studies: Links and Connections." In *Cultural Studies and Communication*, edited by James Curran, D. Morley, and V. Walkrerdine. London: Arnold.

Stein, Shayla. 1996. Essay from English 370, University of Missouri: ⟨http://www.missouri.edu/engbob/courses/370/archives/essay3/sse3.html⟩.

Stent, Gunther. 1975. "Limits to the Scientific Understanding of Man." *Science* 187:1052–57.

Stocking, George. 1974. *The Shaping of American Anthropology, 1883–1911: A Franz Boas Reader*. New York: Basic Books.

Stoller, Paul. 1992. *The Cinematic Griot*. Chicago: University of Chicago Press.

Strecker, Ivo. 1988. "Filming among the Hamar." *Visual Anthropology* 1, no. 4:369–78.

Sullivan, Nancy. 1993. "Film and Television Production in Papua New Guinea." *Public Culture* 5, no. 3:533–56.

Sussex, Elizabeth, ed. 1975. *The Rise and Fall of British Documentary: The Story of the Film Movement Founded by John Grierson*. Berkeley: University of California.

Taureg, Martin. 1983. "The Development of Standards for Scientific Films in German Ethnography." *Studies in Visual Communication* 9, no. 1:9–29.

Taylor, Lucien, ed. 1994. *Visualizing Theory: Selected Essays from V.A.R., 1990–1994*. New York: Routledge.

———. 1998. "Visual Anthropology Is Dead, Long Live Visual Anthropology!" Review essay. *American Anthropologist* 100, no. 2:534–37.

Taylor, Robert Lewis. 1949. "Profiles" (of Robert Flaherty). *New Yorker*, 11 June, 30–41; 18 June, 25–40; and 25 June, 28–43.

Tsing, Anna Lowenhaupt. 1993. *In the Realm of the Diamond Queen: Marginality in an Out-of-the-Way Place*. Princeton, N.J.: Princeton University Press.

Turnbull, Colin. 1979. "Anthropology and Drama: The Human Perspective." In *Anthropology, Drama, and the Human Experience*, edited by Colin Turnbull and Nathan Garner, 1–4. Washington, D.C.: George Washington University.

Turner, Terence. 1990. "Visual Media, Cultural Politics, and Anthropological Practice: Some Implications of Recent Uses of Film and Video among the Kayapo of Brazil." *Commission on Visual Anthropology Review* (spring):8–13.

———. 1991. "The Social Dynamics of Video Media in an Indigenous Society: The Cultural Meaning and the Personal Politics of Video-Making in Kayapo Communities." *Visual Anthropology Review* 7, no. 2:68–76.

———. 1992. "Defiant Images: The Kayapo Appropriation of Video." *Anthropology Today* 8, no. 6:5–16.

Turner, Victor. 1969. *The Ritual Process: Structure and Anti-Structure*. Ithaca, N.Y.: Cornell University Press.

———. 1974. *Dramas, Fields, and Metaphors: Symbolic Action in Human Society*. Ithaca, N.Y.: Cornell University Press.

———. 1976. "Social Dramas and Ritual Metaphors." In *Ritual, Play, and Performance: Readings in the Social Sciences/Theater*, edited by Richard Schechner and Mady Schuman, 97–120. New York: Seabury Press.

———. 1982a. "Dramatic Ritual/Ritual Drama: Performative and Reflexive Anthropology." In *A Crack in the Mirror: Reflexive Perspectives in Anthropology*, edited by Jay Ruby, 83–97. Philadelphia: University of Pennsylvania Press.

———. 1982b. *From Ritual to Theater: The Human Seriousness of Play*. New York: Performing Arts Journal Press.

———. 1986. *The Anthropology of Performance*. New York: Performing Arts Journal Press.

Van Dongen, Helen. 1965. "Robert J. Flaherty, 1884–1951." *Film Quarterly* 18, no. 4:2–14.

van Gennep, Arnold. 1960. *The Rites of Passage*. Chicago: University of Chicago Press.

Vertov, Dziga. 1923 (1984). "Kinoks: A Revolution," translated by Kevin O'Brien. In *Kino Eye: The Writings of Dziga Vertov*, edited by Annette Michelson. Berkeley: University of California Press.

———. 1972. "The Vertov Papers," translated by Marco Carynnyk. *Film Comment* 8:46–51.

Vonnegut, Kurt, Jr. 1974. *Wampeters Foma and Gran Falloons*. New York: Delta Books.

Wambaugh, Joseph. 1973. *The Onion Field*. New York: Delacorte Press.

Wardlow, Holly. 1996. "Bobby Teardrops." *Visual Anthropology Review* 12, no. 1:30–46.

Warren, Charles. 1996. *Beyond Document: Essays on Nonfiction Film*. Hanover, N.H.: University Press of New England.

Waugh, Thomas. 1988. "Independent Documentary in India: A Preliminary Report." *SVA Newsletter* 4, no. 2:13–14.

Weatherford, Elizabeth. 1990. "Native Visions: The Growth of Indigenous Media." *Aperture* 119:58–61.

Weatherford, Elizabeth, and Emelia Seubert. 1988. *Native Americans on Film and Video*. Vol. 2. New York: Museum of the American Indian.

Webster, Steven. 1980. "Realism and Reification in the Ethnographic Genre." *Critique of Anthropology* 6, no. 1:39–62.

Wholstein, Ronald T. 1977. "Filming Collective Behavior and the Problem of Fore-shortened Perspective: A Corrective Method." *Studies in the Anthropology of Visual Communication* 4, no. 2:81–85.

Whyte, William. 1964. *The Slum: On the Evolution of Street Corner Society*. New York: Wiley.

Wilden, Anthony. 1972. *System and Exchange: Essays in Communication and Exchange*. London: Tavistock.

Wilk, Richard. 1993. "It's Destroying a Whole Generation: Television and Moral Discourse in Belize." *Visual Anthropology* 5:229–44.

Willmot, Eric. 1987. "Aboriginal Broadcasting in Remote Australia: Review of Aboriginal Invention of TV." *Media Information Review* 43:38–40.

Winston, Brian. 1988. "The Tradition of the Victim in Griersonian Documentary." In *Image Ethics*, edited by Larry Gross, John Stuart Katz, and Jay Ruby. New York: Oxford University Press.

———. 1995. "Part Four: Actuality as Science." In *Claiming the Real: The Documentary Film Revisited*, 127–247. London: BFI Publishing.

Witek, Joseph. 1989. *Comic Books as History*. Jackson: University of Mississippi Press.

Wolf, Gotthard. 1967. "Organization and Aims of the Encyclopedia Cinematographica." In *Catalog*, 4–11. Göttingen: Institut für den Wissenschaftlichen Film.

Wolfe, Tom. 1979. *The Right Stuff*. New York: Farrar, Straus, and Giroux.

Woodhead, Leslie. 1987. *A Box Full of Spirits: Adventures of a Film-maker in Africa*. London: Heinemann.

Worth, Sol. 1966. "Film as Non-art: An Approach to the Study of Film." *The American Scholar* 35, no. 2:322–34.

———. 1972. "A Review of *You Are on Indian Land*." Draft of a review later published in a revised form in the *American Anthropologist* 74, no. 4:1029–31.

———. 1976. "Margaret Mead and the Shift from 'Visual Anthropology' to the 'Anthropology of Visual Communication.'" *Studies in Visual Communication* 6, no. 1:15–22.

———. 1981. "Toward an Anthropological Politics of Symbolic Form." In *Studying Visual Communication*, edited by Larry Gross. Philadelphia: University of Pennsylvania Press.

Worth, Sol, and John Adair. 1970. "Navajo Filmmakers." *American Anthropologist* 72:9–34.

———. 1972. *Through Navajo Eyes*. Bloomington: Indiana University Press.

Worth, Sol, and Larry Gross. 1981. "Symbolic Strategies." In *Studying Visual Communication*, edited by Larry Gross. Philadelphia: University of Pennsylvania Press.

Worth, Sol, with Jay Ruby. 1981. "An American Community's Socialization to Pictures." In *Studying Visual Communication*. Edited and with an Introduction by Larry Gross, 200–203. Philadelphia: University of Pennsylvania Press.

Wright, Chris. 1998. "The Third Subject: Perspectives on Visual Anthropology." *Anthropology Today* 14, no. 4:16–22.

Young, Colin. 1976. "Observational Cinema." In *Principles of Visual Anthropology*, edited by Paul Hockings. The Hague: Mouton.

———. 1986. "Observational Film." *Cilect Review* 1, no. 1:69–79.

Young, Colin, and Edmund Carpenter. 1966. *Films Made by Americans in the Pacific Which May Have Any Anthropological or Ethnographic Significance*. Presented at Round Table Conference on Ethnographic Film in the Pacific Area, UNESCO, Paris.

Zavattini, Cesare. 1953. "Some Ideas on the Cinema." *Sight and Sound* 23 (July):64–70.

Index

as visual art, 22, 110–11, 168, 178; non-representational, 144

visual explanation vs. sound in, 110

"Film as Non-Art," 22, 111

Film Australia, 15

Film Comment, 239

Film studies, 268

canons, theories of, 273

documentary theory in, lack of, 272–73

and literary models, 268

postmodernism in, 268; real vs. representation, 269

Film Study Center. *See* Harvard University

Film Theory and Criticism, 272

Filmmaking

decentralization of access, 213

ethics, moral, politics of, 137–49

historical uses of, 45–46

as industry, 18

professional vs. anthropological needs, 21, 23

profit motive of, 21–22, 23

static camera in, 177–78

technical advances in, 9, 12, 42, 149

technical skills for, 19, 53

technology of, 19, 41, 118, 119, 176, 180, 203, 249, 278; advances, 226, 227, 238; costs of, 19, 20, 76, 124; ideology of, 149; limits of, 58–59; video, 20

Films for Anthropological Teaching, 3, 25

Fine, Elizabeth, 245

Fires in the Mirror, 261

Firesign Theatre, 152

First Contact, 15

Firth, Raymond, 183, 250

Fischer, Michael, 224, 258

Fish, Stanley, 184

Fitterman, Joseph, 81

Flaherty, Frances, 57, 69, 73, 284n. 3

and Franz Boas, 83

connections to anthropologists, 83–85

excerpts from diary of, 72–74, 78–82, 84

fundraising efforts of, 71–72, 78–83

Flaherty, Robert, 7, 9, 19, 27, 39, 57, 68, 70, 119, 143, 144–45, 168, 171, 198–99, 200, 211, 272, 283–84n. 2, 284n. 3.

as America's "native son," 77

Arctic photographs of, 67, 74

as artist, 69, 74

Baffin Island expedition of, 87

as collaborator with Inuit, 76, 88–92, 102, 104

contributions to film, 69, 78–80, 91–92

as explorer, 74

as father of documentary, 69, 71, 83, 92; anthropological methods, ethnological theory in films, 86–88, 90; importance of, 85–86

formative period of career, 78

fundraising efforts of, 71–72, 77–83, 85

"Harvard print," 67, 74–75, 82

influence on Jean Rouch, 12, 69

as interpreter of Inuit, 74–75

knowledge of Curtis's work, 72–74

lack of anthropological training, 83, 85, 86

as lecturer, 74

as movie-goer, 71

persona and myth of, 69, 76–77

pre-*Nanook* films, 67, 74–75, 82

as professional filmmaker, 74–75, 83

screening of *Nanook*, 73–74; subjects' response, 197

as storyteller vs. scientist, 71, 85

travelogues, adventure films as models for, 71, 75–76, 169

Fogo Island people, 209

Fonda, Peter, 185

For a Cultural Future: Francis Jupurrurla Makes TV at Yuendumu, 227

Forest of Bliss, 95, 102

as aesthetic masterpiece, 110

culture of Benares, 111–12

Gardner's intentions in, lack of, 110

as personal, not ethnographic, 110

Fort Apache, the Bronx, 139

19, 57, 132; with indigenous people, 236–37
ethics, morals, politics of, 14, 143, 230
as ethnographers, 27, 29
influence on ethnographic film, 244
lack of anthropological knowledge, training, 4, 256
marketplace considerations of, 4, 37–38
single-author view of, 197, 198
Professional organizations, 25–26. *See also under names of organizations*
Program in Ethnographic Film (PIEF), 11, 19, 25, 96
Psychological Cinema Register. *See* Audiovisual centers, Pennsylvania State University
Public Broadcast Lab (PBL), 130. *See also* U.S. Public Broadcasting Service
Public Culture, 183
Pudovkin, Vsevolod, 170

Quimby, George, 72

Rabemananjara, Jacques, 214
Rabinow, Paul, 157, 158
Ramos, Alcida, 286n. 13
Ray, Nicholas, 27
Raymond, Alan, 206
Raymond, Susan, 206
Realism
    in film. *See under* Documentary films; Ethnographic film; Film and video
    premise of, 274
    as positivist philosophy, 274
    as social construction, 274–76
Reality as social construction, 201
Reassemblage, 288n. 1
Reception studies, 36–37, 39, 134, 181, 199, 217, 227
    codes, cultural assumptions of makers in, 185, 190, 192
    context of, 182
    ethnographic methods in, 182–84
    of film and television, 183–84, 187–89, 193; in classrooms, 189–92, 193; by

families, 188–89, 190; interpretive strategies for, 188–89, 190; participant/observation in, 188
    lack of, 3, 184, 268, 276
    model for, 192–93
    of photographs, 183
    psychological paradigms for, 182
    quantitative methods in, 182
    role of, 184
    "symbolic strategies" for, 184–85
    theory of, 183
    understanding, 182; author, text, audience, 182
Reflections on Fieldwork in Morocco, 157, 158
Reflexivity, 202, 203, 209, 242, 246, 255
    in anthropology, writing, film, 169, 172, 176; lack of, 151–52, 156–57, 163, 176, 179
    definition of, 154–56, 166–67; vs. autobiography, 156, 158, 160, 172
    effects on readers/viewers, 67, 152, 156, 169
    in ethnographic film, 266, 276
    example of, 153–54
    as narcissism, 160
    producer, process, product, reader/viewer in, 154, 156, 160
    purpose of: to reveal process of production, 67, 144, 148, 152, 169, 170, 172, 177; to reveal producer/maker, 67, 147, 148, 149, 152, 162, 169, 172, 177; to understand product/ethnography, 67, 152
    relationship with anthropology, film, 151, 152–53, 159–61, 167, 171
    See also under Anthropology; Boas, Franz; Documentary film; Ethnographic film; *Nanook of the North*; Rouch, Jean
Regnault, Félix-Louis, 7, 8, 44, 46, 48–49, 57, 168, 278
Regnier, Sebastian, 283–84n. 2
Reichard, Gladys, 55
Reichert, Julia, 148

Index